Contemporary Perspectives on the Detection, Investigation and Prosecution of Art Crime

Australasian, European and North American Perspectives

Edited by

DUNCAN CHAPPELL
University of Sydney, Australia

SASKIA HUFNAGEL
Queen Mary University of London, UK

ROUTLEDGE
Routledge
Taylor & Francis Group
LONDON AND NEW YORK

First published 2014 by Ashgate Publishing

Published 2016 by Routledge
2 Park Square, Milton Park, Abingdon, Oxfordshire OX14 4RN
711 Third Avenue, New York, NY 10017, USA

First issued in paperback 2016

Routledge is an imprint of the Taylor & Francis Group, an informa business

British Library Cataloguing in Publication Data
A catalogue record for this book is available from the British Library

The Library of Congress has cataloged the printed edition as follows:
Chappell, Duncan.
Contemporary perspectives on the detection, investigation and prosecution of art crime : Australasian, European and North American perspectives / by Duncan Chappell and Saskia Hufnagel.
pages cm
Includes bibliographical references and index.
ISBN 978-1-4094-6313-9 (hardback : alk. paper)
1. Art thefts--Law and legislation. 2. Art thefts--Investigation. 3. Art--Forgeries. 4. Cultural property--Protection (International law) I. Hufnagel, Saskia. II. Title.

K5219.C43 2014
364.16'287--dc23

2014015352

ISBN 13: 978-1-138-63769-6 (pbk)
ISBN 13: 978-1-4094-6313-9 (hbk)

CONTEMPORARY PERSPECTIVES ON THE DETECTION, INVESTIGATION AND PROSECUTION OF ART CRIME

Contents

PART III INTERNATIONAL AND REGIONAL OVERVIEWS

Figure and Tables

Contributors

Ludo Block is a director at Grant Thornton Forensic & Investigation Services in the Netherlands prior to which he was a senior police officer in the Netherlands, first in the Amsterdam Police where he held various commanding positions, including Detective Chief Inspector in the serious and organized crime division. From 1999 until 2004 Ludo spent almost six years working in Moscow as the Dutch police liaison officer for Russia and surrounding countries. Ludo completed a Masters in Social Sciences in 1998 and a PhD (Public Administration) in 2011, both at the Vrije Universiteit, Amsterdam.

Neil Brodie graduated from the University of Liverpool with a PhD in Archaeology in 1991 and has held positions at the British School at Athens, the McDonald Institute for Archaeological Research at the University of Cambridge, where he was Research Director of the Illicit Antiquities Research Centre, and Stanford University's Archaeology Center. Since February 2012 he has been Senior Research Fellow at the Scottish Centre for Crime and Justice Research, at the University of Glasgow, where he is researching the criminology and economics of the antiquities market as part of the ERC-funded Trafficking Culture project. He has published widely on issues concerning the antiquities market, and was co-author (with Jennifer Doole and Peter Watson) of the report *Stealing History*, commissioned by the Museums Association and ICOM-UK to advise upon the illicit trade in cultural material. He also co-edited *Archaeology, Cultural Heritage, and the Antiquities Trade* (2006, with Morag M. Kersel, Christina Luke and Kathryn Walker Tubb), *Illicit Antiquities: The Theft of Culture and the Extinction of Archaeology* (2002, with Kathryn Walker Tubb), and *Trade in Illicit Antiquities: The Destruction of the World's Archaeological Heritage* (2001, with Jennifer Doole and Colin Renfrew).

Duncan Chappell, an Australian lawyer and criminologist, is currently an Honorary Professor in the Faculty of Law at the University of Sydney, and a Conjoint Professor in the School of Psychiatry at the University of NSW. He is also the past Chair of the International Advisory Board of the Australian Research Council's Center of Excellence in Policing and Security. A past President of the NSW Mental Health Review Tribunal; a former Deputy President of the Federal Administrative Appeals Tribunal; and a former Director of the Australian Institute of Criminology, he has also held senior academic posts in Australia, Canada and the US. Chappell has researched and published widely on a range of crime and criminal justice topics, including art crime and trafficking in cultural property. Among his most recent publications on this subject is a book, *Crime in the Art and Antiquities World: Illegal Trafficking in Cultural Property* (2011) published by Springer, New York, and co-edited with Stefano Manacorda of the University of Paris.

Noah Charney is a professor of art history, specializing in art crime. He teaches for Brown University, American University of Rome, and on the ARCA Postgraduate Program in Art Crime and Cultural Heritage Protection, run by the Association for Research into Crimes against Art, an international research group that he founded. He is also a best-selling author of fiction and non-fiction, an award-winning columnist, and editor of *The Journal of Art Crime.*

Craig Forrest is a Reader in law and Fellow of the Centre for Public, International and Comparative Law, TC Beirne School of Law, University of Queensland, Australia. He is a member of the International Law Association's Cultural Heritage Law Committee, and in that capacity his recent research has focused on the immunity of art works on loan. He also has a research interest in the protection of the underwater cultural heritage, and served as a member of the South African delegation to UNESCO that negotiated and adopted the 2001 UNESCO Convention on the Protection of the Underwater Cultural Heritage. He has acted as an advisor to UNESCO on its adoption by states.

Stefan Gruber is an associate professor at the Hakubi Center for Advanced Research of Kyoto University. Previously, he was a lecturer at Sydney Law School and regularly teaches and researches at universities in China. His current research concentrates on sustainable development law and policy, the conservation of cultural heritage, and the illicit trafficking of cultural property and other forms of art crime with a regional focus on East and Southeast Asia.

Damien Huffer is currently a post-doctoral fellow at the Smithsonian National Museum of Natural History and Museum Conservation Institute. He completed his PhD in Archaeology/Bioarchaeology at the Australian National University in 2013, with a dissertation entitled 'The Ties that Bind: Population Dynamics, Mobility and Kinship during the mid-Holocene in Northern Vietnam'. He has ongoing research interests in Southeast Asian and Central Asian archaeology, bioarchaeology, human osteology, the application of stable isotope geochemistry to investigating the human past, as well as cultural property law, anti-looting outreach, and the development of new scientific methods to monitor and document the global antiquities trade.

Saskia Hufnagel is a qualified German legal professional and accredited specialist in criminal law. She currently works as Lecturer in Criminal Law at Queen Mary University of London. She previously worked as a Research Fellow at the Australian Research Council Centre of Excellence in Policing and Security, Griffith University, Australia, and was a Leverhulme Fellow at the University of Leeds. Her main research areas encompass law enforcement cooperation in Asia, North America, the EU and Australasia, comparative constitutional and human rights law with a focus on terrorism legislation and emergency management and the policing of art crime. Her monograph *Policing Cooperation Across Borders: Comparative Perspectives on Law Enforcement within the EU and Australia* (Ashgate) was published in 2013. Saskia was awarded an LL.M. (2004) and a PhD in Law (2011) by the Australian National University.

Stephen Nall is a lawyer, art consultant and exhibition curator in private practice in Sydney and a member of a provincial Local Authority Arts Board. As an art consultant and former gallery proprietor in the Australian art market, he has an intimate understanding of the strengths and weaknesses of the trade in art works and objects. He is a frequent commentator in Australian media reports on art crime.

Patrick J. O'Keefe is Honorary Professor in the School of Law and the School of English, Media Studies and Art History at the University of Queensland. He has been particularly interested in art theft and illicit traffic, advising governments, international organizations and private clients on the implications of these activities. The third edition of his *Commentary on the 1970 UNESCO Convention* will be published in 2014. The second edition of his *Commentary on the UNESCO Convention* on underwater cultural heritage (published February 2014) contains in-depth analysis of illicit traffic in such heritage and the concept of 'commercial exploitation'.

Vicki Oliveri specializes in art crime research. The 2007 theft of the Frans van Mieris painting, *A Cavalier (self portrait)*, was the focus of her 2012 Honours thesis. She has recently teamed with University of Western Sydney academic Dr Pamela James to research the acquisition of illicit Indian antiquities by Australian galleries.

Kenneth Polk is Professor of Criminology at the University of Melbourne. Although now retired from teaching, he continues to engage in research and writing on various topics of crime in the art market. Polk received his BA from San Diego State, his MA from Northwestern University, and his PhD from UCLA. Before coming to Melbourne he was Professor of Sociology at the University of Oregon. Among his previous books were *When Men Kill* (Cambridge University Press) and *Children as Victims of Homicide* (with Dr Christine Alder, also published by Cambridge University Press). Polk is a former member of the Australian Governments National Cultural Heritage Committee.

Lyndel V. Prott, former Director of UNESCO's Division of Cultural Heritage and former Professor of Cultural Heritage Law at the University of Sydney, is currently Honorary Professor at the University of Queensland. She has written over 300 items on cultural heritage law and is currently Honorary Professor at the University of Queensland.

Robyn Sloggett is Director of the Centre for Cultural Materials Conservation, which delivers industry-focused teaching, research and consultancy programs related to cultural preservation. Her current research incorporates art authentication, the scientific and cultural analysis of painting and medium used in Australia, art market development and the impact of art fraud, cultural conservation in Southeast Asia, and the preservation of cultural material and archives held in remote and regional communities. In 2003 she was awarded the AICCM's Conservator of the Year Award for 'Services to the Conservation Profession'.

Preface and Acknowledgements

Duncan Chappell and Saskia Hufnagel

The origins of this book are to be found in a workshop on art crime held in the Australian city of Brisbane, Queensland, in May 2012. The workshop, coordinated by the present editors, was titled 'Contemporary Perspectives on the Detection, Investigation and Prosecution of Art Crime'. The workshop was funded by a Griffith University International Workshop Award and the Australian Research Council's Center of Excellence in Policing and Security (CEPS) based at Griffith University in Queensland.

The workshop's aim was to gather international and Australian scholars and experts in the field of art crime detection, investigation and prosecution to discuss contemporary issues and developments. It was directed in particular at assessing the areas of art theft, fraud and illicit trafficking of cultural property, which have not so far received significant attention in the field of Australasian criminal law and policing research. It also sought to uncover more about the nature and scope of the art crime problem in an Australasian context, and examine how such crime is currently dealt with by criminal justice agencies within this region.

To inform this assessment the workshop applied a comparative perspective from Europe and North America regarding law enforcement and legal methods used to detect, investigate and prosecute art crime. It combined invited international academic and practitioner perspectives on the art crime problem to foster collaborative present and future research and linkages. The ultimate objective of the workshop was to address similarities and differences between the different regions and determine whether similar problems exist and common solutions can be identified.

The described aims and objectives of the workshop are now very much those which have motivated this book which incorporates chapters contributed by many of those who participated in the gathering. We believe that its publication is of particular significance not only because of the apparent lack of systematic scholarly research in the field of art crime in Australia and the region but also because European and North American studies reveal that art crime is becoming a broadening and highly profitable area of criminal activity.

This book, like the workshop that preceded it, could not have been published without the on-going support and encouragement of CEPS and its Director Professor Simon Bronitt. We wish to express our deep gratitude and thanks to Professor Bronitt who supported this project with growing enthusiasm.

We would like to thank all contributors for their considerable efforts and patience. In particular we would like to thank Alison Kirk (Publisher) from Ashgate Publishing for her enthusiasm for the project from its first hour and the reviewers for their very supportive feedback.

Chapter 1
Law Enforcement's Still Evolving Role in Art Crime: Some Introductory Remarks

Duncan Chappell and Saskia Hufnagel

Theft of an Icon

Just over a century ago one of the world's most iconic works of art, Leonardo da Vinci's painting of Lisa del Giocondo, the wife of a wealthy Florentine merchant, disappeared from the salon where it had been on display in the Louvre Museum in Paris, France.[1] The disappearance on 21 August 1911 of the Louvre's prime masterwork, known as *La Jocondo* or *Mona Lisa*, was soon recognized to be a theft which prompted immediate worldwide publicity and attention. French police were quickly notified and a massive investigation commenced, led by the Paris police chief, Louis Lepine, under the supervision of a presiding magistrate, Henri Drioux. Also involved was Alphonse Bertillon, now generally recognized as one of the founders of modern forensic science,[2] who searched the crime scene for clues and dusted for fingerprints – a method of identification of criminals that had only very recently been invented. A suspicious thumb print was in fact detected by Bertillon on the frame of the painting which had been discarded by the thief (or thieves). However, the print did not match those of any of the persons identified initially as possible suspects in the case, who included current and past employees of the Louvre.

Despite the best efforts of Lepine, Bertillon and their retinue of investigators the search for the painting and those responsible for its theft produced no results. It was believed that a gang of skilled art thieves must have been behind the theft of *Mona Lisa* but their motive was unclear since, as Lepine is reported to have said, 'it is generally conceded that even a dull person would realize the impossibility of selling such a famous work'.[3] Lepine's words proved to be prophetic, to a degree, for the crime was ultimately solved more than two years later when a prominent

---

1 In what follows we have relied, unless otherwise noted, upon the excellent and recent description of the theft of the painting and the investigation that ensued provided by Rita Angelica Scotti in her book *Vanished Smile. The Mysterious Theft of Mona Lisa* (Vintage Books 2010).

2 See in general Ron Fridell, *Solving Crimes: The Pioneers of Forensic Science* (Franklin Watts 2000).

3 Scotti (n 1) 61.

art dealer in Florence, Italy, who had advertised that he would 'pay generously for fine artwork',[4] received a written response from a person who signed himself as 'Leonardo'. The writer stated that:

> The stolen work of Leonardo da Vinci is in my possession. It seems to belong to Italy since its painter was an Italian. My dream is to give back this masterpiece to the land from which it came and to the country that inspired it.[5]

The art dealer, in company with the then director of the Uffizi gallery in Florence, subsequently met with 'Leonardo', established that he did indeed possess the missing *Mona Lisa*, and immediately notified the Italian authorities who quickly arrested the man. 'Leonardo' proved to be Vincenzo Peruggia, 32, an Italian house painter and migrant to France who had been involved in prior work at the Louvre, including assisting with the construction of the special frame for *Mona Lisa* on which Bertillon had found the suspicious fingerprint. Peruggia had in fact been interviewed by investigating police as a former employee but no fingerprints were taken from him and no attempt was made to check his professed alibi concerning where he was at the time of the theft. Further, the French police already possessed on their files a complete criminal dossier on Peruggia who had been twice arrested previously for unrelated crimes. The dossier included identity photographs as well a full set of fingerprints.

The Significance and Relevance of Art Crime to Law Enforcement

We refer to these details of the police investigation into what is still probably one of the most dramatic and sensational art crimes to occur during the past century because they continue to illustrate many of the themes that are central to the focus of this book. First and foremost this is a book which seeks to emphasize to those engaged in law enforcement, whether as practitioners or policy makers, the ongoing significance and relevance of art crime to their work as well as the nature of the challenges they are likely to encounter when responding to such crime. It is quite apparent that over a century ago French law enforcement officials were ill-prepared and ill-equipped to meet these challenges when responding to the theft of *Mona Lisa*. Not only did they lack any expertise in art crime but their investigation – as just noted – seems to have been deficient in many ways, despite having the assistance of one of the leading forensic experts of his time, Alphonse Bertillon.[6]

---

4 Ibid., 157.

5 Ibid., 158.

6 Bertillon died shortly after Peruggia's arrest and Lepine had retired before he came to trial in June 1914. Peruggia was convicted of the theft and ultimately sentenced to seven months and nine days imprisonment for a crime which the court assumed had been committed by him alone. Subsequent commentators have suggested that this was a

We suggest from the evidence presented in this book that in general law enforcement officials in many parts of the world almost certainly remain today as ill prepared and ill equipped as their French counterparts were in the early 1900s when dealing with all forms of art crime. Some indication of this can be found in the fact that clearance rates alone for stolen art masterpieces are said by the US Federal Bureau of Investigation (FBI) to be as low as five per cent of reported offences.[7] While there are a number of notable exceptions, identified in succeeding chapters, law enforcement agencies in large part do not regard art crime either as a separate category of offence, or as one deserving of specialist attention. Art theft of the type described, when it occurs, is also usually subsumed within the category of property crime or larceny making it virtually impossible to obtain systematic and reliable statistical data about the nature and extent of this particular aspect of art crime. The same situation prevails in relation to other aspects of art crime like fraud and forgery which also get swept into more generalized fraud and fakery offence categories.

Just what is encompassed within the term 'art crime' is in itself a matter of some contention as has been stated by a number of criminologists who have studied this topic.[8] Criminological interest in and attention to art crime is of relatively recent origin with the first major published English language text on the subject only emerging in the United States (US) in 1994.[9] The author of this text, John Conklin, adopted a typology utilized by the International Foundation for Art Research (IFAR) to define art. The IFAR's list comprised fine arts, decorative arts, antiquities, ethnographic objects, Oriental and Islamic art and miscellaneous items including armour, books, coins and medals.[10] The FBI has also adopted an expanded version of this IFAR typology for tracking stolen art objects. The FBI list includes archaeological material as well as stamps, musical and scientific instruments.[11]

While statistical data about art crime may be in thin and tenuous supply there is sufficient secondary evidence to suggest that it does represent a significant and expanding aspect of the overall crime burden. Much of this secondary evidence is explored in chapters of this book. It remains true, however, that much more

---

false assumption and various theories have been advanced suggesting Peruggia both had accomplices and was only a minor player in a much more devious conspiracy. See in particular Scotti (n 1).

7 Brad Lendon, 'Reward Beats Risk for Art Thieves' *CNN* (2008) <http://edition.cnn.com/2008/CRIME/02/14/art.theft/index.html> accessed 3 November 2013.

8 See in general Thomas Bazley, *Crimes of the Art World* (Praeger 2010), Chapter 1.

9 John Conklin, *Art Crime* (Praeger 1994).

10 IFAR, 'Stolen Art Alert' *IFAR* (2013) <http://www.ifar.org/stolen_art_alert.php?docid=1190985411> accessed 3 November 2013. See also in general Jonathan Sazonoff, 'Reporting Stolen Property' *Museum Security Network* (2013) <http://www.museum-security.org/reporting_stolen_property.html> accessed 3 November 2013.

11 FBI, 'National Stolen Art File' *FBI* (2013) <http://www.fbi.gov/about-us/investigate/vc_majorthefts/arttheft/national-stolen-art-file> accessed 3 November 2013.

empirical research still needs to be done across many parameters to document the nature, magnitude and impact of art crime. These parameters should include not only geographic or jurisdictional boundaries but also links with serious and organized crime; money laundering offenses and tax fraud; and the trafficking of weapons and drugs.

Book Structure and Content

We have arranged the book in three parts. Part I contains five chapters devoted to case studies of three forms of art crime – antiquities theft, art theft and art fraud. The studies, which set the stage for what follows in Part II and III, cover different areas of the globe but make it clear that much of art crime has transnational roots and dimensions. In Part II, which comprises four chapters, aspects of criminal law and procedure relevant to art crime are considered including the types of scientific evidence available to assist in prosecuting art fraud; the role played by UNESCO in developing international laws to protect cultural heritage from criminal exploitation; the dilemmas confronting law enforcement when seeking to deal at the international level with the investigation of art crime and the recovery of plundered objects; and the specific problems associated with granting immunity for seizure of works of art on loan across international boundaries. Finally in Part III, five chapters review contemporary efforts at the regional and international level to enhance the scope and calibre of law enforcement efforts in regard to art crime.

Attention is now turned briefly to some of the major themes and issues that are raised by individual chapters in each part of the book.

Part I: Case Studies

In the absence of detailed empirical research regarding so many aspects of art crime reliance often has to be placed upon case studies to illustrate its characteristics. In Chapter 2 Neil Brodie, a highly experienced archaeologist, by means of four case studies considers the problems and issues surrounding the antiquities trade. The first and most dramatic of these case studies involves the story of the now famous Euphronios krater purchased by the New York Metropolitan Museum of Art in 1972 for US$ 1 million. The krater was eventually identified as being looted from Italy and its recovery and ultimate return to its country of origin forms a gripping tale in its own right.[12] But as Brodie stresses the looting of objects like the Euphronios krater, or less valuable items from sites in Jordan and elsewhere, damages archaeological heritage, thereby compromising or weakening historical

12 The tale is eloquently told in the book by Peter Watson and Cecilia Todeschini, *The Medici Conspiracy: The Illicit Journey of Looted Objects from Italy's Tomb Raiders to the World's Greatest Museums* (Perseus Books Group 2006).

scholarship. Such looting is now becoming endemic, especially in past and present conflict zones like Iraq, Afghanistan, Libya and most recently Syria.[13] It is also behaviour which is currently subject to minimal attention from law enforcement because it is usually low on the list of national and international political priorities.

In Chapter 3 Duncan Chappell and Ken Polk turn attention to the 'Peculiar Problem of Art Theft'. As they indicate this is a most puzzling form of crime because above all else a successful theft produces for the criminal an object which is so well known that it is not only impossible to sell but also places the thief at serious risk of being subject to police investigation. Such an outcome was, as has already been described, the fate of Vincenzo Peruggia following his theft of the *Mona Lisa* in 1911, and many other art thieves since that time.[14] Chappell and Polk discuss a number of different patterns that the theft of art can take with a view to increasing our understanding of this crime and the measures that might be taken to combat it.

In Chapter 4 Duncan Chappell and Saskia Hufnagel examine a number of cases of art fraud occurring in two very different settings – Europe and Australia. Their focus is upon the way in which such crimes are detected, investigated and prosecuted by law enforcement agencies at a time when, largely because of the huge prices many works of art now attract in the market place, the incentive to inject fakes into that market has probably never been greater. As Chappell and Hufnagel suggest, the risks of being detected for producing and selling fake works of art appear quite negligible in the contemporary international art market where those seeking to acquire valuable paintings, sculptures and other forms of cultural heritage are no longer knowledgeable connoisseurs or patrons of artistic endeavour but rather more akin to commodity traders bent upon securing a maximum profit from their activity.

In Chapter 5 Vicki Oliveri makes a detailed comparative study of the investigation of two high-profile art thefts which remain unsolved in two quite different locations – Boston, Massachusetts in the US and Sydney, New South Wales in Australia. The 1990 art theft at Boston's Isabella Stewart Gardner Museum (the Gardner) has been described as 'the biggest, most confounding art heist in American history'. A total of 13 paintings were stolen, valued now at more than $500 million, by artists of international renown and stature like Rembrandt, Vermeer and Picasso. Despite a major police investigation of the theft, including active involvement by the FBI's specialist Art Squad, those responsible for the theft remain at large and none of the stolen paintings have been recovered. The theft still remains an open, active case and a top priority of the Gardner which

---

13 See, for example, Mathew Bogdanos, 'Thieves of Baghdad: The Global Traffic in Stolen Iraqi Antiquities' in Stefano Manacorda and Duncan Chappell (eds), *Crime in the Art and Antiquities World: Illegal Trafficking in Cultural Property* (Springer 2011).

14 For a review of some of these notable thefts and their perpetrators see Sandy Nairne, *Art Theft and the Case of the Stolen Turners* (Reaktion Books 2011).

together with the police continues to pursue regular leads and remain confident that the artworks will eventually be found.

The Australian art theft studied by Oliveri is much more recent and only involves the loss of a single painting – a canvas by the 17th century Dutch artist Frans van Mieris titled *A Cavalier (self portrait)*. The painting, said to be worth about $1.4 million, was stolen from the Art Gallery of New South Wales (AGNSW) on 10 June 2007. As in the case of the Gardner theft a major police investigation ensued without producing any positive results. However, unlike the Gardner theft it would seem that having failed to detect the criminal(s) involved, or recover the painting, the police investigators have now put the case on an inactive list. Oliveri is critical of this defeatist attitude, contrasting it with the much more positive and ongoing activity associated with the long-standing Gardner theft investigation. She also points to the significant deficiencies in the current Australian law enforcement environment when dealing with art crime where investigative expertise is absent and the priority given to this category of crime is minimal.

In the final chapter in Part I, Stephen Nall, an Australian art dealer and consultant as well as a lawyer, provides an 'insider's view' of the problems associated with dealing with fakes in the contemporary art market place. The Australian art market is of course only miniscule compared with those of North America, Europe and Asia but it still attracts the attention of fakers and forgers bent upon sharing some of the spoils of the booming sales in contemporary art. These sales have, in particular, had international connections within the vibrant market for Australian Aboriginal paintings and it is this component of the Antipodean art scene which has also experienced the most public exposure of fakes.[15]

In his chapter Nall does not concentrate on indigenous art fraud but he describes in some detail his personal involvement in securing a landmark legal ruling by an Australian higher court ordering the destruction of fake works falsely claimed to have been produced by two of the nation's leading contemporary artists. Nall is critical of the current law enforcement response to art fraud. He also offers a number of suggestions about actions that might be taken by art dealers and others involved in the art market to offer better protection against the scourge of forgery and deception it is currently experiencing.

Part II: Criminal Law and Procedure

In Part II of the book three of the four featured authors are lawyers. The exception is Robyn Sloggett, the author of Chapter 7, who is an art conservation scientist and specialist. Sloggett's knowledge and skills have made her one of Australia's most

15 For more on the subject of fraud within the market for Australian indigenous art see Chapter 4 as well as Christine Alder, Duncan Chappell and Kenneth Polk, 'Frauds and Fakes in the Australian Aboriginal Art Market' (2011) 56 *Crime Law and Social Change* 189-207.

respected experts in authenticating works of art – an expertise much in demand given the prevalence already referred to of fraud and fakery in the contemporary art market.

In her chapter Sloggett discusses ways in which evidence can be gathered and presented in a legal context where art crime fraud is alleged. As she states, building the chain of evidence for art authentication is a complex and carefully constructed activity that ensures that works can be legitimately, and verifiably, linked to the artist who is purported to be their source. This evidential chain may be constructed from the time the work is created; in the main by due diligence in documentation provided by the artist or their representative. This secures provenance. On the other hand this evidential chain may be constructed from investigation that takes place after the work has been called into question. In both cases what is at stake is the ability to claim that the work is authentic and that its descriptor matches the conclusion that can be drawn from the evidence at hand. In this way considerations of authenticity are context dependent and if new evidence comes to light then the conclusion must be revisited and revised.

In Chapter 8 attention is given to developments in international criminal law designed to afford greater protections against the scourge of cultural heritage looting referred to earlier in Chapter 2. Lyndel V. Prott, its author, was for many years a senior official with the United Nations Educational, Scientific and Cultural Organization (UNESCO), the chief international body concerned with rule making in this field. As Prott stresses, like many other areas where international organizations are active, UNESCO is frequently asked to perform tasks for which it is neither equipped nor given competence. UNESCO has no policing powers and no police force at its disposal. Even so, as Prott demonstrates, the agency has had a considerable impact on criminal law, national and international, and has set standards for behaviour for both nation states and their citizens through the passage of instruments like the 1970 UNESCO Convention on the Means of Prohibiting and Preventing the Illicit Import, Export and Transfer of Ownership of Cultural Property (UNESCO Convention, 1970).

Chapter 9 is also concerned with international issues in the area of art crime and in particular with the challenges of investigating the illicit trafficking of cultural objects and securing their recovery and repatriation. Patrick J. O'Keefe, its author, was also involved for many years with UNESCO. As he emphasizes there are for several possible reasons few examples of criminal or civil law proceedings involving the trafficking of cultural objects. Thus persons caught in wrongful possession of cultural objects are often willing to give them back in order to avoid adverse publicity and attention arising from legal action; or the crime may not be reported, or followed up; and there are many difficulties associated with any enforcement activity that has an international dimension.

Having identified these various factors O'Keefe goes on to examine a number of significant cases where legal proceedings have occurred. Anyone who wishes to recover the proceeds of art crime can draw lessons from this analysis by O'Keefe on how to avoid the numerous pitfalls that litter the road towards success. Certainly a successful prosecution or recovery will often be difficult and any litigant must know what to do and anticipate the problems that can arise. But a successful action must be seen not only for its own value, but as acting as a deterrent to other thefts and illicit traffic in general. That is why a badly prepared case, or a case where there is little likelihood of success so that an adverse decision is highly possible, can hurt the prospects for other claims.

In Chapter 10, the final chapter in Part II, Craig Forrest explores further legal hurdles that can arise when art objects travel beyond their national borders for exhibition or allied purposes. Increasingly lenders of works of art have become reluctant to loan them to institutions in other States fearing their seizure at the behest of third-party claimants taking advantage of the change in jurisdiction brought about by the movement of the art objects. Claims by third parties may arise primarily in one of two ways. First, a claimant may seek to have the art seized to enforce a judgment made against the owner. Secondly, and perhaps most commonly, a claimant (whether a government, company or individual) may claim to be the owner, or entitled to possession, of the work of art, and bring legal proceedings to have that ownership or possession recognized and then to take possession of the work of art. This civil action may be complemented by a criminal action, requiring the seizure of the art as part of a criminal investigation.

To facilitate the exchange of works of art in general, a number of jurisdictions have enacted immunity from seizure legislation. Immunity from seizure legislation essentially seeks to immunize a borrowed work of art from seizure by court order or from some other legally-imposed restraint on its physical movement. The extent to which immunity should apply to seizures pursuant to a criminal investigation or breach of a criminal law requires a careful balancing of interests: the direct interest of facilitating the exchange of culture by providing immunity versus the need to fully investigate crimes and to give full effect to the criminal law. In his chapter Forrest examines the manner in which a number of States in Australasia, Europe and North America have addressed this issue in their national legislation.

Part III: International and Regional Overviews

In Chapter 11 Ludo Block, a highly experienced police officer and crime investigator, provides an overview of the law enforcement approach taken to art crime across the 27 member states of the European Union (EU). As Block states at the outset of his chapter,

> In popular culture […] policing art crime tends to be portrayed as a thrilling area of police work performed by officers with seemingly unlimited resources. Reality, however, is, as usual, far less exciting. Even though worldwide treaties acknowledge the importance of cultural heritage protection and recognise that the damage caused by such crimes as art theft and looting can be irreversible, in most countries, art crime policing is accorded little priority.

Block goes on to provide more detailed descriptions of the state of art crime policing in specific EU member states. He concludes that although 18 of the 27 member states maintain centralized expertise, in only eight member states is actual investigative capacity allocated to the area of art crime. The size of these investigative units varies from one officer in Lithuania to a few hundred in France and Italy. At the EU level, although the prevention and investigation of art crime has been discussed in the political arena on several occasions over the past three decades, only recently has such discussion led to tangible policy instruments. Moreover, Europol – in contrast to its popular image – in fact undertakes no activities in relation to art crime.

As Noah Charney indicates in Chapter 12 the somewhat parlous and unfocused situation described in the EU regarding the policing of art crime is mirrored to a significant degree in North American climes. Charney, a highly respected and knowledgeable commentator on art crime and the founder of the influential Association for Research on Crimes Against Art (ARCA), notes that while the US Department of Justice and other reliable sources make clear the severity and extent of art crime worldwide this aspect of crime remains little known and little regarded in North America, even among police and governmental agencies. Efforts in recent years to promote the study of art crime have resulted in an increased understanding of the phenomenon internationally, from better-informed media coverage to the addition of several new art squads in countries that never before had any dedicated art police. Two such relative newcomers to the field in North America are the FBI Art Squad, founded in 2004, and the Quebec Art Squad, founded in 2008. Charney goes on to discuss the extent of art crime in North America, as well as the efforts to curb it. He also presents three case studies, two from the US and one from Canada, and summarizes the successes of the new art squads in both the United States and Canada.

In Chapter 13 Stefan Gruber, an academic lawyer who has specialized in the study of Chinese law and particularly that relating to the protection of the environment, considers the nature and patterns of art crime in Asia, a vast region of the world which has tended to be given far less prominence in the past in discussion and debate about this topic. As Gruber reminds us many Asian nations have experienced in the past the systematic plunder of their cultural heritage by colonial occupiers. This plunder has in many cases continued into the modern era as illustrated by the looting of Khmer treasures that took place in Cambodia during that nation's period of turmoil in the 1970s and the relentless flow of illegally excavated antiquities from China.

Gruber's chapter explores existing forms of art crime in those parts of Asia where looting and trafficking of regional artefacts have developed extensively in contemporary times. The sophisticated methods of looters and middlemen, the highly efficient smuggling networks which support them, and the involvement and resources of international art dealers collectively make the detection, investigation and prosecution of this art crime very difficult. Globalization, the simplified circulation of goods, and the diversity of political and legal systems in Asia are other aspects which add to the challenges facing cross-border regulation of the art trade and the tracking of cultural artefacts. The last part of the chapter examines several mechanisms and issues which are relevant to the prevention of art crime in Asia.

Chapter 14, by Duncan Chappell and Damien Huffer, continues with the Asian theme and connection by exploring, among other things, the ways in which illicitly obtained and trafficked artefacts from a number of Asian countries have found their way to Australia. Australia, an affluent and economically advanced nation which is much closer geographically to Asia than Europe or North America, has in recent years fostered deeper relationships with its Asian neighbours. At the same time evidence has emerged of looted objects from Asia reaching Australian shores and entering public and private collections. Chappell and Huffer consider two cases in particular in which such objects have been detected and efforts made to repatriate them to their country of origin. Their analysis of these cases suggests that the contemporary Australian legal regime for the protection of cultural property is far from effective, as are the mechanisms for enforcing that regime.

Chapter 15, the concluding contribution by Saskia Hufnagel describes the work performed by Interpol in the field of art crime. As is apparent from her description, Interpol's involvement has been expanding over recent years despite the general lack of interest in art crime already noted among many law enforcement agencies around the globe. Interpol has been quick to recognize that despite this less than enthusiastic attitude this is an area of crime where international law enforcement cooperation and collaboration can deliver dividends in the form of enhanced rates of detection and recovery of stolen items. It seems very likely that this cooperation and collaboration will become stronger as new services provided by Interpol to its members, like the PSYCHE program referred to by Hufnagel, come on stream.

Some Concluding Thoughts

As noted in the preface to this book its origins are to be found in a workshop, coordinated by the present editors, on the topic of 'Contemporary Perspectives on the Detection, Investigation and Prosecution of Art Crime'. The workshop, which was held in the Australian city of Brisbane in May 2012, was attended by an invited group of participants from both Australia and overseas, many of whom have contributed to the content of this book.

It is clear from these contributions that a great deal still needs to be done not only in Australia, but much farther afield to bolster law enforcement responses to art crime. It is also apparent that law enforcement alone cannot tackle a form of crime whose tentacles extend across international borders and whose impact can affect the integrity and dignity of an entire nation's cultural heritage. It is also somewhat ironic, but quite telling that the art crime with which this chapter commenced, the theft of the *Mona Lisa* more than a century ago, demonstrates these very same things with a lacklustre performance by law enforcement being added to by the failure to recognize the theft's cross-border dimensions and the involvement of a perpetrator who was seeking to return to his country from France what he incorrectly perceived to be an illicitly acquired Italian treasure. It is to be hoped that it will not be another century before some concerted action is initiated to remedy the situation which has been described.

Part I
CASE STUDIES

Chapter 2
The Antiquities Trade: Four Case Studies

Neil Brodie*

Introduction

Antiquities are generally held to comprise individual objects or parts of larger objects or structures that were made in ancient times (antiquity). Examples might include ceramic or metal vessels, statues or parts of statues, or broken off pieces of architecture. Although the term 'antiquities' is in general usage, and seems to enjoy some consensus of understanding, there is no agreed date-threshold for separating antiquities from 'non-antiquities', and so it should be born in mind that the term is subject to a certain fluidity of meaning. Since at least the eighteenth century, antiquities have been taken from archaeological sites, monuments and museums and traded internationally. Over time, as the material damage caused by the looting of antiquities came to be recognized, proliferating national and international laws placed the antiquities trade under progressively stronger statutory regulation, so that increasingly it has been made illegal. Nevertheless, this regulation has not succeeded in controlling or reducing the trade, and since the 1950s the material volume and monetary value of the trade have risen at an alarming rate. And while traditionally, the antiquities trade has been in the hands of specialist dealers, the increasing availability of illicit antiquities on the open market has opened opportunities for more routine criminal involvement and profit.

This chapter examines by way of four case studies various harmful manifestations of the antiquities trade. First, it recounts the tale of the now famous Euphronios krater, bought by the Metropolitan Museum of Art in 1972 for $1 million, and explains how the looting and trade of antiquities like the Euphronios

* This chapter was prepared in response to a kind invitation by the ARC Centre of Excellence in Policing and Security at Griffith University to present a paper at the workshop Contemporary Perspectives on the Detection, Investigation and Prosecution of Art Crime in May 2012. The author would like to thank Saskia Hufnagel and Duncan Chappell for extending this invitation, and along with their staff for making the workshop such an enjoyable and worthwhile occasion. The chapter was written while the author was funded by the European Research Council under FP7, grant number ERC StG-2011 283873 GTICO as part of the Trafficking Culture project.

krater can damage archaeological heritage, thereby weakening or compromising historical scholarship. Not all traded antiquities are as valuable as the Euphronios krater, nor are they important enough to be named individually, but the second case study, examining archaeological site looting in Jordan, shows how the trade of less valuable antiquities can still be profitable, and how their extraction can still cause enormous damage. The third case study moves away from questions of archaeological damage and historical scholarship, and considers how antiquities might be exploited by more commonplace episodes of financial crime, in this case the possible misuse of material donations to Californian museums for tax fraud. Finally, following and elaborating upon the problem of fraud, the fourth case study introduces the subject of fake antiquities by way of a description of the so-called Persian Mummy, discovered in Pakistan in 2000, and the further challenges to historical scholarship that they pose.

The Euphronios (Sarpedon) Krater

The Euphronios (Sarpedon) krater is a red-figure calyx krater made in Athens *circa* 515 BC, 46 cm high and 55 cm in diameter, signed by Euxitheos as potter and Euphronios as painter. It is decorated on the front with a scene depicting the death during the Trojan War of Sarpedon, who is attended by Hypnos and Thanatos with the god Hermes looking on. On the reverse are three Athenian youths arming themselves for battle. The krater was bought by the Metropolitan Museum of Art in 1972 for the then record-breaking price of $1 million, and is now thought to have been excavated illegally in Italy in 1971. In 2006, the Metropolitan restored ownership of the krater to Italy.

The krater is generally believed to have been discovered in December 1971 by tombaroli digging illegally in the ancient Etruscan cemetery of Cerveteri, in Italy.[1] They are said to have sold the krater to Italian dealer Giacomo Medici for something in the region of $88,000, with Medici, in turn, arranging for the krater to be smuggled into Switzerland, where he sold it to US dealer Robert Hecht for $350,000.[2] In February 1972, Hecht alerted the Metropolitan Museum to the existence of the krater, and in August 1972, after some haggling, the Metropolitan, under the directorship of Thomas Hoving, agreed to buy the krater from Hecht for $1 million.[3] The krater arrived in the United States on 31 August 1972.

Hecht claimed to be acting on ten per cent commission as agent for the krater's owner, whom he identified as Lebanese collector and dealer Dikran Sarrafian.[4]

1 Vernon Silver, *The Lost Chalice* (HarperCollins 2009) 287-90.

2 Ibid., 37-52, 287-90.

3 Thomas Hoving, 'Super art gems of New York City: "Hot Pot" part II – Unexpectedly, the money source opens up' (*artnet.com*, 2001) <www.artnet.com/magazine/features/hoving/hoving7-2-01.asp> accessed 19 July 2012.

4 Ibid.

Hecht supplied two documents of provenance in support of his claim. First was a letter dated 10 July 1971, written by Sarrafian to Hecht, in which Sarrafian declared that he would deliver the vase to Hecht in expectation of a final sale price of $1 million. Second was another letter from Sarrafian to Hecht, dated 9 September 1972, stating that Sarrafian's father had obtained the krater in 1920 in London and that because it was in fragments it had been sent [to Switzerland] for restoration, three years before the writing of the letter.[5]

On 12 November 1972, the *New York Times* announced the Euphronios (Sarpedon) krater's acquisition with a cover story for its Sunday magazine.[6] The price and provenance of the krater were both withheld, with the Metropolitan claiming that it was maintaining secrecy in order to protect a potential source of future acquisitions.[7] On 19 February 1973, however, a more critical account of the krater's provenance was published,[8] heralding a series of articles that questioned the museum's account and suggesting instead that the krater had been excavated illegally at Cerveteri in late 1971. The names of Hecht and Sarrafian leaked out and the $1 million price tag was revealed.[9]

The new and potentially damaging allegations of illicit provenance caused the Metropolitan to send lawyers to visit Sarrafian in Beirut.[10] They obtained documents from Sarrafian confirming that he had received payment for the krater including one dated to 19 October 1972 recording his receipt of $909,000 in Swiss francs. They also obtained testimony from a clerk who had seen the vessel in fragments with Sarrafian in Beirut in the early 1960s. The Metropolitan's legal team also collected affidavits from Bürki, confirming that he had received a fragmentary krater from Sarrafian in August 1971, and a photographer in Basel who had seen the fragments in September 1971.[11] This accumulated evidence was made public in June 1973, and seemed to confirm

5 Thomas Hoving, *Making the Mummies Dance: Inside the Metropolitan Museum of Art* (Simon and Schuster 1993) 319; Thomas Hoving, 'Super art gems of New York City: The "Hot Pot" III – The shit hits the fan' (*artnet.com* 2001) <www.artnet.com/magazine/features/hoving/hoving7-5-01.asp> accessed 19 July 2012.

6 James Mellow, 'A new (6th Century B.C.) Greek vase for New York' *New York Times Magazine* (New York, 12 November 1972) 42, 43, 114-16.

7 Nicholas Gage, 'Farmhand tells of finding Met's vase in Italian tomb' *New York Times* (New York, 25 February 1973).

8 Nicholas Gage, 'How the Metropolitan acquired "the finest Greek vase there is"' *New York Times* (New York, 19 February 1973).

9 Gage (n 7).

10 Thomas Hoving, 'Super art gems of New York City: The "Hot Pot" V – Utterly unexpected good news' (*artnet.com* 2001) <www.artnet.com/magazine/features/hoving/hoving7-13-01.asp> accessed 19 July 2012.

11 Nicholas Gage, 'Dillon stands by vase' *New York Times* (New York, 27 June 1973); Thomas Hoving, *Making the Mummies Dance: Inside the Metropolitan Museum of Art* (Simon and Schuster 1993) 333; Hoving (n 10).

that the krater was in Switzerland before the suggested December 1971 date of illegal excavation, as well as refute allegations of illicit provenance.[12]

In July 1973, Hoving received from art collector Muriel Newman a copy of a letter she had sent to Sarrafian stating that she had seen a fragmentary Euphronios vessel with him in Beirut in 1964. Newman subsequently signed an affidavit confirming this statement.[13]

By the end of 1973, therefore, the question of provenance seemed settled in favour of the Hecht/Metropolitan account of Sarrafian's ownership, and thus legitimate provenance. Matters rested there until the Italian Carabinieri began investigating Giacomo Medici and Robert Hecht in the 1990s. In September 1995, they raided Medici's Geneva storerooms, recovering 3,800 whole or fragmentary antiquities, more than 4,000 photographs of looted antiquities in various stages of restoration, and thousands of documents relating to his business. Among the photographs were two, taken in May 1987, one showing Medici standing next to the Euphronios (Sarpedon) krater on display in the Metropolitan, the second showing Hecht in a similar pose.[14] On 16 February 2001, the Carabinieri raided Hecht's apartment in Paris. They recovered a handwritten 'memoir' of Hecht's, setting out an autobiographical account of his life in the antiquities trade. It contains two accounts of the Sarpedon Euphronios: the first admitting to the fact that Hecht had bought the krater from Medici and that it had been excavated illegally in 1971; the second reiterating the Sarrafian provenance as provided to the Metropolitan. Finally, in June 2001, Marion True of the J. Paul Getty Museum informed Italian investigators in a sworn deposition that Dietrich von Bothmer, curator at the Metropolitan at the time of the krater's acquisition, had pointed out to her on an aerial photograph the location of the looted tomb from which the krater was allegedly taken, though von Bothmer subsequently denied this allegation.[15]

On 3 February 2006, the Metropolitan reached an agreement with Italy about the return of twenty objects, including the Euphronios (Sarpedon) krater, which Italian investigators had shown to have passed through the hands of Medici and to have been illegally exported (that is, stolen) from Italy. Although for the Euphronios (Sarpedon) krater the evidence for illegal excavation and trade was still largely circumstantial, the Metropolitan's director Philipe de Montebello clearly thought it was convincing when he was quoted as saying that it was 'highly probable' that the vessel had been stolen from an Etruscan

12 Gage (n 11).

13 Thomas Hoving, *Making the Mummies Dance: Inside the Metropolitan Museum of Art* (Simon and Schuster 1993) 335-6; Hoving (n 10).

14 Peter Watson, and Cecilia Todeschini, *The Medici Conspiracy* (2nd edn, Public Affairs 2007) 107.

15 Jason Felch and Ralph Frammolino, *Chasing Aphrodite: The Hunt for Looted Antiquities at the World's Richest Museum* (Houghton Mifflin Harcourt 2011) 209 211; Watson and Todeschini (n 14) 206-7.

tomb.[16] The krater arrived back in Italy on 18 January 2008, where it was put on display with other returned objects at the exhibition *Nostoi: Capolavori Ritrovati*, before being curated permanently at the Villa Giulia in Rome.[17]

Hoving has written since leaving the Metropolitan in 1977 that for a long time in private he harboured doubts about the krater's Sarrafian provenance, largely because, in various statements, Sarrafian had referred to the krater as comprising a hatbox of fragments thereby implying that it was incomplete.[18] The krater bought by the Metropolitan, though fragmented, was complete, and was considered by Hoving to be too large, even in fragments, to have fit into a hatbox. By 1993, Hoving had come to believe that there were in fact two Euphronios kraters: the Sarpedon one that had been illegally excavated in 1971 and subsequently acquired by the Metropolitan, and a second less-well-preserved one that had been in the possession of Sarrafian as claimed and documented, but that had subsequently turned up in the collection of Nelson Bunker Hunt.[19] Hecht had simply taken the provenance and documentation from the Sarrafian/Bunker Hunt krater and attached it to the illegally-excavated and better-preserved Sarpedon krater bought by the Metropolitan. Sarrafian had been killed in a car crash in 1977,[20] and so was unavailable for further comment. When challenged by Hoving about a possible switch, Hecht himself was ambivalent.[21] The Bunker Hunt krater, however, was bought by Leon Levy and Shelby White in 1990, and returned to Italy in 2010 when evidence emerged that it too had been illegally excavated.[22] Thus if Sarrafian had indeed possessed a Euphronios krater, as the evidence collected by the Metropolitan suggests, then it would have constituted a third example of the artist's work, though its identity and whereabouts remain unknown.

The now well-documented case of the Euphronios krater has much to reveal about the operation of the antiquities trade, and about its harmful effects on historical scholarship. First, as regards the trade itself, the krater started life as a stolen object in Italy, its country of origin. Unauthorized excavation of antiquities has been a criminal offence in Italy since 1939.[23] After transportation

16 Randy Kennedy and Hugh Eakin, 'Met agrees tentatively to return vase in '08' *New York Times* (New York, 4 February 2006).

17 Elisabetta Povoledo, 'Ancient vase comes home to a hero's welcome' *New York Times* (New York, 19 January 2008).

18 Gage (n 7); Gage (n 11); Hoving (n 10); Thomas Hoving, 'Super art gems of New York City: The "Hot Pot" VI – The old switcheroo' (*artnet.com* 2001) <www.artnet.com/magazine/features/hoving/hoving7-16-01.asp> accessed 19 July 2012.

19 Thomas Hoving, *Making the Mummies Dance: Inside the Metropolitan Museum of Art* (Simon and Schuster 1993) 338-9; Hoving (n 18).

20 Hoving (n 10).

21 Hoving (n 18).

22 Elisabetta Povoledo, 'Repatriated art in Rome' *New York Times* (New York, 29 March 2008).

23 Giovanni Pastore, 'The looting of archaeological sites in Italy', in Neil Brodie, Jenny Doole and Colin Renfrew (eds), *Trade in Illicit Antiquities: The Destruction of*

to Switzerland, a so-called transit country, its legal identity was altered or laundered by the attachment of false documents of provenance, or ownership history, providing the appearance of an object that had been out of Italy since at least the 1920s and probably earlier, which would facilitate its onward trade. It is likely too that from then on customs forms accompanying the krater would have listed Switzerland as its country of origin, and not, as would have been correct, Italy. Once safely out of Italy, and with new documents of provenance disguising its illicit trade, the krater became a legitimate acquisition for the Metropolitan Museum, in its destination country of the USA. The routing of material through transit countries to provide the appearance and perhaps after a sufficient period of time even the substance of legitimacy in destination countries is a characteristic feature of the antiquities trade, a feature that distinguishes it from most other transnational criminal trades, such as drugs trafficking, for example, which tend to be illegal from source through destination.[24] A possible parallel to the object laundering that characterizes the antiquities trade might be found in the trafficking of blood diamonds.[25]

Where the Euphronios (Sarpedon) krater might have been exceptional was in the production of a false provenance that was able to withstand reasonably serious scrutiny by the Metropolitan Museum once the *New York Times* had embarrassed the museum with its allegations of looting and smuggling. Most antiquities appearing for sale outside their countries of origin are sold with only minimal or even no provenance. They are mixed in with licit antiquities similarly being sold without provenance as 'unprovenanced antiquities', a category destined if not designed to obstruct law enforcement and to frustrate any attempts by law-abiding collectors or collecting institutions to confine their acquisitions to objects that are demonstrably licit. Collectors and institutions are forced instead to choose whether to believe that all unprovenanced antiquities are illicit, unless proven otherwise, or that they are all licit, unless proven otherwise. Many if not most have in the past chosen the latter assumption, falling back in their defence on the criminal law (and inappropriate in this context) principle of 'innocent until proven guilty'.[26]

---

the World's Archaeological Heritage (McDonald Institute for Archaeological Research 2001) 155.

24 Simon Mackenzie and Penny Green, 'Introduction: A context for the engagement of criminology and archaeology' in Simon Mackenzie and Penny Green (eds), *Criminology and Archaeology: Studies in Looted Antiquities* (Hart 2009) 4; Ken Polk, 'Whither criminology in the study of the traffic in illicit antiquities?' in S. Mackenzie and P. Green (eds), *Criminology and Archaeology: Studies in Looted Antiquities* (Hart 2009) 14-17.

25 Edgar Tijhuis, 'The trafficking problem: A criminological perspective' in Stefano Manacorda and Duncan Chappell (eds), *Crime in the Art and Antiquities World* (Springer 2011), 88.

26 James Ede, 'The antiquities trade: towards a more balanced view' in Kathryn Walker Tubb (ed), *Antiquities: Trade or Betrayed* (Archetype 1995) 211.

The facts that

1. the legal appearances of antiquities change according to their associated documentation and their point in the trading chain;

2. dealers like Hecht might simultaneously be doing business with smugglers like Medici and respected cultural institutions like the Metropolitan Museum; and

3. licit and illicit antiquities become inseparable as unprovenanced antiquities;

have caused criminologists to characterize the antiquities trade as a 'gray trade' or 'gray market'.[27] This characterization seems particularly appropriate for the destination market, and has implications for policies aimed at regulating or reducing demand.

The commercial agents and institutions that constitute the antiquities trade like to distinguish between a legal and an illegal trade, and object strongly to the idea that the trade should be viewed as singular undifferentiated 'gray' entity. One dealer, for example, has written that the 'attempt to unify the whole trade has as much validity as grouping back street abortionists with the consultants at Guys Hospital'.[28] The legal trade, dealers suggest, is in material that was excavated decades or even centuries ago, and that has been in collections ever since. The illegal trade, by contrast, the trade in illegally excavated and exported antiquities, is in the hands of a few rogue dealers, the few bad apples that are tainting the contents and reputation of the larger trade barrel.[29] Public policy, dealers suggest, should be aimed at extracting the bad apples, thereby leaving legitimate dealers to conduct their business free from outside interference, for the good of themselves and their customers, and more generally for the cultural and economic benefit of the trading country. Yet even dealers who propound this vision of the trade have on occasion been caught holding material that was originally stolen,[30] showing that the sharp distinction between licit and illicit that they like to draw is not warranted. The separation of licit and illicit trades should be a primary goal of public policy, not its assumed point of departure. Once a

27 Simon Mackenzie, 'The market as criminal and criminals in the market: Reducing opportunities for organized crime in the international antiquities market' in Stefano Manacorda and Duncan Chappell (eds), *Crime in the Art and Antiquities World* (Springer 2011) 71-3.

28 Ede (n 26) 211.

29 Jerome Eisenberg, 'Ethics and the antiquity trade' in Kathryn Walker Tubb (ed), *Antiquities: Trade or Betrayed* (Archetype 1995) 216.

30 Neil Brodie, 'Smoke and mirrors, in *Who Owns Objects?*' in Eleanor Robson, Luke Treadwell and Chris Gosden (eds), *The Ethics and Politics of Collecting Cultural Artefacts* (Oxbow 2006) 7-8.

recognizably illicit market is isolated it will be easier to tackle by a combination of law enforcement and moral rejection.

The case of the Euphronios (Sarpedon) krater also illustrates the damage that the looting of archaeological sites causes to historical scholarship. Attic red-figure pottery was made in Athens from about 530 BC to 360 BC. Large quantities were exported to the Etruscan city states of central Italy, where it was used as tableware at banquets and ultimately deposited in graves alongside the dead.[31] Because of their preservation in Etruscan tombs, most whole vases are found in Italy, and not, as might be expected, in Greece. They started to be excavated in large numbers during the nineteenth century, when many private and public collections of Attic pottery were assembled.[32] Unfortunately, because of the rudimentary state of excavation methodology at the time, there are few surviving records of the excavation contexts – records of where the vases were found and what was found accompanying them. Contextual information of this sort is vital for interpreting the value, function and symbolism of the pottery in ancient Etruscan society, and thus for the study of Etruscan society more generally. In view of the scientific shortcomings of early excavations, then, it is particularly regrettable that the many tombs containing Attic pottery that have been discovered since the development of a more mature archaeological methodology have been excavated by looters, so that again no contextual information has been recorded. The tomb in which the Euphronios (Sarpedon) krater is thought to have been found is believed from the later testimony of eye-witnesses to have contained statues of a winged sphinx and a panther, and 'all manner of painted ceramic vessels',[33] though as the people present at the robbing of the tomb were attending to what might have been saleable material, their testimony contains no account nor memory of any unsaleable or perishable material that might also have been present – material that is now lost to scholarship.[34] Italian archaeologists did in fact excavate the tomb in 1974, but by that time there was nothing left for them to find.[35]

Hoving described the Euphronios (Sarpedon) krater as ' … a work that would force the history of Greek art to be rewritten',[36] and it is a fact that since the time of their rediscovery in the eighteenth century, the artistic worth of Attic vases has been and continues to be highly regarded. Their well-executed scenes of mythological, ritual and everyday life are seen to have prefigured the Renaissance 'discovery' of mimesis, and the practice of celebrated painters such as Euphronios of signing their products suggests to modern scholars that ancient society held visual art and individual artists in high regard. The presence of Attic vases alongside ancient

31 Nigel Spivey, 'Greek vases in Etruria' in Tom Rasmussen and Nigel Spivey (eds), *Looking at Greek Vases* (Cambridge University Press 1991).

32 Brian Sparkes, *The Red and the Black* (Routledge 1996) 34-63.

33 Silver (n 1) 42.

34 Ibid., 48.

35 Ibid., 111-16.

36 Hoving (n 19) 318.

sculpture and European paintings in the collections of the nineteenth-century royal and early-twentieth-century capitalist nobilities[37] also shows how after rediscovery they were received as luxury commodities, encouraging a view among scholars that as highly-regarded artworks they would have fulfilled a similar social role of luxury good in ancient Greece and Etruria.[38]

It is now recognized, however, that to some extent at least, the modern high regard for Attic pottery might be colouring perceptions of its past importance. It is worth remembering, for example, that in 1972 the Euphronios (Sarpedon) krater was worth more than an equivalent gold vessel,[39] whereas in ancient Athens, and presumably in ancient Etruria too, such equivalence would have been unthinkable. The price of ceramic vessels would have been only a small fraction of that of gold vessels.[40] Furthermore, if, as has been argued, pottery was made in imitation of precious metal vessels, their artistic originality might have been less obvious and the social status of their painters lower than previously thought, despite their practice of signing work.[41] Given these counter-arguments, the assumption that Attic red-figure pottery might have functioned as a luxury good in antiquity is now regarded with some suspicion, and given the seeming importance of pottery for Athens as an export commodity, scholarly doubts and debates over the value of the pottery inevitably confound broader studies of the ancient economy.[42] Thus the full and correct historical interpretation of an antiquity such as the Euphronios (Sarpedon) krater depends to a greater or lesser extent upon the context of its discovery, but in the absence of any such contextual information, not only is its interpretation likely to be flawed, it is more likely to be led astray by the presuppositions of the scholar.

Early Bronze Age Sites of Jordan

The case of the Euphronios krater is notorious on account of what appeared at the time to be an exorbitant purchase price paid by a prestigious institution in the major commercial and cultural hub of New York. Objects like the Euphronios krater populate the public imagining of the antiquities trade, which is conceived as an affair of precious 'treasures' and extravagant deals, with their attendant risk

37 Vinnie Nørskov, *Greek Vases in New Contexts* (Aarhus University Press 2002) 58-71; Michael Vickers and David Gill, *Artful Crafts: Ancient Greek Silverware and Pottery* (Clarendon Press 1994) 1-32.

38 Vickers and Gill (n 37) 2-4.

39 In 1991, the collector Michael Steinhardt paid $1.2 million for a gold bowl or phiale discovered in Sicily and made sometime between 323 BC to 146 BC. When corrected for inflation, by 1991 the $1 million paid for the Euphronios krater, which is just over twice as large as the phiale, would have been worth $3.3 million.

40 Vickers and Gill (n 37) 85-8.

41 Ibid., 105-190.

42 Sparkes (n 32) 144-5, 164-6.

of celebrity hubris. It is a conceptualization that owes much to the fictional worlds of Indiana Jones and Thomas Crown, and encourages the erroneous belief that the goals of ameliorating policy or regulation should be to prevent the theft and secure the recovery of ancient 'masterpieces'. It comes as no surprise then to find that policy responses to the trade sometimes seem to offer better protection to 'treasures' and the property rights of their dispossessed owners than they do to what appear at first glance to be more mundane objects of no particular artistic or monetary value. Article 2.5 of the British Museum's acquisitions policy, for example, makes a distinction between objects of major and minor importance:

> The Museum will normally only acquire those archaeological and heritage objects that have documentation to show a legal history back to November 14th 1970 (the date of the UNESCO Convention) and this policy will apply to all objects of major importance. The Museum recognises, however, that in practice many minor items are not accompanied by detailed documentary history or proof of origin and reserves the right for the Museum's curators to use their best judgement as to whether such objects should be recommended for acquisition.[43]

As the case of the Euphronios krater shows, the monetary value of an object is no guarantee of its good provenance, and there is no reason why the documented provenance of 'minor items' should be inherently inferior to that of major items. What Article 2.5 does reveal, in fact, is that the British Museum applies a less stringent test of provenance to the acquisition of minor items, perhaps born out of a belief that the degree of archaeological damage caused by looting correlates in a positive fashion to the importance of the object, or perhaps more simply because of a (probably realistic) fear that the risk of scandal and public embarrassment is more acute for acquired major items that are subsequently found to be illicit in some way. The British Museum takes its definition of 'minor items' from the UK government's *Combating Illicit Trade: Due Diligence Guidelines for Museums, Libraries and Archives on Collecting and Borrowing Cultural Material*, which has the following to say:

> 'Minor items' are not easy to define comprehensively, since most categories of material, from manuscripts and coins to porcelain and Greek vases, necessarily include both minor and major items. Nor is it appropriate to use financial value as the main criterion, since items which are very cheap and which may seem insignificant can have major archaeological and cultural significance. However, they share the following characteristics:
>
> - may be of common types, or may be items of which multiple examples were made and have survived.

43 Policy on Acquisitions (British Museum 2007) <www.britishmuseum.org/pdf/Acquisitions.pdf> accessed 6 September 2012.

- are usually made of relatively cheap or plentifully available materials
- are often (but not always) small in physical size
- may lack conventional beauty or other appeal
- tend to be (but are not always) of relatively low monetary value.[44]

Thresholding antiquities according to their perceived importance is also a feature of some laws. Council Regulation (EEC) No 3911/92 of 9 December 1992 on the export of cultural goods, for example, is intended to control the export of antiquities, artworks and other cultural objects from the European Union by a system of export licensing. Paragraph 2, however, states that:

> However, without prejudice to paragraph 4, the Member State which is competent in accordance with the two indents in the first subparagraph may not require export licences for the cultural goods specified in the first and second indents of category A1 of the Annex where they are of limited archaeological or scientific interest, and provided that they are not the direct product of excavations, finds and archaeological sites within a Member State, and that their presence on the market is lawful.[45]

The objects referred to in the first and second indents of the Annex are archaeological objects more than 100 years old which are the products of excavations and finds on land or underwater, or of archaeological sites.

The exclusions allowed by Paragraph 2 of the EEC Regulation suggest a third reason for discriminating against 'minor items'. It might simply be a misguided though well-intentioned attempt to maximize the effectiveness of what scarce law enforcement resources are available to combat the trade by deciding a hierarchy of object importance or interest. Presumably, the hope is that by focusing regulatory protection on 'more important' objects, the problem will be diminished. However, as explained for the Euphronios krater, the main problem caused by the looting of antiquities is not the act of theft itself, but the harm to scholarship caused by the destructive circumstances of the theft. There is no guarantee, and indeed it is highly unlikely, that the damage caused by looting of 'minor items' will be related to the monetary value, artistic importance or archaeological significance of the objects themselves. This point is easily demonstrated by a brief discussion of the looting of Early Bronze Age (EBA) cemetery sites of Jordan.

Archaeological research on the ground and remote survey by means of satellite imagery have characterized the severe looting of EBA cemetery sites in

---

44 *Combating Illicit Trade: Due Diligence Guidelines for Museums, Libraries and Archives on Collecting and Borrowing Cultural Material* (Department for Culture, Media and Sport, 2005) 10. <www.culture.gov.uk/images/publications/Combating_Illicit_Trade05.pdf> accessed 7 September 2012.

45 Council Regulation (EC) 3911/92 on the export of cultural goods [1993] para 2.

west-central Jordan from the mid 1990s through into the 2000s.[46] For one site in particular, Bâb edh-Dhrâ', the combination of information derived from the different methodologies has proved particularly illuminating, both in terms of assessing the scale of the archaeological damage caused by looting, and estimating the monetary profit made from the sale of what are, by the DCMS definition at least and probably any other definition, minor objects.

The cemetery at Bâb edh-Dhrâ' was in use throughout the EBA, but the most numerous and commonly excavated tomb is the EB IA shaft tomb. Sixty of these shaft tombs were excavated officially between 1965 and 1981, and are in the process of being published.[47] Each tomb was likely to contain several interments, usually accompanied by some small, undecorated ceramic vessels (jugs, cups, bowls and the like), with maximum dimensions between 10 to18 cm. On the London market in the late 1990s, these pots were selling for prices in the range £70 to £175, depending upon size – so not Euphronios prices by any stretch of the imagination. In 2007, examination of a Google Earth image of Bâb edh-Dhrâ' showed that the total area looted was 74,377 sq. m., an area encompassing between 600 and 670 tombs, which could have contained in total between 9,000 and 28,000 pots.[48] At late 1990s prices, assuming a mean price of £122 for each pot, the sale of the Bâb edh-Dhrâ' pottery on the London market would have realized something between £1 and £3.4 million.[49] Thus although not one of these 'minor items' of pottery was monetarily valuable in itself, in aggregate, their total resale value would have presented an enticing prospect for the unscrupulous dealer. And whereas the looting of the Euphronios krater occasioned the loss and destruction of the contents of only a single tomb, the Jordanian pottery would have been acquired from hundreds of tombs, which between them would have contained thousands of burials – nothing less in fact than an ancient population. The destruction was made worse, if that is possible, by the arid environment of Bâb edh-Dhrâ' which

46 Ghazi Bisheh, 'One damn illicit excavation after another: the destruction of the archaeological heritage of Jordan', in Neil Brodie, Jenny Doole and Colin Renfrew (eds), *Trade in Illicit Antiquities: The Destruction of the World's Archaeological Heritage* (McDonald Institute for Archaeological Research 2001); Daniel Contreras and Neil Brodie, 'The utility of publicly-available satellite imagery for investigating looting of archaeological sites in Jordan' (2010) 35 *Journal of Field Archaeology* 101-14; Konstantinos Politis, 'Dealing with the dealers and tomb robbers: the realities of the archaeology of the Ghor es-Safi in Jordan' in Neil Brodie and Kathryn Walker Tubb (eds), *Illicit Antiquities: The Theft of Culture and the Extinction of Archaeology* (Routledge 2002).

47 Donald Ortner and Bruno Frohlich, *The Early Bronze Age I Tombs and Burials of Bab edh-Dhra', Jordan* (Altamira 2008); Thomas Schaub and Walter Rast, *Bab edh-Dhra: Excavations in the Cemetery Directed by Paul W. Lapp* (1965-67) (Eisenbrauns 1989).

48 Contreras and Brodie (n 46) 109.

49 Neil Brodie and Daniel Contreras, 'The economics of the looted archaeological site of Bâb edh-Dhrâ': a view from Google Earth' in Paula Lazrus and Alex Barker (eds), *All The Kings Horses: Looting, Antiquities Trafficking and the Integrity of the Archaeological Record* (Society for American Archaeology 2012) 22.

favours the preservation of perishable materials such as textiles and other organic objects, which usually do not survive in archaeological sites. The loss to historical scholarship caused by the looting of Bâb edh-Dhrâ' and its neighbouring EBA cemeteries is incalculable.

Museum Donations and Tax Fraud

The cases so far considered have shown how the antiquities trade converts archaeological artifacts into expensive artworks or more modestly priced collectables, at the cost of damaged or destroyed archaeological sites and compromised historical scholarship. The harm does not stop there, however. The fact that unprovenanced antiquities have no verifiable evidence of previous ownership renders them particularly vulnerable to fraudulent transaction. The following two case studies explore this broader area of criminality by examining in turn the suspected use of antiquities for tax fraud, and the ease with which antiquities can be faked and passed onto the market as genuine.

In January 2008, US federal agents raided the premises of two antiquities dealers and four museums in California, on suspicion of theft and conspiracy to commit tax fraud.[50] The dealers were Robert Olson and the husband and wife partnership of Jonathan and Cari Markell. The museums were the Los Angeles County Museum of Art (LACMA), the Bowers Museum, the Pacific Asia Museum (PAM) and the Mingei International Museum. The raids were the culmination of an investigation that had commenced in April 2003, and were justified by evidence collected by an undercover agent, posing as 'Tom Hoyt', said to be an IT specialist interested in purchasing antiquities and donating them to museums in return for a tax deduction. Federal agents also seized 16 international cargo shipments destined for Olson. The investigation focused on transactions of antiquities believed to have been illegally excavated and exported from Ban Chiang and associated archaeological sites in Thailand.

Olson, 79 years old at the time of the 2008 raids, was proprietor of Bobbyo Imports, and clearly considered himself to be a 'wholesaler', importing antiquities to be sold to collectors or to other dealers.[51] The affidavit issued against Olson alleged that he had purchased, received and sold Thai antiquities in violation of California and federal criminal laws, and that he had engaged in a conspiracy to assist others in preparing false tax returns. Olson claimed to have started importing Thai antiquities after a meeting in 1979 with Armand Labbé,[52] curator at the Bowers Museum, who could arrange for any material imported by Olson

50 Jason Felch, '4 Southland museums raided in looting probe' *Los Angeles Times* (Los Angeles 24 January 2008).

51 Search warrant affidavit, *United States v 18624 Del Rio Place*, 08-0090M (Central District of California 18 January 2008).

52 Labbé died in 2005.

to be exhibited. Olson is quoted as saying that after a major exhibition of his material at the Bowers in 1985, he paid $24,000 of his own money to print a catalogue,[53] and that in consequence of bringing his material to the attention of a larger audience, the market 'exploded'.[54] Olson started importing 'hundreds and hundreds of pieces' of Ban Chiang pottery, with sales to museum curators and collectors, and to the Markells. Olson claimed to sell the Markells antiquities and also to help them import. A shipment intercepted by ICE in 2003 was addressed jointly to Olson and the Markells.[55] Markell himself stated that he had started dealing in Thai material in 1988, at first through Olson.[56]

US federal law allows tax deductions for tangible, non-monetary donations to non-profit organizations, including museums.[57] The donor is permitted to claim a deduction equal to the fair market value of the donated material. The federal investigation into Olson and the Markells alleged that they were enabling customers to evade tax by supplying them with antiquities intended for charitable donation to museums, and providing them at the same time with an appraisal of fair market value far in excess of cost price. Thus Olson and the Markells would profit from the sale of looted and smuggled antiquities, the customers would benefit financially by claiming a deduction equal to an inflated appraised value while paying only cost, and the museums would acquire new material for their collections free of charge. The undercover agent 'Tom Hoyt' made eight separate purchases of antiquities on different occasions (Tables 2.1 and 2.2), with Olson and J. Markell supplying both material and appraisal and arranging introductions to relevant museum staff. At first, Olson used another California dealer (Joel Malter) as appraiser, but after Malter stopped, he approached Susan Lerer, who was said by Olson to be Labbé's girlfriend.[58] Markell prepared his own appraisals of material he supplied himself, but validated them with an electronic copy of the signature of Roxanna Brown, curator of Bangkok University's Southeast Asian Ceramics Museum. 'Hoyt' also ascertained that Markell had prepared donations for the Los Angeles County Museum of Art in the name of his brother-in-law Allan Schore, and for at least one other named client. In January 2013, Olson was indicted on charges of conspiracy and trafficking in stolen goods.[59]

---

53 Armand Labbé, *Ban Chiang: Art and Prehistory of Northeast Thailand* (Bowers Museum 1985).

54 Jason Felch, 'Little glamour surrounds alleged smuggler' *Los Angeles Times* (Los Angeles 31 January 2008).

55 Search warrant affidavit, *United States v Los Angeles County Museum of Art*, 08-0100M (Central District of California 18 January 2008).

56 Ibid.

57 Erin Thompson, 'The relationship between tax deductions and the market for unprovenanced antiquities' (2010) 33 *Columbia Journal of Law and the Arts* 241-265.

58 Search warrant affidavit, *United States v 18624 Del Rio Place*, 08-0090M (Central District of California 18 January 2008).

59 Jason Felch, 'Stolen-artifacts case has cost much, yielded little, critics say' *Los Angeles Times* (Los Angeles 18 May 2013).

Table 2.1 Donations to museums made by 'Tom Hoyt' of material purchased from Robert Olson

Date	*Purchase price ($)*	*Appraised value ($)*	*Appraiser*	*Museum*
Dec 2003	12,000	44,700	Malter	Bowers
Mar 2004	12,000	44,700	Malter	Bowers
Dec 2005	6000	18,775	Lerer	PAM

Table 2.2 Donations to museums made by 'Tom Hoyt' of material purchased from Jonathan and Cari Markell. Purchase price includes cost of material and appraisal fee paid to Markell

Date	*Purchase price ($)*	*Appraised value ($)*	*Appraiser*	*Museum*
Mar 2006	1,500	4,990	J. Markell	PAM
Jun 2006	1,500	4,985	J. Markell	Mingei
3rd quarter 2006	1,350	4,900	J. Markell	Mingei
4th quarter 2006	1,500	4,850	J. Markell	Berkeley
Mar 2007	1,500	4,915	J. Markell	Mingei
Sep 2007	1,500	6,000	J. Markell	Mingei

It was estimated that for a maximum rate taxpayer in 2008, the saving on a typical $5000 donation would have been $700.[60] Most donations comprised more than one object, and the objects themselves were usually of low monetary value and seemingly of limited artistic interest. Again, like the Jordanian EBA pottery, the bronze and stone weapons and tools from Ban Chiang sourced through Olson and Markell that are now illustrated in museum collections' databases are a far cry in both market value and artistic merit from the Euphronios krater. Again, though, the scale of the archaeological damage caused by their looting can only be guessed at.

The role of the museums in this affair deserves more than a little attention. Most published criticism has centred upon the apparent readiness of the museums concerned to acquire material of dubious provenance. Yet by the early 2000s, due in no small part to scandals such as the one generated by the acquisition of the Euphronios krater, museums and their professional associations had

60 Matthew Wald, 'Tax scheme is blamed for damage to artifacts' *New York Times* (New York 4 February 2008).

developed ethical guidelines for museum acquisitions of antiquities, with the express purpose of preventing the large-scale acquisition of looted or smuggled material. The British Museum's code is one example, as previously discussed. At the time of the investigation into the Californian museums, the relevant ethical guidance as regards art museum acquisitions in the United States was contained in the June 2004 Association of Art Museum Directors (AAMD) guidelines regarding archeological material and ancient art, which required that: 'Objects which have not been out of their probable country of modern discovery for at least the preceding 10 years should not be acquired.'[61] Yet, with the apparent exception of LACMA,[62] the museums concerned seemed to have ignored that recommendation, which raises questions about museum attitudes to ethical guidance more generally, and about the inclination, duty and ability of museum associations to enforce that guidance in particular. But the AAMD acquisition guidelines had nothing to say about the possible abuse of gifting arrangements for tax fraud, even though a large percentage of museum acquisitions are through donation or bequest.

Figure 2.1 shows the importance of gift acquisitions for three of the museums concerned, which have on-line catalogues of their collections that are open to searching. The histogram shows clearly that virtually all acquisitions of antiquities from prehistoric Thailand were donated. The museums between them made hardly any purchases of material during the periods in question. The histogram also shows that more than half of all gifts were sourced through Markell. Thus on the face of it, the dependence of museums on material donations for building their collections renders them vulnerable to entanglement, knowingly or not, with conspiracies intending to commit tax fraud. One way for museums to protect themselves from involvement in tax frauds would be for them to adopt voluntarily a stronger appraisal process than is currently acquired under US law. For example, most donations identified during the investigation were of material worth less than $5000. For donations worth more than $5000, US law requires a detailed appraisal including information about provenance and reasons for appraisal.[63] The voluntary adoption by museums of this stronger standard of appraisal would augment the regular due diligence process recommended in the revised AAMD (2008)[64] and other museum association guidelines, and adhere to the spirit if not the letter of ethical codes.

---

61 Report on acquisition of archaeological materials and ancient art (Association of Art Museum Directors 2004).

62 Search warrant affidavit, *United States v Los Angeles County Museum of Art*, 08-0100M (Central District of California 18 January 2008).

63 Publication 561: Determining the Value of Donated Property (Internal Revenue Service 2007).

64 Report of the AAMD task force on the acquisition of archaeological materials and ancient art (revised 2008) (Association of Art Museum Directors 2008).

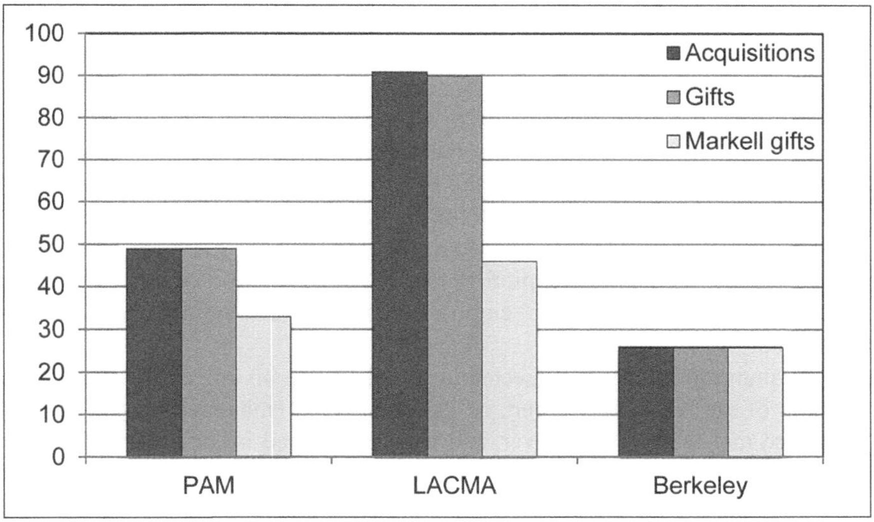

Figure 2.1 Acquisitions of objects from Thailand dating to before 500 AD by three museums (PAM 1980-2002; LACMA 1974-2005; Berkeley 1991-2007)

Persian Mummy (Persian Princess)

In March 2000, Amanollah Riggi of New Jersey sent Oscar Muscarella of New York's Metropolitan Museum four Polaroid photographs of what appeared to be a mummy, together with a translation of a cuneiform inscription that could be seen on the mummy's gold breastplate. Riggi claimed to be acting on behalf of a Pakistani acquaintance, and said that the mummy was available for purchase. The translation, prepared by a 'cuneiform expert at a major American university',[65] identified the mummy as the daughter of the fifth-century BC Achaemenid Persian King Xerxes. Muscarella soon discovered, however, that he had been supplied with only a part of the expert's full translation and report, which in its entirety judged the inscription to be fake. In any case, Muscarella was skeptical of the mummy's authenticity because of his own doubts about the iconography of carving visible on its wooden sarcophagus, and did not pursue the matter any further.

A few months later, in October 2000, Pakistani police in Karachi arrested one Ali Akbar on suspicion of selling a mummy, along with tribal leader Wali Mohammad Reeki of Quetta, who was in possession of it. This mummy was later found to be the one featured in the photographs seen by Muscarella. Both

65 K.M. Romey and M. Rose, 'Saga of the Persian Princess' 54 *Archaeology* January/February 2001, 24-5; 'The mystery of the Persian Mummy' (BBC 20 September 2001) <www.bbc.co.uk/science/horizon/2001/persianmummy.shtml> accessed 17 July 2012.

men were charged with contravening Pakistan's Antiquity Act. Reeki claimed to have received the mummy from an Iranian named Sharif Shah Bakhi, who since the accusation has never been located. The mummy was taken to the National Museum of Pakistan in Karachi, where at a preliminary press conference it was presented as the mummified remains of a Persian princess dating to about 600 BC. In the wake of the press conference, a debate broke out between Iran and Pakistan over the rightful ownership of what was seen to be an unparalleled archaeological find. No royal burials had ever been found in the vicinity of Xerxes' capital Persepolis, in present-day Iran, and given that Egypt was part of Xerxes' empire the practice of mummification was not totally out of the question.[66]

The mummy itself was subjected to an exhaustive investigation led by Asma Ibrahim of the National Museum of Pakistan.[67] The embalmed body was lying on a reed mat with a stone cover, and had been placed inside a carved wooden sarcophagus. It was decorated with a gold mask and crown, and bore an inscribed gold breastplate declaring 'I am the daughter of the great King Xerxes ... I am Rhodugune.' But as the investigation progressed, doubts about the authenticity of the mummy began to accumulate. Although the sarcophagus was carved with royal symbols, closer examination revealed lead pencil marks that had been made to guide the carving. A CT scan of the body showed that the internal organs, including the heart, lungs and brain, had been removed prior to embalming, which was counter to Egyptian practice. There were grammatical errors on the breastplate's inscription, and, crucially, the inscriber had used the later Greek version of the princess's name Rhodugune, instead of the Persian Wardegauna. Finally, radiocarbon dates of the reed mat showed it to be only fifty years old at most.

With the mummy's accoutrements shown to be fake, attention shifted to the body itself, which was that of an adult woman. The CT scan showed that the body had a fractured spine, caused by a blow with a blunt instrument, but an autopsy determined the probable cause of death to have been a broken neck. Radiocarbon dates suggested a date of death around 1996. The autopsy could not show whether the woman's neck had been broken deliberately or not, but Pakistani police launched a murder investigation. As of 2008, no progress had been made with the case.[68] Meanwhile, it was rumoured that two related mummies were being offered for sale on the international market.

66 Kristin Romey and Mark Rose, 'Saga of the Persian Princess' 54 *Archaeology* January/February 2001, 24-5; 'The mystery of the Persian Mummy' (BBC 20 September 2001) <www.bbc.co.uk/science/horizon/2001/persianmummy.shtml> accessed 17 July 2012.

67 'The mystery of the Persian Mummy' (BBC 20 September 2001) <www.bbc.co.uk/science/horizon/2001/persianmummy.shtml> accessed 17 July 2012.

68 Abbas Naqvi, 'Fake "mummy" still awaits burial' (*BBC News* 24 February 2008) <http://news.bbc.co.uk/1/hi/world/south_asia/7206526.stm> accessed 17 July 2012.

On 20 December 2001, the BBC science series Horizon screened a TV documentary on the mummy.[69] The programme drew attention to the resources and organization that must have supported the fabrication of the mummy: a person with knowledge of anatomy and embalming techniques, a cabinet maker, a stone carver, a goldsmith, and someone with a rudimentary knowledge of cuneiform. There would need to have been a facility to conduct mummification, which in itself would have taken half a ton of drying chemicals. The act of mummification must have taken place within 24 hours of the woman's death. Oscar Muscarella suggested it had most probably taken place in Iran.[70]

Fakes are the 'double whammy' of the antiquities trade. They are produced with the intention to defraud an innocent purchaser, but at the same time they undermine historical scholarship by reducing confidence in the material remains of the past. At first sight, the resources and organization supporting the manufacture of the Persian Mummy might appear to be unusual, but police investigations of other faking operations have revealed similar organizational efforts. The difference is that the effort is expended on producing a larger number of less valuable pieces. In February 2012, for example, it was reported that Italian police had arrested several people on suspicion of faking antiquities, including an archaeologist, an antiquities dealer and a ceramics expert, who between them most probably possessed the artistic and technical expertise necessary to produce convincing fakes, but also a nurse, who could arrange for fake ceramic pieces to be X-rayed in a hospital so as to fool authenticity tests based on thermoluminescence dating. One victim of the gang is said to have spent €1 million on its worthless products, while a police raid on the premises of one of the accused recovered 3,000 allegedly fake pieces.[71]

Some faking operations are organizationally less complex, sometimes coming down to the work of an unusually gifted individual. Brigido Lara, for example, by his own admission, is believed to have produced 40,000 objects purporting to be from various Mexican Precolumbian cultures before his arrest in 1974.[72] In 2006, the artworld looked on in disbelief when police arrested the 82-year-old George Greenhalgh, his 81-year-old wife Olive and their 45-year-

---

69 'The mystery of the Persian Mummy' (BBC 20 September 2001) <www.bbc.co.uk/science/horizon/2001/persianmummy.shtml> accessed 17 July 2012.

70 Ibid.

71 Tina Lepri and Ermanno Rivetti, 'Police raid criminal gang suspected of faking antiquities' (*Art Newspaper* February 2012) <http://www.theartnewspaper.com/articles/Police-raid-criminal-gang-suspected-of-faking-antiquities/25583> accessed 6 September 2012.

72 Nancy Kelker and Karen Bruhns, *Faking Ancient Mesoamerica* (Left Coast Press 2010) 66-71; Jesse Lerner, 'Brigído Lara, post-pre-Colombian Ceramicist' (Spring 2001) *Cabinet Magazine* <http://cabinetmagazine.org/issues/2/brigadolara.php> accessed 6 September 2012.

old son Sean on charges relating to faking antiquities and other artworks. Sean was said to have 'knocked them up' in the family's garden shed at their unprepossessing home in Bolton, England.[73] Nevertheless, Sean Greenhalgh's fakes were good enough to fool experts for nearly 18 years, during which time they are thought to have earned the family at least £850,000.[74] His most celebrated piece was the 52 cm-tall headless alabaster torso of the so-called Amarna Princess, said to date from fourteenth-century BC Egypt, perhaps representing a daughter of Pharaoh Akhenaten and his queen Nefertiti. It had taken Sean Greenhalgh three weeks to make, and was then authenticated by the British Museum and sold through Christie's London to Bolton Museum for £500,000, with funding obtained from the UK's National Art Collections Fund and National Heritage Memorial Fund. It came complete with fake provenance, attesting to its sale at auction in 1892.[75] The Greenhalghs were convicted in 2008.[76]

Fake provenances and forged documents of provenance are a common accompaniment of fake artifacts, seen for example in the case of the so-called Getty Kouros, a 2 m-high marble statue bought by the J. Paul Getty Museum in 1985 for $9.5 million. The statue's provenance comprised several letters that contained mention of it, but that were subsequently shown to be counterfeit. Consequently, the authenticity of the statue also fell under suspicion, and has never since been decided in a satisfactory manner.[77]

The owners of the Persian Mummy were unsuccessful in their attempt to sell it to the Metropolitan Museum, but as the Amarna Princess and Getty Kouros show, museums are not immune to the possibility of acquiring fakes. One study of ancient Near Eastern antiquities in major museums has provided a long catalogue of possibly fake objects held in their collections.[78] Museum collections of Precolumbian antiquities from Central and South America are also thought to be badly compromised by fakes.[79] Fake antiquities add another layer of uncertainty to any historical research that is based partly or wholly on unprovenanced material. As already described for the Euphronios krater, the absence of contextual information both hinders the correct sociocultural

---

73 '"Artful Codger" spared jail over counterfeit art' *Guardian* (London 28 January 2008).

74 Ibid.

75 Martin Bailey, 'How the entire British art world was duped by a fake Egyptian statue' *Art Newspaper* (London May 2006) 4.

76 '"Artful Codger" spared jail over counterfeit art' *Guardian* (London 28 January 2008).

77 Thomas Hoving, *False Impressions: The Hunt for Big Time Art Fakes* (Andre Deutsch 1996); Kenneth Lapatin, 'Proof? The case of the Getty Kouros' (2000) 20 *Source: Notes in the History of Art* 43-53.

78 Oscar White Muscarella, *The Lie Became Great. The Forgery of Near Eastern Cultures* (Styx 2000).

79 Karen Bruhns and Nancy Kelker, *Faking the Ancient Andes* (Left Coast Press 2010); Kelker and Bruhns (n 72).

interpretation of an object and weakens the constraints on any interpretations that may be unduly influenced by the subjectivity of the researcher. These threats to historical scholarship ramify when it cannot even be known for certain that the objects under study are genuine. But uncertainties over the authenticity of antiquities held in museum and other collections add one further and perhaps even more insidious threat to historical scholarship. Expert knowledge as regards the stylistic and technical characteristics of a particular class of antiquities is indispensible for their study and interpretation, and is only acquired through a long and close familiarity with the material in question. It forms the basis for the practice of connoisseurship, which is important for, among other things, distinguishing the genuine article from the fake. It is for this reason that museums assemble study collections, which comprise large numbers of whole and fragmentary objects representing the range of stylistic, technical and material variation typically displayed for individual classes of objects. If these collections are infiltrated by unidentified fakes, their reliability is compromised, and any knowledge obtained through studying or handling them is similarly rendered unreliable. A vicious circle sets in as the knowledge required to distinguish genuine artifacts from fake becomes less dependable, and it becomes easier for fakes to enter the market and collections.

Conclusion

This chapter has presented by means of four case studies an overview of the problems and issues surrounding the antiquities trade, which confound historical scholarship and offer opportunities for criminal involvement and profit. For these reasons, the trade is considered harmful and is subject to national and international regulation. The chapter has mentioned regulatory frameworks in passing, but has not considered them in any critical detail. There is an ongoing debate over the relative merits of strong or weak statutory regulation, and a parallel debate over the effectiveness of implemented regulation, particularly that of the 1970 UNESCO Convention on the Means of Prohibiting and Preventing the Illicit Import, Export and Transfer of Ownership of Cultural Property, which remains the most widely applied international instrument in this context. Implemented regulation is often vitiated by poor enforcement, possibly because the antiquities trade is not seen to be a political priority and in consequence policing is under-resourced. Alternative, non-regulatory options of trade control have hardly been explored, and although, as this chapter has demonstrated, ethical restraint on the part of museums and collectors cannot be relied upon, one positive development is the establishment of cooperative agreements between museums and source countries aimed at meeting the demand for antiquities by loan exhibitions. Recent introductions to these debates and developments can be found in Cuno,[80] Manacorda and Chappell,[81] Nafziger and Nicgorski,[82] and in chapters in this present volume. The interested reader should enquire further there.

80 James Cuno (ed), *Whose Culture? The Promise of Museums and the Debate Over Antiquities* (Princeton University Press 2009).

81 Stefano Manacorda and Duncan Chappell (eds), *Crime in the Art and Antiquities World* (Springer 2011).

82 James Nafziger and Ann Nicgorski (eds), *Cultural Heritage Issues: The Legacy of Conquest, Colonization, and Commerce* (Martinus Nijhoff 2009).

Chapter 3
The Peculiar Problem of Art Theft

Duncan Chappell and Kenneth Polk

Introduction

In these pages we will be examining the puzzling topic of art theft. Above all else, it often seems to be a crime that makes little sense, since in many situations a successful theft produces for the criminal an object which is so well known that it not only is impossible to sell on either a legal or illegal market, but the very presence of the object becomes a source of danger to the thief if for some reason circumstances provoke a police investigation. As is true for many forms of crime, however, there are actually a number of different patterns that the theft of art can take, and one of the tasks here will be to examine the major ones we can identify, and then define the major characteristics of each.

As we proceed, it will become necessary to provide some basic information about the contemporary art market,[1] and art theft.[2] The art market can be seen as consisting of two major components. There is, first, the primary art market which is made up of the initial point of sale after the work has been created. This can be done basically through two processes. One is where the artist sells directly to the customer, while the second is where the art passes through the hands of a dealer, with the artist paying a fee to the dealer. After some artists develop reputations for their art, they may sign an exclusive contract with a particular dealer. However the art market works, it is relatively rare that this primary sector is the target for thieves for the simple reason that most live artists still producing and selling their works rarely make enough money out of their art to attract the attention of potential thieves. As we shall see, unfortunately some elderly artists are an exception to this observation (see the cases involving Tucker and Picasso below). The secondary market is where art re-enters the market after an initial sale. It is here that we find virtually all of the expensive art, as, for example, in the major

1 Don Thompson, *The $12 Million Stuffed Shark – The Curious Economics of Contemporary Art* (Palgrave Macmillan 2008); Sarah Thornton, *Seven Days in the Art World* (Granta Books 2008).

2 John E. Conklin, *Art Crime* (Praeger 1994); Simon Mackenzie, 'Criminal and Victim Profiles in Art Theft: Motive, Opportunity and Repeat Victimisation' (2005) 10 *Art and Antiquity Law* 353, 370; Keith Middlemas, *The Double Market: Art Theft and Art Thieves* (Saxon House 1975); Bonnie Burnham, *The Art Crisis* (Collins 1975); Milton Esterow, *The Art Stealers* (2nd edn, Macmillan Publishing 1973).

auction houses of the developed world. Expensive art which has been stolen, if it is to enter the legitimate art market, must gain access to this secondary market, with the most likely points of entry being either an art dealer or an auction house. To be successful in terms of moving an object onto this secondary market, then, the potential art thief, first, must have access to works of art (which can be stolen), then after the theft has been carried off, the thief must, second, have a 'portal' or entry point into the secondary market if he/she is to realize an economic gain through the market, and then if there is to be an economic benefit from the theft, third, the stolen object(s) have to be sold to an ultimate consumer.

It can be pointed out, as an additional introductory matter that according to most official statistics there is no art theft, or any art crime for that matter. Currently in countries such as Australia and the United States, the major statistical bodies of information regarding crime have no way of recovering information about the specific topic of art crime. Essentially, all of art theft falls into the area of the 'Dark Figure' of crime, that is, that figure which is unknowable based on official statistics. To be sure, some countries have some information on art theft. In Italy, the Carabinieri have an extensive file on art and cultural heritage material stolen in that country, and in the United States there is some information on art theft available from specific policing units such as the Los Angeles Police Department and the FBI (both have units devoted to the topic of art crime). Nonetheless, there is no systematic assessment of the total volume of art theft in most nations.[3] For our investigation, then, we will have to seek out alternative approaches to examine the problem. For present purposes, which concern primarily attempting to delineate major patterns of art theft, we will draw upon various basically qualitative reports, including accounts found in media outlets, and where possible, referral to police or court records.

Scenario 1: Bent Dealers in the Art Market

The Case of Albert Tucker: A first form of art theft to be addressed consists of those rare examples where the instigator of the theft is positioned as a dealer within the art market. At the time the thefts in our first case occurred, the victim, the well-known Australian artist Albert Tucker, was quite elderly. He had been befriended by an established art dealer in the Melbourne market, Max Joffe. The thief, who was asked to order and catalogue Tucker's private collection, was given complete personal access to what amounted to a treasure trove of art which contained in addition to major works by Tucker others by such noted artists as Arthur Boyd, Daniala Vassilieff and Joy Hester. For Joffe, the temptation was too great, and he first stole large numbers of works, and then sold them on to the market in his role as dealer. For the thefts, Joffe was charged with stealing 57 works, many of which have not been recovered. He was ultimately convicted of

3 Mark Durney, 'Art Theft Statistics: A Need for Reliability' (2010) 1 *Cultural Heritage and Art Review* 13, 16.

24 counts of theft, and received a custodial sentence (the thefts occurred in 1994, and the conviction was recorded in 1998). The artist's biographer, Janine Burke (2002), indicated that Tucker was 'crushed' by the revelations of the thefts and that it had a 'devastating' impact on his life.[4]

The Case of 'Cornelius M': The noted Dutch expert on art and antiquities crime, Tijhuis,[5] provides a description of the complex form of art theft engaged in by a person he identifies as 'Cornelius M'. The thefts targeted large, wealthy French estates (apparently personally scouted and selected by Cornelius M), and involved at least 15 individuals who stole paintings, valuable antiquities, tapestries and furniture. The thieves themselves were never caught in the acts of theft. Once stolen, the goods were transferred to locations in The Netherlands and Belgium by special chauffeurs (one of whom provided crucial information to the police). After being moved, the mastermind of the operation ('Cornelius M') sold the items to what Tijhuis describes as 'complicit dealers' who then sold the items to customers primarily in Belgium and the south of The Netherlands. These dealers had shops mostly in areas remote from city centres, but one feature of the laws where they did their business was that since they were apparently legitimate dealers they were able to pass on what Tijhuis refers to as 'good title'[6] to the objects sold to their customers. Interestingly, 'Cornelius M' twice previously had been charged with offences involving receiving stolen antiquities, and had even served a prison sentence. In fact, the start of the thefts involving this gang began when he was released from this prior sentence. Cornelius M was sentenced to 14 years in prison in France, and 15 of his accomplices were given prison sentences which ranged from 1 to 6 years. This case is a bit more complicated, but again demonstrates the damage that can result when an apparently legitimate art dealer becomes directly involved in theft. In this case, the central dealer was able to check out the territory to identify targets for the thieves who essentially stole to order. This central dealer then worked through other dealers (providing the portal), and from there they were able to move their works onto the legitimate market and into the hands of customers.

In these two cases we see how the presence of a complicit dealer eases the problems of art theft. Their work as dealers gives them both information about where art objects might be found that can be stolen, as well as knowledge of which of these objects are likely to sell. The role as dealers provides the valuable portal into the art market, and their apparent legitimacy as dealers

4 Janine Burke, *Australian Gothic: A Life of Albert Tucker* (A. Knopf 2002); Virginia Trioli, 'Stealing from Aladdin's cave of art' *The Age* 11 April 1998 (in 'News Extra').

5 Antonius Johannes Garhardus Tijhuis, 'The Trafficking Problem: A Criminological Perspective' in Stefano Manacorda and Duncan Chappell (eds), *Crime in the Art and Antiquities World: Illegal Trafficking in Cultural Property* (Springer 2011) 87, 92-4, 98.

6 See ibid., 93.

eases any problems of not only providing access to customers, but doing so with the expectation that they will be able to obtain full market value for the goods (that is, they do not have to 'knock down' the price which they might be expected to do if they were selling goods where the customers knew they had been stolen).

Scenario 2: Successful Thieves Who are Not Good at the Business of Art

The Mona Lisa *Theft*: Probably the most famous art theft was the successful lifting of the Mona Lisa from the Louvre just over 100 years ago. In that case, the thief had both inside knowledge (having been employed for work inside of the museum) and very good luck in managing the theft itself. The painting disappeared on a day the Louvre was closed, and in which the security was even more lax than normal. The thief simply took the painting out of its frame, rolled it up, and made his way out of the museum (that this last was successful was where the luck, and quiet wits of the thief, entered). At that point we have the situation of many art thieves: the theft has been successful, but now how do they convert that to some economic advantage? If you have stolen the most famous painting in the western world, you do have a problem. While it might be worth huge amounts of money if it were possible to place it on the market, many thieves, as did this one, find that converting the work into spendable funds is simply not possible. In fact, for two years this thief had no choice but to leave the painting rolled up in his closet. While he tried to claim that his act was one of patriotism (a retaliation for the original theft from Italy, he believed wrongly, by Napoleon), in fact what brought him undone (as it has done for scores of art thieves) was his misguided attempt to sell the painting.[7]

The Troubles with The Scream: There are four renditions of Edvard Munch's *The Scream*, and two different ones have been the object of what were ultimately unsuccessful art thefts. The first of these began with the theft of one of the renditions from the National Gallery in Oslo in February 1994. This was a classic example of a group of thieves (four men were ultimately convicted of the theft) who had hoped that they could make a large amount of money from the theft. Initially they demanded a ransom of US$ 1million from the Gallery, which refused to pay this amount. This was followed in March, 1994 by the Norwegian police seeking the assistance of the British police in setting up a sting operation (which was successful), where an undercover member of the British Art Squad unit posed

---

7 Natalie Evans, 'Who's Smiling Now? Mugshot of Mona Lisa Thief to be Auctioned in Paris' *Mirror* (13 March 2012) <http://www.mirror.co.uk/news/world-news/mugshot-of-mona-lisa-thief-vincenzo-759890> accessed 18 April 2012; Richard Lacayo, 'Art's Great Whodunit: The Mona Lisa Theft of 1911' *Time Magazine* (27 April 2009) <http://www.time.com/time/arts/article/0,8599,1894006,00.html?artId=1894006?contType=article?chn=arts> accessed 14 April 2012.

as a civilian buyer representing the interests of the Getty Museum. The painting was recovered undamaged, and the offenders arrested in May, 1994.

The second version of *The Scream* was stolen in 2004 from the Munch Museum also in Oslo, along with an additional Munch painting, *The Madonna*. Some eight months later, in April, 2005 authorities made an initial arrest in the case, and three further suspects also were in custody by June, 2005. Despite the fact that the two paintings had not been recovered (although the city authorities offered a substantial reward for information about the works), six men went on trial for the crime in early 2006. Of these, three were convicted and were sentenced to between four and eight years in prison. Just a few month later in 2006, the two paintings were recovered, with both suffering some damage as a result of their ordeal.[8]

The Strange Case of Russborough House: Located in County Wicklow, Ireland, Russborough House has been the scene of four major thefts, none of which proved successful for the thieves. The first case involved a group of IRA members who, after tying and gagging the owners, stole 19 old masters (including works by Vermeer, Rubens, Gainsborough and Goya), and afterwards sent a large ransom note, and, in addition, the demand for the release of two IRA members then held in prison. Within a week the paintings were found in the boot of a car, and the perpetrators ended up in prison. One of the most notable of the Russborough thefts was the second, which took place twelve years after the first, in May 1986. Led by Martin Cahill, an Irish criminal gang stole 18 of the Russborough works (the Vermeer was once again taken). Some of the works were smuggled out of Ireland, and ended up in a variety of locations, including Istanbul (where three individuals were arrested in possession of one of the works). In fact, all but two of the works were recovered, including the Vermeer which was part of a successful undercover sting in Antwerp, Belgium. Russborough House was the setting for two later thefts, one involving two paintings stolen in 2001 (both recovered in 2002), the other took place in 2002 and involved five paintings, all of which were recovered within a few weeks of the theft. While the four thefts were initially successful as criminal acts, what is notable across all of these is the inability of the criminals to reap any economic rewards from their crimes.[9]

Some Other Examples: There are a large number of cases which have a similar appearance to these. The now famous FBI figure, Robert Wittman, for one example, participated in a number of undercover operations which lead to the

8 Kevin Sullivan, 'Stolen "Scream" Painting Recovered after 2 Year Search' *Washington Post* (4 September 2006) <http://www.washingtonpost.com/wp-dyn/content/article/2006/08/31/AR2006083100783.html> accessed 8 April 2012.

9 Brian R. Williams, 'Mobsters in the Manor House: What the Four Russborough Robberies Taught Us about Art Theft & Organized Crime' (Damforst Museum: The Online Museum of Damaged, Forged & Stolen Art 2011) <http://www.damforstmuseum.org/mobsters_manor_house.html> accessed 9 April 2012.

recovery of important works, including a small Rembrandt self-portrait that had been stolen from the National Museum in Stockholm. In that venture, an initial tip-off that occurred in the United States ultimately led to the arrest of some of the thieves in Copenhagen as they were, they thought, selling the work to what they took to be a mobster from the United States (that is, Wittman) and then the return of the Rembrandt to Stockholm.[10] In this pattern, what we see are individuals who are somehow successful in negotiating the theft of art, only to come undone by their lack of knowledge and connections with the art market.

In the case of the theft of several paintings by the popular English painter L.S. Lowry, the criminal group held the works for a bit over three years before they were recovered by a police raid. Four of the gang received prison sentences, although apparently three of the individuals involved in the armed theft were still at large. This case was notable in that those arrested were also involved in major drug dealing. Again, however, there was no indication of any profit as a result of the thefts of the art works.[11]

Scenario 3: Insider Thieves

Not all art thieves are likely to view themselves as criminals in the traditional sense. Some who become involved do so because their work, at least initially, gives them legitimate access to the art they eventually steal.

The Case of Stephen Biear: In March, 2012, the FBI announced that Stephen Biear, 51, Ossining, New York, had been sentenced to 10 years in prison for stealing art work and money from his elderly and wealthy employer. The art included works by Warhol, Duchamp and Picabia, among others. The length of the sentence is in part explained by the fact that in addition to the art, Biear stole over 3 million dollars from his employer by transferring money from the employer's accounts to his own.[12]

The Case of the Stolen Works of Mervyn Smith: When he was in his late 80s, for a period of time one of the carers of Mervyn Smith was Lilya Flaks. Smith was a reasonably successful Australian painter (living in Adelaide) who had sold works

10 Robert Wittman and John Shiffman, *Priceless: How I Went Undercover to Rescue the World's Stolen Treasure* (Crown Publishers 2011).

11 Helen Nugent, 'Victim of LS Lowry Paintings Robbery Relieved After Thieves Jailed' *The Guardian* (22 March 2012) <http://www.guardian.co.uk/artanddesign/2012/mar/22/ls-lowry-paintings-robbery> accessed 28 March 2012.

12 FBI, 'Former Caretaker of Elderly Millionaire Sentenced in Manhattan Federal Court to 10 Years in Prison for Stealing $3.2 Million and Valuable Artwork' (29 March 2012) <http://www.fbi.gov/newyork/press-releases/2012/former-caretaker-of-elderly-millionaire-sentenced-in-manhattan-federal-court-to-10-years-in-prison-for-stealing-3.2-million-and-valuable-artwork> accessed 12 April 2012.

for as much as $30,000 in the 1980s. Flaks was convicted of stealing a total of 28 watercolours worth more than $500,000 from Smith's Adelaide home. The details of the theft came to light when Flaks's former partner, who had been given the art as a gift, attempted to have the works valued so that they could be sold.[13]

The Case of Picasso's Electrician: Insiders can take various forms. In an emerging case in France, an electrician has argued that Picasso offered him as a personal gift 271 previously unseen works in return for work carried out at the artist's houses between 1971 and 1973. All of this came to light when they approached the Picasso Administration, which manages the Picasso estate, to have the works authenticated (the works had been stored in a garage near Cannes for close to 40 years). The son of the artist, Claude Picasso, is convinced that the works were stolen, and referred the matter to authorities, who ultimately indicted the electrician and his wife.[14]

The Case of the St Louis Museum Tour Guide: There are many examples of museum or library insiders who work as tour guides, curators, or security guards using their inside access to steal from their employing organization. In this St Louis case, James H. Strassner (who had been a tour guide at the museum) was sentenced to three years on probation after pleading guilty to stealing six Civil War-era coins worth over $18,000. The coins, dating from 1849 and 1862 had disappeared the day before a travelling exhibit was to open for the public (in mid-2011). This resulted in a wide public information campaign regarding the thefts, after which the coins were returned anonymously about a month later.[15]

The Case of the Missing Paintings from the Hermitage: After several concerns were raised about security and possible theft at the Hermitage Museum in St Petersburg, a nation-wide museum audit was ordered by President Vladimir Putin. The audit at the Hermitage found that more than 200 items were missing from the Russian medieval art section. It was then established that the individual responsible for the thefts was actually the custodian entrusted with safeguarding the unit's holdings, assisted as an accomplice by her husband and son. The works went missing in 2001, and some were recovered in 2007. The museum employee died of a heart

---

13 Sean Fewster and Andrew Dowdell, 'Woman Accused of Stealing Mervyn Smith's Art Claims Ownership' *The Advertiser (Adelaide)* (18 June 2008) <http://www.adelaidenow.com.au/news/south-australia/accused-art-thief-claims-ownership/story-e6frea83-1111116669252> accessed 4 April 2012.

14 Michel Guerrin, 'His Chauffeur, An Electrician and the Mysterious $50 Million Stash of Picassos' *Le Monde* (13 March 2012) <http://www.worldcrunch.com/his-chauffeur-electrician-and-mysterious-50-million-stashpicassos/4936> accessed 14 April 2012.

15 Jennifer Mann, 'Museum Tour Guide Admits to Theft of Civil War-era Coins' *St Louis Post-Dispatch* (15 March 2012) <http://www.stltoday.com/news/local/crime-and-courts/museum-tour-guide-admits-to-theft-of-civil-war-era/article_b09ebb4e-6ee1-11e1-87f4-001a4bcf6878.html> accessed 4 April 2012.

attack shortly after the investigation was undertaken.[16] These cases involving various forms of 'insiders' are instances where the role of the individual provides direct, legitimate access to works of art. Few such insiders take advantage of their position. When they do, if their intention is to derive direct economic benefit from the theft, they may find themselves in the same position as criminals who are knowledgeable about how to steal things, but who are ignorant in terms of how to derive any financial return from the thefts. Since they are often not aware of the basic dynamics of the secondary art market, their attempts to enter that market may result in the ready identification of the art as stolen, and their arrest as a consequence. Lest we think this a unique contemporary phenomenon, Esterow[17] tells the tale of a late 19th-century butler in The Netherlands who actually made a prisoner of his elderly master, and proceeded to sell many of his most valuable works of art.

Scenario 4: Stealing for Pleasure

The Case of the French Waiter: There are a few known instances where persons have stolen art essentially for their own consumption. Such thefts simplify the problems faced by the criminal, of course, because they remove the issue of working through a portal to reach a market. One of the most notorious recent cases was that of Stephane Breitwieser, a waiter from France who stole over 200 works of art between 1995 and 2001 with a combined estimated value of over 1 billion US dollars. He stole from over 172 museums, and tended to specialize in 16th- and 17th-century artists. The most valuable work among the thefts was by Lucas Cranach the Elder (*Sybelle, Princess of Cleves*), where the estimated value at auction was in the 5 million English pounds. Typical of this type of theft, Breitwieser's worry of apprehension was not at the danger point for most art thieves, which is when the work is placed on the market, but rather his problem was that of avoiding arrest during the theft itself. And, in fact, he was arrested close by a museum in Switzerland where he had stolen an object two days before, when a passerby became suspicious of his behavior outside of the museum and reported him to authorities. Breitwieser was sentenced in 2005 to three years in prison, of which he served 26 months.[18]

The Case of the New York Waiter: A similar pattern was revealed with the arrest and sentencing of Mark Lugo (like Breitwieser, a restaurant waiter) for the theft of over $700,000 in art works stolen in New York and California. Lugo was first jailed

---

16 'French Painting Returns to Russia's Hermitage 6 years after Theft' *RAI Novosti* (29 January 2007) <http://en.rian.ru/russia/20070129/59831884.html> accessed 4 April 2012.

17 Esterow (n 2) 136.

18 John Hooper, 'Connoisseur Turned Crook who Plundered Europe's Galleries for the Simple Love of Art' *The Guardian* (5 February 2003) <http://www.guardian.co.uk/world/2003/feb/05/arts.artsnews2> accessed 4 April 2012.

in California for the theft of a work by Picasso from a gallery in San Francisco, but then was sentenced to from one to three years in New York for thefts that included a work by Fernand Leger from a gallery in Manhattan's Carlyle Hotel. There is no mention in the accounts of any attempts by Lugo to sell the works, and, in fact, he displayed them on the walls of his New Jersey apartment (according to the brief account in the *New York Post*, 2012).[19]

The Odd Case of Mr William M. V. Kingsland, or was that Melvyn Kohn? One of the most unusual cases of art theft is found in the odd story of the late William M. V. Kingsland. For openers, his birth name, apparently, was Melvyn Kohn, but it seemed he thought his new name better fit his aspirations of status. In what appeared to be an attempt to elevate his image, Kingsland falsely had claimed that he lived on Park Avenue (his small New York apartment was on the East Side on 72nd), that he had attended Groton and Harvard (he had been to neither) and that he had previously been married to French royalty (he had not). After his death in 2006 at age 58 (it might have been 62), when public administrators began to assess the many paintings that were crammed into his small apartment, including works by Copley, Henri, Corot, Lely, Toulouse-Lautrec and Picasso, among others, many were found to have been stolen, most apparently in the 1960s and 1970s. One work, for example, a 1790 portrait by Copley of the Second Earl of Bessborough, had been stolen in 1971 from the Fogg Art Museum at Harvard University. Unfortunately, that is about all that is known. In fact, at this point it is not possible to say how many of the over 300 works actually were stolen (although it is known that several, such as the Copley, were). Important for present purposes, it further is not known who actually was responsible for the actual thefts. There is no mention in the available records of any acquaintance, friend, or relative ever seeing any of the works in the apartment, so however they came into his hands, Kingsland was not one who boasted to anyone about the rare collection of art he has accumulated. He seems to have been, in short, a true 'gloater', one who apparently possessed art for his own pleasure, or at least his own reasons. In common with others who gather such works for their own enjoyment (or reasons, since in his case we know neither how, nor why, he came by the hundreds of works), there is no record of him ever placing a work onto the art market, and thereby exposing himself to the risks of discovery. The work by Copley, for example, was quickly exposed as previously stolen when the art dealer who acquired it after Kingsland's death checked on its provenance, a simple process than anyone might have undertaken had the work been placed on the open market.[20]

19 *New York Post*, 'Hotel art thief is prison-bound' *New York Post* (8 February 2012) <http://www.nypost.com/p/news/local/hotel_art_thief_is_prison-bound_OORzxN+rezA8zEVgBEjNnL> accessed 4 April 2012.

20 Eric Konigsberg, 'Two Years Later, the F.B.I. Still Seeks the Owners of a Trove of Artworks' *New York Times* (12 August 2008) <http://www.nytimes.com/2008/08/12/nyregion/12kingsland.html?pagewanted=print&_r=0> accessed 26 September 2013.

The Case of the Connoisseur Thief: In his survey of art theft, Esterow[21] (1973, pp. 239-242) recounts the story from the 1920s in Paris of an art thief with impeccable taste. At that time, there were a series of extraordinary thefts where the victim was extremely wealthy, and of what was termed 'exceptional taste', and the items taken were always either a valuable painting or distinctive art object. Money or other valuables were not touched. The investigating police discovered that where an art work was stolen, it was the finest item in the collection. In a scene worthy of fiction, a trap was laid for the thief that involved creating a lavish evening party at the home of a supposed South American millionaire who just happened to have purchased recently a golden chalice. The ruse worked, and the police were able to follow the thief to a villa on the French Riviera. In the drawing room was a 'breathtaking' scene where the walls were filled with stolen art treasures.

In these various cases, we see a distinctive and different pattern from virtually all other forms of art theft. While the thief must face the difficulties of any thief in terms of the dangers posed by process of taking the art into their possession, once that has been gained, the thief avoids the problems faced by many criminals who seek some monetary gain from their theft. This means that the point of danger, as seen in these cases, comes with the theft itself. In three of the four cases, the criminal has come to grief because he went once too often to the well. Had any of the three been content with the number of works possessed up to the last theft, they may have, like Kingsland, left for us the same mystery we face in his case. That is, a house stuffed full of stolen art, and confusion regarding how that art found its way to that particular location (of course, we must hasten to add that part of the confusion here is that because of his death we are unable to assert with assurance that Kingsland was either a thief or a 'gloater').

Scenario 5: Creating a Portal into an Illegal Market

If thieves have a problem in terms of access to the legitimate secondary art market, a possible option, of course, is to seek out some illegitimate outlet for the sale of the stolen art works. One logical possibility that arises is that the works are 'stolen to order' by a 'Mr Big' with deep pockets who is willing to take the risks of purchasing such art.[22] Those knowledgeable about the theft of art tend to be skeptical that such individuals exist. However, considerable evidence is available about the existence of a wide spread illicit market for stolen works. In March, 2012, Italian police arrested three persons (a fourth was able to escape) who had worked a scheme for over ten years whereby they broke into villas in Venice and replaced valuable paintings with works that were actually touched up photographs.

21 Esterow (n 2) 239-242.

22 Philip Cornford, 'A Cavalier Frame of Mind' *Sydney Morning Herald* (13 April 2007). <http://www.smh.com.au/news/arts/a-cavalier-frame-of-mind/2007/10/12/1191696171884.html> accessed 13 April 2012.

The originals were then, according to accounts, sold 'on the black market'.[23] Over 40 works were stolen over the decade, including paintings by Canaletto and Guardi. In Spain, also in 2012, two ancient bronze statues were stolen, only to be recovered just as they '...were about to be sold on the black market to an Italian buyer...', the account adding that, consistent with a black market sale. The thieves were planning to sell the art for half of its value.[24] Another earlier case from the 1980s involved a band of Italian art thieves who used high-tech cutting tools and alarm avoidance devices and were able to carry off a perfect burglary at the Hungarian national museum in Budapest and cart off several works of art. The criminals were later arrested in Italy before they were able to deliver the paintings into the hands of a 'Greek olive oil baron' who seems to have paid a considerable sum up-front for the purpose of having the works to hang in his home.[25]

In a more recent example (April, 2012), several individuals in northern England were arrested after thefts of two objects from an Oriental museum in Durham. The group was alleged by police to consist of 'specialist criminals who knew exactly what they were after'. While it was initially thought that the two items were headed for 'overseas buyers with very deep pockets' who have created what was termed a 'thriving market for such items',[26] in fact the objects were recovered in England a few days later.[27]

The Balkans region has become a focal point for recent attention in terms of organized criminal activity around art theft. While there has been some amount of theft from regional sources (such as the recent loss of a Caravaggio copy taken from a museum in Odessa), there has been wider concern for the emergence of illicit trade in all manner of goods, and one observer has alleged that what is termed the 'Balkan mafia' has been '...using stolen art in bigger drugs and arms deal since as far back as the mid-1980s'.[28] The Caravaggio copy was recovered two years later when three Ukrainians and a Russian were arrested as they

---

23 Kate Deimling, 'Italian Police Dismantle a High-Tech Art Crime Ring Led by a Fugitive Venetian Prince' *Artinfo* (24 March 2012) <http://artinfo.com/news/story/780130/italian-police-dismantle-a-high-tech-art-crime-ring-led-by-a-fugitive-venetian-prince> accessed 11 April 2012.

24 'Roman Statues Rescued in Spain' *The Olive Press* (24 March 2012) <http://www.theolivepress.es/spain-news/2012/03/28/roman-statues-rescued-in-spain> accessed 4 April 2012.

25 Thomas Bazley, *Crimes of the Art World* (Greenwood Publishing, 2010) 52.

26 Martin Wainwright, 'Specialist Criminals Stole £2m Chinese Artefacts from University, Say Police' *The Guardian* (11 April 2012) <http://www.guardian.co.uk/uk/2012/apr/11/2m-chinese-artefacts-durham-university?newsfeed=true> accessed 12 April 2012.

27 Nelson McKay, 'Good Work of Police Led to £2m Stolen Treasure Find' *Evening Chronicle* (17 April 2012) <http://www.chroniclelive.co.uk/north-east-news/evening-chronicle-news/2012/04/17/good-work-of-police-led-to-2m-stolen-treasure-find-72703-30776169/> accessed 18 April 2012.

28 Thomas Flynn, 'Caravaggio Copy Snatched from Odessa Museum', *Artknows* (August 5, 2008). <http://tom-flynn.blogspot.com.au/2008/08/caravarrio-copy-snatched-from-oddessa.html>accessed 11 April 2012.

were negotiating the sale with a buyer in Berlin.[29] A recent report asserts that the Balkan region has become an important transit portal for art works stolen throughout Europe (including France, Switzerland, Austria, Germany, Belgium and The Netherlands among others) and makes reference to 'well known gangs' who are based in Serbia, Macedonia, Kosovo and Montenegro.[30] Supporting the observations by Pryor, the BBC (13 April 2012) reported that three people had been arrested in Serbia in connection with the theft of a painting stolen from a Swiss museum in 2008.[31] In the original theft, four paintings were taken, but two of these were found abandoned in a parked car in Zurich shortly after the robbery.[32] A further report[33] indicated that the police involved were part of Serbia's Anti-Organized Crime unit supported by elements of the Swiss police, and that over a million dollars was seized as well.[34]

It is still difficult, unfortunately, to pin down exact details of the amount of well organized criminal activity which is involved in the theft of art, and its consequent movement onto a market. A case which illustrates this point perhaps better than most, as well as pointing to the complexities of distinguishing between rewards, ransoms, buy backs and payments for information is that of the theft in July 1994 of two high-profile paintings by the British artist J.M.W. Turner from an exhibition in Frankfurt, Germany. The paintings, valued then at £24 million, were fully insured and on loan from the Tate in London. Following the theft an extensive international police investigation ensued lasting more than eight years and resulting eventually in the return of both paintings to the Tate. The story of this investigation and the associated negotiations that occurred between the Tate and the shadowy criminals in possession of the paintings is told in depth by Nairne.[35] Acting through a German lawyer who was in contact with these criminals, and in close consultation with the police as well as the oversight of the British courts, the Tate was able to facilitate this return while paying various 'investigative' and

29 RIA Novosti, 'Stolen Caravaggio Painting Found in Berlin' *RIA Novosti* (28 June 2012) <http://en.rian.ru/art_living/20100628/159610936.html> accessed 11 April 2012.

30 Riah Pryor, 'Balkans Targeted in Hunt for Stolen Art' *Art Newspaper* (19 January 2012) <http://www.theartnewspaper.com/articles/Balkans+targeted+in+hunt+for+stolen+art/25391> accessed 4 April 2012.

31 'Stolen Cezanne Found by Serbian Police' *BBC News* (12 April 2012) <http://www.bbc.co.uk/news/entertainment-arts-17687963> accessed 13 April 2012.

32 'Stolen Paintings found in Zurich' *BBC News* (19 February 2008) <http://news.bbc.co.uk/2/hi/entertainment/7252142.stm> accessed 13 April 2012.

33 'Serbian Police Retrieve Stolen Masterpiece' *The Age* (14 April 2012) <http://www.theage.com.au/world/serbian-police-retrieve-stolen-masterpiece-20120413-1wyvy.html?skin=text-only> accessed 26 September 2013.

34 For additional details, see 'Serbian and Swiss Police Raid Nets Stolen Cezanne Painting; Four Men Arrested' *New York Daily News* (13 April 2012) <http://www.nydailynews.com/news/world/serbian-swiss-police-raid-nets-stolen-cezanne-painting-men-arrested-article-1.1061145.> accessed 14 April 2012.

35 Sandy Nairne, *Art Theft and the Case of the Stolen Turners* (Reaktion Books 2011).

allied expenses of £3.5 million. By this time the paintings were said to be valued at least £20 million each. The Tate had earlier received payment from the insurers for the loss of the paintings, and had purchased from the insurers for a small sum their acquired rights to possess them should they ever be discovered and reclaimed from the thieves.

From the perspective of the Tate the outcome was a stellar success with both paintings being recovered undamaged and with a substantial additional sum in hand from the proceeds of their insurance deal. Concern was expressed, however, in some sections of the British media about the ethics involved and in particular the payment of what seemed to be a ransom for the return of the art works. The Tate rejected this criticism, claiming nothing of the kind had occurred and that all of the payments had been made for legitimate purposes and without benefiting the criminals in any way. Even so the criminals who eventually handed over the paintings have never been identified publicly and remain at large, probably somewhere in the Balkans, although two offenders involved in the theft itself were caught and imprisoned. The case does suggest that on occasions some well organized and patient criminals can benefit from art theft. What also remains unclear is how frequently arrangements for the return of stolen art works may be negotiated directly behind the scenes by their original owners, or insurance companies.

There are without question situations where those involved in art theft are also demonstrated to be directly involved with drug trafficking, as in the case of some of those convicted in the Lowry theft noted above where three of the individuals were convicted of drug-related offences as well as the art theft.[36] In the second of the Russborough House thefts, the crime involved a well-known criminal group headed by Martin Cahill that had international links with such locations as the Isle of Man, Istanbul, Antwerp and Luxemburg (among others) which involved, in addition to the movement (or attempted movement) of art, money laundering and drug trafficking.[37]

While all of this can be documented, it is still not possible to state in any precise way how common such involvements are where art theft is concerned. We have seen here that, in fact, art theft can take many forms. One of these, among many, consists of organized criminals attracted by the potential for high economic returns represented by expensive art.

Scenario 6: The Art Disappears

While the many accounts reviewed above permit us to establish some of the outlines of the forms that art theft can take, it has to be admitted that this information is available from cases where the art, or the criminals, have been recovered or identified. In an unknowable percentage of cases, the theft has not been

36 Nugent (n 11).

37 Williams (n 9).

solved, and we therefore are ignorant of the details of the events surrounding the loss of the art. According to the FBI, only about 5 per cent of stolen art works are ever recovered.[38] This is, of course, hardly more than a guess, although the FBI is one of the few organizations that maintain a data base of stolen art from which such estimates might emerge. A recent account lists the 'Top 10 Art Heists of All Time', and among these ten, in seven cases the art works had been returned, in another case the thieves had been arrested but the art work had not been recovered, and another of the cases (the thefts from the Iraqi Museum) had been partially solved.[39] In only one case (the thefts from the Gardner Museum in 1990) of this 'top 10' list was there absolutely nothing known about the circumstances of the theft. If these were used as a standard, then, the clear-up rate (depending upon how it was calculated) would be somewhere between 70 and 90 per cent, considerably higher than the FBI estimate. We are not attempting to argue that even a majority of art thefts are, in fact, cleared up by either a recovery or an arrest, rather we point out again how uncertain quantitative statements are regarding art crime. Certainly, examples abound of the theft of art where the works have not been recovered.

The Case of the Gardner Museum Theft: One of the most well-known examples of art theft consists of the break-in by two thieves into the Isabella Stewart Gardner Museum in Boston in the early morning hours of 18 March 1990. The two criminals had dressed themselves as Boston police officers, and managed to trick the security guards at the museum into giving them entry. Once inside, the thieves bound and gagged the guards, and then managed to walk off with 13 of the most valuable works of art to be found in the Western world, including a Vermeer and works by Rembrandt, Degas and Manet. In the more than two decades since there have been many theories about who might have done this crime, but to date there has been no sign of either the thieves or of the missing art works.[40]

The Case of the Lost Cavalier: The Art Gallery of New South Wales in Sydney was the setting for one of the other stories of unrecovered stolen art. In June of 2007, while the museum was open for visitors in the morning hours, a thief managed to unscrew two wall fastenings, probably in about 60 seconds, and walk out of the museum with a 17th-century Dutch masterpiece insured for $1.4 million dollars. There was no CCTV camera. The work, *A Cavalier*, by Frans van Mieris has not been seen since, nor has there been any word about who was responsible for the crime.[41]

---

38 Julia Layton, 'How Could Someone Steal a Painting from a Museum?' *How Stuff Works* (2012) <http://people.howstuffworks.com/steal-painting-from-museum.htm> accessed 18 January 2012.

39 Graphic Design Degrees, 'Top 10 Art Heists of All Time' (2009) <http://graphicdesigndegrees.org/top-10-art-heists-of-all-time/> accessed 18 January 2012.

40 Bazley (n 25) 16.

41 Cornford (n 22).

The Case of the Lost Exhibition: Sydney also was the setting thirty years before of one of the more notable examples of an unsolved art theft. In the early hours of 4 April 1977, thieves not given to subtlety literally smashed their way into the Macquarie Galleries in King Street, Sydney and made off with 28 paintings by Grace Cossington Smith, making their getaway in a maroon Holden sedan. The works made up the entire exhibition. In the more than three decades since, there has been no arrest of any of those involved in the theft, and there has been no sighting of any of the 28 works.[42]

Scenario 6a: But Sometimes After Many Years a Stolen Painting is Discovered

In Australia a case fitting this description is the recovery of a painting by Rupert Bunny in 2010 after it was stolen in 1991. Acting on a tip off from a member of the public the police found the painting, titled *Girl in Sunlight*, hanging on the wall of a Melbourne resident's home.[43] Art stolen from the National Museum of Fine Arts in Buenos Aires by the junta in Argentina in December 1980 was found twenty-one years later when objects surfaced at Sotheby's in 2001.[44]

Scenario 7: When Art is Stolen for Political Reasons

The Case of the Weeping Woman: There are a handful of cases of art theft where the motivations for the theft appear to be purely political. As such, there is no question of disposing of the stolen works on either a legitimate or an illegitimate market. One such case is that of the theft of the *Weeping Woman* from the National Gallery in Melbourne, in August, 1986. The painting had been purchased less than a year before, amid considerable controversy, for $1.6 million. The burglary itself could serve as a textbook example of a successful art theft. The theft probably occurred during a Saturday night, and wasn't even noticed on Sunday, the director of the Gallery finally being told on Monday that the Picasso was gone (security staff had been fooled by a card put in the painting's place saying that it had been temporarily removed). It appeared that the thieves knew what they were up to. They used what was described as a 'security tool' to unscrew the painting from a wall, carefully took the painting from its frame without damaging the canvas, then rolled the painting up so that it could be easily taken from the Museum without attracting attention. Immediately afterward, letters of demand and ransom began arriving

42 Bruce James, 'Who Stole the Show? The Daring – and still Unsolved – Theft of an Entire Exhibition 20 Years Ago Changed the Australian Art World Forever' *The Age Good Weekend* (26 July 1996) 90, 95.

43 Gabriella Coslovich, 'Picking up paintings for a steal' *The Age* (8 May 2010) <http://www.theage.com.au/national/picking-up-paintings-for-a-steal-20100507-ujtg.html> accessed 12 April 2012.

44 Jonathan Webb, *Stolen: The Gallery of Missing Masterpieces* (Madison Books 2008) 47.

demanding more money for the arts from persons calling themselves 'Australian cultural terrorists'. After a short period of negotiating, and some serious pressure being applied to some young artists in Melbourne, the painting was found in a locker at a local railway station. Interestingly, the Victoria Police played virtually no role in solving the theft, at one point stating flatly to museum figures that 'We are not getting involved.'[45]

Pulling the Threads Together

In many situations, art theft is a puzzling crime. While the art involved may be worth many millions of dollars, it is far from clear how a theft will result in any profit whatsoever for those involved. Time and time again, individuals have been able to carry off the actual theft of an art work, only to find themselves in serious trouble when they attempt to convert the stolen art into monetary reward. Successful negotiation of stolen works, we have seen, generally involves both access to art, and access to a market. Given their position in the market, case material informs us that dealers willing to engage in illegal activity are ideally placed since they have direct knowledge that they can draw upon in terms of identifying candidate works and planning successful thefts, and they have direct access to the legitimate market for the disposal of these stolen works.

In the case of organized crime, knowledge of how to carry off such crimes as burglary on the part of the criminals gives them access to art works, and emerging data suggests that at least some well-organized criminals find lucrative avenues in an illegal, black market for the disposal of the stolen goods (although the length of time some of the goods remain in the hands of the criminals hints at problems of negotiating an economically rewarding outcome). In very different ways, then, these two different approaches are designed to 'solve' the problem of arranging access to a market to dispose of the stolen works of art.

In some art thefts, of course, there is no need to seek out a portal, illegal or otherwise, for the disposal of the goods. So-called 'gloaters' who are also thieves steal for their own pleasure, and thereby are not interested in a market for the stolen material. For the cases that we know about, then, the risks to these individuals are found in the thefts themselves, and in the cases of both Breitwieser and Lugo, we know about their activities because they were arrested in connection with a theft of art (not its disposal). While we have to be careful in the case of Kingsland because we know little about how he came to possess so much stolen art, the fact that most of the known stolen works in his collection had been taken in the 1960s and 1970s suggests that for some reason he withdrew from any connection with a stolen art market before he could be apprehended and charged with any crime. Similarly, art that is stolen

45 Justin Murphy, 'Stolen Picasso' *ABC News* (broadcast 19 September 2004) <http://www.abc.net.au/tv/rewind/txt/s1199862.htm> accessed 14 April 2012.

for political reasons, such as the *Weeping Woman*, is not intended for later sale, and thus once stolen, the thief or thieves are not exposed to the dangers that result from attempts to enter either a licit or illicit art market.

For many who become involved in art theft, however, while the act of theft itself might be successful, they find that any attempt to sell the work on the legitimate market is not only unsuccessful, but dangerous in that a common consequence is exposure and arrest. As Wittman is fond of saying, many art thieves are successful criminals, but they make poor businessmen. Time and again, we see that what has been a successful burglary is followed by a botched attempt either to ransom the work, or to sell it onto the market.

It needs to be said that a major barrier to the sale of stolen art works in present times is the rapid flow of information onto the market regarding works that are stolen. In many countries, including Germany, France, Italy and the United States, policing agencies have extensive files of stolen art works that can be consulted when an object is placed on the market. At the international level, within law enforcement circles Interpol has a large file dedicated to identifying art works that are stolen. For private citizens there is ready access to the Art Loss Register. Most major auction houses now routinely consult with the Art Loss Register as they prepare for an auction, and there are numerous examples of how this has resulted in the successful identification of stolen art works, sometimes in cases that are 20 or more years old.[46]

There are some implications of our analysis for the potential control and prevention of art crime. For one, we would urge states and international bodies to strengthen existing data bases of stolen art. States such as Australia which have virtually no presence either in terms of a national data base or such collections as the Art Loss Register should move to plug this gap. Time and again the presence of such information has resulted in the discovery of stolen art, even decades after the original theft. For another, it would appear that recent decades have seen a stronger presence in art theft of internationally organized criminal groups, such as is suggested by the recent arrests in Belgrade. Prevention and control where organized criminal groups are involved presents complications. Simplistic 'target hardening' efforts, such as using increasingly sophisticated technological devices in major public collections, are likely either to generate in response technologically sophisticated criminals who overcame security barriers, or a 'displacement' effect so that expensive art is searched out in less well protected places, such as the homes of often elderly wealthy collectors, or perhaps as we have seen in some of our case material, a shift to smaller museums with less adequate security processes in place. Ultimately prevention in terms of involvement of sophisticated criminals may be better served by engaging in a public education campaign that makes clear, as seems to be true, that even well-prepared criminals rarely reap economic benefits from art theft.

---

46 Jonathan Webb, *Stolen: The Gallery of Missing Masterpieces* (Madison Books 2008).

That is, perhaps criminals in the know might be persuaded away from art theft if they are convinced that there is little or no money in it.

In the foregoing, we have attempted to refine the analysis of art crime by calling attention to the diversity of forms that this crime can take. Put simply, there is no one pattern that this crime can take. Others who follow may find other approaches to the task of differentiation. We have found it useful for our purposes to identify three basic questions: (1) what access is found to art which can be stolen? (2) is there access to a portal such as made available by a recognized art dealer or auction house? and (3) what access is sought to buyers for the stolen art? The specific forms we have identified result from the specific interplay of these issues. Essentially, the 'variations' we have identified result from how different individuals resolve the problems posed by these three questions. Thus, in our First Scenario, the 'bent dealers' are persons who have direct access to valuable art as a consequence of their occupation, and the same role solves the problem of seeking a portal (although it may also provide access to other dealers who become complicit in the disposal of stolen art), and through their dealership they will have direct access to potential customers who may remain ignorant of the illicit character of the art works they buy. There are other ways of addressing these problems. Thus, some avoid the issue of attempting to enter a market for the stolen art, either because they steal for their own pleasure (Scenario 3), or perhaps because the motivation for the theft is political, and therefore there is no question of seeking a sale for the work (Scenario 6). Some connected with forms of organized crime through their illicit networks solve the problem of finding customers by moving the work into an illegal, or black, market.

It goes without saying that others, applying different criteria or questions, might suggest quite different scenarios in order to describe the differences we have observed in the forms that art crime can take. From our earlier work, for two examples, we have to admit that two major scenarios of art theft do not emerge easily from the framework we have applied:

Scenario 8: When Art Is Stolen as an Act of Conquest[47]

Probably the single most successful art thief over recent centuries was Napoleon Bonaparte, who removed a huge volume of material from the territories he had conquered, some of which remain in the Louvre in Paris to this day. In turn, however, the German Government in World War II elevated such theft to an exceptional level when it removed literally thousands of works of art from both individuals and states. There is nothing new in all of this, of course, as evidenced by the Roman era where they carted off a huge amount of material from states they had brought under their control. So effective were they, that it

47 See in general Margaret M. Miles, *Art as Plunder: The Ancient Origins of Debate about Cultural Property* (Cambridge University Press 2008).

has been claimed that there are now more obelisks in former Roman territory than there are remaining in Egypt.[48]

Scenario 9: The Theft of History

A major issue confronting the art world in present times is the flow into the developed world of cultural heritage material which tends to flow mostly from heritage rich but economically less advantageous nations of the world. This illicit traffic begins most often with what is now in most countries defined as a theft of cultural heritage material (and, of course, it constitutes a theft of history). We have expressed a view elsewhere[49] that these share many features with some of the other forms of art theft we have examined here.[50] Thus, for an example, a major problem faced by those engaged in this illicit traffic is to gain access to the large, international and legal market for such objects. In many respects, the process involves a movement of materials through an access portal located in a transit point such as Hong Kong, and thereby gains papers which appear to make the items legitimate to flow onto the licit antiquities market.

We have not included these two scenarios in the body of our analysis because initially at least, these seem to present rather different problems that we confront in addressing most forms of art theft. Recent events in the UK, however, suggest that at least some overlap with the Theft of History scenario and more traditional forms of art theft from museums. Thieves have struck three different collections in the early months of 2012 where the goal has been the theft of Chinese cultural material (in the two examples where the attempts resulted in the successful removal of the material from the museum, the items stolen were Chinese jade objects). In this case the examples involved thieves attempting to gain access to material in public collections (not an unknown problem in art theft), but we do not yet know enough about what follows, or is intended to follow, to know what happens after that. What we can say is that the thefts definitely involve cultural heritage material (Chinese jade objects), and that the techniques involved in the thefts have the appearance of many other thefts where objects have been taken from museum collections.

---

48 Arielle Kozloff, 'The Antiquities Market: When What Where Who Why … and How Much?' in Kate Fitz Gibbon (ed), *Who Owns the Past? Cultural Policy, Cultural Property, and the Law* (Rutgers University Press 2006) 183, 200.

49 Christine Alder and Ken Polk, 'The Illicit Traffic in Plundered Antiquities' in Philip Reichel and Jay Albanese (eds), *Handbook of Transnational Crime and Justice* (Sage 2005) 98, 113.

50 Duncan Chappell and Ken Polk, 'Unraveling the "Cordata": Just How Organized Is the International Traffic in Cultural Objects?' in Stefano Manacorda and Duncan Chappell (eds), *Crime in the Art and Antiquities World: Illegal Trafficking in Cultural Property* (Springer 2011) 99, 116.

In conclusion, we have in these pages attempted to make the point that there is no single pattern of art theft. There are, rather, important variations in the way an art theft proceeds. In many cases and situations, we observe, as many have before us, that in many respects art theft is a puzzling form of crime. Often, individuals are successful in stealing one or another art objects, only to find that there is no way that they are successfully able to convert the theft into income. Stolen expensive works of art are exceptionally difficult to dispose of upon the legitimate art market. To be sure, some thieves have found some ways around this problem. At the same time, however, many successful thieves find that they are no good at the business of art, and either are arrested as proof of this assertion (for example, in a sting operation, as in the case of *The Scream*), or as we often find, the works disappear from sight as the thief rolls them up and puts them in a hidden place (the *Mona Lisa*, for example, was placed in a closet for two years). Understanding art theft, we believe, will require more explication of the differences between the various forms that such thefts can take.

Chapter 4

Case Studies on Art Fraud: European and Antipodean Perspectives

Duncan Chappell and Saskia Hufnagel

Introduction

A Market Ripe for Fraud

> Uncertainty surrounding stock market investments, coupled with a range of stimulus measures around the world, has incentivised property buyers and fuelled an increasing demand for 'investments of passion', including art, luxury collectibles (cars, boats, jets etc), sports investments and wine, jewellery and watches. Unlike many of the great patrons of the past, from the Medicis to the Mellons, who were interested in curating art of earlier periods or in discovering and nurturing new talent, a growing number of those buying art at the highest level now see themselves primarily as investors.[1]

As this excerpt from a recent article published in the authoritative *Financial Times* illustrates, art has now become a much sought after commodity among the wealthy for its economic rather than aesthetic qualities. With international auction houses like Sotheby's and Christie's reporting record contemporary sales of art, and with the prices obtained at auction of the works of individual artists like Picasso, Giacometti and Rothko reaching new highs, this market has attracted to it investors from around the globe.[2] But not surprisingly, given the huge sums these investors have been prepared to pay for their paintings, sculptures and other art works, this market has also attracted those seeking to obtain a share of the perceived financial gains by fraudulent means.

1 See Laura Battle, 'Estate of the Art' *Financial Times* (13 April 2012) <http://www.ft.com/intl/cms/s/2/440ea16e-7e41-11e1-b009-00144feab49a.html#axzz2QK6BNQk2> accessed 21 May 2013.

2 In 2011, for example, Christie's announced sales of $5.7 billion (ibid.) while in November 2012 Sotheby's achieved a record breaking $375 million art sale (see Carol Vogel, '$375.1 Million Art Sale is Sotheby's Record' *New York Times* (13 November 2012) <www.nytimes.com/2012/11/14/arts/design/contemporary-art-sale-is-sothebys-record.html?_r=0> accessed 21 May 2013.

Art forgery[3] has a quite long if not venerable history, which has been richly documented and dissected in a recent scholarly study by Lenain.[4] More typically, in the modern era the career activities of a number of more prominent art forgers have been described in popular literature and film.[5] Some of these accounts have been based on information, which has become available as a result of the detection and successful prosecution of these forgers while others have amounted to autobiographical descriptions of their careers in art crime. In one such recent published autobiography the author claimed to have conducted a highly successful business in art forgery, which lasted more than 30 years and traversed both the United States and the United Kingdom.[6] During this time the forger was able to insert several hundred fake art works into the market place without apparent detection or apprehension by the authorities.[7]

Sources like these suggest that skilled and sophisticated art forgers are able to survive and prosper in the contemporary art market with relative impunity, and even though some are eventually caught and brought to justice many if not most of their fake works of art still remain unidentified. Just how extensive the problem of fakes is in the art market remains a matter of considerable conjecture with scant scholarly research being available on the subject and only secondary and allied sources of information to rely upon.[8] This information includes that still being generated by the recent collapse of the famous Knoedler Gallery in New York City. The Knoedler, New York's oldest gallery which had been in business since 1846, closed its doors in 2012 and went into voluntary administration after allegations emerged that it had been engaged in inserting fake paintings into the market.[9] Following this collapse a number of civil law suits are in progress with former

3 In this chapter the terms art fraud and art forgery are used interchangeably even though in technical terms at common law it is not possible to forge a work of art – only a document; see Duncan Chappell and Kenneth Polk, 'Fakers and Forgers, Deception and Dishonesty: An Exploration of the Murky World of Art Fraud' (2009) 20(2) *Current Issues in Criminal Justice* 2-20. At civil law this situation does not exist.

4 Thierry Lenain, *Art Forgery. The History of a Modern Obsession* (Reaktion Books 2011).

5 See, for instance, Philip Mould, *The Art Detective: Adventures of an Antiques Roadshow Appraiser* (Penguin Books 2009); Laney Salisbury and Aly Sujo, *Provenance: How a Con Man and Forger Rewrote the History of Modern Art* (Penguin Books 2010).

6 Ken Perenyi, *Caveat Emptor. The Secret Life of an American Art Forger* (Pegasus Books 2012).

7 In his book Perenyi admits that he was the subject of an FBI investigation for a number of years, but ultimately no charges were ever laid against him (ibid., 312).

8 For a discussion of some of the estimates made of the incidence of fake works of art existing in the market see Christine Alder, Duncan Chappell and Kenneth Polk, 'Frauds and Fakes in the Australian Aboriginal Art Market' (2011) 56 *Crime, Law and Social Change* 192.

9 Patricia Cohen, 'A Gallery that Helped Create the American Art World Closes Shop after 165 Years' *New York Times* (30 November 2012) <http://www.nytimes.

clients of the Knoedler claiming the gallery sold them for millions of dollars fake paintings of such famous artists as Jackson Pollock, Robert Motherwell, Willem de Kooning and Mark Rothko.[10]

The Knoedler case indicates that even the most prestigious galleries with seemingly impeccable reputations may be the source of fake paintings in the contemporary art market. The full story behind the alleged fakes is yet to be told but it would seem that the paintings the subject of dispute, all of them new to the market, were obtained over more than a decade from a mysterious and obscure art dealer who said that she had acquired them in turn over a long period from an unnamed collector. The Federal Bureau of Investigation (FBI) is apparently still examining these claims.[11]

Role of Law Enforcement

In general a law enforcement body such as the FBI can only be brought in to investigate a case of alleged fraud like this after someone has made a credible crime complaint, or some other form of law enforcement intelligence has revealed its possible existence. Thus, in cases of art forgery at large it may take many years for such a complaint or intelligence to be generated, simply because no one other than the forger(s) involved is aware of the fake work. There may also be other reasons why an official complaint may not emerge, even if someone other than the original forger and his or her accomplice(s) is aware of the fake. Dealers and collectors who unwittingly acquire a fake may be very reluctant to admit this fact because of the financial loss that will occur if a supposedly genuine painting for which millions of dollars may have been paid turns out to be something else. An unscrupulous dealer or collector in this situation may well decide to try and 'pass the parcel' onto some other unwitting purchaser, perhaps through an auction house sale. Alternatively, they may simply hold on to the work, afraid to be embarrassed by admitting to having been duped, but hoping that eventually they may be able to sell it at a reasonable price.

Circumstances like these tend to compound the complexities that surround law enforcement's role in cases of art fraud. It is this role, which forms the substance of this chapter where, using a comparative approach, we consider how law enforcement agencies in certain European jurisdictions and in Australia have handled significant investigations into art fraud during the past decade. First we

---

com/2011/12/01/arts/design/knoedler-art-gallery-in-nyc-closes-after-165-years.html?_r=0> accessed 5 September 2013.

10 Charlotte Burns, 'Knoedler Forgery Scandal grows' *The Art Newspaper* (9 January 2013) <http://www.theartnewspaper.com/articles/Knoedler-forgery-scandal-grows/25427> accessed 5 September 2013.

11 Patricia Cohen, 'Knoedler Gallery Again Accused of Fraud in New Lawsuit' *New York Times* (30 January 2013) <http://artsbeat.blogs.nytimes.com/2013/01/30/knoedler-gallery-again-accused-of-fraud-in-new-lawsuit/> accessed 5 September 2013.

turn to the so-called Beltracchi Case in Germany, which has been the subject of considerable publicity both in the European Union (EU) and abroad. The case is one involving the forging of at least one hundred paintings by contemporary artists, many of which still remain unidentified in the art market and are believed to have been dispersed to a number of European countries as well as to other countries around the globe. Second, we consider a case in Australia where paintings by a famous Aboriginal artist have been faked by a non-Aboriginal forger. From these art fraud cases we go on to discuss the common and disparate threads that emerge from them in regard to the identification, prosecution and punishment of this art crime offence.

The Beltracchi Case

The Beltracchi case is one of the more recent European art forgery cases, which, for a number of reasons, has received a lot of media attention beyond its German origins for a number of reasons. Firstly, the perpetrators of the case were very charismatic and in many ways understood how to play with the emotions of the actors in the art world and the general audience following their case.[12] Secondly, the German police conducted a very thorough investigation that involved expert knowledge of art and the market as well as the use of advanced technology, to prepare a watertight case.[13] Thirdly, the case continues to wreak havoc in the art market with long ensuing civil cases against galleries and experts involved in promoting the forged works.[14] These three aspects are explored in the case study and, though they are not unique in the history of art forgery, they provide a stark contrast to the Australian situation.

The Criminal Masterminds

Wolfgang Beltracchi (born 1951), the painter of the forged works; his wife Helene Beltracchi (born 1958) and her sister Jeanette Spurzem (born 1957) who helped him in various ways; and the 'logistical expert'[15] involved in the distribution of the

12 Joshua Hammer, 'The Greatest Fake Art Scam in History' *Vanity Fair* (10 October 2012) <http://www.vanityfair.com/culture/2012/10/wolfgang-beltracchi-helene-art-scam?currentPage=all> accessed 5 September 2013.

13 Interview with lead investigator at the Landeskriminalamt Berlin on 23 March 2012 (Interview KHK René Allonge, Abteilung Kunstdelikte, LKA Berlin, Tempelhofer Damm 12, 12101 Berlin).

14 Stefan Koldehoff and Tobias Timm, *Falsche Bilder – Echtes Geld* (Galiani Berlin 2012) 183-202.

15 According to the prosecution brief, Otto Schulte-Kellinghaus established the contacts to galleries in Paris, brought most of the paintings onto the market and received a

forgeries, Otto Schulte-Kellinghaus (born 1943), were the accused perpetrators in what the German media have commonly termed the 'Beltracchi Case'.[16] According to the dispassionate factual account in the judgement of the Cologne District Court[17] Wolfgang Beltracchi was born in Germany under the name of Wolfgang Fischer. His father painted churches while his mother was a housewife. He was expelled from school at the age of 17 and went to art school on a scholarship for gifted artists although never completing his artistic studies. Between 1972 and 1983 he travelled as a 'hippie' and sold some of his (original) paintings when he needed money. In 1992 he met his wife and later co-defendant while working on a documentary movie. The couple had a daughter while Beltracchi also had a son from a previous relationship. From 1996 onwards he travelled through the South of Europe with wife and daughter in a camper van, ultimately settling in the South of France in 2000. In 2007 the couple moved into another home in Freiburg, Germany, that had been bought and renovated for about 5,000,000 Euros.

Beltracchi had no criminal record at the time of his arrest by German police in Freiburg in the evening of 27 August 2010. The short account of his life provides no clues as to how he became one of the most notorious art forgers in modern history, nor how he could convince his wife, sister and friend Otto Schulte-Kellinghaus, to help him commit a series of sophisticated crimes over a considerable period of time.

However, it is not difficult to discover information about Beltracchi's charismatic personality. Throughout his criminal trial and beyond all reports on the case agreed that Beltracchi was a somewhat memorable figure.[18] With long hair and in flamboyant style Beltracchi displayed a cheerful mood throughout the trial. His constant stance was that he did not forge paintings for the money involved, but rather as a prank to fool the art world and show its dark side. This stance made him rather likeable to many sections of the media and some journalists even called him the 'Robin Hood' of the art world,[19] stealing from the rich and giving to the poor.

More perceptive German media accounts, however, were able to compare Beltracchi to a typically German folk hero, 'Till Eulenspiegel', who never learned a proper handicraft, stole from anyone and did not share the proceeds with the poor

---

commission of 20 per cent per painting sold. He also established contact to the renowned German art historian Werner Spies, self-proclaimed expert on the works of Max Ernst, who subsequently authenticated a fake Max Ernst produced by Wolfgang Beltracchi. Dorothea Hülsmeier, 'Fälscher blamieren Experten' *Westdeutsche Zeitung* (2 September 2011); Sven Röbel and Michael Sontheimer, 'Forgery Scandal Embarrasses International Art World' *Spiegel Online* (13 June 2011).

16 Author unidentified, 'More about German art scam – High life ends for couple who conned art world' *NZ Herald News* (27 October 2011).

17 Urteil Landgericht Köln vom 27/10/2011, Az. 110 KLS 17/11.

18 See, for example, Joshua Hammer, 'The Greatest Fake Art Scam in History' *Vanity Fair* (10 October 2012) <http://www.vanityfair.com/culture/2012/10/wolfgang-beltracchi-helene-art-scam?currentPage=all> accessed 5 May 2013.

19 Michael Kohler, 'Sammlung Jägers' *Art – Das Kunstmagazin* (28 September 2011).

at all but acted purely to enrich himself.[20] This analogy explains more neatly the psyche of Beltracchi, but does not take away from the fact that he became a forger rock-star for a while. Like Till Eulenspiegel who started to play pranks on the rest of the world because people from his home town had laughed at him when he fell into the river while entertaining them with his walk on a tightrope, Beltracchi might have felt frustrated with the lack of recognition of his own original pieces and therefore started to try and take revenge on the art world.

The accounts given of his case, as well as the views expressed by members of the art world more generally, still seem divided about his actual 'talent' as an artist. The merits of his recent original genuine works, produced in association with his colleague (artist, not forger) Manfred Esser are purely a matter of taste.[21] These pieces are photographic works by Manfred Esser, which are painted over by Beltracchi. However, his forgeries, while highly appraised before the discovery of their true heritage, were later condemned as being simplistic and of rather poor quality, assessments that were no doubt easy to make after the fact by critics who had earlier appeared fully satisfied as to the authenticity of works.[22]

To expand on the actual facts of the case, Beltracchi forged 20th century works of art by numbers of well-known and respected artists including Max Pechstein, Heinrich Campendonk, Kees van Dongen and Max Ernst.[23] The fraudulent activities of Beltracchi and his accomplices remained undetected for a long time as the 'cover stories' given for the forged paintings brought onto the market were found convincing by galleries and buyers and the types of paintings offered for sale were seemingly irresistible to their purchasers. The forgeries were often paintings that had knowingly gone missing during the Second World War (WWII) or that had been displayed in old catalogues, but without a photograph. However, Beltracchi also painted 'new' pictures in the styles of these artists that he claimed should have been part of their *œuvre*.[24]

To convince the art world of their authenticity, the forger group claimed that Werner Jägers, who had died in 1992 and was the grandfather of the two accused sisters, had bought the pieces before WWII from the gallery Alfred Flechtheim and had hidden them in the German Eifel region during the war. Jägers was said to be a friend of the master tailor Johann Wilhelm Knops, the grandfather of the accused Schulte-Kellinghaus, who himself was said to be an art collector. In fact, both grandfathers had never collected art, nor had they been particularly interested

20 Sometimes known as Tyll Owlglass in English literature; see, for example, Kenneth Robert Henderson Mackenzie (ed), *The Marvellous Adventures and Rare Conceits of Master Tyll Owlglass, Newly Collected, Chronicled and Set forth, in our English Tongue* (Trübner 1860).

21 See at www.beltracchi-project.de.

22 Koldehoff and Timm (n 14) 113-15.

23 Nicolette Feiler-Thull, 'Gewiefte Fälscherbande – Prozess um Kunst-Skandal in Köln' *3Sat Kulturzeit* (12 September 2011).

24 Gisela Friedrichsen, 'Eulenspiegel oder Künstler' (2011) 43 *Der Spiegel* 148, 149.

in art during their lifetimes. Nonetheless, both the 'Jägers' and the 'Knops' collections became famous as a part of the legendary provenance for the forged works of art, and the four accused reinforced their authenticity through occasional sales of genuine works of art they pretended originated from these collections, and by some other purchases of real art.[25]

The accused also had a sophisticated way of distributing tasks among the group. While Wolfgang Beltracchi copied the missing paintings (or painted new works in the style of the famous artists), Otto Schulte-Kellinghaus, who appeared as a serious senior businessman, established contacts with renowned art experts, some of whom, like Werner Spies, gave him appraisals for the pieces examined.[26] The wife of Beltracchi posed as the owner of most of the art works and actively traded on the art market with the help of her sister. Additionally, the Beltracchi couple faked photographs to highlight the authenticity of the paintings. Wolfgang had photographed his wife Helene disguised as her own grandmother in their house in France sitting in front of several forged paintings from the 'Jägers Collection' which were later sold as originals. The black-and-white photo had been printed on pre-war developing paper and was slightly out of focus. They even cut a zigzag pattern around the edge of the picture to make it look authentic, but only distributed scans rather than the original so as not to raise suspicion.[27]

Beltracchi himself remained in the background throughout all interactions with the art market.[28] As his name had been changed from Fischer to Beltracchi when he married his wife Helene, and Helene's sister was married and hence also not called Beltracchi anymore, it was difficult for police to establish a link between the different perpetrators bringing the forgeries onto the art market.[29]

Beltracchi and his compatriots in crime have become famous not only because of their theatrical appearance in court, the later self-promotion through the 'Beltracchi Project' – the joint works Beltracchi produced with his friend Esser – or the movie produced about his life and pranks, but also because of the very substantial financial profits they made from their forging activities.[30] Their financial success seriously challenges allegations that 'crime does not pay'. As indicated above they were able to pay 5,000,000 Euros for a house in Freiburg, Germany and they also purchased for 2,000,000 Euros an estate in the South of France.[31] It was alleged by investigators that the actual sum obtained by the group

---

25 Claudia Herstatt and Angelika Kindermann, 'Etikettenschindel' *Art – Das Kunstmagazin* (12 September 2011).

26 Michael Kohler, 'Sammlung Jägers' *Art – Das Kunstmagazin* (28 September 2011).

27 Tony Paterson, 'High life ends for couple who conned art world' *New Zealand Herald* (27 October 2011).

28 Koldehoff and Timm (n 14) 114, 115.

29 Interview Landeskriminalamt Berlin (n 13).

30 Koldehoff and Timm (n 14) 245-70.

31 Urteil Landgericht Köln vom 27/10/2011, Az. 110 KLS 17/11; the estate where the fake photographs of Helene were taken.

from fake paintings totalled 35 Million Euros, but there is every reason to believe that the true sum was significantly higher than this.[32]

But enough about the perpetrators of this major criminal event in the contemporary art world. The more fascinating part of the story for our purposes is how the criminals were identified and eventually brought to justice.

Investigating the Beltracchi Case

The evidence gathered during the criminal investigation into the Beltracchi case was substantial and might ultimately have led to the conviction of the accused without confessions. It was therefore all the more frustrating for investigators that the trial was cut short by a plea bargaining deal and their extensive research never saw the light of the court room.[33] As the German magazine 'Spiegel' reported after the trial, 'the art forger … had reason to smile despite being sent to jail for six years.'[34] The article continued that 'because of his confession, the millionaire fraudster has been given a virtual slap on the wrist, while the truth has been sacrificed for a deal'.

While it is inherent to police work that criminals might get off or receive a light sentence at trial despite considerable efforts on their part to secure a conviction, it seems that in art crime cases this happens more frequently, possibly contributing to a lack of police interest in these matters.[35] Judge William Kremer sentenced Beltracchi to six years in jail; his wife Helene received a four-year term; her sister Jeanette was given a suspended 21-month sentence; and the accomplice Otto Schulte-Kellinghaus was sentenced to five years. Only 14 forged paintings were the subject of counts at the trial, which concluded after only nine days. This was all the more surprising, since the trial had been scheduled originally for 40 days and 168 witnesses were to be heard.[36]

While it can generally be said that low sentences are the order of the day for art criminals, another recent art crime trial in Germany tends to counter this assumption. In the case of the 'Count of Waldstein', a dealer of fake Alberto Giacometti sculptures received a nine-year jail term though the damage caused was a fraction of that in the Beltracchi case.[37] The 'Count' was convicted of 50 counts

32 Markus Huth, '35 Millionen Euro Schaden' mz-web.de (27 January 2012).

33 Interview Landeskriminalamt Berlin (n 13).

34 Michael Sontheimer, 'A cheerful prisoner: Art forger all smiles after guilty plea seals the deal' *Spiegel Online* (27 October 2011) <http://www.spiegel.de/international/germany/0,1518,794454,00.html> accessed 3 September 2012

35 Susanna Partsch, *Tatort Kunst: Über Fälschungen, Betrüger und Betrogene* (C.H. Beck 2011) 169.

36 Sontheimer (n 34).

37 Sven Röbel and Michael Sontheimer, 'Sculptures in a Suitcase: The Fake Count who Flogged Giacometti Forgeries' *Spiegel Online* (18 May 2011) <http://www.

of fraud while being part of a criminal organization. However, considering that the damage involved in these 50 counts only amounted to Eight Million Euros, while the damage in the 14 Beltracchi counts totalled 16 Million Euros, this decision of the Stuttgart district court seems particularly severe for this type of crime.[38]

The police investigators in Berlin had taken the Beltracchi case on because they had been involved previously in making inquiries potentially relating to Wolfgang Fischer/Beltracchi and his compatriots in crime. Further, the Cologne district where the Beltracchi case originated did not, unlike its counterparts in Berlin, Stuttgart and Munich, have a separate art crime unit within its state police force.

Earlier investigations in Berlin suggested that at least 15 Beltracchi forgeries had already been sold by the 1980s, but had become subject to statute of limitations. The limitation period for fraud is five years, but can be ten years for an aggravated offence. Beltracchi's forging activities had nearly been uncovered in 1995 when a potential buyer of some of his fake 1920s Molzahn paintings had discovered that one of the paint pigments used was only invented about 30 years later.[39] Berlin police subsequently received a lead that a painter in the South of France named Fischer was the author of these fakes but could not then make the name change link from Fischer, as Beltracchi was originally called, to Beltracchi.[40]

After many years of investigations, the forged painting that finally unravelled the Beltracchi case was the 'Red Picture with Horses' – a work falsely attributed to Heinrich Campendonk. This picture had been acquired by the Lempertz Gallery in 2006, but because its Director Henrik Hanstein had not considered it necessary to get an expert opinion regarding the authenticity of the work, it was offered directly to a buyer and sold for 2.4 Million Euros. The buyer then sought the advice of experts to authenticate the picture and the painting was subsequently viewed by two art experts who both considered it to be a fake. The picture was then subject to forensic analysis in a laboratory where it was determined that it contained titanium white, which had not existed at the time the picture was claimed to have been painted. The buyer then returned the painting to the Lempertz Gallery where police later came across it by chance when they were in the Gallery pursuing a different investigation.[41]

---

spiegel.de/international/sculptures-in-a-suitcase-the-fake-count-who-flogged-giacometti-forgeries-a-763170.html> accessed 3 September 2012; Anonymous author 'Lange Haftstrafe für Fälscher von Giacometti-Werken' *Pforzheimer Zeitung* (30 June 2011) <http://www.pz-news.de/baden-wuerttemberg_artikel,-Lange-Haftstrafe-fuer-Faelscher-von-Giacometti-Werken-_arid,278140.html> accessed 3 September 2012.

38 Anonymous author (n 37).

39 Joshua Hammer, 'The Greatest Fake Art Scam in History' *Vanity Fair* (10 October 2012) <http://www.vanityfair.com/culture/2012/10/wolfgang-beltracchi-helene-art-scam?currentPage=all> accessed 5 September 2013.

40 Interview Landeskriminalamt Berlin (n13).

41 Ibid.

One of the experts consulted in regard to the 'Red Picture with Horses' painting, a Campendonk expert, had previously judged a number of Campendonk fakes produced by Beltracchi to be genuine. Police nevertheless trusted her opinion in regard to the 'Red Picture with Horses' painting being a fake. As the main police investigator reported, 'there are so many fake Campendonks out there that an expert has probably already studied on fakes in the course of developing expertise'.[42]

With the discovery of the fake 'Red Picture with Horses' painting there now ensued a long and thorough investigation into many other cases of suspected forgery, mainly triggered by the further discovery of a series of false gallery labels that Beltracchi and his colleagues had used to disguise his fakes. These labels specified that the paintings had once belonged to the 'Collection Flechtheim'. The accused had glued them onto several paintings as proof of provenance. Alfred Flechtheim had been a renowned German art dealer in the 1920s. However, he had never produced these, if any, labels to mark paintings in his collection. Police searched assiduously for pictures with these identifying labels and found a vast number of them. These were then examined by experts and laboratories to help establish evidence for a prosecution of Beltracchi and his co-offenders. A total of 53 cases of suspected fake paintings by Beltracchi were investigated, but only 14 could ultimately be established to be forgeries to the point of being the subject of a specific criminal charge.

Another reason why police trusted the Campendonk expert was that she did not take a proportion of the sum for which the painting was sold as commission for her assessment, but a set fee. This was in stark contrast to the Max Ernst expert who had authenticated a number of Beltracchi's works. Werner Spies, an art historian and contributor to the *Frankfurter Allgemeine Zeitung* newspaper, had declared all of them to be genuine, for a significant fee – a proportion of the price for which the paintings had been sold. One of these paintings was eventually purchased by an ex-publisher and art collector, Daniel Filipacchi in New York for €5.5 million.[43] Spies indicated that he had been amazed by the quality of the paintings and even pointed to one of them as being a masterpiece in the artist's *œuvre*.[44]

While the most recent and exhaustive account of the Beltracchi case by two German journalists claims that the pictures were all of poor quality and only the names and stories behind them fooled the art world,[45] this view is considered to be a rather unfair description of the artistic skill of the convicted fraudster. A number of significant experts, including those that worked without commission, had been fascinated by the paintings, their colours and the techniques and while Beltracchi might not be a great artist, he surely was and remains a talented painter.

The forger group was not unmasked by either experts and auction houses or police for approximately 15 years. However, once investigations had started,

42 Ibid.

43 Sontheimer (n 34).

44 Koldehoff and Timm (n 14) 113-15.

45 Interview Landeskriminalamt Berlin (n13).

more and more incriminating evidence was found. Apart from the labels, another very important piece of evidence came from the frames.[46] Some of the frames were made of wood from the same tree, which was very suspicious considering that the forged painters worked in different countries.[47] The frames were also all fabricated with the French technique, which was considered to be rather unlikely for the pictures claimed to be by other than French artists.[48]

Further points that raised suspicion were that the paint did not have small fractures, characteristic for old paintings, and that the 'titanium white' used for the pictures actually did not exist at the time the pictures were dated.[49] Labels from galleries had been tainted to look old, but had been glued to the pictures with a type of glue that was only invented much later.[50]

A further significant issue in the investigation was the level of international cooperation obtained by the German police. The German investigators could have probably found very important evidence in Beltracchi's house in the South of France. However, it was searched long after the properties in Germany and after Beltracchi was made aware of the investigation and had started to destroy evidence. The property in France was scheduled to be searched the same day as the ones in Germany, but, as the French courts were at the time on their annual holidays, no French judge could be found by the German police to issue a search warrant.[51]

Despite these setbacks, and as already stated, the comprehensive German police investigation led to the conviction of the accused, although the sentences they received were low and the vast accumulated evidence presented to the trial court was largely untouched throughout the proceedings. This was in fact the sole criminal investigation of the perpetrators but numbers of civil trials have followed against auction houses and experts associated with the dissemination of Beltracchi's forgeries. The damage has hence been not only financial but also reputational for many members of the art world.

Further Damage Caused by the Beltracchi Group

Major problems and vulnerabilities in the determination of provenance of works of art exist due to the lack of complete and comprehensive catalogues

46 Zeitung Heute, 'Tadellos das Gemälde ist' *Der Tagesspiegel* (31 December 2011).

47 DAPD, 'Kunstfälscher-Skandal: Beltracchis Frau spielte eigene Groβmutter' nachrichten.yahoo.com (28 January 2012); Gabriela Walde, 'Wie man Kunstfälschern auf die Schliche kommt' *Berliner Morgenpost* (2 February 2012).

48 Zeitung Heute, 'Tadellos das Gemälde ist' *Der Tagesspiegel* (31 December 2011).

49 DAPD (n 47); Walde (n 47); Eckhard Hoog, 'Beltracchi: Wie viele Bilder des Fälschers sind im Umlauf?' *Aachener Zeitung* (31 December 2011).

50 DAPD (n 47).

51 Interview Landeskriminalamt Berlin (n 13).

of paintings by individual artists as well as those maintained by galleries and museums.[52] The accused in the Beltracchi case exploited this situation to their advantage. They forged the labels that indicated the gallery from which the pictures had been obtained, and also relied upon the fact that there existed few catalogues relating to the forged works or galleries, and that if they did exist they did not contain photographs or reproductions of the faked pictures.[53]

One of the civil trials that ensued as a result of the Beltracchi case was brought against the Lempertz Gallery by the company that had purchased the 'Red Picture with Horses' painting attributed to Campendonk. The case was settled and the company received 2.8 Million Euro in compensation.[54] Similarly, the Paris Gallery Cazeau-Beraudiere had to settle a law suit brought against it by Daniel Filipacchi who had purchased from it a painting attributed to Max Ernst. Werner Spies, the Max Ernst expert who had authenticated a number of paintings for extensive sums of money was sued in Nanterre, France, for writing an authentication certificate on the back of a photograph of the fake Max Ernst painting 'Tremblement de Terre' by Beltracchi. The court decided in the first instance that Spies and the Geneva Gallery which sold the painting had to pay 652,883 Euros compensation (each 50 per cent of the sum) to the buyer. Werner Spies has not been prosecuted for this conduct even though by authenticating this painting from a photograph by writing on its back, he received a considerable percentage of the actual price paid by the future buyer. However, it seems that all of this is now history and Spies is back on his feet this year having organized an important Max Ernst retrospective.[55]

We will discuss in the comparative analysis whether these practices of authentication should be banned, or whether further legal restrictions on experts will lead to a situation where they will not want to give any opinion on a piece for fear of legal repercussions. What could be agreed upon though here is that they should not receive a percentage of the price, but like other professions be bound to an hourly rate depending on the level of their expertise.

52 Partsch (n 35) 180.

53 Joachim Hauschild and Ute Thon, 'Henrik Hanstein – Interview: "Die Experten sind mitverantwortlich"' *Art – Das Kunstmagazin* 19/05/2011.

54 Koldehoff and Timm (n 14) 139, 235; Alexander Forbes, 'Tentacles of Europe's Biggest Art Fraud Case Entangle Max Ernst Museum' *BlouinARTINFO* (25 January 2012) <http://www.blouinartinfo.com/news/story/757318/tentacles-of-europes-biggest-art-fraud-case-entangle-max-ernst-museum> accessed 4 November 2013.

55 Julia Michalska, 'Werner Spies rehabilitated with Max Ernst show in Vienna' *The Art Newspaper* (28 January 2013) <www.theartnewspaper.com/articles/Werner-Spies-rehabilitated-with-Max-Ernst-show-in-Vienna/28493> accessed 5 September 2013.

Indigenous Art Fraud in Australia

The Antipodean Indigenous Art Market

In travelling from the European continent, and our discussion of the Beltracchi case forgeries, to Australia we not only cover an immense physical distance but also enter an entirely different art market and environment. In many ways Australia may well be seen as something of a byway on the international art scene. With only a relatively small population of around 23 million persons its art market cannot in any way emulate those seen in Europe and North America with their multibillion dollar sales. Nonetheless, as a developed and prosperous nation with strong links to the burgeoning economies of Asia the Australian art market is still quite substantial.[56] This is especially the case in regard to the market for works produced by Aboriginal artists.[57]

Since the 1970s Indigenous visual arts and crafts in the country have grown exponentially and become the dominant element in both the local and international market for Australian art.[58] In a far-reaching review of this Indigenous industry conducted by the Australian Senate in 2007 it was estimated that its annual value amounted to between AU$100 and AU$300 million.[59] The Senate review also examined claims that questionable practices in the industry, including quite widespread fraud and fakery, had the potential to undermine confidence in the Indigenous art market and damage the reputations of individual artists and art centres. The Senate review concluded that there was considerable substance to these claims, and that in particular fraud and related illegal activity was commonplace and extremely difficult to investigate and prosecute. The Senate review stated that even where existing laws provided opportunities to prosecute, successful outcomes had been poor, mainly through a lack of evidence and the poor education of the artists involved. Submissions made to the review suggested that there had only been one known conviction, obtained in a case in 2001.[60]

The 2001 case referred to by the Senate review was that of *R v John Douglas O'Loughlin* (*O'Loughlin*), dealt with in the District Court of New South Wales (NSW).[61] We turn now to consider this case in more detail since it provides an

---

56 Major international auction houses like Sotheby's and Christie's maintain offices in Australia while there is a quite extensive network of art museums and galleries throughout the country.

57 See in general *Senate Standing Committee on Environment, Communications, Information Technology and the Arts, Indigenous Art – Securing the Future. Australia's Indigenous Visual Arts and Craft Sector* (Commonwealth of Australia, 2007).

58 Ibid., 3.

59 Ibid., 9.

60 Ibid., 105.

61 *R v O'Loughlin* (2002) Unreported, NSWDC, 13/2/2002. In what follows considerable reliance has been placed upon the description of proceedings in *O'Loughlin*

important glimpse into the fraudulent activity committed by certain persons engaged in the Indigenous art sector as well as illustrating the challenges faced by law enforcement in tackling this area of art crime in Australia.

O'Loughlin

The *O'Loughlin* case was concerned with alleged forgeries of paintings claimed to have been produced by Clifford Possum Ttjapaltjarri, one of Australia's most distinguished Indigenous artists.[62] In February 1999 an art gallery in Sydney held what purported to be a retrospective of Possum's work. The artist himself came to the exhibition which comprised 22 paintings said to have been painted by him. After viewing these works Possum identified 18 of them as 'not mine'. Subsequently Possum was also shown a number of other paintings said to be by him which were in the possession of the Art Gallery of NSW and the Museum of Contemporary Art, both located in Sydney. Possum indicated that several of these paintings were also 'not mine'. Most of the paintings held by the various galleries had signatures on the back by Possum.

Possum's allegations concerning the authenticity of the paintings triggered an investigation by the Commercial Crime Agency (CCA) of the NSW Police Force (NSWPOL). The choice of the CCA seems to have been based upon the element of fraud involved rather than any expertise among its members in art crime. Indeed at that time (1999) NSWPOL, together with its law enforcement counterparts in each Australian jurisdiction, lacked any specialist art crime unit or investigators to deal with a case like this – a situation which in fact continues up until the present day. The detectives assigned to the case were experienced in conducting investigations into business and allied frauds but they had to acquire any additional knowledge and assistance required about art fraud from other sources.

Initial inquiries by police suggested that the source of the fake paintings was to be found in the South Australian city of Adelaide, and in the business of a non-Indigenous wholesaler in Aboriginal art, John O'Loughlin. O'Loughlin had a long commercial association with Possum and he was identified as the supplier of the paintings included in the gallery exhibition as well as those in the hands of the other two art institutions involved in the case. The police then interviewed O'Loughlin who claimed he had obtained all of the paintings directly from Possum. The police also interviewed a former associate of O'Loughlin who admitted that both he and O'Loughlin had produced a number of Aboriginal style 'dot paintings' over the years.

Possum, in the evidence he provided to the investigators, admitted that on several occasions he had been asked by O'Loughlin to sign canvases with paintings

---

contained in Tania Johnson, 'When is a Forgery not a Forgery' (2006) 6 *Journal of Indigenous Policy* 83 and Chappell and Polk (n 3).

62 See Vivien Johnson, *Clifford Possum Tjapaltjarri* (Art Gallery of South Australia 2003).

'that not my work' and 'not my story' because he was drunk at the time and also fearful of possible reprisals by O'Loughlin if he refused these requests. As Johnson (2006) has indicated, in making these statements Possum was asserting as clearly as he could in his limited English that the paintings he had signed for O'Loughlin were forgeries.[63]

Following these interviews the CCA obtained a warrant[64] to intercept the phone communications of John O'Loughlin and subsequently learned from this source that he kept certain paintings and art supplies and equipment at a farm house near Adelaide. When police searched this farmhouse they found a number of completed and partially completed Aboriginal style 'dot paintings' as well as paint and paint brushes.

In October 1999 the police arrested and charged O'Loughlin with 19 counts of 'obtain money by deception' and three counts of 'use false instrument' pursuant to the provisions of the *NSW Crimes Act 1900.* A committal proceeding followed which resulted in O'Loughlin being committed for trial on all 22 counts. However, before this trial commenced the prosecution offered a plea bargain, which O'Loughlin accepted, and he subsequently pleaded guilty in February 2001 to five counts of 'obtain money by false and misleading statements' with a further five such counts taken into consideration. As a result of this plea O'Loughlin not only reduced the number of counts for which he eventually stood convicted, but also faced lower maximum sentences for what were more minor offences than those originally charged.

The tactic by the prosecution of accepting a plea of guilty to these lesser offences seems to have been driven by the belief that it would have been very difficult to prove beyond a reasonable doubt that O'Loughlin had the requisite 'dishonest intent' required to be convicted of the more serious offences for which he had originally been committed for trial. This belief was re-enforced at the subsequent sentencing of O'Loughlin in the District Court of NSW where mitigating evidence was led suggesting that O'Loughlin had been acting under the assumption that he had been initiated by Possum into a position that allowed him to assist with his paintings and to reproduce his stories. As is well documented, Indigenous collaborative practices like this are prevalent in traditional art of the type engaged in by Possum.[65] The misleading statements made to the investigating police as well as to others, and that led to O'Loughlin's convictions, were that each of the paintings the subject of a charge had been produced entirely by Possum.

---

63 Johnson (n 61) 91.

64 One of the authors, Duncan Chappell, was at the time a Deputy President of the Australian Commonwealth Administrative Appeals Tribunal in Sydney and involved in the issue of this warrant, as subsequently disclosed in the criminal proceedings that followed. To the best of our knowledge this remains the first and only occasion in Australia that phone interception has been used successfully in this way in an art crime investigation.

65 See in general Johnson (n 62); Alder, Chappell and Polk (n 8).

O'Loughlin was ultimately sentenced to a good behaviour bond for a period of three years – a remarkably lenient penalty given the circumstances of the case and one which was certainly most discouraging to the police who had invested very considerable resources and time in investigating the matter. As several commentators have observed[66] the case revealed significant deficiencies in the laws relating to fraud and their application to art crime of the type engaged in by O'Loughlin. The case also failed to convey a strong deterrent message to those engaged in art fraud either in the Indigenous art market, or in the broader art market in Australia. The sentencing judge in the O'Loughlin case said that he was not persuaded that this was a matter where 'the concept of general deterrence looms large, primarily in my view because of the amount of money involved and the circumstances in which the offences were committed with regard to the long standing relationship the prisoner had with the artist'.[67] This observation suggests that the prosecution failed in its sentencing submissions to draw judicial attention to the importance of the Indigenous art market and its economic benefits for Aboriginal communities throughout Australia. It also failed to note the very significant worldwide publicity given to the O'Loughlin case in media like the British Broadcasting Corporation[68] and the *Guardian* newspaper[69] – publicity which must surely have affected international confidence in the provenance of Aboriginal art claimed to be produced by leading artists like Clifford Possum.

Post the O'Loughlin case there has been only one further investigation and prosecution in Australia of a case involving fraud in regard to Aboriginal art. This case arose in Melbourne in the southern Australian State of Victoria and led to fraud charges being brought against a non-Indigenous husband and wife team, Ivan and Pamela Liberto, who over a period of several years had engaged in the sale of a number of paintings claimed to be produced by another famous Aboriginal artist, Rover Thomas.[70]

Suspicion as to the authenticity of one of these works was raised in 2005 by a curator at Christie's, the international auction house, and the Victoria Police (VICPOL) were called in to investigate. In a manner similar to that just described in the O'Loughlin case this investigation and subsequent prosecution was handled by officers with no prior experience of dealing with art crime. Nonetheless, the Liberto's were ultimately convicted in 2008, at a trial before a jury, of a number of counts of obtaining or attempting to obtain money by deception dishonestly from

66 See Johnson (n 61); Chappell and Polk (n 3).

67 Cited in Johnson (n 61) 96.

68 BBC News, 'Aboriginal Art Under Fraud Threat' *BBC News* (28 November 2003) <http://news.bbc.co.uk/2/hi/entertainment/3246474.stm> accessed 3 November 2013.

69 Patrick Barkham, 'Dealer Convicted of Fraud as the Aboriginal Art World Fights Back' *The Guardian* (24 February 2001) <http://www.guardian.co.uk/world/2001/feb/24/patrickbarkham> accessed 3 November 2013.

70 *R v Ivan Liberto and Pamela Yvonne Liberto* (2008) VCC 1372.

the sale of forged paintings, said by them to be genuine works by Rover Thomas.[71] The trial judge, in sentencing the Liberto's to a cumulative total of three years imprisonment, observed that the jury's verdict included a finding that the paintings had in fact been produced by the defendants and their offences had been deeply premeditated and highly planned.[72] He also noted that the offences had caused significant cost to 'innocent third parties, in this case the auction houses, and at another general cost to the integrity of the art industry, in particular the Aboriginal art industry which must suffer when this sort of activity is brought to light'.[73]

Protecting the Integrity of the Art Market

If nothing else our analysis of certain prominent art fraud cases in two entirely different settings and geographical environs illustrates how damaging such activities can be not only to those immediately duped by fraudsters but also to the international art market at large whose integrity must be called into question by the presence of identified fakes like those described. Even more troubling is the knowledge that there are almost certainly significant numbers of other forged works lurking in this market, produced by skilled forgers like Beltracchi, which as yet remain unidentified.

We have already referred to the reluctance among some of those involved in the art market to draw attention to works of art that may be suspected or even known to be fakes. Those who are prepared to speak out may run the risk of lawsuits for defamation, or if they wrongly assess a fake work to be genuine to large claims for damages because of their faulty judgement. For these reasons it is now suggested that many experts who in the past may have been prepared to offer a learned opinion about the authenticity of an art work no longer wish to engage in such actions. As one art expert has stated in the wake of the Knoedler scandal:

> There is a basic asymmetry in the system. You can say with impunity that a work is by Motherwell and it is not actionable [...] But if I say it is not genuine you can sue me. (Foundations and scholars) are even constrained from giving free opinions about whether there have been problems with certain dealers [...] Now is the time for legislation to protect free speech for scholars and writers of catalogues raisonnés. Without courage, honesty and open communication, forgeries will distort art history and pollute the market.[74]

---

71 Ibid. See also Alder, Chappell and Polk (n 8); Chappell and Polk (n 3).

72 *R v Ivan Liberto and Pamela Yvonne Liberto* (n 70).

73 Ibid., 3.

74 These are the remarks of Jack Flam, President of the Dedalus Foundation that oversees the estate of the late Robert Motherwell, one of the artists whose forged works have allegedly been among those uncovered in the Knoedler scandal. See Laura Gilbert, 'Art Expert Contradicts Knoedler Gallery' *The Art Newspaper* (15 November 2012) <http://

It remains to be seen whether or not legislators will have the courage to affect law reform of this type, and if the notoriously secretive and opaque art market will become more transparent in order to expose problematic work when it first surfaces, rather than concealing or ignoring its existence. The Beltracchi case, like no other, seems to have prompted considerable alarm in the art market place regarding the risks associated with purchasing high value art and has prompted fresh searches for technological devices that might minimize these risks. It has been reported, for instance, that the German auction house caught up in the Beltracchi affair, Kunsthaus Lempertz, has invested in an expensive 'Thermo Scientific Niton X ray fluorescence analytic machine' which may be used in the future on a routine basis to examine the types of pigments used in a painting and matching those with those known to have been adopted by a particular artist.[75] However, such testing will only be of assistance if the forger did not use the correct pigment – something which the more sophisticated offenders appear unlikely to do. Technology may provide some measure of risk avoidance, but other preventive measures are also needed, not the least of which is an enhanced law enforcement presence in the art market devoted to early investigation and detection of fakery and the apprehension and prosecution of those involved.

Enhancing Law Enforcement

The cases we have examined in some depth in this chapter did involve the successful intervention of law enforcement agencies in Europe and Australia. In the Beltracchi case this intervention came at a quite late stage in the lifespan of the forgery team who were able to operate with seeming impunity for many years even though there were suspicions raised about the authenticity of some of the paintings they injected into the market. Once alerted to the possibility of fraud the German police acted in a proficient and comprehensive way to bring the perpetrators to justice. Their investigative work was assisted by the use of specialist detectives in the area of art crime – a situation which was in marked contrast to that described in Australia in the O'Loughlin and Liberto cases even though the police who did gain responsibility for the investigations produced favourable outcomes.

As Block has indicated elsewhere in this book,[76] within the European Union specialization in art crime investigation is becoming more prominent and important. A number of countries now have such specialist units including Italy, a world leader in this area, as well as Germany, the United Kingdom and France. While systematic evaluation of these units is lacking, at least in the published scientific literature, there is strong anecdotal evidence that having a specialist unit

www.theartnewspaper.com/articles/Art-expert-contradicts-Knoedler-gallery/28061> accessed 5 September 2013.

75 Ibid.

76 See Chapter 10 of this collection.

available to handle art crime investigations of all types increases confidence in the integrity of the related art market, and almost certainly encourages more reporting of art crimes including fraud and fakery.[77] Units of this type are also able to offer expert advice on security measures that might be taken to prevent art theft and fraud.

The formation of specialist art crime law enforcement units alone will not be a universal salve for all forms of art crime. It is not just police who need to be better resourced and organized when dealing with such crime, but also prosecutors. Lawyers are required to lead prosecutions who understand the intricacies of the art market and are able to advise and assist in bringing appropriate charges against offenders when they are caught. We have referred to some of the difficulties experienced by those involved in the Beltracchi and O'Loughlin cases in settling upon the particular charges which best fitted the prosecutions.

We have also mentioned the possibility of law reform, especially in Australia where the existing laws regarding offences of fraud and forgery are lumbered with archaic and confusing principles that make prosecutions difficult. Prosecutors have also seemed reluctant to utilize more flexible and modern laws designed to combat money laundering and organized criminality in the art crime arena. As the Beltracchi case illustrates in particular the activities of the forging team were well planned and coordinated, fitting the description of organized crime contained in the *United Nations Convention Against Transnational Organized Crime 2004*.[78] However, the conviction for fraud while being part of a criminal organization received by Beltracchi is as far as German law can go for these types of organized crimes. It would also seem likely that the significant sums of money obtained by Beltracchi and his colleagues for their forged works might well have brought them within the framework of German anti-money laundering provisions.[79]

Conclusion

We have sought in this chapter, through a review of several contemporary cases of art fraud, to draw attention in particular to the problems of detecting, investigating and prosecuting this form of art crime. The problems we believe are not unique to any single nation, region or hemisphere although some jurisdictions seem better prepared than others in the way they manage cases of art fraud, often because they

77 Ibid.

78 See Jessica Dietzler, 'On "Organized Crime" in the Illicit Antiquities trade: Moving Beyond the Definitional Debate' (2012) *Trends in Organized Crime* <http://traffickingculture.org/wp-content/uploads/2013/01/2013-Dietzler-On-organized-crime-in-the-illicit-antiquities-trade_moving-beyond-the-definitional-debate.pdf> accessed 5 September 2013.

79 See Janet Ulph, 'The Impact of Criminal Law and Money Laundering Measures Upon the Illicit Trade in Art and Antiquities' (2011) 16(1) *Art, Antiquity and Law* 39-52.

are located in places where such fraud appears to be both endemic and threatening to the burgeoning international market in art works of all types.

Those trading in this market are especially sensitive to unanticipated fluctuations in the quality and price of the commodities they are buying and selling, often for huge sums of money. Fakery and forgery are an anathema to the integrity and stability of any commodity market. In the art marketplace, which at present remains largely free of any regulation, the risks of being snared by one of the fraudulent works of an artist like Beltracchi appear to be increasing, despite some law enforcement successes in capturing and punishing the forgers. These successes must be tempered by the realization that the forgers have in many cases been able to operate with seeming impunity for years before being detected, and that the punishment they have received, when measured against the damage they have caused, seems minimal.

Resolving this situation is clearly well beyond the remit of both law enforcement and this chapter, and will require the development of far greater transparency and trust in the art market, most probably through the establishment of regulatory regimes that contain some real, substantial and credible powers of compliance.

There seem to be two significant problem areas in the detection, investigation and prosecution of art fraud/forgery. Both problems relate to regulation, but the responsibility of the market and the state can be distinguished. First, it is apparent that particularly in the detection phase of art fraud, experts and auction houses play a significant role. Experts, because they might have higher financial incentives not to detect a forgery than to do so and auction houses, because they have predominantly financial motivations and rely on expertise of others rather than following their own suspicions. With regard to both actors it can therefore be concluded that the detection of a forgery comes at a financial loss and the likelihood of detection – and ensuing investigation and prosecution of the forgers – is potentially diminished. The answer to the question as to what can be done to increase the detection rate of forgeries lies therefore within the market itself and its self-regulation.

With regard to the investigation and prosecution phases the Australian examples have shown that art fraud cases present significant challenges to police, judges and prosecutors as the relevant expertise is often not present within their ranks. While many European and North American countries have therefore commenced to create such expertise within specialist art crime units, other countries do not have such an advantage.[80] In the area of art theft, the lack of public policing expertise has opened the market to private investigators as the police have neither the knowledge, nor the resources to pursue such crimes over a prolonged period of time.[81] As a consequence, police acquire even less possibilities to be confronted with art crime cases and the focus shifts to private security, which again is linked to financial incentives, rather than bringing the perpetrators to justice. However,

80 See Chapters 10 and 11 in this volume.

81 See, for example, Chapter 5 in this volume.

as long as art crime remains a low priority within policing, this trend cannot be stopped.

A first starting point in increasing detection, investigations and prosecutions of art fraud could be the enhancement of self-regulation of the art market with regard to expertise and forensic detection methods. A second step could be to increase police awareness and expertise and a third step to adapt national laws in this area to facilitate prosecution and conviction. The cases that do come to light are widely published on in the media and lead to considerable damage to the reputation of the art market. This should be an incentive for the market to change its practices more actively. The investigation and prosecution of such cases do usually find very positive resonance in the media and provide good publicity, especially for police. This should enhance police enthusiasm to investigate such cases. However, as long as the art market and governments do not consider the existing problems to be serious the current situation will not change.

Chapter 5
A Tale of Two Cities, A Tale of Two Art Thefts

Vicki Oliveri

Introduction

As the title suggests this chapter is concerned with the tale of two very different and still unsolved art thefts which took place in cities far apart from one another. The most recent of these thefts occurred in Sydney, Australia, where the Frans van Mieris painting, *A Cavalier (self portrait)*, had been on display at the Art Gallery of New South Wales since 1993. Fourteen years later, in 2007, the unthinkable happened: it was stolen. The earlier robbery happened in the United States (US) in 1990 at Boston's Isabella Stewart Gardner Museum. This was not your usual art theft, with a roll call of purloined paintings which included Rembrandt, Vermeer, Manet and Degas amongst the artists whose works were stolen. More than twenty-three years later the intrigue surrounding this particular unsolved theft continues, as does the speculation.

In examining and comparing these two cases of art theft, the qualitative approach is applied – an approach determined by the problem of art crime statistics. The term 'chiaroscuro', which is 'the Italian technical term for light and shade',[1] is a useful one to apply here as there is plenty of light and shade concerning art crime statistics. In terms of 'shade', art crime can be referred to as a 'dark figure crime'[2] within the criminology field. That is, there exist crimes which cannot 'be found in official statistics of crime'.[3] According to Chappell and Polk, this could be because statistics may not have categories that specifically target art crime and so these cases may be grouped with general cases of fraud and property crime.[4] Another explanation for the low statistical representation of art crime is that the victims may not be willing to report the crime because 'identifying the work as fraudulent [or stolen] may have the

1 Ernst Gombrich, *The Story of Art* (16th edn, Phaidon Press 1995) 37.

2 Duncan Chappell and Ken Polk, 'Fakers and Forgers, Deception and Dishonesty: An Exploration of the Murky World of Art Fraud' (2009) 2(3) *Current Issues in Criminal Justice* 16.

3 Ibid., 16.

4 Ibid.

instant result of seeing a large investment of money disappear'.[5] Additionally, cultural institutions have a history of not reporting thefts as they fear this can draw attention to weaknesses in their security.[6] Simon Mackenzie refers to this as the 'flag effect'.[7] That is, 'certain properties stand out as attractive to thieves',[8] with weak security measures being one of them. By announcing a robbery a gallery would be metaphorically raising a flag for potential thieves, signalling the gallery's vulnerabilities. All these factors combine to create a significant gap in quantitative data. Consequently there has been a reliance on the qualitative approach. To again utilize the term 'chiaroscuro', this is where the 'light' enters to counter the 'shade' cast by the problematic nature of art theft statistics. To that end, this chapter will endeavour to shed some 'light' on these two instances of art theft through addressing the following questions: What does a comparison of these two cases, with particular emphasis on the policing perspective, reveal about the Australian experience of art theft at a cultural institution? Are there differences in approaches to the investigation process? What key lessons emerge?

Gaps on the Walls: The 2007 Theft of *A Cavalier (self portrait)*

An art theft takes place, generating a series of headlines:

- $1.4m Cavalier art theft probably an inside job[9]
- 'Expert' snatched masterpiece from NSW gallery[10]
- Dutch master stolen[11]
- Police investigate theft of 17th-century artwork[12]

---

5 Ibid.

6 Noah Charney, 'Art Crime in Context' in Noah Charney (ed), *Art and Crime: Exploring the Dark Side of the Art World* (Praeger 2009) xxii-xxiii.

7 Simon Mackenzie, 'Criminal and Victim Profile in Art Theft: Motive, Opportunity and Repeat Victimisation' (2005) 10 (4) *Art, Antiquity & Law* 362-3.

8 Ibid., 363.

9 Clare Morgan, '$1.4m Cavalier Art Theft Probably An Inside Job' *The Age* (15 June 2007) <http://www.theage.com.au/news/national/14m-cavalier-art-theft-probably-an-insidejob/2007/06/14/1181414466910.html> accessed 8 November 2011.

10 Anonymous author, '"Expert" Snatched Masterpiece From NSW Gallery' *ABC News* (15 June 2007) <http://www.abc.net.au/news/2007-06-14/expert-snatched-masterpiece-from-nsw-gallery/69298> accessed 8 November 2011.

11 Richard Jinman and Clare Morgan, 'Dutch Master Stolen' *The Sydney Morning Herald* (14 June 2007) <http://www.smh.com.au/news/arts/dutch-master-stolen/2007/06/13/1181414383922.html> accessed 8 November 2011.

12 Art Gallery of New South Wales, 'Police Investigate Theft of 17th Century Artwork from the Art Gallery of New South Wales' <http://archive.artgallery.nsw.gov.au/media/archives_2007/mieris> accessed 21 November 2011.

The headlines, usually associated with the museums and galleries of Europe and North America, were home-grown on this occasion. At 10:30am on the 14 June 2007, The Art Gallery of New South Wales (the Gallery) announced via a media release[13] that the police were investigating the theft of a painting. *A Cavalier (self portrait)*[14] by Frans van Mieris, had been 'stolen from the Gallery between 10:00am and 12:30pm on Sunday 10 June'.[15] The painting was described as 'a valuable 17th century work'.[16] The Gallery's Director at the time, Edmund Capon, stated, 'I am deeply shocked. Well over a million people visit the Gallery each year and this is a very rare occurrence as the security measures at the Gallery are sound and proven.'[17] Despite Capon's assurances, the issue of CCTV cameras and security as a whole would prove to be contentious, drawing criticism from the media.

Using the details in the police report, supplemented with details garnered from the media coverage, a timeline of the theft could be interpreted as follows:

- **Saturday 9 June 2007, 8:00pm-10:00pm:** Two security guards stated they had entered the room, at separate times, between 8:00pm and 10:00pm. According to the report, however, the first security guard to enter the room explained that owing to a storm that night he 'did not particularly pay attention to the missing artwork as he was concentrating on checking for water damage'.[18] Consequently, he could not be '100% certain the piece was present at the time'.[19] The second security guard who checked the room did not notice anything of concern.[20] In light of the security guards' statements, the police determined that, 'it can therefore not be confirmed exactly when the piece was last sighted, however it is believed to have gone missing between 10:00pm 9/6/2007 and 12:30pm 10/6/2007 and taken by person/s not known'.[21] This statement would indicate that *A Cavalier*'s absence was noticed at 12:30pm on June 10. If, according to their own report, police believed the painting had gone missing between 10:00pm on Saturday night and 12:30pm on Sunday afternoon, why would one news story claim that, 'Police believe the painting … was stolen sometime between 10:00am and 12:30pm on Sunday'?[22] Similarly, why did

13 Ibid.

14 Frans van Mieris I, *A Cavalier (self portrait)* 1657-1659, oil on oak panel, 20 × 16 × 1 cm, Gift of James Fairfax AO 1993, Art Gallery of New South Wales, Sydney.

15 Art Gallery of New South Wales (n 12).

16 Ibid.

17 Ibid.

18 New South Wales Police Force, 'Police Report' (The Rocks Local Area Command, 11 June 2007) 2.

19 Ibid.

20 Ibid.

21 Ibid.

22 Karen Barlow, 'NSW Gallery Defends Security System After Theft of 17th Century Artwork' *The World Today* (14 June 2007) <http://www.abc.net.au/worldtoday/content/2007/s1951612.htm> accessed 4 November 2011.

the Gallery's media release specify a timeframe of 10:00am and 12:30pm? Aside from one news story which stated that 'It is unclear when the small painting ... was plucked from the Gallery's walls',[23] the Gallery's specified timeframe was repeated in other news stories:

- It was taken some time between 10:00am and 12:30pm.[24]
- [It was] ... removed ... between 10:00am and 12:30pm last Sunday.[25]
- The painting was taken during viewing hours on Sunday.[26]

On 10 June, a thief walked into a small room of the Art Gallery of New South Wales ... [and] unscrewed from the wall *A Cavalier (self portrait)* ... and walked out of the Gallery.[27]

The repetition of this timeframe suggests that an after-hours robbery had possibly already been ruled out at this early stage of the investigation. As the timeline continues a significant area of concern emerges: the delay in notifying law enforcement agencies, such as the NSW Police Force and the Australian Customs Service.

- **Sunday 10 June, 3:30pm:** It was at this time the Gallery's General Manager, Anne Flanagan, 'indicated she was advised of the missing piece'.[28] The police report signified that the painting was noted missing at 12:30pm, a fact reiterated by a newspaper report which stated that the loss had been noticed by 'a Gallery security guard doing his rounds at 12:30pm on Sunday afternoon'.[29] This leaves a three-hour gap between the discovery of the loss and the General Manager being advised, which is perhaps due to the Gallery staff conducting checks to determine the painting's whereabouts. Certainly, the performance of these checks was, according to the police report, the 'initial reason the matter had not been reported to police'[30] at that stage. This is also confirmed by a

23 Jinman and Morgan (n 11).

24 Anonymous author, 'How Was Painting Stolen' *The Daily Telegraph* (15 June 2007) <http://www.dailytelegraph.com.au/news/sydney-nsw/how-was-painting-stolen/story-e6freuzi-1111113749872> accessed 8 November 2011.

25 Morgan (n 9).

26 Nick Bryant, 'Brazen Heist at Australia Gallery' *BBC News* (14 June 2007) <http://news.bbc.co.uk/2/hi/asia-pacific/6752147.stm> accessed 18 November 2011.

27 Peter Coleman, 'The Great Australian Art Heist' *The Wall Street Journal* (22 June 2007) <http://online.wsj.com/article/SB118246120253743938.html> accessed 21 November 2011.

28 New South Wales Police Force (n 18) 1.

29 Dan Box and Matthew Westwood, 'For a Cavalier, He Went Quietly' *The Australian* (15 June 2007) <http://www.theaustralian.com.au/news/nation/for-a-cavalier-he-went-quietly/story-e6frg6nf-1111113753566> accessed 8 November 2011.

30 New South Wales Police Force (n 18) 2.

report in *The Australian*[31] where Flanagan explained that 'the initial delay was due to an internal investigation, and search of the building inside and out, to establish whether the painting had not simply been mislaid. "Clearly by Sunday evening, things were not looking good", she said'.[32]

- **Monday 11 June, 12:00nn:** Approximately twenty-four hours after the Gallery discovered the painting was missing, police were notified of the theft and attended the scene soon after to interview staff.[33] Forensic Services were also brought in to examine the area where the painting had been displayed.[34] It was during the police interviews that the Gallery's General Manager requested that, 'investigators do not notify the public or media at this point. The foregoing reasons being that Flanagan wishes to advise James Fairfax [the painting's donor] of the loss as well as the insurance agency, NSW Treasury Managed Funds, prior to them finding out via the media which would have a negative impact on the Gallery'.[35]

- **Wednesday 13 June, 3:24pm:** Police met with Gallery staff 'in regard to a controlled release of information to the Media in an effort to seek assistance from members of the public'.[36] At the meeting Flanagan disclosed that all 'interested parties (Fairfax and Insurance Company) had now been informed of the theft'.[37] Consequently, police released details of the crime to 'Law Enforcement Agencies Australia wide including the Australian Customs Service'.[38]

- **Thursday June 14:** Information about the theft was released to the public media via a press conference at the Art Gallery of New South Wales.

The Gallery's delayed notification of the crime was canvassed in the media coverage. *The World Today*, an Australian Broadcasting Commission (ABC) national current affairs program, stated that the Gallery's Director, Edmund Capon, was 'not concerned that it has taken five days for the theft to become public'.[39] As Capon explained, 'That's not to say that nothing's been done. Monday was the police; secondly, I was away; thirdly I had to speak to the donor; and fourthly

31 Box and Westwood (n 29).

32 Ibid.

33 New South Wales Police Force (n 18) 1. Police attended the scene from 12:06pm to 13:00pm on 11 June 2007.

34 Ibid., 2. Forensic services examined the scene for fingerprints.

35 Ibid.

36 Ibid.

37 Ibid.

38 Ibid.

39 Barlow (n 22).

there's a lot of work been done in the last two days, believe me.'[40] *The Australian*[41] pointed to how the instances of notifications were staggered throughout this period, confirming that:

> NSW Police were not called in until Monday – although Gallery staff had telephoned Mr Capon in Italy the night before to say they thought there might have been a theft – and Customs was not told of the loss until Wednesday … Even after the Police were called, the Gallery requested a delay until yesterday, after Mr Capon had returned to Australia, before the loss was made public – in which time they broke the news to the state Minister for the Arts, Frank Sartor, James Fairfax, and the Gallery's board of trustees.[42]

It is understandable that, prior to notifying the police, the Gallery wanted to ensure the painting had not been relocated to another section of the building. However, as an article in the US-based *Wall Street Journal*[43] observed, 'The price for this cautious delay was high indeed. When the police were brought in, the trail was cold.'[44] This 'cautious delay', coupled with the yet to be deployed media spotlight, bought the thief extra time to disappear with the valuable painting unimpeded. It should be noted here, however, that the private consultant, Michael Maher, who was undertaking a NSW state government sanctioned contemporaneous and autonomous investigation of the theft, offers an alternative view regarding the delayed notification. He recollects that police were informed close to when the painting's absence was first noticed.[45] When his attention was drawn to the fact that the relevant police report was dated Monday 11 June, whereas the painting was discovered missing on Sunday 10 June, Maher explained that the detectives were not working that weekend and therefore completed the report on their next working day, which was Monday 11 June.[46]

That a theft occurred at all had the media scrutinizing the Gallery's level of security, and especially so given that the theft took place less than two weeks out from the start of a major exhibition of Islamic Art[47] which, according to media reports, had precipitated the Gallery's 'biggest security operation in its history'.[48] Although a Gallery media release had stated that 'CCTV cameras

40 Ibid.

41 Box and Westwood (n 29).

42 Ibid.

43 Coleman (n 27).

44 Ibid.

45 [Telephone] Interview with Michael Maher, Independent Investigator of the theft *A Cavalier* (Sydney, 6 June 2012).

46 Ibid.

47 Art Gallery of New South Wales, 'The Arts of Islam: Treasures from the Nasser D Khalili Collection, 22 June – 23 September 2007' <http://www.artgallery.nsw.gov.au/sub/islam/index.html> accessed 4 June 2012.

48 See: Box and Westwood (n 29). The theft came at a 'sensitive time for the gallery, which had already planned to mount the biggest security operation in its history for an

within the Gallery are being reviewed',[49] the police investigation revealed that 'the area from where the painting was taken did not have any CCTV cameras or any other security devices installed'.[50] In actuality, the nearest CCTV cameras were located at the 'entrance/exits'[51] of the Gallery and with approximately 6000 to 10 000 visitors[52] on a weekend, detecting any suspicious entries and exits was a challenging task.

The theft led to harsh criticism of the Gallery's security measures although, according to Michael Maher, this criticism was totally unfounded because security at the Gallery was on a par with security at other equivalent galleries overseas.[53] Furthermore, as was noted in their 2007 annual report, the Gallery has had 'a long and successful security track record'.[54] The regular exhibitions held at the Gallery can be seen as a testament to that track record, for if the security was not of a sufficient standard then other galleries would not be loaning them their works. Maher also discounted the criticisms generated by the lack of CCTV cameras, contending that such surveillance equipment would not necessarily prevent a theft or crime. He agreed, however, that security surveillance can be useful after a crime in identifying perpetrators, except when they have concealed their identities such as through wearing hooded clothing.[55] Nonetheless, in the aftermath of the theft, and the criticism that ensued, reviewing and upgrading security at the Gallery became an understandable priority.

When art thefts occur speculation arises naturally as to the motivation for the crimes and the whereabouts of the stolen works. Michael Maher, when weighing up the little evidence available regarding the disappearance of *A Cavalier*, said he believed it was unlikely the theft was opportunistic.[56] The specialized tools needed to remove the painting ruled this out, he said, as it would have required the thief to have prior knowledge of how the painting was fastened in order to determine how to best remove it.[57] He also believed the painting was still in Australia.[58] It is worth noting that *A Cavalier* was not the only artwork to have been removed illicitly from the Gallery, which has been the victim of at least three prior robberies. In

---

exhibition of Islamic arts, opening next week'; and Jinman and Morgan (n 11). 'The robbery comes at an embarrassing time for the gallery, which recently revealed details of the biggest security operation in its history for an Islamic arts exhibition opening in eight days.'

49 Art Gallery of New South Wales (n 12).

50 New South Wales Police Force (n 18) 2.

51 Ibid.

52 See ibid. and Morgan (n 9).

53 [Telephone] Interview with Michael Maher (n 45).

54 Art Gallery of New South Wales, 'Art Gallery of New South Wales Annual Report 2007' 14 <http://www.artgallery.nsw.gov.au/media/uploads/reports/AGNS> accessed 4 November 2011.

55 Ibid.

56 [Telephone] Interview with Michael Maher (n 45).

57 Ibid.

58 Ibid.

1942 a William Dobell painting, *Study of a Woman Dozing*, was removed from its frame and taken from the Gallery.[59] It was believed at the time to be 'the first theft of a picture from a national gallery in Australia'.[60] More recently, in 2004, a 'wood carving of a pink magnolia by Tokyo-based artist Yoshihiro Suda',[61] valued at $35 000, went missing. It has never been found.[62] Apart from these two incidents, a 2007 article reported that Edmund Capon believed *A Cavalier*'s theft was 'the first time an artwork has been stolen from the Gallery in about 15 years'.[63]

Even though delving into the past may reveal more instances of loss at the Gallery, it can also provide hope for the future recovery of missing artworks. Consider the fate of another artwork by Frans van Mieris. His painting, *Man at a Window Smoking a Pipe* (1658),[64] was one of four paintings recovered in 1998, thirty years after being stolen from Romania's Brukenthal National Museum.[65]

Unfortunately at the present moment, the chances of recovering *A Cavalier* seem to have diminished. The NSW police have indicated that while technically the case does remain open[66] they have suspended their investigations into the matter since June 2008.[67] Just as the Gallery's role in the theft came under scrutiny, so too the police investigation is not without its criticism. As a former experienced police officer himself, Maher recognized that a well-run law enforcement investigation is dependent on the qualities of the individual police officers involved. Detective work is a very personally driven process and Maher questioned the level of 'drive' shown by police throughout the *A Cavalier* investigation. He also reiterated the familiar point that Australia still lacks a specialized art crime investigation unit

59 Anonymous author, 'Art Gallery Theft: Painting Taken from Frame' *The West Australian* (10 June 1942) <http://nla.gov.au/nla.news-article47335718> accessed 12 February 2012.

60 Ibid.

61 Anonymous author, 'Thieves targeted NSW art gallery before' *The Sydney Morning Herald* (6 August 2007) <http://www.smh.com.au/news/National/Thieves-targeted-NSW-art-gallery> accessed 24 October 2011.

62 Ibid.

63 Jinman and Morgan (n 11). Note: to date I have been unsuccessful in finding further information about this theft.

64 Details sourced from <http://www.brukenthalmuseum.ro/img/europeana/etajII/04_18.jpg> accessed 2 June 2012. Also known as *Soldier at a Window, Smoking Pipe*, details sourced from: <http://www.parisartstudies.com/index.php?option=com_content&task=view&id=236&Itemid=1> accessed 2 June 2012.

65 William Honan, 'Stolen Old Masters Surface in US' *The New York Times* (9 July 1998) <http://www.nytimes.com/1998/07/09/arts/stolen-old-masters-surface-in us.html?pagewanted=all&src=pm> accessed 23 May 2012.

66 Email from Detective Senior Constable Alison Acock (NSW Police Force – The Rocks Local Area Command) to author (27 June 2012). 'It is technically still an open police investigation.'

67 New South Wales Police Force (n 18) 4. Report states, 'No further investigation 02/06/2008 – case suspended.'

and believes one is needed. He did concede that police inquiries do, by necessity, get prioritized and a more serious offence (for example, murder, sexual assault) will be given a higher investigative priority than property crime, which is what an art theft is categorized as being. Overall, he asserted that property crime is 'down the ladder'[68] when it comes to policing priorities. *A Cavalier* remains lost property, leaving a gap in the wall[69] and a gap in art history, particularly of the Dutch Golden Age – the era during which Frans van Mieris worked.[70]

Empty Frames: The 1990 Robbery at the Isabella Stewart Gardner Museum

The 1990 art heist at Boston's Isabella Stewart Gardner Museum (the Gardner) left not only gaps in the walls but, quite literally, the empty frames from which a selection of the paintings were forcibly removed.[71] The Gardner robbery is a frequently cited and well-documented case which has generated countless articles over the twenty-three year period since the artworks disappeared. It has been referred to in various books,[72] including that seminal text by John Conklin, *Art Crime*. Indeed, the opening lines of Conklin's introduction make direct reference to this theft.[73] It has featured in a documentary, *Stolen*,[74] and has been the basis of a book, *The Gardner Heist: The True Story of the World's Largest Unsolved Art Theft*.[75]

---

68 Ibid.

69 Barlow (n 22). References Edmund Capon's reaction to the loss of *A Cavalier*, 'How would you feel? It's like … if you walk home and find a gap on your wall, that's how I feel. And I don't like gaps on the wall.'

70 M. Westwood and C. Perkin, 'Art Heist Overshadows Whiteley Record' *The Australian* (14 June 2007) <http://www.theaustralian.com.au/news/nation/art-heist-overshadows-whiteley-record/story-e6frg6nf-1111113744881> accessed 4 November 2011.

71 Fox Butterfield, 'Boston Museum Says It Was Uninsured for Theft' *The New York Times* (19 March 1990) <http://www.nytimes.com /1990/03/20/arts/boston-museum-says-it-was-uninsured-for-theft.html?pagewanted=all&src=pm> accessed 23 October 2011. 'Some of the paintings and at least one Rembrandt were cut from their frames.'

72 Examples include: Matthew Hart, *The Irish Game* (Chatto and Windus 2004); Simon Houpt, *Museum of the Missing: The High Stakes of Art Crime* (Madison Press Books 2006); Jonathan Webb, *Stolen: The Gallery of Missing Masterpieces* (Madison Press Books 2008); Anthony Amore and Tom Mashberg, *Stealing Rembrandts: The Untold Stories of Notorious Art Heists* (Palgrave Macmillan 2011); Stefano Manacorda and Duncan Chappell (eds), *Crime in the Art and Antiquities World: Illegal Trafficking in Cultural Property* (Springer 2011).

73 John Conklin, *Art Crime* (Praeger Publishers 1994) 1.

74 Rebecca Dreyfuss (Director), *Stolen* (Persistence of Vision Films, USA 2006).

75 Ulrich Boser, *The Gardner Heist: The True Story of the World's Largest Unsolved Art Theft* (Collins 2009).

While thirteen works were stolen in total, two pieces in particular, Rembrandt's *Storm on the Sea of Galilee* (1633)[76] and Vermeer's *The Concert* (1658-1660),[77] tend to dominate the headlines and understandably so. While Rembrandt (who incidentally was a contemporary of Frans van Mieris)[78] may have left the world around two thousand artworks,[79] *Storm on the Sea of Galilee* is his 'only known seascape'.[80] Unlike Rembrandt, however, Vermeer's output as a painter was very low. There are approximately 36[81] of his artworks in existence and so consequently they are considered rare and precious items. However *all* 13 stolen pieces are worthy of being recognized. This is not just because they are each irreplaceable, but because they reflect the aesthetic tastes of Mrs Gardner and so were (and are) an integral part of her personal collection. Therefore, to mention them here is to honour her aesthetic legacy. The other 11 artworks stolen on 18 March 1990 (along with the Rembrandt and Vermeer already mentioned) were:

- Rembrandt, *A Lady and Gentleman in Black*, 1633[82]
- Rembrandt, *Self-Portrait*, ca. 1634[83]
- Manet, *Chez Tortoni*, 1878-1880[84]
- Govaert Flinck, *Landscape with an Obelisk*, 1638[85]
- Five gouache drawings by Edgar Degas:[86]
- Degas, *La Sortie de Pesage*[87]
- Degas, *Three Mounted Jockeys*[88]

76 Isabella Stewart Gardner Museum, 'Fact Sheet: Stolen Artworks – Theft of Thirteen Artworks, March 18, 1990' <http://www.gardnermuseum.org> accessed 23 October 2011), 'oil on canvas, 161.7 × 129.8 cm. Inscribed on the rudder: Rembrandt (sic). f::/1633'.

77 Ibid., 'oil on canvas, 72.5 × 64.7 cm'.

78 Otto Naumann, *Frans van Mieris (1635-1681) The Elder* (Davaco, Doornspijk [Netherlands] 1981) 13. 'Frans van Mieris's name might not be a household word like that of his famous contemporary Rembrandt, but his fame was equally widespread in the seventeenth century.'

79 Amore and Mashberg (n 72) 2.

80 Isabella Stewart Gardner Museum (n 76).

81 Ibid.

82 Ibid., 'oil on canvas, 131.6 × 109 cm. Inscribed at the foot: Rembrandt.ft: 1633- A double portrait of a lady and gentleman in dramatic black and white'.

83 Ibid., 'etching, 1 3/4 × 2 in. (Bartsch 2, Rovinski 2, Hind 57)'.

84 Ibid., 'oil on canvas, 26 × 34 cm. Inscribed at the foot on the left: Manet'.

85 Ibid., 'oil on oak panel, 54.5 × 71 cm. Inscribed faintly at the foot on the right: R. 16.8 (until recently attributed to Rembrandt)'.

86 Ibid.

87 Ibid., 'pencil and watercolor on paper, 10 × 16 cm'.

88 Ibid., 'black ink, white, flesh and rose washes, probably oil pigments, applied with a brush on medium brown paper, 30.5 × 24 cm'.

- Degas, *Cortège aux Environs de Florence*[89]
- Degas, *Program for an artistic soirée*, 1884[90]
- Degas, *Program for an artistic soirée*, 1884[91]
- Finial in the form of an eagle[92]
- Chinese bronze beaker or *Ku*[93]

The thieves' eclectic bounty had investigators and the public alike all wondering who was behind 'the biggest, most confounding art heist in American history'.[94] The investigation (and speculation) continues to this day.

When it comes to investigating the art heist, the Gardner provides the following details on their website:

> Over the last 20 years, the investigation has been shepherded by Security Directors at the museum in cooperation with the FBI Boston Bureau. The theft remains an open, active case and a top priority of the museum (and of the FBI/Art Recovery Squad, who lists it on its 'most wanted art' list) … The Museum and authorities continue to pursue regular leads and remain confident that the artworks will be recovered.[95]

In recent times the Gardner has developed a good working relationship with both the Federal Bureau of Investigation (FBI) and the Office of the US Attorney – the two key law enforcement agencies involved in the case. Certainly, the FBI's establishment of an Art Crime Team[96] in 2004 would have helped in providing more expertise, as 'Art Crime Team agents receive specialized training in art and cultural property investigations.'[97] However, as

89 Ibid., 'pencil and wash on paper, 16 × 21 cm'.

90 Ibid., 'charcoal on white paper, 24.1 × 30.9 cm'.

91 Ibid., 'A less-finished version of the above, charcoal on buff paper, 23.4 × 30 cm'.

92 Ibid., 'gilt metal (bronze), French, 1813-1814, approx. 10 in. high. This originally sat on the top of the pole support of a silk Napoleonic flag … which was not taken by the thieves'.

93 Ibid., 'Chinese, Shang Dynasty, 1200-1100 B.C. H. 10 1/2 in. Diam. 6 1/8 in. Wt. 2 lbs. 7 oz. An ancient bronze beaker … This is the oldest artwork taken by the thieves'.

94 Steve Lopez, 'The Great Caper: Is the Heist of the Century About to Be Solved, Two Cons May Hold the Answer' (1997) 150 (21) *Time* 74 <Academic One File, http://find.galegroup.com, Gale Document Number: A19966911> accessed 19 October 2011.

95 Isabella Stewart Gardner Museum, 'Theft Overview' <http://www.gardnermuseum.org/resources/theft/> accessed 10 June 2012.

96 FBI, 'Art Crime Team' <http://www.fbi.gov/about-us/investigate/vc_majorthefts/arttheft/art-crime-team/ accessed 12 July 2012. The team is headed up by Archaeologist/Art Historian, Bonnie Magness-Gardiner, who is the Director of the FBI's Art Theft Program.

97 Ibid.

the Gardner's current Director of Security, Anthony Amore, has explained, it was one of his aims to encourage a good inter-agency working relationship when he started at the Gardner, and his background in Federal Government security helped in doing this.[98] According to Amore, one of the main reasons a good working relationship is so important is for the simple fact that museums and galleries are not set up to conduct criminal investigations.[99] Added to this, museum staff is often required to contend with the different views and opinions given by interested parties, such as board members and trustees, on how best to approach a response to the theft.[100] Amore acknowledged that the machinations of the investigation process created a complex situation, especially in the case of the Gardner where 'it's a three-fold approach'[101] with each law enforcement entity having their particular focus:

> The FBI has assigned an agent to investigate the theft – although their focus is usually crimes such as bank robberies and violent crime. They can also provide anonymity for the informant.[102]
>
> The Assistant US Attorney is also involved and their responsibility is in the area of prosecutions, and in offering potential immunity from prosecutions and protection to any witnesses and informants.[103]
>
> Anthony Amore's area of responsibility, as Director of Security at the Gardner, is overseeing the reward, fielding any information the public sends him and also providing expertise about the stolen artwork.[104]

This harmonious working relationship was acknowledged in an article in *The Boston Herald*[105] on the twentieth anniversary of the Gardner theft. In reporting that the 'key investigators are redoubling efforts to publicize an offer of full and unconditional immunity to anyone who helps locate or return 13 stolen items valued at a half-billion dollars',[106] journalist Tom Mashberg noted that this was a 'far cry from the 10th and 15th anniversaries, when there was a spotty cooperation among the FBI, museum investigators and federal prosecutors and

98 [Telephone] Interview with Anthony Amore, Director of Security, Isabella Stewart Gardner Museum (Sydney-Boston, 14 June 2012).

99 Ibid.

100 Ibid.

101 Ibid.

102 Ibid.

103 Ibid.

104 Ibid.

105 Tom Mashberg, 'Gardner Heist Sleuths: Immunity for the Art!' *The Boston Herald* (18 March 2010) <http://www.bostonherald.com/news/regional/gardner_heist/news/view/20100314gardner_heist_Sleuths> accessed 19 October 2011.

106 Ibid.

no such promise of immunity'.[107] Such a state of affairs, according to Mashberg, 'was before Gardner Museum security director Anthony M Amore, the lead sleuth on the case, forged ties with the FBI and Brian T. Kelly, an assistant US attorney in Boston who has long advocated the immunity idea'.[108]

Compounding the initial 'spotty cooperation' was the speculation which had attached itself to the Gardner theft, no doubt help fuelled by the curious nature of the crime perpetrated by two thieves dressed up as Boston police officers[109] at a time when criminal gangs and mobsters were active in the city.[110] Understandably, in light of the relentless speculation, Amore uses the analogy of the needle in the haystack to explain his approach to investigating the theft.[111] 'The goal', he says, 'is to reduce the size of the haystack until you can eventually see the needle.'[112] Key to reducing the size of the haystack is the commitment shown by The Gardner's staff and the investigating team to remain dedicated to recovering the stolen works. To be hopeful in the early days following the theft was commendable. To maintain that hope twenty-three years later is testament to the dedication and energy of all involved.

This show of positive spirit which has enveloped the Gardner since the theft is evidenced by this declaration on their website: 'The Museum and authorities continue to pursue regular leads and remain confident that the artworks will be recovered.'[113] Against a backdrop of empty picture frames,[114] the visible scars left from the theft, the museum has used this air of hope and dedication to move forward – and in this spirit the empty frames have transformed into symbols of hope that one day the artwork will be returned[115] and the gap in art history repaired.

---

107 Ibid.

108 Ibid.

109 Isabella Stewart Gardner Museum, 'Theft Overview' (n 95).

110 Bill Van Siclen, '2 Decades Later, Mysteries Remain of the Gardner Museum Art Theft' *The Providence Journal* (14 March 2010) <www.projo.com/art/content/artssun_Gardner_Theft14_03-14_10_LIHNH4H_v2> accessed 19 October 2011. Anthony Amore stated: 'Actually, I don't think you have to go outside the Boston area to find people who had the ability to pull off the Gardner theft […] People tend to forget that back in the 1980s and 1990s, Boston was a spawning ground for all sorts of criminal enterprises: drug dealing, gun running, extortion, home invasions, property theft – you name it.'

111 [Telephone] Interview with Anthony Amore (n 98).

112 Ibid.

113 Isabella Stewart Gardner Museum, 'Theft Overview' (n 95).

114 Amore and Mashberg (n 72) 200-201. 'The ornate gilded frames that held the art now hang empty in the spaces that the paintings once occupied.'

115 Ibid., 201. 'While some view the frames as a symbol of mourning, the Gardner Museum sees them as placeholders for works that they trust will be returned.'

Gaps on the Walls and Empty Frames: A Comparative Analysis of the Theft of *A Cavalier* and the Gardner Robbery

'It's like stealing history'[116] the FBI states on its dedicated art crime website. This sentiment has been acknowledged and followed from the outset of this comparative analysis despite the stark difference in the monetary value of the two thefts: $500 million[117] for the Gardner works contrasted with $1.6 million[118] for *A Cavalier*. When it comes to safeguarding cultural history, an artwork's economic value should not be the dominant determinant of how much attention[119] it receives when tragedy strikes and it is stolen.[120] One lost Frans van Mieris painting should be as much of an investigative priority as any other stolen work when its cultural and historical significance is taken into consideration. The title of this section, with the words 'Gaps on the Walls'[121] and 'Empty Frames',[122] references the visible signs of loss that resulted from the thefts at the Art Gallery of New South Wales and the Isabella Stewart Gardner Museum, respectively. This comparative analysis will demonstrate that while there are commonalities between the Gallery and the Gardner's experiences with art theft, there are also clear differences.

The most obvious point of difference is the present status of both cases. While both remain open, only the Gardner case is being actively pursued and the US Federal Government is considering mounting a public awareness campaign to

116 FBI, 'Art Theft' <http://www.fbi.gov/about-us/investigate/vc_majorthefts/arttheft> accessed 14 July 2012.

117 See: Mashberg (n 105). 'The thirteen pieces are valued at a half-billion dollars'; Van Siclen (n 110). The 'estimated $500 million in stolen art'.

118 Art Gallery of New South Wales Trust, 'Auditor General's Report to Parliament 2007' (5) 49 <http://www.audit.nsw.gov.au/Publications/Financial-Audits/2007/Volume-5-2007> accessed 4 November 2011. 'The [Art Gallery of NSW] Trust's insurer accepted a claim for the amount of $1.6 million which will be used to procure a similar work.'

119 Nikos Passas and Blythe Bowman Proulx, 'Overview of Crimes and Antiquities' in Stefano Manacorda and Duncan Chappell (eds), *Crime in the Art and Antiquities World: Illegal Trafficking in Cultural Property* (Springer 2011) 55. 'When art theft makes news, the focus is on high-value thefts from museums or private collections.'

120 Anonymous Author 'Missing Masterpieces' *Security: Solutions for Enterprise Security Leaders* (2000) 37 (6) 14-17 <http://web.ebscohost.com/ehost/pdfviewer/pdfviewer?sid=2df31f66-e23f-4939-87e9-1c6845828401%40sessionmgr10&vid=5&hid=18> accessed 9 October 2011. Robert Koverman made this observation, 'I think there's a misunderstanding about the value of art and how that relates to museum security […] There are so many consequences if a piece is damaged or stolen and that's irrespective of value. Value escalation increases public awareness as well as copy-cat theft, but value does not affect how we in museum security protect our artwork and cultural artifacts […] We have a responsibility to do that regardless of value.'

121 Barlow (n 22 and n 69).

122 Amore and Mashberg (n 72) 200-201.

generate greater attention about the 1990 theft.[123] In contrast, *A Cavalier* has not only disappeared from the walls of the Gallery, it has all but disappeared from memory save for some continued interest in the case which helps it maintain some level of public profile. This interest, however, does not come from Australia but rather, it comes from the United States.

Firstly, the FBI has the painting listed on its 'Top Ten Art Crimes List',[124] and secondly, the Gardner's Anthony Amore has set up a website with the aim of recovering it. He had read the article written in the weeks leading up to the fifth anniversary of *A Cavalier*'s disappearance which had reported that 'after exhausting all avenues of investigation'[125] all parties involved had 'given up'.[126] This motivated Amore into action, but it also left him asking, 'Can the police not spare even one officer to pursue the painting? Is there not a single other investigation in the whole of Australia that can do with one less officer?'[127] Amore's questions draw attention to the fundamental differences between the Australian and the US experience of art theft evident primarily in the area of policing. The suspended status of *A Cavalier*'s investigation highlights the under-resourced policing environment in Australia – which is compounded by the non-existence of a specialized art crime unit within the country. Admittedly, the investigation process for the Gardner theft had a patchy beginning, but what emerged from this was a positive show of cooperative interagency engagement between the Gardner, the Office of the US Attorney and the FBI. The US, unlike Australia, does have an art crime unit, the FBI's Art Crime Team.[128] The Art Crime Team can and does provide expert policing skills to cases like the Gardner robbery, where an FBI Lead Agent[129] has been assigned. Extending from this, the team has a dedicated site within the FBI's website which provides a medium through which to raise the profile of art and cultural

123 Milton Valencia and Stephen Kurkjian, 'Public's aid sought in '90 Gardner Museum heist' *The Boston Globe* (11 June 2012) <http://articles.boston.com/2012-06-11/news/32177551_1_robert-guarente-heist-investigation> accessed 18 June 2012.

124 FBI, 'Art Theft' (n 116).

125 Andrew Taylor, 'Search for stolen masterpiece ends' *The Sydney Morning Herald* (20 May 2012) <http://www.smh.com.au/entertainment/art-and-design/search-for-stolen-masterpiece-ends-20120519-1yxis.html> accessed 7 June 2012. 'Acting Sergeant Chris Nash said NSW police had suspended their investigation in 2008 after exhausting all avenues of investigation.'

126 Ibid. 'Four-and-a-half years after *A Cavalier*, a 17th-century Dutch masterpiece insured for $1.4 million, was stolen from the gallery, Australian authorities have stopped trying to recover the painting.'

127 Anthony Amore, 'Giving Up on a Masterpiece' *The Huffington Post* (14 June 2012) <http://www.huffingtonpost.com/anthony-amore/giving-up-on-a-masterpiec_b_1594834.html> accessed 14 June 2012.

128 FBI, 'Art Theft' (n 116).

129 Isabella Stewart Gardner Museum, 'Theft Overview' (n 95). Lead Agent Geoff Kelly.

property crime. Two initiatives which assist the team are their Top Ten Arts Crime List,[130] created in 'November 2005 to help publicize and locate stolen masterworks around the globe',[131] and more essentially, the establishment of a National Stolen Art File.[132] This database of stolen objects is another key component missing from the Australian policing landscape. The calls for the establishment of an art loss register have, to date, remained unanswered.

The interagency cooperation that marks the Gardner case is not only bolstered by the specialized policing resources at its disposal, but also through the governmental support it receives. The Office of the US Attorney has assigned an Assistant US Attorney[133] to work the case and the office itself helps to maintain public awareness about the artworks stolen from the Gardner, stating that it 'will be zealous and chase any leads'.[134] A review into the theft of *A Cavalier* showed up no similar attitude or approach, but rather the suggestion that the investigating officers lacked the necessary drive essential for running a dedicated and thorough investigation,[135] although one has to consider this critique within the context of an under-resourced policing environment. The NSW State Government did add to those resources by appointing a private firm, Michael Maher and Associates, to provide an independent investigation into the theft.

The policing perspective of this comparative analysis points to what Conklin and Polk refer to as the 'guardianship'[136] component in the protection and safeguarding of cultural objects. As Conklin explained:

> Art and antiquities thefts result from the convergence of three factors: artworks that are suitable for stealing, the absence of effective security measures to protect those works, and the presence of people who are motivated to steal…

---

130 FBI, 'Art Crime' <http://www.fbi.gov/news/stories/2007/july/artcrime_073007> accessed 16 August 2012. 'The top ten list was developed by our Art Crime Team, a dozen special agents with extensive training in sleuthing stolen artworks and three Department of Justice trial attorneys. The team works in major art markets around the country and has helped locate more than 850 items worth over $65 million.'

131 Ibid.

132 FBI, 'National Stolen Art File' <http://www.fbi.gov/about-us/investigate/vc_majorthefts/arttheft/national-stolen-art-file> accessed 15 August 2012. 'The National Stolen Art File (NSAF) is a database of stolen art and cultural property. Stolen objects are submitted for entry to the NSAF by law enforcement agencies in the U.S. and abroad.'

133 Isabella Stewart Gardner Museum, 'Theft Overview' (n 95). Assistant US Attorney Brian Kelly.

134 Valencia and Kurkjian (n 123).

135 [Telephone] Interview with Michael Maher (n 45).

136 Conklin (n 73) 119; Ken Polk, 'Art Crime and Prevention: Best Practices' Paper presented at the *Art Crime Protecting Art, Protecting Artists and Protecting Consumers Conference* convened by the Australian Institute of Criminology, Sydney, 2-3 December 1999 <http://www.aic.gov.au/en/events/aic%20upcoming%20events/1999/~/media/conferences/artcrime/polkart.pdf> accessed 11 November 2011.

> those components are referred to as target suitability, guardianship and motivated offenders.[137]

For both the Gallery and the Gardner, the thefts prompted a security review and upgrade, and while criticisms were levelled at both institutions for their supposedly inadequate security, these were not wholly founded. Maher was quick to correct this uninformed view regarding the Gallery, whose security was actually on a par with that found in other galleries overseas,[138] while Amore explained that 'the standards, personnel, and technology at the Gardner were at least as good – and usually better – than those in place at other institutions'.[139] The thefts did, however, reveal weaknesses in the guardianship measures at both institutions which the security upgrades were able to rectify. Unlike the Gardner, however, the Gallery is a public entity and falls under the auspice of the NSW State Government, and so the government is a key stakeholder in maintaining adequate security at the Gallery and the other cultural institutions it has responsibility over. The Gallery's former Director, Edmund Capon, explained that 'the NSW government had ignored the Gallery's pleas for more money to guard against theft',[140] adding further that:

> We were very conscious of the fact that we were understaffed and had no technology in terms of security and yet we had all these priceless paintings … That situation has been rectified but it should have been rectified without it having to pay that price.[141]

Whether a public entity or not, the guardianship of cultural property should not be considered the sole responsibility of the cultural institution. It requires both interagency and interdisciplinary support and cooperation.

That cooperation can face challenges when the parties involved have divergent views on how to best respond to an art theft. For both the Gallery and the Gardner the issue of offering a reward saw two different responses. Within days of the Gardner theft, and at the urging of law enforcement agencies, a reward was announced.[142] The Gallery was also advised by police to offer a reward, but declined.[143] Certainly

---

137 Conklin (n 73) 119.

138 [Telephone] Interview with Michael Maher (n 45).

139 Amore and Mashberg (n 72) viiii.

140 Andrew Taylor, 'Thieves with Cavalier Attitude' *The Sydney Morning Herald* (30 May 2010) <http://news.smh.com.au/action/printArticle?id=1522077> accessed 22 November 2011.

141 Ibid.

142 Fox Butterfield, 'Auctioneers Underwrite Reward in Art Theft' *The New York Times* (21 March 1990) <http://www.nytimes.com/1990/03/21/arts/auctioneers-underwrite-reward-in-art-theft.html> accessed 23 October 2011. The museum 'decided to offer the reward at the urging of the Federal Bureau of Investigation'.

143 Gemma Jones, 'Art gallery refuses to offer reward for stolen painting' *The Daily Telegraph* (21 August 2007) <http://www.dailytelegraph.com.au/news/sydney-nsw/art-

there are arguments both for and against the offering of rewards, with the more dominant view being that rewards encourage more thefts.[144] In the case of the Gardner, though, the law enforcement agencies were hoping for a quick recovery of the objects, fearful that they may be taken overseas.[145] In the case of the Gallery, they were adhering to a NSW Government policy that did not accommodate the issuing of rewards.[146] As a public institution it would be public funds financing any reward, and the harsh realities of government economics is a significant factor that comes into play. In a climate where public spending and priorities are constantly being scrutinized, for a government to be seen to be doing deals over an object (cultural significance aside) is not usually a popular platform for re-election. This was not an issue in the Gardner's case, where the initial reward was underwritten by two privately run auction houses.[147]

When considering the components of guardianship, one factor mentioned by the Gallery's former Director, Edmund Capon, is worth noting. While reflecting on the theft of *A Cavalier*, which he characterized as 'probably one of the blackest moments'[148] in the Gallery's history, Capon reaffirmed his belief that 'creating that public goodwill is our greatest insurance and it's one of our greatest assets'.[149] The public too has a role in safeguarding cultural property, through supporting the cultural institutions in their community. Both the Isabella Stewart Gardner Museum and the Art Gallery of New South Wales continue to cultivate that public support through their art collections, exhibitions and artistic and cultural programs.[150]

---

gallery-refuses-reward-offer/story-e6freuzi-1111114226659> accessed 22 November 2011. 'The Art Gallery of NSW has ignored police advice to offer a reward which could secure the return of a $1.4 million dollar painting.'

144 The following excerpts present both sides of the argument: Anthony Amore and Tom Mashberg (n 72) 22. 'Cases involving cash handovers have prompted much debate about the propriety of rewards ... Critics ... question whether they set the stage for further instances of artnapping and extortion.' Dorit Straus, 'Implication of Art Theft in the Fine Art Insurance Industry' in Noah Charney (ed), *Art and Crime: Exploring the Dark Side of the Art World* (Praeger 2009) 97.'Rewards can encourage information leading to recovery.'

145 Butterfield (n 142) Sotheby's and Christie's were advised by the FBI that 'a quick offer could be crucial, before these things get out of the country'.

146 [Telephone] Interview with Michael Maher (n 45). Maher explained that the gallery was required to adhere to state government policy and the state government does not make deals in regards to ransoms or rewards.

147 Butterfield (n 142) The reward 'was made possible by a highly unusual agreement between Sotheby's and Christie's, the art auction houses, which will underwrite the reward'.

148 Shelley Gare, 'One Last Question, Mr Capon' *The Sydney Morning Herald*: the (Sydney) magazine (December 2011) 52.

149 Ibid.

150 Two notable examples illustrate this: The Gallery's exhibition, *Picasso: Masterpieces from the Musée National Picasso*, Paris, held 12 November 2011-25 March 2012, broke 'the record for the highest attended exhibition in the Gallery's history' (See: 'Picasso has broken AGNSW attendance record'<http://www.artgallery.nsw.gov.au/media-office/picasso-to-break-attendance-record/> accessed 19 August 2012; and the Gardner

The public's 'goodwill' is just as vital to the life of a cultural institution as a good security system.

Conclusion

The 2007 theft of *A Cavalier* shows Australia is not immune from art theft, and the comparative analysis illustrates that there still exist opportunities to enhance both the minimization and policing of art theft. This finding reiterates the recommendations held by Australian scholars of art crime which were first publically espoused at the 1999 art crime conference convened by the Australian Institute of Criminology (AIC).[151] That is, the policing of art crime in Australia is hampered significantly by the lack of expertise, training and dedicated attention that a specialized art crime unit could offer.[152] This links back to Bryan Hanley's claims made during the 1999 AIC conference, where he stated that, 'in their strategies for dealing with crime Police will generally choose an approach that is either proactive or reactive in concept'.[153] It could be asserted that the establishment of an art crime unit would be seen as a proactive strategy to employ in the policing of art crime, while the lack of such a unit arguably both facilitates and contributes to a non-standardized approach to policing practices in this area. Furthermore, the continuing non-

---

recently opened its '$114 million new wing', which was designed by architect Renzo Piano and 'more than doubles the Gardner's footprint'. (See: Geoff Edgers, 'Museum Director Anne Hawley Weathered Some Storms to See the Expansion Through' *The Boston Globe* [15 January 2012] <http://www.boston.com/ae/theater_arts/articles/2012/01/15/ for_gardner_museum_director_anne_hawley_patience_is_rewarded_with_new_wing/?p1=News_links> accessed 19 August 2012).

151 *Art Crime Protecting Art, Protecting Artists and Protecting Consumers Conference* convened by the Australian Institute of Criminology and held in Sydney, 2-3 December 1999.

152 Brian Hanley, 'Law Enforcement Issues in Art Theft' Paper presented at the *Art Crime Protecting Art, Protecting Artists and Protecting Consumers Conference* convened by the Australian Institute of Criminology and held in Sydney, 2-3 December 1999 <http://aic.gov.au/events/aic%20upcoming%20events/1999/~/media/conferences/artcrime/hanleyle.pdf> accessed 11 November 2012. 'We have yet to establish a specialist art and cultural property investigation unit in any State or allocate a single officer to that task on a full time basis' 2; 'Art theft as an investigation is rarely simple. It is often linked to other offences such as receiving, fraud, extortion, smuggling and money laundering. The more complex the investigation, the greater the level of experience and training required to address the liability' 4.

153 Brian Hanley, 'Crime Prevention' Paper presented at the *Art Crime Protecting Art, Protecting Artists and Protecting Consumers Conference* convened by the Australian Institute of Criminology and held in Sydney, 2-3 December 1999 <http://aic.gov.au/events/aic%20upcoming%20events/1999/~/media/conferences/artcrime/hanleyle.pdf> accessed 11 November 2012 2.

existence of an art loss register[154] hinders the ability to routinely check off and 'quickly identify stolen material, and thereby close off access to the art market of such illegal works'.[155] It also limits the collection of specific data on stolen objects[156] and, more importantly, it makes the likelihood of recovering stolen art 'very low because we have no loss register to serve as our memory'.[157] Given that art loss registers are already in existence in other countries, the expertise is there waiting to be accessed, as well as advice on the costs of implementing and operating such a database.

Another initiative that the comparative analysis raises, and one that is not widely canvassed (if at all) in the Australian experience of art theft, is that of public awareness campaigns. Throughout the period since the 13 artworks were stolen from the Gardner there has been a lot of media attention which has kept the theft in the spotlight. While this may attract a certain amount of false information, it could potentially lead to a breakthrough. In contrast to the situation in the United States, there has been little attention cast on *A Cavalier*'s disappearance in Australia. In cases like the theft of *A Cavalier*, where the investigation was suspended owing to no leads, perhaps targeted public awareness campaigns staggered over a nominated period may assist in procuring new information. Unlike the Gardner, however, there is no reward on offer to act as an incentive for providing information leading to the recovery of *A Cavalier*. Nevertheless, the website set up by Anthony Amore, http://stolencavalier.wordpress.com (along with a more recent *facebook* page, 'Stolen Cavalier')[158] provides a model of how the internet and social media can be utilized to both engage and interact with the public on cases of stolen artworks, even without the offer of a monetary reward.

The comparative analysis between the Australian experience of art theft and that of the United States highlights the obvious differences between the two

154 See Polk (n 136) 2. 'If such a register were available to both dealers and auction houses, and further if the art consumers knew of its presence as well, then the routine checking of works would quickly identify stolen material, and thereby close off access to the art market of such illegal works.' And Ken Polk, Lisette Aarons, Christine Alder and Duncan Chappell, 'An Exploration of the Illegal Art Market of Australia' A Report Submitted to the Criminology Research Council (15 March 2000) <http://www.criminology researchcouncil.gov.au/reports/8-98-9.pdf> accessed 11 November 2011 iii. 'The Australian art market is unique in the developed world in not having available a stolen works register.' See also pages 5, 22 and 25.

155 Polk (n 136) 2.

156 Chappell and Polk (n 2) 16. According to Chappell and Polk, cases of art crime may be grouped with general cases of fraud and property crime, making it difficult to collate a listing of stolen art objects.

157 Taylor (n 140): 'Criminologist Professor Kenneth Polk said the probability of finding art stolen in Australia was very low because we have no loss register to serve as our memory.'

158 See <https://www.facebook.com/#!/pages/Stolen-Cavalier/396558823760740> accessed 10 January 2013.

countries: Australia, unlike its US counterpart, lacks the benefit of having an art crime unit, an art loss register and public awareness campaigns. The primary difference, however, is that after more than twenty-three years all involved with investigating the 1990 theft at the Isabella Stewart Gardner Museum still maintain their dedication and hope that the works will be returned. The key lesson they teach, the lesson *A Cavalier* wants us all to learn is: Don't give up the search.

Chapter 6
An Australian Art Dealer's Perspective on Art Crime

Stephen Nall

Organised Crime in Australia

In describing the 'face of contemporary organised crime in Australia' the 2011 Australian Crime Commission (ACC) has stated

> Organised crime is sophisticated, resilient, highly diversified and pervasive. Current patterns of organised crime are more complex now than at any point in history.
>
> Organised crime groups are entrepreneurial and unrestrained by legislation, borders, morality or technology. They are adaptable, innovative and fluid – infiltrating a wide range of industries and markets, well beyond areas generally considered vulnerable.[1]

It is the author's view that these elements describe precisely the conditions that have ramped up art fraud into one of the most pervasive organised illicit activities in the current Australian art market. Disturbingly, these crimes are committed by criminals who are able to operate with a sense of impunity and invincibility since there is no effective law enforcement directed to their detection and criminal prosecution.

The ACC Report also describes the typical relationships that create the environment for this level of criminality:

> Organised criminal groups and networks operating in Australia, whether transnational or domestic, can be formidable in terms of their capabilities, resources and resilience. They exploit existing opportunities and create new ones. Many rely heavily on enablers including identity crime, communications technologies and access to professional expertise, while some benefit from access to corrupt officials.[2]

1 Australian Crime Commission, *Organised Crime in Australia* (ACC 2011).
2 Ibid.

As the organisational relationships described above have existed in the Australian art market for decades, there is an urgent need to take significant steps to eradicate the conditions that allow art fraud to be carried out with such impunity. It is hoped that this chapter will serve as a clarion call to art market professionals, law enforcement agencies and government to make an equal and concerted effort to undertake the reforms necessary to detect and prosecute the criminals whose activities prejudice the future of this important market.

Context: Some Unmasked Forgers

In the United Kingdom (UK) in 1999, painter John Myatt and art dealer John Drewe were convicted of art crimes.[3] Together, and with a few lesser accomplices they constituted a team of organised criminals who defrauded numerous highly reputable art market professionals in New York, London and other European cities. Over ten years they sold approximately 200 artworks, wrongly attributed to master painters, for millions of pounds. In the process, Drewe became an influential art dealer, a patron of the arts and a wealthy individual.

Although John Myatt was sentenced to one year in jail for a conspiracy to defraud, he now hosts the British Sky Arts television series called 'Fame in the Frame'. John Drewe was sentenced to six years in prison and served two. He has recently been convicted of a further fraud involving mortgages and is serving a further prison term.

How did they do it? The skill of a painter, the hubris of a con man and the organised, planned co-operation of a team of lesser accomplices is all it takes. The artist, Myatt who answered a newspaper advertisement, was recruited by Drewe to paint 'reproductions'. The impecunious artist needed the money and was a competent but unknown painter. His ability to reproduce art works or 'innuendos' of artist's works was rewarded by Drewe with ever greater frequency and higher reward. He was 'commissioned' by Drewe to reproduce specific artist's works and in a particular colour palette. Once Myatt became aware that the works were being sold by Drewe as genuine original works, the artist was complicit in the crime to defraud a victim purchaser. They were finally discovered when Myatt tried to sell a fake at auction himself.

Drewe, on the other hand, was the mastermind in this series of organised crimes from the beginning. He recruited the artist to produce the fakes, the intermediaries to sell fake artworks on commission and he faked the provenance documents that supported a fake authenticity by 'gaining the trust' and unlimited access to the Victoria & Albert Museum and the Tate Gallery London archives that held European commercial gallery records and photographs of genuine art works.

3 Andrew Buncombe, 'Art forger convicted of "brilliant" fraud art forgery' *The Independent* (13 February 1999) <http://www.independent.co.uk/news/art-forger-convicted-of-brilliant-fraud-art-orgery-1070405.html> accessed 6 January 2014.

When questioned by the media about the number of unknown fake works still in circulation, Myatt said there were hundreds but that he would not be naming them.

Australian Fakes

In June 2009 in Australia, two admitted Australian art fakers, William Blundell and Wayne Casbold, appeared and were interviewed on the Australian Broadcasting Commission current affairs program *Four Corners*.[4] The program, titled 'Fake', sought to establish the incidence and prevalence of fakes in the art market and expose the actions of one of Australia's leading art dealers, Ronald Coles, who it was alleged was heavily involved over many years in the commission of art fraud, but had not at the time been charged, as his whereabouts were unknown.

In an unreported decision, Casbold was convicted in 2009 for obtaining monies by deception after selling a drawing falsely attributed to renowned Australian artist Robert Dickerson (b. 1924) at auction. Soon after the program was broadcast he established a website offering his services as a convicted criminal to the public and claims to be the 'poacher turned gamekeeper'. In the website, www.isitfake.com.au, he claims to be able to identify fakes and offers to provide advice on provenance. In the program, both he and Blundell proudly declare their ongoing abilities to fool the unwitting art buying public with their fakes. William Blundell even has an entry in Wikipedia which states that he admits in the *Four Corners* program to painting at least 400 pictures in the style of Whiteley alone and that he had undertaken 'innuendos' of many other Australian artists.[5]

As a postscript to the *Four Corners* program, on 22 August 2013, Coles pleaded guilty to 15 counts of fraud as a Director and Larceny as a bailee. The extent of his fraudulent activities is estimated by art market sources to be in the tens of millions and it is noteworthy that the police case against him is reported to have involved 77 charges.[6]

So why all the fuss? After all, the cultural history of the western world is replete with stories of master artists signing their names to 'supervised' works in which they took only a minor 'hands-on role'. Picasso is said to have remarked of fake works attributed to him, 'If I like it I say its mine. If I don't, I say it's a fake.'[7]

4 ABC Television, *Four Corners* 'Fake' (8 June 2009).

5 See at <en.wikipedia.org/wiki/William_Blundell> accessed 14 November 2013.

6 Paul Bibby, 'Art dealer Ronald Coles guilty of multi million dollar fraud' *Sydney Morning Herald* (22 August 2013) <http://www.smh.com.au/nsw/art-dealer-ronald-coles-guilty-of-multimilliondollar-fraud-20130822-2sdo9.html> accessed 6 January 2014.

7 Simon Caterson, 'The fine art of faking it' *Inquirer, The Weekend Australian* (12 August 2006).

Today, as part of this scholastic tradition, art students are encouraged to copy the masters to hone their skills. So what tips the balance from student with integrity intact to an artist with the requisite *mens rea*, or criminal intention? Indeed based on my ten years as an art dealer and discussions had with many artists, it is more usual that an artist will not be selling fake artwork or wrongly attributed work for sound ethical reasons. But when they do, it appears from anecdotal evidence from many victims, the usual scenario is almost identical to the facts in the Myatt and Drewe case:

- An artist is recruited by an art market professional;
- An intermediary is recruited to sell the work after assurances of authenticity;
- There is a Mastermind and a planned crime if not a targeted victim;
- False provenance documentation is created and employed to support the authenticity;
- Challenges to authenticity are resolved by expensive and protracted litigation or immediate payment with secrecy attached;
- The criminality of these activities is disguised by civility and the claimed lack of criminal intention or 'innocence';
- After the authenticity of an artwork is expertly challenged as 'problematic', owners act out of self-interest and fail to declare the problematic work or its source publicly.

Identifying and Describing Problematic Art Works?

The current 'best fit' theory in art authentication supports the proposition that no painting can have 100 per cent provenance without a complete catalogue raisonné.

The Centre for Cultural Materials Conservation (CCMC) at the University of Melbourne and its Director Robyn Sloggett has succeeded, in establishing, in a relatively short time an international reputation for forensic analysis of artworks. However, notwithstanding the reputation and expertise of the staff and results, there is still an admitted subjectivity in the results and the theory of 'best fit' they promulgate. The theory is reliant on an accurate and complete database of the artists' materials techniques and range of work. The application of the theory will result in an art work as 'problematic' to a certain degree based on the 'best fit' of a specific work within that artists' *œuvre*.

Positively, this scientific methodology provides continuity of succession, a necessary aspect of any authentication service, because, as the value of an artist's works increases the attraction of faking and forging their work and supporting provenance also increases. Negatively, this methodology is expensive due to the expertise and technology employed and misses the significant volume of faked art work that falls in the lower range of sale values of $5000-$40,000.

Explaining Fakes and Forgeries (Also 'Attributions' and 'Innuendoes')

A **Fake** is something not genuine or presented fraudulently. **To fake** is to cheat, swindle, steal or rob manipulate fraudulently. It is 'problematic', if it is suspected to be fake.

A **Forgery** is a document made or adapted to imitate a genuine thing with intent to deceive.[8] Thus, a forgery differs from a fake in so far as the forgery is a 'copy' of an original work of the artist but a fake might simply be in the 'style' of the artist. Again, a forgery is 'problematic'.

An **Attribution** is an acknowledgement of original authorship and an **Innuendo** is an indirect or subtle reference, especially one made maliciously. Australian faker William Blundell first misused these two 'descriptive' terms in an attempt to trivialise his intent when painting the many faked art works sold as originals by Sydney art dealer and socialite Ann Curvers in the 1980s.[9] The analysis of these types of works are important as they go to the intention of the person handling the work and will be most certainly 'problematic' if represented to be authentic, at a later stage. At the very least, it is disingenuous of artists that paint innuendoes to believe they will not be used for fraudulent purposes.

The Meaning of Provenance

Provenance is the origin, source of something or history of ownership or location of an object.[10] Knowledge of the provenance of an artwork is the clear responsibility of all art market professionals. Without good provenance, an object cannot be certified as authentic. It therefore must be 'problematic' to some degree, even if it looks like an authentic work. It is possible to fake or forge a document which if genuine, would 'establish provenance' of an object. Therefore in undertaking an authentication or valuation, one must always be on the look out for 'false provenance' which can be an indication of intent to deceive and therefore lead one to a conclusion that the object is 'problematic'. One significant issue has emerged with the inclusion in auction catalogues of fake art works that have been withdrawn from sale. In Australia, when an art work published in an auction catalogue is alleged by an authoritative source as wrongly attributed, auction house practice is to withdraw it from the auction and return it to the owner. The owner is then able to re-offer the art work for sale and use the catalogue image to support a claim of good provenance albeit falsely and perhaps with the intention to commit a fraud.

---

8 See definitions of Fake, Forgery, Attribution, Innuendo, Provenance at Wikipedia.org.

9 ABC Television, *Four Corners* 'Fake' (8 June 2009).

10 Oxford English Dictionary 10th edn: **Provenance** n 1. the place of origin or earliest known history of something, 2. a record of ownership of a work of art or an antique.

Restored Art Works

Sloggett gives examples of art works that start innocently, but over time can become 'problematic' through a change in destiny. One of the most common ways in which this occurs is through restoration to the point where 'very little of the original work is extant'.[11]

In the 2010 judgement of the Supreme Court of Victoria in *Blackman & Anor vs Stewart and Anor*, Justice Peter Vickery exercised his discretion in favour of two famous Australian artists, Charles Blackman and Robert Dickerson to order the destruction of three faked art works wrongly attributed by art dealer Peter Gant, to be work of the artists.[12]

During the case, a prominent art restorer in Melbourne confirmed his involvement in the restoration of several Charles Blackman authentic paintings for a client, a prominent doctor and collector. He advised that they were discovered when Blackman the artist vacated the studio he once occupied in the good doctor's stables. The paintings had suffered extensive water damage, such that as art works they were virtually non-existent. It is quite common, as in this case, for such restored works to be sold at auction for vast sums with a bare acknowledgement of restoration, if at all. Anecdotal evidence suggests that restorers are also persuaded by clients to 'restore' more than just the original subject matter of the work sometimes enhancing artworks to improve the prospects of sale.

Signed: True or False?

Signatures can also create opportunities for an artwork to be considered problematic. There is further anecdotal evidence that a now high-profile Melbourne art dealer who was previously acting as a 'runner' for auction houses early in his career produced to another local art dealer, a painting signed by the famous Australian artist 'Tom Roberts'. The dealer recognised the work as a painting she observed three weeks earlier in an out-of-town charity sale but at that time 'without a signature'. Sloggett refers to this type of 'strengthening' of work as 'problematic', as it clearly alters the context of the work.[13] Salvador Dali is said to have signed many blank sheets of paper, in a production line at a luxury hotel, leading to the proliferation of 'problematic' Dali lithographs.[14] But forensic

11 Robyn Sloggett, 'All that Glitters' Paper presented at *Art Crime, Protecting Art, Protecting Artists and Protecting Consumers Conference*, convened by the Australian Institute of Criminology, 2-3 December 1999, Sydney.

12 *Blackman and Anor (Dickerson) vs Stewart and Anor (Gant)* 2010 VSC 299, 1 June 2010.

13 Sloggett (n 11).

14 Mick Brown, 'My weekend with Salvidor Dali' *The Daily Telegraph* (21 May 2010) <http://www.telegraph.co.uk/culture/art/art-features/7750501/My-weekend-with-Salvador-Dali.html> accessed 18 January 2014.

analysis can determine whether a signature has been applied after varnish, which helps in determining the type of behaviour that results in a 'problematic' finding.

Who Determines Authenticity?

> The history of art fraud is scattered with stories of experts who 'got it wrong', and not just wrong, but terribly wrong. This subjective nature of connoisseurship has led to an interest in scientific enquiry as a possible benchmark in authentication.[15]

Robyn Sloggett is the Director of the CCMC and says that we can never be 100 per cent sure if work has been produced by a particular artist. Indeed, the absence of a complete recording system or 'catalogue raisonné' that is guaranteed by the artist makes this statement a truism.

Proving fakes both 'beyond a reasonable doubt' (criminal standard), or 'on the balance of probabilities' (the civil standard), is possible with the direct testimony of the artist. But for the most part, the artist that is faked is a deceased artist, for two simple reasons:

1. The deceased artist cannot challenge the authenticity; and
2. The notional value of the fake work wrongly attributed to an established deceased artist is often higher than a similar artwork by a living artist due to its rarity.

The Role of Experts

The common law has for many years recognised the need for 'experts' to make determinations on matters of dispute that involve esoteric judgements, scientific facts or just unusual experiences. However, there are a number of hurdles (including the Supreme Court Rules) that must be scaled before the court will accept a person's expertise.

Prominent Australian artists like Blackman, Brack, Dickerson, Nolan, Olsen, Rees, and Whiteley have all been prolific in the production of drawings that sell in the lower price range ($5000-$40,000). The vast majority of these art works are authenticated through a rudimentary examination of materials and an assessment of the aesthetic values of the work. The examination of these works for authentication is done by artists, their survivors (widows and offspring) and art market professionals who are 'experts' in the artist's *œuvre*. Although there usually exists an enormous reservoir of expertise and goodwill in each authentication, there is often a variable standard applied which leads to doubt and uncertainty.

15 Sloggett (n 11).

In Australia the federal government also has a system of Commonwealth appointed valuers who are able to value works gifted to public institutions and which attract a tax deduction. The problem with this system is that the criteria for appointment may not be as rigorous as it should be to ensure that the works being examined are authentic.

It has been shown in the recent past that many 'expert' art market professionals are also not able to make accurate assessment of authenticity. This therefore brings into question the process by which the authentication of artwork is accurately determined.

In the Victorian Supreme Court civil action referred to earlier of *Blackman & Anor vs Stewart and Anor*, the issues associated with the establishment of the authenticity of works of art came under consideration. The civil action was commenced against a local art dealer in Melbourne, Peter Gant who it was alleged had been offering for sale fake works of art which were claimed to be produced by the artists Charles Blackman and Robert Dickerson. Dickerson was able to testify in person concerning the lack of authenticity of the works attributed to him, but Blackman, because of ill health could not give testimony and it was thus left to experts to establish that the works said to have been produced by him were in fact fakes. Justice Peter Vickery, the trial judge, was in no doubt after hearing evidence from these art experts for Blackman and from Dickerson himself, that the artworks were faked. In its judgement the court held:

> They were fakes masquerading as the genuine article. What is more, they were deliberately contrived to deceive unsuspecting members of the public... The false signatures drawn on each work could have had no other purpose.[16]

Where Are the Fakes Now?

The short answer is – everywhere. They are waiting to be discovered in private homes, public and private art galleries and museums, private collections, auction houses, storage units, safes, banks and in the possession of criminals waiting for the opportunity to commit fraud by offering them for sale. They will always be around. Sloggett estimates that 10 per cent of Australian art is fake or problematic[17] – a figure which is probably quite conservative. Only a fraction of these problematic works are ever identified, and even when they are, those possessing the knowledge are often reluctant to disclose it to others since they may suffer financial and other losses as a result.

---

16 *Blackman and Anor (Dickerson) vs Stewart and Anor (Gant)* 2010 VSC 299, 1 June 2010.

17 ABC Television, *Four Corners* 'Fake' (8 June 2009).

Who Has Been Prosecuted?

In Australia reported criminal cases of art fraud are extremely rare. Indeed in the past three decades or more only five such cases appear to have reached the criminal courts:

- In 1977, a Melbourne art dealer, Peter Sparnay was convicted of five counts of dishonestly obtaining money from the sale of art works he knew to be fakes and the artist Russell Drysdale had to give evidence that they were not by his hand.[18]
- In 1999, John O'Laughlin, an art dealer based in Adelaide, was convicted pursuant to the NSW Crimes Act for obtaining a benefit by deception when he was discovered selling a whole exhibition of fake paintings purported to have been produced by the distinguished Aboriginal artist Clifford Possum. He received a three-month suspended sentence.
- In 2007, Ivan and Pamela Liberto, a Toorak socialite couple were convicted in Melbourne of four counts of obtaining property by deception and two counts of attempting the same. They served nine months in jail of a three-year custodial sentence.
- In an unreported case in 2009, Wayne Casbold was convicted in a Magistrates court in Sydney of receiving money by deception for the sale of an artwork at auction that he claimed to be produced by artist Robert Dickerson. He now hosts a website (www.isitfake.com.au) where he prominently features the very same work and claims to be a 'poacher turned gamekeeper'.[19]
- On 22 August 2013 in the District Court in Parramatta west of Sydney, Ronald Coles was convicted of 15 charges of fraud relating to his activities as an art dealer for over 20 years. At the time of writing he remains on bail without being sentenced to attend medical specialists to determine the cause of an as yet undiagnosed medical condition.[20]

These persons may be the criminals but there are many more people with the requisite *mens rea*, who practice deceit to defraud unwitting buyers, experts and bargain hunters. They commit crimes that go un-discovered and un-reported and un-prosecuted due in large part to a pall of inaction on the part of the majority of art market professionals, government agencies and the public.

18 Paul Baker, 'Policing Fakes' Paper presented at *Art Crime, Protecting Art, Protecting Artists and Protecting Consumers Conference*, convened by the Australian Institute of Criminology, 2-3 December 1999, Sydney.

19 ABC Television, *Four Corners* 'Fake' (8 June 2009).

20 Paul Bibby, 'Art dealer Ronald Coles guilty of multi million dollar fraud' *Sydney Morning Herald* (22 August 2013) <http://www.smh.com.au/nsw/art-dealer-ronald-coles-guilty-of-multimilliondollar-fraud-20130822-2sdo9.html> accessed 6 January 2014.

The legislation in Australia that deals with fakes and fraud is inadequate and archaic, bearing no relationship to technological advancements in domestic and industrial printing, that have made the task of falsification of provenance records and the production of false art works so simple and frequent. In particular, the majority of the secondary art market has failed to take proper precautions in the face of growing numbers of art fraud incidents which might lead one to the conclusion that many art market professionals are themselves complicit in this illicit activity.

Who Are the Victims of Art Fraud?

In 2002, the present author put the proposition that the falsely 'attributed' artist and the public are the primary victims of art fraud and the various types of art market professionals are all secondary victims.[21] The most compelling reason for this proposition is the fact that the sale of a fake artwork can be repeated indefinitely to defraud further innocent persons and so compound the original damage to the artist's reputation again and again, until the fake is impounded or destroyed.

The Victorian Supreme Court recognised that the faking of an artist's work does not only defraud an innocent purchaser, 'it results in a contraction of the artist's market, once the presence of such works circulating in the market becomes public knowledge. In the result, potential purchasers will understandably have reduced confidence in the authenticity of this artist's genuine artworks and be less prepared if not reluctant to invest in the works of the artist the subject of the deception. In short, such activity undermines the confidence of the public in the artist's work'.[22]

The majority of fake art works sold, however, are in the range of $5,000-$40,000. These works are bought by ordinary people who invest their savings and, more often, funds from their self-managed super funds. Beyond the artist whose work is faked, the average victim is a hard-working citizen with a love of art and a trust in the art market professional.

Taking Fakes Out of Circulation

It is of major importance to artists and the market that fakes are identified and taken out of circulation. It was for this reason that the artists Blackman and Dickerson brought the civil suit against the Melbourne art dealer Peter Gant who they alleged had offered for sale three drawings, valued at $24,000

21 Stephen Nall, 'Protecting the Artist' Paper presented at the *Problematic Paintings Symposium* 26/27 September 2002.

22 *Blackman and Anor (Dickerson) vs Stewart and Anor (Gant)* 2010 VSC 299, 1 June 2010.

which were fakes. Both artists, Blackman and Dickerson, are eminent in the Australian visual arts community.

Together the artists have devoted over 120 years to the development of their art and the market that had sustained and nurtured their careers. Many of the owners of their art works and offspring are close personal friends. From the beginning, Dickerson regarded any failure on his part to prosecute his case as a personal failing, because in his words 'the picture was wrong. It is a bad little picture and it makes me look stupid'.

Both artists were in for a full-on fight, if that was necessary. They obtained estimates of legal costs and engaged lawyers, who in turn sought assistance from experts. They did not anticipate however that it would be necessary to deal with numerous efforts by Gant to take technical points in interlocutory applications which served to delay the prosecution of the case and add significant additional expense.[23]

Another potential avenue of redress in removing fake art works from the market place might be expected to be found in the *Australian Copyright Act 1968* (Cth) which was amended in 2000 to adopt substantially the 1957 French codified version of 'moral rights' for visual artists, authors and performing artists. In particular the right to NOT have art works falsely attributed to an artist was enshrined in the Australian law with suitable remedies for artists.

Copyright Amendment (Moral Rights) Act 2000 (Cth), Division 7, Section 195AZA, Remedies for infringements of moral rights:

1. Subject to section 203, the relief that a court may grant in an action for an infringement of any of an author's moral rights in respect of a work includes any one or more of the following:

   (a) an injunction (subject to any terms that the court thinks fit);
   (b) damages for loss resulting from the infringement;
   (c) a declaration that a moral right of the author has been infringed;
   (d) an order that the defendant make a public apology for the infringement;
   (e) an order that any false attribution of authorship, or derogatory treatment, of the work be removed or reversed.

2. In exercising its discretion as to the appropriate relief to be granted, the court may take into account any of the following:

   (a) whether the defendant was aware, or ought reasonably to have been aware, of the author's moral rights;
   (b) the effect on the author's honour or reputation resulting from any damage to the work;

23 Stephen Nall, 'An Artist's point of view' Paper presented at the *ACGA/CCMC Forum*, Melbourne, 26 July 2010.

(c) the number, and categories, of people who have seen or heard the work;
(d) anything done by the defendant to mitigate the effects of the infringement;
(e) if the moral right that was infringed was a right of attribution of authorship – any cost or difficulty that would have been associated with identifying the author;
(f) any cost or difficulty in removing or reversing any false attribution of authorship, or derogatory treatment, of the work.

However, for practical purposes it is unlikely that this legislation will be much used by artists as the remedies available under the Copyright Act require expensive legal intervention and artists are traditionally shy and private by nature.

The solution is to address the need for a simple action available to artists who are having their authorship falsely attributed, whether intentionally or unintentionally. The answer lies in the revision of the Copyright Act (moral rights) legislation to incorporate as a crime 'receiving and retaining wrongly attributed artworks', or amend Criminal codes to simplify the prosecution of art fraud. Other government support mechanisms for artists could include an art fraud register.

However, the solution does not lie in the exclusive use of civil remedies. Criminal sanctions are also a powerful deterrent and should be used where appropriate to send a message to those that would seek to wreck the Australian art market, or defraud a person, that such behaviour will not be tolerated. For example, art market professionals claiming expertise or years of experience and vendors who value art works should all be considered in a special role of authority. In the event that proof is required of involvement in the sale of a fake artwork by these persons the onus of proof could be reversed to require they prove that they did not intend to commit a fraud.

The Supreme Court action brought by Blackman and Dickerson against Peter Stanley Gant has resulted in a major step forward. In addition to a number of technical legal principles the case appears to have established several important practical principles for the visual arts market including:

- The standing of artists' (including their representatives/survivors) to seek injunctions to restrain the sale of, or seek the destruction of fakes;
- The use of expert evidence to determine authenticity in the absence of first hand evidence of an artist;
- The importance of reliable evidence of provenance of artworks;
- That valuations are based upon the presumption of authenticity, without which no valuation should be provided; and
- The exercise of the court's discretion using generic consumer protection statutes to order the destruction of fake artworks to ensure the future protection of consumers.

What Are the Stakeholders' Responses?

The response by key stakeholders in the Australian art market to art fraud and the constituent elements of this form of criminal behaviour provides the basis for making recommendations that, if adopted, could largely eliminate this menace from the Australian art market.

Public Response to Fakes

The public response is not uniform. Since the media exposure of the Gant action in which a businessman from a wealthy demographic gave evidence that Gant had sold him pictures and represented them falsely to be authentic, the present author has met another buyer of a fake falsely attributed to Dickerson purchased from the same source. Art dealer, Mrs Stewart, who was a party to the Gant action, was also supplied with the fake artworks by Peter Gant.

Psychological issues abound. Indecision about action that victims of art fraud might take to recover purchase monies is affected by the prospect of large legal costs to recover relatively small sums and the hurt and betrayal felt by some at the hands of 'friends' who brokered the transaction. There may also be some sense of complicity if there was reliance placed on the artwork being a bargain, and there is always the feeling of embarrassment at being gullible.

The solution is in establishing 'crime-stoppers' education of the public through art market businesses and professionals and the media, legislative reform and government support of the visual arts industry.

Police/Government Response to the Issues

It is evident from communications with Australian police that they are unaware of the severity of the art fraud problem. More disturbingly, they have sometimes responded by trivialising the issue. There are clearly insufficient resources devoted to the problem of art fraud which is regarded as the poor cousin of 'white-collar' fraud. It is also a 'niche' crime with its own jargon and personality types, often targeting victims who are wealthy, aspirational individuals who are self conscious of the potential for embarrassment and ridicule at the disclosure of their gullibility. The government is apathetic and largely unaware of the nature and dimension of the art fraud problem faced by the public and art market professionals.

Initial inquiries with the police before the commencement of a civil action against the art dealer Peter Gant revealed that the value of the artworks sold, or the amount of the fraud that was alleged to have been committed, was not sufficient to interest the Victorian Police. It seemed that the Major Fraud Squad was 'too busy' to deal with anything as trivial as art in this price bracket. This reaction was understandable if not acceptable.

A lot of work undoubtedly goes into a successful police prosecution of cases involving fraud. Consequently in a case that has a low value art work at stake and where the onus of proof on the prosecution to prove the guilt of the accused 'beyond a reasonable doubt' seems a bit risky, there is unlikely to be any enthusiasm to become engaged with the matter. By way of contrast the facts of the Liberto case (2007) mentioned earlier, which was successfully investigated and prosecuted, were much clearer and the evidence much stronger. The accused were caught 'red-handed' with all the materials needed to fake art works and to pass off a fake Rover Thomas painting for over $200,000. The evidence presented to the court by the police and CCMC was sufficient to prove beyond a reasonable doubt an intention to deceive.

In Australia, as other chapters in this book illustrate, police agencies are required to work with outmoded legislation that is anything but specific to art fraud. Furthermore, there is no specific art crime training available to police other than that which is available to the public. This is a situation that needs redress if victims of art fraud are to be better served by law enforcement.

Artist Responses to Being Faked

Artists' reactions to art fraud are often no less self interested than the general public, and for the most part, unless they can see a direct and detrimental impact on them or their market, they are inclined to be somewhat blasé. Young artists who have no experience of being 'faked' see it, ignorantly and misguidedly, as a 'badge of honour'.

Serious and more mature artists will often be indignant, hurt, and shocked at the ignorance of the public for being fooled by the fake work and some are physically affected. They are often 'sickened' by the 'abuse of their name and reputation' in the act of falsely attributing them to such work. The so-called 'Picasso response' mentioned above is rare, but only a few take action. They most often hope that it will be an isolated occurrence and avoid the confrontation and annoyance. Most fakes are attributed to deceased artists and their heirs, are loathe (usually in advancing years) to become involved in remedial litigation.

In these cases there is a need for a public defender of the cultural heritage of the nation that is charged with the task of initiating remedial litigation to protect the cultural and financial value that resides in maintaining the integrity of these artists' markets.

How Do Art Market Professionals Respond to Fakes?

For many years the response by art market professionals was one of denial, anger and fear. Many denied there were any problems and refused to discuss it. They were angry with those few who wanted reform and transparency and maintained that there was no need for action. As the time passed it emerged that the very same people had been the subject of elaborate frauds and were embarrassed by their ignorance and gullibility and fearful that this would be exposed.

In essence the responses vary according to the degree of exposure and the roles they play.

- **Primary market dealers** are not as exposed because they are mostly dealing with living artists and holding exhibitions of recent art works. However the biggest players in this sector can be exposed as they might have significant secondary art works in stock and often handle secondary sales on commission. It is interesting to note that the present author has been the most active in pressing for reform in this area through a primary market dealer. This activity resulted in the Australian Commercial Galleries Association (ACGA) producing draft educational material on the importance of many issues but in particular, ethical art dealing and provenance. The document is still available on the ACGA website, www.acga.com.au.

- **Secondary market professionals,** including both dealers and auction houses, are the most vulnerable to fakes, forgeries and problematic art works, with the lesser known and 'lower profile' players being the target for criminals to 'off-load' these problematic art works. Although most auction houses have 'experts' to assess works taken in for sale, it is regrettable that the 'expertise' of these staff members is quite variable and often leads to fakes being sold.

Unfortunately the ACGA series of discussion papers on the issues of ethical art trading and the importance of provenance, has not yet resulted in a sustainable solution emerging, notwithstanding the increased level of investigative journalism and media coverage devoted to the subject. The solution may be founded in the strengthening of an industry-wide culture based on the maintenance of integrity and honesty of art market professionals and if necessary the licensing of participants. An organised approach to the recording and data storage of problematic and stolen art works is also necessary, as is legislative reform establishing extended moral rights of artists and their heirs.

The Anatomy of a Fraudster – The Crime of Broken Trust

Just how art fraud has become such a problem in Australia is also an interesting question.

Art market professionals undertake various roles. They may be curators, restorers, valuers, dealers, auction house staff, artist's assistants and art couriers. In their working life, all of these people are regularly placed in positions of trust and often as custodians of valuable art work. History attests, that the temptation to commit crimes of opportunity is often so overwhelming, that many people succumb. The art market is made up of ordinary people and more often than not the people who have greeted you warmly, shared a meal or kissed you on both cheeks may have been those engaged in art fraud. They are people in positions of trust, and often the recipients of great generosity from the people they defraud. However, in other walks of life the crimes and misdemeanours of such individuals have been exposed and prosecuted systematically, often successfully and often with the assistance of enabling criminal legislation.

The Metamorphosis of Art Fraud into Organised Crime

In recent years the appearance of substantial artworks in the Australian art market with high nominated values (between $100,000 and $2,200,000) and provenance that supports the attribution to a famous artist has increased alarmingly.

The Age newspaper has reported that art dealers Peter Gant and John Playfoot have been involved in the sale of a major artwork falsely attributed to Brett Whiteley where the attribution claims were supported by alleged false provenance documents for at least one work titled *Orange, Lavender Bay*. This transaction was supported by a gallery catalogue which was published by Peter Gant Fine Art, as evidence of provenance for the painting sold. The report says that the catalogue appears to be fabricated.[24] The present author is aware that the dispute over the authenticity of the painting was settled out of court by a reimbursement of the monies paid by the purchaser.

More recently, there have been further media reports of a civil suit undertaken by a Sydney merchant banker, Andrew Pridham against a former auction house employed auctioneer and art consultant Anita Archer who has been regarded by many as an 'expert art consultant'. Archer was sued by Pridham for deceptive conduct in the sale of a $2.2M painting attributed to 'Brett Whiteley', titled *Lavender Bay 1988*. In this proceeding the present author is aware, Peter Gant was joined as a third-party defendant.[25] The same Age Newspaper report also states that Sloggett did test the earlier Whiteley painting *Orange, Lavender Bay* and found in her preliminary report the painting could not be ascribed to Whiteley and that the paint behaved like recent paint. The present author is aware that this claim was listed for trial in August 2013, and the matter was settled by confidential agreement between the parties.

---

24 Gabriella Coslovich, 'A Striking similarity, but spot the suspected fake' *The Age* (19 July 2010) <http://www.smh.com.au/entertainment/art-and-design/a-striking-similarity-but-spot-the-suspected-fake-20100718-10g32.html> accessed 18 January 2014.

25 Wendy Frew, 'Big Blue sparked by doubt over Whiteley paintings' *Sydney Morning Herald* (18 February 2012).

This civil action and the previous matter of the fake Whiteley, suggest an organisation responsible for producing a more substantial level of problematic art in Australia with correspondingly significant consequences.

The response of the media has been to expose the activities of these dealers and to 'out' the images of the fake works where possible. Although CCMC has purportedly provided its confidential service to the purchasers of these paintings, the Whiteley painting *Orange, Lavender Bay* that has allegedly been returned to Melbourne art dealers John Playfoot and Gant purportedly remains in the art market and available for sale.

It is clear that organised crime has invaded the lucrative art market with substantial sums being invested in the manner of the 'Myatt and Drewe exemplar'. Problematic and fake pictures of famous Australian artists including Brack, Streeton, Tucker, Whiteley, Williams and Olsen are believed to have been sold for many hundreds of thousands, if not millions of dollars.

It is commonly held within art market circles that the art market has long been used as a method of laundering money gained by illegitimate means (most often undeclared income). With the desirability of cash as a driving force in the art market where large sums of money change hands for desired artworks, the market has attracted wealthy people whose activities are sometimes illegal.

Because of the absence of an ethical basis for proclaiming expertise as an art market professional, and the nature of the 'crimes against trust' that enable art fraud, legislation is needed which specifically addresses the crime of 'art fraud' and gives appropriate weight to the breach of trust element involved. Unless this occurs, it is unlikely that successful prosecutions will occur at a faster rate than one every ten years, or that organised crime of art fraud will be discouraged. For Australia, this failure of the art market is a national shame.

Conclusion

There are still a number of changes necessary to establish effective roadblocks to this type of criminal behaviour.

The following are a few possible suggested changes that deserve further research:

- An education program aimed at stakeholders including the public, the artist, the art market professionals and the Police Services;
- An art loss register to display stolen art works;
- A problematic art register to record all 'problematic' art work that does not meet minimum standards of provenance or is regarded as 'fake' (not of the hand of the artist) by an agreed authority;
- An efficient single authentication service that will administer the above registers and note any status change;
- Legislation that encourages the prosecution of art fraud;

- Legislation requiring notification of artists and their heirs of fakes discovered.

Although the Copyright Act provides for the prosecution of persons falsely representing authenticity of art works, there are no known actions taken under that legislation. It has to be questioned whether further legislative amendment should be made to facilitate this type of action.

Part II

CRIMINAL LAW AND PROCEDURE IN ART CRIME

Chapter 7
Considering Evidence in Art Fraud

Robyn Sloggett

Introduction

If Australian self-proclaimed 'innuendo-ist' William Blundell is to be believed, then a significant amount of the 4,000 paintings and drawings which he produced as 'innuendoes', are now attributed to some of Australia's greatest artists.[1] Clearly these works cannot have a secure provenance, and are unlikely to stand up to forensic scrutiny. How then is it possible that they could ever have been sold as genuine works representing the artists whose names they now bear? Unfortunately, there is one very simple explanation, which is that within the art market the proposition that a particular artwork is authentic is not always assessed with sufficient rigour to ensure that it will stand up to scrutiny. In numerous cases such a proposition is really no more than a suggestion, and the unwary buyer assumes that there must be evidence, to which they are not privy, that supports it. In such cases the new owner is often astonished to learn that the evidential chain that should link the work to a particular artist is non-existent, and they have spent a large amount of money on the basis of an ill-conceived and unsubstantiated opinion.

Securing the evidential link between the work and the artist who is purported to have produced it requires a rigorous analytical approach; one that not only accepts particular evidence that may support the assertion of authenticity, but which can also contest evidence that is not correct. Such an approach is by its very nature multidisciplinary, often bringing together knowledge of art history, the art market, cultural materials conservation, chemistry, law and policing. What constitutes evidence of authenticity is generally based on considerations of provenance, art historical context, including facts about the artist and scientific enquiry. Of the three, provenance is the most effective, yet, substantial resources are required to provide a verifiable and rigorous provenance. In addition, faked works are generally accompanied by fake provenance; but as the link is neither necessary nor sufficient, it follows that faked provenance does not mean that the work is fake and a fake work does not imply that the provenance is faked. This leaves art historical and scientific enquiry as the two areas in which to pursue and provide rigorous assessment of the materials and techniques not only of the artwork, but also of the provenance documentation associated with it.

---

1 Ben Hills, 'Oils ain't oils: the one-man Whiteley machine' *Sydney Morning Herald* (18 July 1998).

This chapter examines the standard investigatory hierarchy that is generally called into play when a work is presented as being problematic. It outlines the processes that are necessary when one of these three platforms, the provenance, the history, or the materials and techniques, is shown to be problematic. It examines provenance as both a corruptible and non-corruptible form of evidence; art history as a form of scholarship that can be rigorous and effective, or subjective and problematic; and scientific enquiry as an interdisciplinary tool which may provide additional information, or which may present results that lead to unsatisfactory conclusions. An assessment of the nature of evidence, and its role in art fraud investigations, draws together the discussions of these three investigatory and evidential platforms.

What is Art Fraud?

Before assessing what constitutes evidence in a particular case, it is necessary to understand what the proposition is that the evidence is supposedly supporting (or disproving). 'Art fraud' describes the crime of obtaining benefit (financial) from the deliberate and intentional deception by passing off a work that is not authentic as if it were; that is the act has to be aligned to intention and outcome. Understanding how intention, particularly the intention to deceive, is formed, manifested and assessed is difficult, but if evidence is properly collected, described and presented then the chain of intention generally becomes apparent.

This establishes the first determinant of evidence, and that is that the evidence must be understood as being relevant to the case at hand within the context in which the work was produced. This is important, as what may be described as 'fraudulent' in one context will not be considered so if it is being offered in a different context, and it is clearly possible for the same work to be considered authentic in one context, but fraudulent in another. A case in point is the works presented in the British Museum exhibition *Fake? The Art of Deception* and its accompanying catalogue. As editor Mark Jones explains:

> Not a single object has been included here merely because it deceived an untutored layman. Most have been validated thrice over, on initial purchase by an experienced collector, on publication by a leading scholar and on acquisition by a great museum.[2]

Clearly, documented in an exhibition entitled *Fake,* these objects, which were at one time accepted as authentic examples of original art, archaeological objects or antiquities, now read in the context of this exhibition as something entirely different. While the objects remain the same, the context in which these works are

2 Mark Jones, Paul Craddock and Nicholas Barker (eds), *Fake? The Art of Deception* (University of Californian Press 1990) 11.

viewed changed; and it changed on the basis of evidence that demonstrated that the supposed history of the object could not be substantiated. *Fake? The Art of Deception* indicated the significance of context in determining what label could be properly attached to what object.

Terminology is critical to how evidence is collected, provided and assessed. If a work is identified as authentic then evidence may be collected to be used for scholarship and developing an understanding of the *œuvre* of the artist. If a work is identified as a copy then evidence may be collected to identify the production of copies in art training in the nineteenth century, for example. If, however, the work is identified as fraudulent, then the evidence could be collected for use in a criminal case. It is important therefore to understand that the use of these terms as evidence is only always relevant to the context and, as *Fake? The Art of Deception* indicates, context can be variable.

The terms of most interest are: authentic, original, fake and fraudulent. There are of course more, such as copy, proof, edition, facsimile, reproduction and a raft of others, but for the purposes of understanding evidence, these four suffice. They operate along a sliding scale of acceptability and, as descriptive terms, are often misused, or misunderstood. It is worthwhile therefore taking a short detour to understand what is meant and where confusion may lie.

'Authentic' is a descriptor of a work that is genuine, and indicates that its descriptor is correct. In this respect it is possible for a copy to be 'authentic' but only if it is labelled as a copy. If it is labelled as if it were by the artist whose work was copied then it may be either a fake, a forgery or fraudulent, depending on the context in which the claim is made. 'Original' describes the first, created work (which for prints will mean not the first print made but the series which is approved by the artist and might contain fifty or one hundred identical prints). The term 'copy' is used to describe a work that is made on the basis of a work that already exists. These descriptors do not imply an intention to deceive. 'Fake', 'forgery' and 'fraudulent', however, do. These descriptors are used interchangeably to describe works that are presented as genuine but are intentionally produced, or evidence relating to them is produced in order to deceive. This includes copies that are presented as if they were by the artist who painted the original and works that have been 'strengthened' by the addition of signatures and dates. Faking works is not a crime unless benefit and deliberate and intentional deception can be proven, at which point the work represents an act of attempted fraud. Unfortunately, these terms are used interchangeably in much of the discussion about the art market and therefore the data set of what constitutes authentic work and what constitutes problematic work is not clear.

What is Evidence?

Information that is claimed as evidence has very particular requirements. Despite Thomas Hoving's claim that art authentication involves 'a pull in the gut or a warning cry from a voice deep inside … nurtured and refined only by saturation'[3] evidence for art authentication has the same standards as other evidence. So what are these standards and what is required for an observation or conclusion to be admissible as evidence?

According to fraud investigator David Walker,[4] there are three questions that relate to the procurement and proffering of evidence. These are:

1. Is it relevant? (Does it prove or disprove a disputed fact?)
2. Is it admissible? (Can the evidence be given?)
3. Is the witness competent? (Can the witness understand the oath?)

According to Walker evidence may consist of facts, oral testimony, documents and physical exhibits. In the case of art fraud evidence comes from three main sources, each of which reflects Walker's criteria. These are art historical, provenance, materials and techniques. Within these groups evidence may be collected through interviews, assessment of primary and secondary document sources, visual comparison and scientific analysis. The Locard Principle, ascribed to the work of Edmond Locard, who is known as the 'father of forensics' claims 'Every contact leaves a trace.'[5] This may be true, but it is not always possible to secure the chain that tracks every trace back to its original source. For this reason the investigation of art fraud relies on building a case within an appropriate contextual framework and in order to use a trace as evidence it is necessary to determine what the theory is that the evidence is supporting. This is essential if an investigation is to determine what is the chorus and what is the main performer in a cacophony of possible evidentiary noise.

The proposition may be put forward, for example, that a particular work is by Rembrandt van Rijn. In this case, given that Rembrandt lived from 1606 to 1669 it makes sense to test the work for evidence that it was 'produced in the Netherlands between 1620 and 1669'. If it clearly contains materials that could have only been in existence in the twentieth century, then there is sufficient information to disprove the proposition. In this case proving an anomaly in materials may be enough to disprove the proposition. Things are rarely so clear-cut, however, particularly when a forger has worked hard to use materials and techniques that reflect Rembrandt's materials and techniques. A broad proposition such as this is often not useful and more specific evidential parameters need to be provided, such as 'the original paint in the painting contains pigments produced prior to 1669'. The fact is that neither sets of evidence are sufficient, even though necessary. There are plenty of works produced in the Netherlands between 1608 and 1699

3 Thomas Hoving cited in Frank Wynne, *I Was Vermeer: The Forger Who Swindled the Nazis* (Bloomsbury Publishing Plc. 2006) 147.

4 David Walker 'Rules of Evidence' *Lecture for the Graduate Certificate in Art Authentication*, The University of Melbourne, 1 June 2012.

5 Kenneth Pye, *Geological and Soil Evidence* (CRC Press 2007) 4.

that are not by Rembrandt van Rijn and a large number of pigments that have been used in the Netherlands prior to 1669 that exist in paintings not by Rembrandt. Identifying a piece of evidence as one that would involve a link to Rembrandt van Rijn requires knowledge of what constitutes a work by Rembrandt. For these reasons it is essential to be able to identify those characteristics that serve to define a work by Rembrandt van Rijn. The existence of verifiable provenance is therefore critical in determining a benchmark for what would constitute acceptable evidence in supporting a claim of authenticity.

A work that is purported to be by Rembrandt will need to have a set of assessable characteristics that position it not only in the Netherlands in the seventeenth century, not only within the workshop of Rembrandt, but within the very particular set of works that have been painted by the hand of Rembrandt. In this case, while it is necessary that the evidence available in the work aligns with the theory that the work was produced in the seventeenth century this is not sufficient. Thousands of works will align with this theory. On the other hand if the work exhibits characteristics that indicate a later date of production, that, for example, it appears to be produced from an acrylic emulsion paint, then this is sufficient to indicate that the work cannot be by Rembrandt. For this reason the most effective pathway in the attribution process is one that can prove an anomaly, and the most effective theory is one that identifies such an anomaly.

The Authentication Pathway

The first step in attribution and authentication is therefore to establish the theory. From this baseline an investigatory pathway can be mapped and a hierarchy of testing developed. At this stage the weight given to the various fields of evidence: provenance, art historical investigation and scientific analysis, can be determined. Regardless of the weighting in these areas it is essential that the working theory be contested at every point that evidence is being examined. This involves testing the theory via observation and experimentation, then assessing any results against the theory and, if the theory is shown to be flawed, replacing it with a new theory or modifying it so that the data that contested the original fits with the theory. Critical to any investigation is the need to have a body of defined, verified and verifiable data that fits with a defined category. We need to know what characteristics an authentic work by Rembrandt exhibits, if we are to know what characteristics would constitute a forged Rembrandt.

Attribution and authentication examinations seek to establish:

- How the object was made;
- What it was made of;
- When it was made;
- Where it was made.

Forensics may provide information to support these points, but forensics will not answer the question: Who made this painting? Forensics will merely determine which data sets can be usefully aligned to a particular theory.

How is Evidence Collected?

Art fraud investigations, by necessity, take as the point of departure an investigation of the object, and then proceed within the structure of a defined investigatory hierarchy. Usually this hierarchy will proceed along the following lines:

1. Initial examination of the object;
2. Development of the proposition about the object;
3. Assessment of primary sources that relate to the artist or the object;
4. Assessment of secondary sources that relate to the artist or the object;
5. Non-invasive visual examination including using a range of advanced light sources to enhance the visual acuity of the investigator;
6. Invasive examination including the removal of samples and cross-sections in order to undertake microscopic examination or investigate solubility or other characteristics of the material;
7. Lab-based techniques that may involve invasive or non-invasive examination;
8. Instrument analysis, often at a nanotechnology level that will assist in identifying the materials used in the artwork, and perhaps also provide evidence of trace elements, or contaminants.

In the initial examination, details about the object are recorded within a strict format. This often takes the form of a condition report, a standard document used in museums and galleries worldwide. In order for the report to be admissible as evidence it must clearly identify the work in question (including accurate measurements and a good image). This document details the frame, support, paint and other layers and inscriptions that relate to the work, and it is critical in ensuring there is a benchmark for all other documentation. This is also the document that verifies that the work in question is the work that has been examined, thereby ensuring the value of the evidence has not been compromised by an inability to provide an evidential link between the work in question, the evidence provided and the assertions drawn from that evidence.

Provenance (as a Corruptible and Non-Corruptible Form of Evidence)

Provenance is the history of the artwork that exists in documentary form and which provides the evidential chain that links the artist and the work in question. The most secure provenance is provided by a sequence of interconnected documents that can verify the link to the artist, but which also serve to verify other documents within that evidential chain. Such documentation may include:

- Exhibition catalogue from an artist's exhibition which clearly identifies the artwork;
- A letter or bill of sale from the gallery representing the artist, which details the artwork;
- Identification of the artwork in a scholarly catalogue raisonné;
- Official acquisition record from an institution;
- An auction or gallery sale record of the artwork with verifiable ownership prior to and after sale;
- An official exhibition sticker attached to the work;
- A statement from the artist that the work is by them.[6]

An example of strong provenance is the paperwork accompanying the gifting of the painting by Sir Arthur Streeton, *Domes of St Mark* to the University of Melbourne. Streeton painted this in 1908 when he was on his honeymoon. Letters in the Streeton Archive at the State Library of Victoria, and subsequently published in Ann Galbally and Anna Gray's edited volume of Streeton's letters, *Letters from Smike: The Letters of Arthur Streeton 1890-1943*, record Streeton discussing the production of works in this series with his patron Baldwin Spencer.[7] There are a series of works from this period including preparatory drawings and oil sketches.[8] The work is listed in the Streeton catalogue of the exhibition of the Venetian works held in the Guildhall, Melbourne in 1909.[9] The work was purchased by Melbourne resident Dr Samuel Ewing, who is the owner noted in Arthur Streeton's self-published 1935 catalogue. Ewing subsequently gifted his art collection, including this work, to the University of Melbourne, and there are a number of letters from Ewing to the University, from Ewing to Streeton and from Streeton to Ewing discussing the condition and treatment of this work prior to the handover from Ewing to the University.[10] The University has catalogued the work and since coming to the University it has hung in a number of exhibitions, with associated catalogue entries.[11] The work was treated at the University's Conservation Centre and these

6 ACGA, '*ACGA Fact Sheets 1, Draft for Discussion, Provenance*' <http://www.acga.com.au/resources/cid/61/parent/0/pid/61/t/resources/title/problematic-art-works-fact-sheets> accessed 1 November 2012.

7 Letter from Arthur Streeton to Baldwin Spencer (8 October 1908) in Ann Galbally and Anna Gray (eds), *Letters from Smike: The Letters of Arthur Streeton 1890-1943* (OUP Australia 1989) 114-115.

8 Arthur Streeton, *The Arthur Streeton Catalogue* (Osboldstone & Co. Pty. Ltd 1935).

9 Arthur Streeton, *Arthur Streeton's Venice* (Catalogue to exhibition July 13th to 27th 1909, Guildhall, Melbourne, accessed from the Exhibition Catalogue Database at the Centre for Cultural Materials Conservation compiled by Lucy Harper 2004).

10 Letter from Arthur Streeton, Letter to Dr Samuel Ewing (9 October 1937) Copy from the NGV Ewing Gift file and provided by Jane Clark, Curator Australian Art at the National Gallery of Victoria, 18 February 1994.

11 Judy Annear and Merryn Gates, *The Ewing Collection* (Ewing Gallery, Melbourne University Union 1981).

records identify and document interventions by both Streeton and conservators during the history of the work.[12] The work was also the subject of scientific investigation, which was published in a peer-reviewed journal.[13] Many works held in public institutions have similar types of provenance documentation.

Other works may not have such good pedigree. Authentic works that have been held within a family, such as those that may have originally been obtained as a gift from an artist, for example, often have no documentation. Other works with no links to the artist whatsoever, claim a significant provenance trail. In such cases, as in the first where family oral history is provided as provenance and in the second where the provenance is as fake as the painting, the asserted provenance cannot be relied on to validate the authenticity of the artwork and art historical investigation and analysis of materials and techniques are required. The fact that many forged works are accompanied by forged provenance indicates the need to have several forms of validation, as well as the ability to cross-reference a proposed provenance with other documentation.

Art History (as a Form of Scholarship that can be Rigorous and Effective, or Subjective and Problematic)

Employing art historical evidence in attribution cases is only as valuable as the rigour with which the historical research has been conducted. In this respect the value of primary documents as source material cannot be over-emphasized. Art historical evidence will include information such as the genre of works produced by an artist, and places where an artist worked, who they dealt with for the sale and distribution of their works, and similar information. For example, if the provenance asserts that a particular work was painted at a particular date and in a particular location and sold to a particular person, then art historical investigation should be able to produce evidence that corroborates this assertion, or at least provides evidence of the likely probability that the assertion is correct. Catalogues raisonnés are very useful in that they provide an overview of an artist's *œuvre*, but they remain, despite their merit, secondary documents and their value resides in the rigour of the scholarship that produced them.

Materials and Techniques (and the Role of Science in Authenticating Artworks)

There is no substitute for looking at art when undertaking any authentication, and if closer and well-informed examination of artwork was undertaken prior to purchase there would be fewer problematic paintings circulating in the art market and hanging on walls in homes, offices and public spaces. There is also no substitute

---

12 Centre for Centre Materials Conservation, 'Condition report – Arthur Streeton's *Domes of St Mark*' (Centre for Centre Materials Conservation, The University of Melbourne 2002).

13 Robyn Sloggett, 'Making The Domes of St Mark' (2005) 29 *AICCM Bulletin* 47.

for being able to access information about an artist and their working methods from data sourced from securely provenanced works. When examining an artwork or an antiquity for its authenticity the assessor will be interested in a number of areas of investigation and will generally begin with a macro investigation, moving to utilize micro and perhaps nano technologies.

The Manufacture of the Object

Of significant interest is the way the object has been produced. This will involve an assessment of the frame or other accessories, to see whether the work has ever been re-presented or whether all its aspects are original. A work that is purported to be from the nineteenth century, and is in a late twentieth-century frame, will raise questions if there is no evidence of previous framing. The issue of artist's choice is also relevant. Is the frame, or the support on which the painting is produced, in keeping with the type known to have been favoured by the artist? A common mistake made by people purchasing art is to assume that the image contains the most relevant information about the artist and the authenticity of the work. For a forger the focus will be on making sure the image looks right so it is not always a good place to focus investigations.

Knowledge about the materials that the artist in question may have preferred is also important. Artists do not, generally, have an unlimited range of paints and brushes, and many, such as Australian expatriate artists, Rupert Bunny[14] or John Peter Russell[15] and British artist John Constable[16] preferred particular colours from particular suppliers. Comparison of the work in question with securely provenanced works from that period will tell the investigator whether the work was produced using the range of paints or the type of brushes favoured by the artist at a particular time. Information such as this can be gathered by good examination techniques, using a good-quality microscope and a raking light (a light source that is held at ninety degrees and shone across the surface of the work).

The various layers that comprise the image are also worth investigation. Is there evidence of a number of layers, and if so what kind? Does the paint appear to have dried between applications? If so, is this in keeping with the evidence in securely provenanced works? Is there evidence of a previous varnish layer? Does this sit between the paint layer and the signature? The answer to such questions progresses an understanding of the way a particular work has been produced.

---

14 Lois Matheson and Robyn Sloggett, 'Rupert Bunny: Surface and Structure' (1993) 19 *AICCM Bulletin* 11.

15 Ann Galbally and Robyn Sloggett, '"Duty points to Paris …" John Peter Russell's Portrait of Dr William Maloney as Talisman' (1996) 37 *Art Bulletin of Victoria* 7; Paula Dredge, 'Paint, Brush & Canvas', in *Belle-Île: Monet, Russell & Matisse in Brittany* (Art Gallery of New South Wales 2011).

16 Sarah Cove, 'Constable's Oil Painting Materials and Techniques' in Leslie Parris and Ian Fleming-Williams (eds), *Constable* (The Tate Gallery 1991).

Other areas that are of interest include any evidence of particular choices made by the artist during the manufacture of the work, such as changes in the composition or the image during construction. Finally, in assessing the authenticity of a work evidence of later additions, restorations or alterations can be very helpful. Some works are simply in too good condition to have lived the life that is claimed for them.

In such circumstances the first step is to undertake a thorough visual examination. A range of visual enhancement tools can then be used such as an ultra violet (UV) light to determine if there are any remnants of existing varnish (various varnishes fluoresce in UV); or infra red (IR) light to view layers that exist below the top layer (IR light, which is the invisible heat component of light can, with the help of relevant imaging equipment, reveal underdrawing or changes that are made with charcoal, graphite or other dark pigments). In some cases X-rays are used to examine the structure of underlaying layers, for example revealing the way worm-holes weave their way through a wooden support, or the types of nails used in panel paintings, or changes that have been made to the composition.[17] In some cases a cross-section will be taken from the paint. This is a small section comprising several paint layers, usually about the size of an average full stop, which can then be examined under a microscope to indicate the structure of the painting. This cross-section can also be analysed using analytical instrumentation such as a scanning electron microscope (SEM) to investigate the pigments[18] or fourier transform infrared spectroscopy (FTIR) to examine the varnish.[19]

Apart from investigating the materials and techniques in the work in question and comparing these findings with the materials and techniques known to have been studied by the artist in question, the authentication process also requires an understanding of material behaviour. The famous Vermeer forger, Hans van Meegeren, produced fake craquelure in his paintings by using phenol formaldehyde (Bakelite) to produce a hard paint surface, which he then baked and rolled to produce fake age craquelure. He then filled the resultant crack with Indian ink to simulate the accretion of dirt. Examination with a good magnifying glass would have shown that these works were 'tricked up'.[20] Natural resin varnishes, and a

17 Giles Robertson, 'The X-Ray Examination of Titian's "Three Ages of Man" in the Bridgewater House Collection' (1971) 113 *Burlington Magazine* 721; Oliver Millar, 'Rubens's Landscapes in the Royal Collection: The Evidence of X-ray' (1977) 119 *Burlington Magazine* 631.

18 Katrien Keune, Annelies van Loon and Jaap Boon 2011 'SEM Backscattered-Electron Images of Paint Cross Sections as Information Source for the Presence of the Lead White Pigment and Lead-Related Degradation and Migration Phenomena in Oil Paintings' (2011) 17 *Microscopy and Microanalysis* 696.

19 Marika Spring, Camilla Ricci, David Peggie and Sergei Kazarian, 'ATR-FTIR imaging for the analysis of organic materials in paint cross sections: case studies on paint samples from the National Gallery, London' (2008) 392 *Analytical & Bioanalytical Chemistry* 37.

20 Wynne (n 3) 111-113.

number of modern synthentic varnishes discolour as they age, and evidence of previous varnish layers may reveal evidence of incomplete cleaning or other forms of restoration. Aged oil paint may darken or discolour, and drying oils may become transparent with time. Pigments may also alter their colour, or fade, depending on their production, storage and display environment and materials with which they are in contact.[21] Works on paper often exhibit foxing (staining from mould or rust spots) and overall discolouration, as the natural tendency of paper to increase in acidity leads to a darkening of the paper. A simple pH test for acidity will indicate whether the darkening is in keeping with the expected pH of the paper, or whether the darkening has been produced in some other way. Most materials used in artwork become embrittled with age. This is true of oil and acrylic paints, cotton and linen canvas, many types of varnish and paper.

For any work that has the appearance of ageing then assessing the characteristics of the work in question with our knowledge of how materials of this kind behave is critical. Different mechanical damage produces different types of cracking in paint layers, as does different effects from environmental changes. Finally materials have their own inbuilt deterioration mechanisms, known as 'inherent vice', and each material has a distinctive deterioration signature. In attribution, the story about the history of the work and the evidence of the history of the work gleaned from examination, should align with our knowledge of the way certain materials behave over time. Any misalignment raises questions that require further investigation.

Scientific Analysis

In some cases assessment of provenance, art historical context and visual examination is not enough to determine whether the work is a good fit with securely provenanced works. At this point examination using a range of scientific instrumentation is required. Scientific analysis only provides answers to very specific and targeted questions, and most information that supports the attribution process is available without the need to resort to high-level scientific analysis. Nevertheless in some instances the answer to one question reveals the smoking gun that determines the validity, or otherwise, of the work in question.

The range of questions that are dealt with by scientific means include questions about the type of material that may have been used in the production

21 Rosamond Harley, 'Field's Manuscripts: Early Nineteenth Century Colour Samples and Fading Tests' (1979) 24 *Studies in Conservation* 75; Paul Whitmore and Glen Cass, 'The Fading of Artists' Colorants by Exposure to Nitrogen Dioxide' (1989) 34 *Studies in Conservation* 85; Christa Brosseau, Francesca Casadio and Richard Van Duyne, 'Revealing the invisible: using surface-enhanced Raman spectroscopy to identify minute remnants of colour in Winslow Homer's colorless skies' (2011) 42 *Journal of Raman Spectroscopy* 1305.

of the work, the characteristics of the constituents (including the pigments or colourants, the carrier, binder or medium) in the material such as trace elements that may identify particular recipes or batches, the age of the material and the type of environment to which the material has been subjected. Scientific analysis can be both qualitative (what kind of material is under examination) and quantitative (how much of particular type of material exist in the sample). In addition to identifying types of materials and their constituents scientific analysis can also assist in determining how a particular material has been manufactured, for example whether a particular pigment has been hand or machine ground (generally by examining the morphology of individual grains of pigment). Quantitative analysis may assist in determining the recipe that was used to produce the paint, and what kinds of additives (modifiers, driers, extenders) have been added to alter its behaviour or characteristics (such as van Meegeren's phenol formaldehyde for example).

Scientific analysis follows a very strict testing regime moving from non-destructive analysis, to micro-sampling for testing that results in the destruction of the sample. Examples of non-destructive scientific analysis include in-situ microscopic examination and UV and IR examination. Sometimes chemical spot tests will help determine whether a particular material such as lead white is present.

If basic examination and in-situ analytical techniques are not effective in providing information, sampling will need to be undertaken and the samples subjected to instrumental analysis. SEM for example, can identify the chemistry of the paint sample, but it can also provide high-level photomicrographs, with magnification as high as one million times. This visual information can be used to understand pigment morphology, which in turn will explain whether a particular pigment has been ground by hand, or by machine, and perhaps the level of technology involved (such as early or late nineteenth century or twentieth-century technology). X-ray diffraction can provide a fingerprint of the crystalline structure of materials, particularly useful for identifying different types of inorganic pigment, ceramics, corrosion products and similar crystalline materials. Other instruments identify organic components of paint such as Gas Chromatography Mass Spectrometry (GCMS), but there are many other instruments that provide information on most components found in paintings including Raman spectroscopy, Laser Induced Fluorescence Spectroscopy (LIF), Laser Induced Breakdown Spectroscopy (LIBS) and Particle Induced X-ray Emission (PIXE).

Conclusion

Building the chain of evidence for art authentication is a complex and carefully constructed activity that ensures that works can be legitimately, and verifiably, linked to the artist who is purported to be their source. This evidential chain may be constructed from the time the work is created; in the main by due diligence in documentation provided by the artist or their representative. This secures provenance. On the other hand this evidential chain may be constructed from investigation that takes place after the work has been called into question. In both cases what is at stake is the ability to claim that the work is authentic and that its descriptor matches the conclusion that can be drawn from the evidence at hand. In this way considerations of authenticity are context dependent and if new evidence comes to light then the conclusion must be revisited and revised. In short, the two platforms of evidence, truth and proof, can only be understood in context, and data is not evidence until it can be securely used to inform a hypothesis. The art of art authentication rests in the crafting of an elegant and effective hypothesis.

Chapter 8
UNESCO's Influence on the Development of International Criminal Law

Lyndel V. Prott

International heritage law is developing rapidly and the question arises as to the use of international criminal law as a means of enforcement of the principles now adopted by international organizations, such as UNESCO's conventions on protection of cultural heritage threatened by conflict, trafficking, neglect and exploitation. The original responsibility of States to enforce the Hague Convention for the Protection of Cultural Property in the Event of Armed Conflict 1954 and its First Protocol have been reinforced by the Second Protocol 1999 and the attribution of competence to the International Criminal Court to deal with serious crimes against cultural heritage. While UNESCO, the chief international body concerned with rule-making in this field, has to date had little enforcement power of its own, it has had an impact on national criminal law, since a number of States are enforcing national legislation in conformity with the UNESCO Conventions. Unfortunately there are inconsistent interpretations of the Convention on the Means of Prohibiting and Preventing the Illicit Import, Export and Transfer of Ownership of Cultural Property, so that the level of enforcement varies greatly between the States, and some States appear not to have legislated at all to sanction breaches of its principles. However, UNESCO's standard-setting is now also reinforced by sanctions meted out by other international organizations which have jurisdiction over criminal matters, such as the International Criminal Court. This article discusses national legislation and its effectiveness in dealing with illicit traffic in cultural objects by criminal or administrative penalties. It looks at the terminology used in national and international law and also touches on new efforts to restrain demand in the States where collectors and dealers in art and antiquities are most represented.

International criminal law began with certain specialized crimes such as piracy, genocide, later war crimes and crimes against humanity. However, we are now experiencing developments in other areas of law which have traditionally been handled as national matters but are now within the purview of various international organizations and, even more importantly, subject to judgment by international courts. These developments also involve certain organizations whose mandate does not specifically confer competence in criminal matters but whose activities inevitably produce effects on international criminal law itself.

UNESCO's Mandate

UNESCO is the United Nations specialized agency with responsibility for education, science and cultural matters. I confine myself here to its cultural mandate. The Constitution commissions the organization to

> Maintain, increase and diffuse knowledge: By assuring the conservation and protection of the world's inheritance of books, works of art and monuments of history and science, and recommending to the nations concerned the necessary international conventions.[1]

It will readily be seen that this, the only statement in the Constitution relevant to this discussion, confers a very general competence on UNESCO, but does not endow it with any punitive power. UNESCO has no policing powers and no police force, though it is from time to time requested by members of the public or even national administrators to take this kind of action. It does its best to prevent threatened action, for example, it made intensive diplomatic efforts to prevent the destruction of the Bamiyan Buddhas and movable cultural objects in Afghanistan[2] and has been active with its Member States to implement the United Nations Security Council Resolution on the return of stolen cultural objects to Iraq.[3]

Two of its earlier Conventions, The Hague Convention For the Protection of Cultural Property in the Event of Armed Conflict and its Protocol of 1954 and the Convention on the Means of Prohibiting and Preventing the Illicit Import, Export and Transfer of Ownership of Cultural Property of 1970, are now reinforced by provisions in other international agreements such as treaties of mutual legal assistance, by improved extradition treaties and by enforcement through international criminal courts, and, in the case of The Hague Convention 1954, improved by a significant and detailed Second Protocol.

Despite this lack of punitive power, UNESCO is deeply concerned in the area of criminal activity relating to cultural heritage because the whole problem of illicit traffic in this domain is highly complex. With the interpenetration of licit and illicit trade it is impossible to avoid dealing in some ways with criminal matters.

---

1 Constitution of UNESCO 1946 Article 1(c).

2 Lyndel V. Prott, 'Protection of Cultural Movables from Afghanistan: Developments in International Management' in Juliette van Krieken-Peters (ed), *Art and Archaeology of Afghanistan: Its Fall and Survival* (Brill 2006) 189-200.

3 UN Security Council Resolution 1483 of 22 May 2003 concerning Iraq.

UNESCO's Activity in the Development of International Criminal Law

The Hague Convention for the Protection of Cultural Property in the Event of Armed Conflict 1954, which UNESCO administers, sets out rules to protect cultural sites and objects and requires States to train their military in these principles, to include them in their military rules (Art. 7) and 'to take, within the framework of their ordinary criminal jurisdiction, all necessary steps to prosecute and impose penal or disciplinary sanctions upon those persons, of whatever nationality, who commit or order to be committed a breach of the present Convention' (Art. 28). Unfortunately, very few of the States Parties to this Convention have passed national legislation to ensure its application. Experience in this and other conventions in force since the Second World War has in any event made it clear that national States are reluctant to take action against wrongdoers in their own jurisdictions despite their agreement to such an international obligation in a broadly accepted multinational convention. Even where a State has prosecuted in its own legal system for a proscribed act such as a war crime[4] (consider the prosecutions in the USA in the case of the My Lai massacre in Viet Nam in 1968[5] or of the torture and abuse of Iraqi prisoners in Abu Ghraib in 2004[6]) there is a clear tendency for national judges to exonerate or punish minimally those responsible for acts declared to be criminal by international treaties.

In 1954 States were not prepared to have an international system for enforcement of criminal law. There were many discussions of this possibility after the First World War and many more after the Nuremberg and Tokyo trials at the end of the Second World War. The 1954 Hague Convention was drawn up at a time when it was clear that States were not ready to allow such a system to develop. The whole of the 1954 Hague Convention has 40 articles, its 'Regulations for the Execution of the Convention for the Protection of Cultural Property in the Event of Armed Conflict' has 21 articles and its Protocol, dealing specifically with movable cultural Heritage, has 15 clauses (assembled as three articles). All this is the successor to the single clause on this subject (Art. 56) in the Hague Convention No. IV Respecting the Laws and Customs of War on Land of 1907 which stated:

> The property of municipalities, that of institutions dedicated to religion, charity and education, the arts and sciences, even when State property, shall be treated as

4 Established by the four Geneva Conventions of 1948.

5 In March 1968, during the war in Viet Nam, between 300 and 500 civilians were murdered by US troops in the village of My Lai. Twenty-six officers were charged with war crimes or obstruction of justice. Only one was found guilty and given a prison sentence. James S. Olsen and Randy Roberts, *My Lai: A Brief History with Documents* (Palgrave Macmillan 1998).

6 Nine US soldiers were ultimately found guilty, *New York Times* at <http://topics.nytimes.com/topics/news/international/countriesandterritories/iraq/abu_ghraib/index.html> accessed 19 August 2012.

> private property. All seizure of, destruction or wilful damage done to institutions of this character, historic monuments, works of art and science, is forbidden, and should be made the subject of legal proceedings.

The last phrase was the only one in the Hague 1907 Convention dealing with sanctions against those who violate the rules as to cultural heritage. Although therefore, the 1954 Hague Convention now looks deficient in its provisions, it was at the time a great step forward.

However, very few States party to the 1954 Convention or to its Protocol have adopted legislation ensuring the implementation of any of its provisions, even for its provisions for the return of cultural objects. The Netherlands, a vigorous promoter of this Convention and its Protocol, found itself in breach of the provisions of the Protocol. Both the Netherlands and Cyprus are party to the 1954 Protocol to the Convention. A legal suit by the Autocephalous Church of Cyprus in the Netherlands failed to recover from two Dutch citizens mosaics looted from the island of Cyprus: the judgment stated that this would be contrary to a rule in the Dutch Civil Code protecting 'good faith' acquirers, on the basis that the 1954 Convention set out obligations between States, but could not overrule the protection of private property of Dutch citizens guaranteed under the Civil Code.[7] (The Netherlands has now passed specific legislation to implement the Convention at the national level.) While this case referred to the Civil Code, the general lack of implementation statutes of any kind means that similar arguments might be made about the provisions of Criminal Codes in force in the great majority of other States Parties.

The existence of the 1954 Convention inspired articles in the 1977 Protocols to the 1949 Geneva Conventions on the law of war. Article 53 of Protocol 1 (relating to the protection of victims of international armed conflicts) prohibits hostile acts 'against the historic monuments, works of art or places of worship which constitute the cultural or spiritual heritage of peoples, to use such objects in support of the military effort or to make them the object of reprisals'. These acts therefore are subject to sanctions under that body of law as well as those prescribed by the 1954 Hague Convention. There is also provision in Protocol 1 for an International Fact-Finding Commission in Article 90, though it may be little used since the founding of the International Criminal Court.

During the 1970s it was suggested that the 1954 Convention was outdated: that its defensive measures for the protection of cultural sites such as painting the symbol of the Convention on the roof of museums or other monuments were of no use when intercontinental ballistic missiles could be used and it

7 Stephan Matyk 'The restitution of cultural objects and the question of giving direct effect to the Protocol to the Hague Convention For the Protection of Cultural Property in the Event of Armed Conflict 1954' (2000) 9 *International Journal of Cultural Property* 341.

would not be possible to identify individual buildings over the horizon from the launch site. However its importance in the prohibition of wanton destruction was only too well demonstrated by developments in the Balkans and Iraq in the 1990s and of wrongful displacement again in Iraq in 2001.

Further major changes had come in the 1990s with the establishment of special war crimes tribunals such as those of Yugoslavia and Rwanda and the discussions on the establishment of an international criminal court. These developments created a very different context for the negotiations concerning the Second Protocol to the Hague Convention in 1999. Chapter IV of this new instrument reinforced the provisions on punishment by including seven detailed articles on 'Criminal Responsibility and Jurisdiction'. 'Serious violations' of the Protocol are defined (Article 15(1)) and each Party is required to:

> adopt such measures as may be necessary to establish as criminal offences under its domestic law the offences set forth in this article and to make such offences punishable by appropriate penalties. When doing so, Parties shall comply with general principles of law and international law, including the rules extending individual criminal responsibility to persons other than those who directly commit the act (Art. 15(2)).

National jurisdiction is recognized if claimed by a State where the offence was committed or where the offender is a national of that State and in some cases also where the alleged offender is present on its territory (Art.16(1)). There are significant provisions on extradition, which will be deemed to be included in an existing extradition treaty between Parties or, in the absence of such a treaty, States may rely on this Protocol as the legal basis for extradition (Art.18(1) and (2)). Parties to the Convention have also agreed to 'afford one another the greatest measure of assistance in connection with investigations or criminal or extradition proceedings' including assistance in obtaining evidence (Art.19), although there is provision to refuse legal assistance or extradition where the prosecution appears to be inspired by political motives or punishing a person on account of their race, religion, nationality, ethnic origin or political opinion (Art. 20). Finally there is a provision requiring each party to adopt such legislative, administrative or disciplinary measures as may be necessary to suppress any use of cultural property in violation of the Convention or the Protocol for any illicit export, removal or transfer of ownership from occupied territory in violation of the Convention or Protocol (Art. 21).

It can be seen from this how much more detail has been legislated in the Second Protocol compared to the single provision in the 1954 Convention. There are, however, elements that still give rise to concern about the application of sanctions. In the first place there are still many States who have not passed implementing legislation and 24 of the 126 States which are party to the Convention are not party to the 1954 Protocol and 62 are not party to the 1999 Second Protocol (as at 4 June 2013). The Committee for the Protection of Cultural Property in the Event of Armed Conflict was set up by Article 14 of the Second Protocol and was established, *inter alia,* to supervise the implementation of the Protocol. It adopted, at its sixth session in September 2011, a Report on the Obligations of the Parties to Implement Chapter 4 (Criminal Responsibility and Jurisdiction of the Second Protocol).[8] Clearly the failure of States to implement sanctions at the national level remains a problem and encourages use of the existing international mechanisms to ensure the punishment of violations.

Furthermore the Second Protocol has not been able to achieve the same level of mandated sanctions in the case of 'armed conflicts not of an international character'. Though clearly the kind of deliberate destruction seen in the demolition of the Bamiyan Buddhas by the Taliban in 2001 or the targeted destruction of monuments now taking place in Timbuktu are seen by many as a crime which should be punished in the same way as those listed in the Second Protocol, certain States negotiating that Protocol were emphatically opposed to setting up any mandatory jurisdiction for these 'non-international' cases. Some States are clearly afraid that such a measure would enable other States to intervene in their internal affairs in times of unrest and factional fighting. Unfortunately it is evident from even these two recent cases that now and in the future one can expect many attacks by non-State entities (including interventions from irregular foreign groups who may, however, have ideological links with groups within a country and may indeed be supported by another State) – leaving a gap which makes prompt intervention to save threatened cultural heritage impossible. It may be that it will take another several decades before States finally come to the conclusion that some such powers must be given if more severe damage is to be avoided. It is ironic that every State, including Afghanistan itself through its exiled government, has agreed that the threatened Bamiyan Buddha should not be destroyed, but that Article 22(2) specifies that the Second Protocol 'shall not apply to situations of internal disturbances and tensions, such as riots, isolated and sporadic acts of violence and other acts of a similar nature'. Although the Taliban regime was not recognized by the international community as the government of Afghanistan, it was in fact the *de facto* government of the country at that time.

A further advance has been the Statute of the International Criminal Court which includes attacks against buildings dedicated to religion, education, art, science or charitable purposes and historic monuments[9] among the war crimes for which it has jurisdiction. This provision led to the prosecution and subsequent imprisonment of Croatian military officers for the destruction of the Mostar

8 UNESCO Doc CLT-11/CONF/211/3.

9 ICJ statute, Article 8 (ix) '...attacks against buildings dedicated to religion, education, art, science or charitable purposes, historic monuments, ... provided they are not military objectives'.

Bridge in Bosnia[10] and Serbian officers for the shelling of Dubrovnik in Croatia.[11] UNESCO provided a good deal of the evidence supporting the investigation and punishment of those acts.

Developments in Civil Law

In 1970 UNESCO adopted the Convention on the Means of Prohibiting and Preventing the Illicit Import, Export and Transfer of Ownership of Cultural Property. It was designed to create reciprocity in the return of cultural objects which had been stolen, clandestinely excavated or illegally exported from their countries of origin. While not directly targeting criminal activity it could not but have a significant impact on it. For example, Article 10(a) requires States Parties to oblige dealers in antiquities 'subject to penal or administrative sanctions, to maintain a register recording the origin of each item of cultural property, names and addresses of the supplier, description and price of each item sold and to inform the purchaser of the cultural property of the export prohibition to which such property may be subject'. Such provisions clearly facilitate the work of police in tracing wrongfully acquired property.

In approving such texts the States were acknowledging the intertwining of civil and criminal aspects in the complex matter of illicit traffic. UNESCO was not the only forum for this debate. In 1985 the Committee of Ministers of the Council of Europe adopted the text of the European Convention on Offences relating to Cultural Property and submitted it to its Member States for signature and ratification. However, the text became extremely controversial. In 1977 the European Committee on Crime Problems (CDPC) decided to establish a Select Committee of Experts on International Co-operation in the Field of Offences (PCROA)[12] Relating to Works of Art, which produced the draft Convention.[13] At that time there were two other committees which could be expected to have had

10 *International Criminal Tribunal for* the Former *Yugoslavia* (ICTY): Indictment of Slobodan Praljak and five other Croatian officers for destruction of protected sites in Bosnia including the Mostar Bridge destroyed on 9 November 1993. Trial commenced 6 April 2006. He was found guilty by the ICTY of this and other crimes and has been sentenced to a 20-year prison term. See at <http://www.icty.org/x/cases/prlic/tjug/en/130529_summary_en.pdf> accessed 29 May 2013. Indictment available at <http://www.icty.org/x/cases/prlic/ind/en/prl-ii040304e.htm> accessed 3 June 2013.

11 ICTY, *Prosecutor v Pavle Strugar*, 2005, sentenced to eight-years imprisonment; *Prosecutor v Miodrag Jokic*, 2005, sentenced to seven-years imprisonment.

12 Bart de Schutter, 'The Harmonization of Criminal Law and International Criminal Co-operation as Instruments of Protection' in *International Legal Protection of Cultural Property* (Council of Europe, Strasbourg 1984) 72-98 at 80.

13 Because it never entered into force this text has been relatively little considered. However, it has been discussed in Lyndel V. Prott and Patrick J. O'Keefe, *Law and the Cultural Heritage: Vol. III, Movement* (Butterworths 1989) 645-6, 676-83.

an interest in this subject: the Committee on Legal Co-operation (CCJ) and the Council for Cultural Cooperation (CCC) which seems not to have been involved in the project[14] despite its obvious relevance. The original text was drafted by the PCROA but its provisions on 'good faith' annoyed some experts in civil (private) law who felt that specialists in criminal (public) law did not have the expertise to deal with this issue, even though they had based their provisions on earlier work of the International Institute for the Unification of Private Law (UNIDROIT). The provision on 'good faith' was dropped before its adoption by the Ministers, thus removing one of the most important provisions in the text. There was also serious disagreement by some scholars at the apparent mixture of public and private law, which they felt must remain separate. These objections were probably the main reason why the Convention ultimately never became law. Only six States signed and there were no ratifications. Hence the Convention never entered into force.[15] Yet recent studies of the complex problem of illicit traffic make clear that it is impossible to completely separate the illicit from the licit: indeed, recent analyses by criminologists[16] show that the antiquities market is best understood not as black and white, but grey.[17]

The model of the antiquities market is a grey market. The reality is that flows of licit and illicit objects are intermixed and therefore that, rather than being a market characterized by a 'clean' public trade and a 'dirty' private or 'underground' trade, the supposedly clean public trade in antiquities is tainted 'grey' by the circulation therein of illicit antiquities.[18]

It seems also that some lawyers still cherished the ideal of sacrosanct principles surrounding the safeguard of private property. Nowadays private property owners and their lawyers seem to be able to live with an array of legal provisions such as those controlling drugs, laundering and confiscation of proceeds from crime, tax fraud, and even criminalization of failure to justify the origin of one's assets clearly, all measures impinging on what once were seen as fundamental property

14 Bart de Schutter, 'The Protection of Cultural Property: Interstate Cooperation of European Perspective' in *The Penal Protection of Works of Art* (International Institute of Higher Studies in Criminal Sciences 1983) 189.

15 Signatories were Cyprus, Greece, Italy, Liechtenstein, Portugal and Turkey. Just three ratifications would have brought the Convention into force. Thanks are due to Christopher Grayson and Candido Cunha, both formerly of the Secretariat of the Council of Europe, who helped me track the history of this draft convention.

16 Ken Polk, 'The Antiquities Trade Viewed as a Criminal Market' (September 2000) *Hong Kong Lawyer* 82; Blythe Bowman Proulx, 'Transnational Crimes Against Culture: Looting at Archaeological Sites and the "Grey" Market in Antiquities' (2008) 24 *Journal of Contemporary Criminal Justice*, 225-42.

17 Simon Mackenzie, 'The Market as Criminal and Criminals in the Market: Reducing Opportunities for Organized Crime in the International Antiquities Market' in Stefano Manacorda and Duncan Chappell (eds), *Crime in the Art and Antiquities World: Illegal Trafficking in Cultural Property* (Springer 2011) 69-86, 70.

18 Mackenzie (n 17).

rights. There is little doubt that the draft Offences Convention was truly forward thinking and was clearly pointing in the right direction: the interlacing of civil, criminal and administrative law has been the inevitable result of efforts to control anti-social acts in a number of fields.

In 1983 UNESCO held a meeting of specialists to discuss the impact of the 1970 UNESCO Convention. The expert panel recommended that UNESCO work with an Institute dealing with the unification of national laws such as UNIDROIT (based in Rome) to work towards the negotiation of what became the UNIDROIT Convention on Stolen or Illegally Exported Cultural Objects 1995. The object of that exercise was to deter the laundering of illegally acquired cultural objects by exploiting dissonant provisions in the different systems of private law and to hinder the use of presumed good faith in cases where there was good reason to believe that the object had been stolen or illegally exported. Stolen cultural objects make up the majority of the illicit trade in heritage items and a high proportion of it is only found when it is advertised (through auctions, exhibitions or incidental discovery) after a series of transactions, some of which clearly involve criminal acts, such as conspiracy or corruption or laundering. It is within UNESCO's remit to deter such activities as much as possible.

The UNIDROIT text includes several crucial provisions to deter the laundering of stolen cultural objects: Article 3(1) provides that the possessor of a stolen cultural object must return it.[19] There will be no compensation for an acquirer who has not exercised due diligence: this requires regard 'to all the circumstances of the acquisition, including the character of the parties, the price paid, whether the possessor consulted any reasonably accessible register of stolen cultural objects, and any other relevant information and documentation which it could reasonably have obtained, and whether the possessor consulted accessible agencies or took any other step that a reasonable person would have taken in the circumstances' (Art. 4(4)). This provision is an important contribution to the prevention of laundering of stolen goods in the art and antiquities market.

The UNIDROIT Convention has no sanctions which could be applied by an international jurisdiction: the States Parties once again are required to take action to enforce its provisions. Nonetheless the UNIDROIT Convention and its approach have had a further influence on international criminal law. The recent prosecution of Giacomo Medici in Italy revealed detailed cross-border planning by dealers and exposed an extensive and lucrative trade in trafficking stolen and clandestinely excavated objects.[20] The dealer Frederick Schultz in New York[21] and

19 Article 3(1).

20 Peter Watson and Cecilia Todeschini, *The Medici Conspiracy: The Illicit Journey of Looted Antiquities From Italy's Tomb Raiders to the World's Greatest Museums* (Perseus Books Group 2006). In 2005 Medici was sentenced to ten-years imprisonment, forfeiture of all the antiquities in his possession, a fine, damages and costs. His appeal against conviction was lost in 2009, though his sentence was reduced from ten to eight years.

21 *United States v Frederick Schultz,* 333 F. 3d 393 (2d Cir. June 25 2003).

his British collaborator Tokeley-Parry in London[22] were charged with conspiracy for smuggling inventoried cultural treasures out of Egypt[23] and both consequently served prison sentences in their respective national jurisdictions.

Further developments in national civil law are also important to support the rules of international criminal law. While theft is universally considered a crime and punishable, illicit excavation is much more difficult to deal with. To prove theft, it is usually necessary to be able to locate the owner. The UNESCO Recommendation on International Principles Applicable to Archaeological Excavations 1956 included a provision that the Member States should 'define the legal status of the archaeological subsoil and, where State ownership of the said subsoil is recognized, specifically mention the fact in its legislation'.[24] Those States who do not claim ownership of undiscovered antiquities, or who have not made their ownership very clear in their legislation, have had difficulties when they try to recover such an object in a foreign jurisdiction. A clear example was the case of *Iran v Barakat*,[25] litigated in the English High Court, where a careful analysis eventually established that Iran did in fact have ownership, but this was through an extended process of accumulating the various incidences of ownership scattered over a range of laws. It was an expensive exercise for the claimant State. In 2008 UNESCO and UNIDROIT established a joint Working Group to provide a simple and very clear provision asserting ownership, which would assist States, if adopted in their legislation, to avoid additional expense and possible loss of a case. That Working Group's recommended clause has now been endorsed by the UNESCO Intergovernmental Committee for Promoting the Return of Cultural Property to Its Countries of Origin or Its Restitution in Case of Illicit Appropriation.[26] It reads as follows:

> *State Ownership*
>
> *Undiscovered cultural objects are owned by the State, provided there is no prior existing ownership.*

---

22 *R.v. Tokeley-Parry* [1999] Crim L R 578.

23 The most exceptional of their thefts was the head of Amenhotep III which was returned to Egypt in 2008. 'The return of Amenhotep III' 927 *Al-Ahram* (Cairo, 25 December 2008) <http://weekly.ahram.org.eg/2008/927/fr3.htm> accessed 2 November 2013.

24 Principle 5(e).

25 Republic of *Iran v Barakat Galleries* [2007] EWCA Civ 1374; Case discussed by Derek Fincham, '*Iran v Barakat*: Iran wins Barakat appeal' in Lyndel V. Prott (ed), *Witnesses to History: Documents and Writings on the Return of Cultural Objects* (UNESCO 2009) 388. Available also at <http://illicit-cultural-property.blogspot.com.au/2007/12/ iran-wins-barakat-appeal.html> accessed 10 November 2013.

26 The text was endorsed by the 17th session of the UNESCO Intergovernmental Committee for Promoting the Return of Cultural Property to Its Countries of Origin or Its Restitution in Case of Illicit Appropriation in July 2011.

Of course, depending on its own history and political philosophy, a State could also omit the last seven words. In either case the intent of the legislator would be absolutely clear for a foreign court. It should be more difficult for thieves and middleman to transfer stolen goods to acquirers in other countries if it is clear that they are subject to seizure because they have been stolen.

The UNESCO Convention on the Means of Prohibiting and Preventing the Illicit Import, Export and Transfer of Ownership Of Cultural Property 1970 and the UNIDROIT Convention on Stolen or Illegally Exported Cultural Objects 1995 both deal with theft, but with the focus on the return of cultural property to its owner rather than with the criminal issues.[27] Article 10(a) of the 1970 Convention requires States Parties to oblige dealers in antiquities subject to penal or administrative sanctions to maintain a register recording the origin of each item of cultural property, names and addresses of the supplier, description and price of each item sold and to inform the purchaser of the cultural property of the export prohibition to which such property may be subject.

The effect of this section is to try to prevent the process of laundering stolen cultural goods. Because a number of the States Parties have not legislated on, or have not implemented this provision, it has not had the essential effect on the widespread practice of laundering stolen property. There is now a move to draft a protocol to the United Nations Convention against Transnational Organized Crime (the Palermo Convention) 2000 to establish an international crime of conspiracy in relation to illicit traffic in cultural objects.

Persuading States to Ratify and Implement the Conventions

Another important obligation for UNESCO resulting from its task of law development is to persuade States to ratify and to implement the conventions. This is sometimes a very difficult job. It has taken more than 30 years to get the major 'art trade' States to ratify the 1970 Convention. France became a party in 1997; Belgium, Germany, Japan, the Netherlands, Switzerland and the United Kingdom have all become party since 2000. Although John Merryman said in 1994 that the 1970 Convention 'is now generally considered to be a failure'[28] (when it then had 80 States Parties), it now has 123 States Parties and is regarded as the international standard on the subject.

In the early years of the 1990s a number of new States emerged from the breakup of the USSR. UNESCO was keen to work with some of these States,

27 All of the cultural heritage conventions and other relevant international instruments can be found in Patrick J. O'Keefe and Lyndel V. Prott (eds), *Cultural Heritage Conventions and Other Instruments: A Compendium with Commentaries* (Builth Wells: Institute of Art and Law 2011), available through <http://www.ial.uk.com/books.php>.

28 John H. Merryman 'The Nation and the Object' (1994) 3(1) *International Journal of Cultural Property* 61-76, 63.

which had had no real experience of international negotiation and knew little about the international cultural conventions available for them to join, while the volatile political situation and borders, which the inhabitants were dissatisfied with, meant that cultural property might be endangered by conflict. The International Committee of the Red Cross was equally concerned to speak to them about the Geneva Conventions. Both organizations felt it to be an important priority to ensure States were aware of and fully informed about the 1954 Hague Convention. A joint workshop was held in Tashkent (where the Red Cross had an office) in 1995. Customs, police, army officers and cultural administrators were invited from Kazakhstan, Kyrgyzstan, Tajikistan, Turkmenistan and Uzbekistan. It proved to be a most rewarding experience for facilitators and participants alike and four of those five States became Parties to the Convention between 1992 and 2012.[29]

The ratification of the UNIDROIT Convention on Stolen or Illegally Exported Cultural Objects 1995 is a particular concern at present. This Convention deals with some of the gaps in the 1970 UNESCO Convention, such as the differing rules on protection of the 'good faith' purchaser, the need for proper searches of provenance and standardization of the rules on time limits for legal pursuit of stolen or illegally exported objects. UNIDROIT, though expert in the field of harmonization of civil law, is a much smaller organization than UNESCO, and UNESCO promotes the UNIDROIT Convention as an essential complement to its own Convention of 1970. Indeed it fulfils the function of a protocol to that Convention.

In encouraging States to ratify the conventions it is often necessary for UNESCO to assist States with the drafting of national legislation to implement these international obligations. When requested, UNESCO provides experts to work with national administrators to devise the best legislation for that State. Such legislation may further develop existing law, particularly to outlaw clandestine excavation and theft, or and it should enhance deterrence by education, retrieval and punishment.

Co-operation with Other International Agencies to Repress Crime

Stolen cultural objects make up the majority of the illicit trade and a high proportion of them are only found when they are advertised (through auctions, exhibitions or incidental discovery) after a series of transactions, some of which clearly involve criminal acts, such as conspiracy or corruption or laundering. It is within UNESCO's remit to deter such activities as much as possible. It does this in many different ways, such as publicizing thefts and losses from the Member States, which are made known to it.

29 ICRC/UNESCO, 'Report on the Regional Seminar on the Implementation of International Humanitarian Law and on Cultural Heritage Law', Tashkent, 25-29 September 1995 (English and Russian).

It has close relationships with the International Council of Museums (ICOM), which publishes '100 Missing Objects' for countries or regions having suffered particularly serious losses, and 'Red Lists' of particular categories of endangered cultural objects, both publications illustrated so as to put the market on notice that they should not buy these objects.

UNESCO also works with Interpol, referring to it aspects of theft and illicit activity, which UNESCO cannot directly deal with, but also helping to publicize losses notified to UNESCO through the Interpol network.[30] It was through the inclusion in Interpol's list of 'The Most Wanted Works of Art' that a 15th-century map based on the work of the classical Greek geographer Ptolemy was identified in Australia as one stolen from the Spanish National Library in whose collection it had been since its foundation 300 years before. There was no prosecution in Australia, since the thief was overseas and was not identified. An unwary purchaser in Sydney had bought it through the Internet.[31]

Raising Awareness of the Problem of Illicit Traffic, of the International Treaties Dealing with It and of the Activity of Bodies such as Interpol and ICOM

This is also a task taken seriously by UNESCO. It has run many regional workshops and seminars on these matters, many of them in partnership with ICOM or Interpol or both. This educational work has also included drafting an International Code of Ethics for Dealers in Cultural Property[32] and the publication of a number of educational kits, which include information on how to ratify the UNESCO and UNIDROIT Conventions on the subject and noting successful returns. Recently it published, with the substantial assistance of several Member States, the book *Witnesses to History: a Compendium of Writings and Documents on the Return of Cultural Objects*.[33] The increasing

---

30 For a fuller discussion of the interface of UNESCO with national police and Interpol see Lyndel V. Prott, 'International Conventions, Databases and the Coordination of Information' invited contribution to the international conference of the Comando Tutela Patrimonio Artistico (Italian Carabinieri), 'La circolazione Illecita delle opera d'arte' 3- 6 May 1999 published as 'Le convenzioni internazionali, le banche dati e l'uniformazione delle informazioni' (English and Italian) in (2000) 34-5 *Bollettino di Numismatica* (Ministero per I beni e le attività culturali, Rome) 33-41.

31 Philip Cornford 'Precious Stolen Map Turns up in Sydney' *The Sydney Morning Herald* (20 October 2007) <http://www.smh.com.au/news/national/precious-stolen-map-turns-up-in-Sydney/2007/10/19/1192301045420.html> accessed 5 June 2013.

32 Available at <http://www.unesco.org/new/en/culture/themes/illicit-traffic-of-cultural-property/legal-and-practical-instruments/> accessed 6 June 2013.

33 Lyndel V. Prott (ed), *Witnesses to History: A Compendium of Writings and Documents on the Return of Cultural Objects* (UNESCO 2009). It has been translated

number of returns which is taking place also has a deterrent effect on those who have until now disregarded appropriate research into provenance.

Terminology

There is another aspect in which UNESCO has been significant and that is in the development of terminology in this area. This has been less conscious and perhaps less helpful. The 1954 Hague Convention did use some language appropriate to criminal law such as 'theft, pillage or misappropriation' and 'acts of vandalism' (Art. 4(3)). Their link to criminal law terminology is evident. 'Reprisals' (Art. 4(4)) are made illegal and subject to prosecution and imposition of 'penal or disciplinary sanctions' (Art. 28). However the UNESCO Convention on the Means of Prohibiting and Preventing the Illicit Import, Export and Transfer of Ownership of Cultural Property 1970 is less clear. In the French text the word '*illicite*' means 'unlawful', illegal or prohibited, although it appears to also have secondary meanings such as '*clandestin*', '*défendu*', or, '*subreptice*'). The use of the English word 'illicit' is less clear. English has two other words available for translation of the French word '*illicite*': 'unlawful' and 'illegal', both of which mean contrary to law, and they are normally the terms used in English language legal drafting. 'Illicit' on the other hand has overtones of 'improper', 'inappropriate' or even 'unethical' or 'immoral' – but not necessarily illegal. It is possible that the word 'illicit' was used in the English version because some of the delegates negotiating at that conference in 1970 were not convinced that illegal export was criminal, although it might well be unethical or undesirable. Be that as it may, the phrase 'illicit traffic' is today very widespread because of the broad ratification of the 1970 Convention and the breadth of English usage in the international community. National legislation implementing the 1970 Convention in English-speaking countries, such as the United Kingdom Dealing in Cultural Objects (Offences) Act 2003 and the Australian Commonwealth Protection of Movable Cultural Heritage Act 1986 as amended (s.14), has in most cases resulted in the creation of a criminal offence.

The use of the word 'restitution' in the name of the UNESCO Intergovernmental Committee for Promoting the Return of Cultural Property to its Countries of Origin or Its Restitution in Case of Illicit Appropriation also needs careful study. While some Continental systems of law believe that 'restitution' may be adequately performed by the payment of damages, English courts for some 400 years have recognized the irreplaceability of certain unique objects which can only be fully remedied by the return of the object itself and not by damages. The word 'return' would have covered either of these meanings, and was also broad enough to include returns not required by law but found

into Chinese and French, a version in Arabic is being prepared and other translations are planned.

to be morally required. The title originally proposed for the committee used only the first 15 words. The addition of the words 'or its Restitution in Case of Illicit Appropriation' was insisted upon by the German delegation at the time of drafting the Committee's Statute in 1978. This has imported an ambiguity allowing States holding different views on the nature of 'restitution' to continue to hold opposing ideas, since 'restitution' in German law occurs only when an illegal taking has occurred while 'restitution' in English is a much wider term and would have included legal and illegal takings in the term 'return'.[34] Fortunately the development of public understanding of the importance of return of the object itself, whatever the means of transfer, and the more broadly accepted understanding that compensation cannot replace a cultural treasure, may make the issue less technical than it was at the time of the Committee's founding.

Conclusion

As in many other areas where international organizations are active, UNESCO is very often asked to perform tasks for which it is not equipped or given competence. I vividly remember receiving an extremely excited Croatian architect in my office at UNESCO in 1991. Having, he thought, at last found the culprit, he leaned on my desk, glared at me and said, 'If Dubrovnik is destroyed, it will be your fault!' Of course I understood his deep anxiety, but I had to explain to him that I had no police force at my disposal, no parachute troop which could be dropped in to defend the city. UNESCO did install observers in Dubrovnik and their evidence provided by UNESCO was used in the subsequent trials of the Serbian officers responsible for the damage done to the city of Dubrovnik.[35]

Control of illicit traffic can only be attempted with a broad range of police, museum and library administrators, lawyers, national governments, police and, as a last resort, military forces and the co-operation of local communities. When all these work together there is a much better chance of preventing criminal activity.

In these seven different ways outlined in the preceding sections, UNESCO has had a considerable impact on criminal law, national and international. However, it is not an instrument for the enforcement of penal law: that has to be done by other bodies. There are now international courts, which can deal with certain criminal offences and there are national courts, which will apply penalties to criminals in accordance with treaty obligations between States. However, it will be readily understood that there is still much work to be done.

34 For a much fuller discussion on the development and use of this term in national and international law see Prott and O'Keefe (n 13) 826-33.

35 ICTY (n 11).

Chapter 9

Difficulties in Investigating Art Crime and Recovering Its Proceeds: An International Perspective

Patrick J. O'Keefe

Art crime, in the sense of theft and smuggling or illicit trafficking, is one of the world's major international crime problems. It is impossible to say just how large a problem it is. Statistics are patchy and unreliable. Most authorities do not distinguish crimes involving art from other crimes, for example, by recording art theft national statistics along with all other kinds of theft. Theft of cultural objects from archaeological sites is, for the most part, clandestine and unrecorded. Nevertheless, what statistics there are, coupled with the views of experienced enforcement authorities, indicate a large and serious problem of world-wide proportions.

That being said, there are few examples of legal proceedings for this crime and particularly few successful ones. There are a number of possible reasons. One is that persons caught in possession of cultural objects are often willing to return them in order to avoid adverse publicity arising from legal action. A second is that the crime may not be reported or, if reported, there is no follow up. A third, and probably the most significant problem, is the difficulties in conducting investigations and prosecution of such crimes when there is an international element.

Secrecy in the Art Trade

Secrecy is endemic in the art trade. Where they can, dealers keep secret the details of those they buy from and those who purchase from them. Auctioneers act in the same way. Unless compelled, they will not reveal the details of those who consigned objects for sale, nor the identity of the buyers. They will avoid legal proceedings if at all possible as these would require making known details of transactions in the object; details that would become public knowledge once the court case commenced. A dealer or auctioneer who handles stolen objects may well be charged with criminal offences. This will attract adverse publicity and discourage potential buyers and sellers. A claim for recovery not of a criminal nature will have the same effect. The dealer or auction house may well consider it best to forego any profit and return the object to the person who presented it. Where there is no hope of recovering any money already paid, the dealer may be able to claim under an insurance policy.

A desire for secrecy will be affected by Article 10(a) of the Convention on the Means of Prohibiting and Preventing the Illicit Import, Export and Transfer of Ownership of Cultural Property 1970 (1970 Convention). It requires States Parties[1] to oblige dealers 'to maintain a register recording the origin of each item of cultural property, names and addresses of the supplier, description and price of each item sold'. This only partly covers the issue of secrecy. For example, it is not necessary to record details of the purchaser. Nor does the register have to be a public document. Indeed, there is nothing in the Article about who is to have access to it. However, the State Party is to impose 'penal or administrative sanctions' for failure to properly maintain the register. This necessarily implies that the register is to be inspected and, through this, details of any suspicious transaction revealed.

Lack of Action

Police or Customs may seize an object on suspicion that it has been stolen or unlawfully exported from another country. They may be able to identify where it originated. However, their efforts will be for naught if the owner refuses to take any action.

A State may appear as owner of a stolen or smuggled object taken from a State collection or clandestinely from an archaeological site. A private collector whether an individual, a museum or a commercial company, may have had part of a collection stolen. An insurance company may appear as owner, having paid out the victim of a theft. The collector or insurance company may pursue the matter personally – at considerable cost – or request the State of which they are citizens to take up the issue on their behalf. The last means is that this State, through diplomatic channels, can request authorities in the State where the object has been found to seize and return it. But many States have very small cultural administrations. Their police and Customs are not specifically trained in procedures for recovery of property from another country. In these circumstances, unless the cultural object is of particular significance, the State may well be hesitant to take the matter further.

It is for the requested State to decide how to proceed. This will be influenced by its own legal system. It may decide to seize the object and launch a criminal prosecution, or it may commence proceedings for recovery under forfeiture rules. Criminal prosecutions are rare as in many cases the person currently holding the object is not the thief and may well not know it was stolen. Also, if the standard of proof for a criminal prosecution is higher than that for civil proceedings, the local authorities may prefer the possibly greater certainty of the latter.

1 As at 7 June 2013 there were 123 States Party to this Convention.

Taking action may involve an element of embarrassment. A museum or other collection may be reluctant to acknowledge that its security has been breached and an object stolen. Donors might be frightened away if they thought that institutional security would not be able to protect their gifts. Another possible source of embarrassment could be the complicity of officials in the theft and/or illicit export. This is not unknown and, if those officials are the ones making the decision whether or not to proceed to recover the object, they are unlikely to take positive action.

Politics will also play a role in the decision making. For example, a State may be reluctant to take any moves to recover a cultural object because it might interfere with relations between the two countries. There is an old saying that 'Our relations are so good we don't want to do anything to damage them' or 'Our relations are so bad that we don't want to do anything to make them worse.' Internal politics can also be significant. An early example of this is provided by the Afo-A-Kom – a wooden statue closely associated with the hereditary ruler of the Kom, a tribal people in the Republic of Cameroon. In 1973 it was found to be held by a dealer in the United States of America, allegedly having been stolen from the Kom in 1966. After some argument involving the dealer and various experts, it was returned to the Kom. However, the Government of Cameroon was initially somewhat reluctant to have it back as it reinforced tribal solidarity at a time when the authorities were trying to form a national identity.[2]

When the Canadian authorities seized textiles they believed were unlawfully exported from Peru and Bolivia, it had them examined by an expert who ruled they were 'cultural property' as defined by both countries. However, the Government of Peru decided it did not want to proceed with the case. It was only after direct intervention by experts from Bolivia who had examined the textiles that Peru changed its mind and agreed to send the witnesses the Canadian authorities needed to build a case. But even then their support was lukewarm.

The late arrival of Peru's witnesses, the inability of one of the witnesses to speak English and the absence of English translations of Peruvian law severely hindered the prosecution of the case.[3]

The Search for Information

On the other hand, the owner might well want to recover the stolen cultural object. However, if a stolen object is easily transportable, it can be out of the

---

2 John Henry Merryman and Albert E. Elsen, *Law, Ethics and the Visual Arts* (3rd edn, Kluwer Law International 1998) 202; Eugenia Shanklin, 'The Odyssey of the Afo-a-Kom' (1990) 23 *African Arts* 62.

3 David A. Walden, 'Canada's Cultural Property Export and Import Act: The Experience of Protecting Cultural Property' (1995) Special Issue *University of British Columbia Law Review* 203, 212.

country and on the other side of the world in a few hours. Finding its location is extremely difficult. Organizations such as the Art Loss Register and Interpol[4] can assist but both these are limited in their coverage. Trade publications may also help. If a number of archaeological objects have been taken from sites within a country it could seek to have the International Council of Museums (ICOM) issue a 'Red List'. These 'classify the endangered categories of archaeological objects or works of art in the most vulnerable areas of the world, in order to prevent them being sold or illegally exported'.[5] But even these sources are of little value if the owner does not know about them. For this reason, UNESCO runs training seminars on a regular basis in various parts of the world. These introduce government officials, museum staff and others to the different means that can help locate stolen material.

But even with knowledge of these institutions, it will be difficult to locate an object. For this reason, the UNIDROIT Convention on Stolen or Illegally Exported Cultural Objects 1995 provides special rules for when a claim to such objects may be brought. The basic rule for stolen objects is that a 'claim for restitution shall be brought within a period of three years from the time when the claimant knew the location of the cultural object and the identity of its possessor, and in any case within a period of fifty years from the time of the theft' (Article 3). Special rules are set out for particular objects such as those from a public collection. The purpose of these rules is to give the claimant an opportunity to locate the object, ask for its return and, if refused, prepare for legal proceedings.

Some objects are stopped at Customs. For example, Customs inspect containers as they come off the ship or plane but this is only done as a spot check or where there is specific information. Many objects will be allowed to enter a country but this does not always mean that the importer is safe. Information may become known to the authorities at a later date; information which results in seizure of the object. For example, the holder of the object may offer it for sale by auction or send it to an expert for conservation. The object is recognized and the authorities notified.

An example of the latter set of circumstances occurred in England in 1994. Papyri had been delivered to the Department of Egyptian Antiquities at the British Museum for translation and assessment. A colleague of the person doing the work recognized them as ones he himself had discovered and had last seen in an Egyptian storeroom. The police were notified and investigated the person who had sent the papyri. They found that this person had a large estate on the grounds of which was a cottage that had been occupied by a person, Tokeley-Parry, who had reported the burglary in 1993 of an Egyptian stone head. The estate and Tokeley-

4 Both discussed in this volume.

5 ICOM – The World Museum Community at <http://www.google.com.au/#hl=en&gs_nf=1&cp=13&gs_id=14&xhr=t&q=icom+red+list&pf=p&output=search&sclient=psy-ab&oq=icom+red+list&aq=0&aqi=g2g-K2&aql=&gs_l=&pbx=1&bav=on.2,or.r_gc.r_pw.r_qf.,cf.osb&fp=df34c9deb5a08d34&biw=1440&bih=661> accessed 6 June 2013.

Parry's new home were raided. A large number of antiquities and records were discovered.[6] Tokeley-Parry eventually admitted to having smuggled some 2000 antiquities out of Egypt. In 1997 he was found guilty on two counts of dishonestly handling antiquities and sentenced to six years imprisonment of which he served three.[7]

The limited ability of Customs to detect cultural objects at entry is recognized in the Australian Protection of Movable Cultural Heritage Act 1986. An object is liable to forfeiture if it is imported into Australia; if it is a protected object of a foreign country and if its export was prohibited by a law of that country relating to cultural property.[8] A person who, knowing these facts, goes ahead and imports the object, is guilty of an offence punishable by gaol or a fine. The object is liable to forfeiture which means that it does not have to be seized by Customs at the border but may be taken at a later time when its whereabouts become known.

A hindrance to the search for information is the lack of communication within a police force and, where two or more countries are involved, between the different police organizations. This was exemplified in the case of Stéphane Breitwieser who, for eight or so years, stole works of art from museums, castles and churches in France, Switzerland, Denmark, Belgium, Germany and the Netherlands.[9] That he was able to evade capture for so long resulted in part from the fact that the police in these various countries did not provide each other with information they individually held. For example, for three weeks in 1996, the French police tracked a series of 14 similar thefts across France from west to east. These implicated Breitwieser and his girlfriend, but the trail disappeared when they moved into Switzerland. The Swiss police were not notified and he continued his career in that country.

Although Stéphane had stolen from all over Switzerland, these crimes were never combined in one list until the formal inquiry began when he was in custody. Had there been a central list, the scale and similarity of the *modus operandi* might have led to earlier investigations. One of the more worrying aspects of Noce's account is the obviously poor co-operation between the different judicial and prosecutorial services, both within and between the states affected.[10]

When this situation can arise in a relatively well organized and homogenous part of the world such as continental Europe, it is even more likely to occur in areas of the world without these characteristics.

6 Facts from Peter Watson, 'The Investigation of Frederick Schultz' (2002) 10 *Culture Without Context: The Newsletter of the Illicit Antiquities Research Centre* 21.

7 *R v Tokeley-Parry* [1999] Crim L R 578.

8 Section 14.

9 His career is described in Vincent Noce, *La Collection Egoiste* (J C Lattès 2005).

10 Lyndel V. Prott, 'Book review: Vincent Noce, *La Collection Egoiste*' (2006) 13 *International Journal of Cultural Property* 115, 118.

Identification

Identification of suspect art can be difficult. For example, if authorities are going to seize objects, they must know which fall within the powers they have been given. But police and Customs officials usually have little knowledge of what constitutes a cultural object. The Canadian case of *R v Yorke*[11] concerned textiles from Bolivia, which, it was alleged, entered Canada with false documentation. Police and Customs officials were sent to seize textiles from Yorke's house. What happened then was explained by the court at his trial.

> During this tour [of Yorke's house], which lasted approximately five to ten minutes, Sergeant White encountered items and would ask the accused questions about their points of origin and their value. As a result of the statements made to Sergeant White on the tour, he decided to seize the items. It is clear from the evidence of Sergeant White and Customs Officers Edwards and Melanson that the accused was with them the entire time and that he explained things to them. His explanations were given as a direct result of questions being put to him by Sergeant White and the questions related to the items being seized and what they were.[12]

Eventually, 6000 textiles were seized. Of these, it was found that 474 were covered by the charge and only 66 were put in evidence.

Identifying the stolen or smuggled cultural object can be difficult but is essential for a successful prosecution and recovery. It is particularly difficult in the case of antiquities taken from an archaeological site. Unless the objects come from a store-house and have already been recorded, no one will know anything about them apart from the person who took them. The claimant will have to prove that they actually did come from a named site or country.

The case *Attorney-General of New Zealand v Ortiz*[13] concerned a Maori carving that had once formed the end wall of a traditional store-house or *pataka* in the Taranaki region of New Zealand. Fearing attack from a neighbouring tribe the owners had buried the carvings in a swamp around 1820. They were defeated and driven off the land although they kept alive the knowledge of where the carvings were located. A person of Maori descent dug them up and sold them in 1972 to an English dealer who took them from New Zealand without an export permit. They were offered for sale at Sotheby's in London in 1978. The New Zealand

11 (1992) 112 NSR (2d) 240; (1992) 115 NSR (2d) 426; (1993) 125 NSR (2d) 238; (1998) 166 NSR (2d) 130; the case is discussed at length in Patrick J. O'Keefe, *Commentary on the 1970 UNESCO Convention* (2nd edn, Institute of Art and Law 2007) 152.

12 (1992) 115 NSR (2d) 426, 251. The Court held that the search and seizure were unreasonable and violated Yorke's rights under the Canadian Charter of Rights and Freedoms.

13 [1982] 1 QB 349; [1982] 3 WLR 571 (CA); [1983] 2 WLR 809 (HL).

Government at this stage had no knowledge the carvings had left the country. However, a television news broadcast in New Zealand showed some of the objects included in the forthcoming sale. This was viewed by a resident of Taranaki who thought the carvings were identical to ones he had seen in a neighbour's garage some six years before. At a social event a few days later he mentioned this to the Director of the Taranaki Museum who contacted a colleague at the National Museum in Wellington who, in turn, brought it to the attention of the Department of Internal Affairs. An auction catalogue was obtained. The excavator of the carvings was questioned and stated that the ones illustrated in the catalogue were the ones he had excavated. This was confirmed by photographs he had taken at the time. Particularly significant was a small gouge mark made by his spade and visible on the images.[14]

In the case *Government of Peru v Johnson*,[15] the plaintiff alleged that it was the owner of antiquities that had been seized from Johnson and others by the United States Customs Service. There was no direct evidence that any of the objects came from Peru. That country's foremost archaeologist in pre-Columbian antiquities gave evidence that each of the objects was of Peruvian style and culture. However, he admitted that that culture spanned not only Peru but also parts of Bolivia and Ecuador. The Court commented: 'In some instances, he admitted that an item may have come from Ecuador or Colombia or Mexico or even Polynesia…'.[16] In these circumstances, the court felt it had no option but to reject the claim by Peru as unproven.

A very different outcome was reached in the English case of *Bumper Development Corporation v Commissioner of Police.*[17] In this case the London Metropolitan Police had gone to the British Museum on a tip-off that work was being done privately in its conservation laboratory on a Shiva Nataraja – a 12th-century statue of the Hindu God Shiva, depicting him in a dancing position surrounded by a circle of flame. The police believed this had been stolen from a Swiss collector. The statue was seized but shortly afterwards Bumper caused a writ to be issued against the police seeking its recovery. India, having been notified of the seizure, wrote to the police alleging the Shiva Nataraja had been stolen from land belonging to a ruined temple in the Indian state of Tamil Nadu. India demanded its return. The police interpleaded before the English court seeking directions. In subsequent legal proceedings, it was alleged that the statue had been excavated as one of a suite of statues in the grounds of the temple by a cowherd seeking mud to build a shelter for his cow. Certainly there was evidence

---

14 These facts are taken from an article written by the person responsible at the time for cultural matters within the New Zealand Department of Home Affairs: Robert R. Cater, 'The Taranaki Panels – A Case-Study in the Recovery of Cultural Heritage' (1982) 34 *Museum* 256.

15 712 F Supp 810 (1989).

16 At 812.

17 [1991] 1 WLR 1362.

that the suite had been dug up, but was the Shiva Nataraja seized in London the same as that excavated in Tamil Nadu? The claimants, led by the Government of India, had to prove this to the satisfaction of the English High Court. The judge was not prepared to accept solely the evidence of the man who found it and those he sold it to (the trail of the statue that had been found in Tamil Nadu petered out in Madras). In fact he found that the finder had, under Indian law, stolen the statue. Evidence was given on a number of points: stylistic resemblance between the one in London and others from the excavation; termite tracks found on the entire suite; scientific analysis of soil attached to the statues; the metal composition of the statues. Of these stylistic resemblance most influenced the judge.

> 'I am satisfied ... that stylistically the two bronzes are a pair ... Metallurgy I have discarded, but the termite runs, the fragments of brick and the similarity in colour of the soil brushed from the idols all strengthen the connection between the Nataraja and Pathur [the identification given to the one found in India]. In size and quality it fits the temple ...'[18]

The court was convinced that the Shiva Nataraja found in Tamil Nadu was that taken by the police in London.

One particular area in which identification has been pursued systematically as a matter of policy is that of Holocaust materials. These consist of objects taken, stolen, or looted by the Nazis during the period 1933 to 1945. At the end of World War II, there was a major effort to return such materials to their owners but a lot had simply disappeared. With the rise of the Cold War with its own set of problems, much of what had happened was forgotten. A generation of museum curators and collectors came into being with no detailed knowledge of the history of the art world during World War II. However, beginning in the early 1990s, events such as the discovery in Russia of objects looted from German museums and a series of books[19] brought the topic back to centre stage for museum staffs and cultural administrations. In 1998 the Washington Conference on Holocaust Era Assets was held and adopted the 15 Washington Conference Principles on Nazi-Confiscated Art. Chief among these were: priority be given to identifying non-restituted art; to facilitate this, records and archives should be opened; encouragement be given to those who lost art to make claims and a fair and just solution be sought to claims even though facts and circumstances might be lacking. The full Parliamentary Assembly of the Council of Europe adopted a Resolution on Looted Jewish Cultural Property on 4 November 1999. Copies of this were distributed to the Parliaments of all Member States in February 2000. Major meetings were then

18 From the transcript of the unpublished judgment of Kennedy J., Queens Bench Division 144.

19 The seminal work was Lynn H. Nicholas, *The Rape of Europa* (Alfred A. Knopf 1994).

held in Vilnius, Lithuania, 2000, and Terezin, Czech Republic, 2009, both of which urged further provenance research.[20]

In the United Kingdom, the results of systematic provenance research for the years 1933-1945 in each national museum, gallery or library were made publicly available on the INTERNET at the end of February 2000. There were 350 objects in national museums with doubtful provenance for the relevant period and many more without any known provenance. Between 1998 and July 2006, 22 works in American Museum collections had been identified as stolen by the Nazis.[21] On the other hand, the Art Loss Register lists 70,000 works lost before and during the war that are still being sought by the owners. At the Terezin meeting, two organizations – the Conference on Jewish Material Claims Against Germany and the World Jewish Restitution Organization – presented a joint paper indicating that only four countries have made major progress towards implementing the Washington Conference Principles.[22] It will be obvious that searching for Holocaust era looted art is no easy task. The available databases are few and seem to only partially cover what is a potentially large number of objects.

But even if, for example, a painting is recognized, a claim will have to be established. In many cases there will be little evidence available. For example, the first matter the British Spoliation Advisory Panel had to investigate involved a painting displayed in the Tate Gallery in London. The claimant recollected it hanging on the wall of the dining room in his parent's house in Düsseldorf before World War II. His mother had sold it to obtain food during the war. There was also a negative of the painting found in his mother's possession that dated to the 1930s. The Panel was prepared to accept that the painting had been owned by the claimant's family. On the other hand, the Hirshhorn Museum and Sculpture Garden in Washington once had a demand made for the return of a small sculpture supposedly looted during the war. The Museum's records did not place the sculpture beyond 1957 although it was thought to have been in an art gallery in Liechtenstein before that date. A request for further details went unanswered. Some years later the Museum established that the sculpture had been in a single private collection in England from the mid-1920s to the 1950s.[23]

---

20 Provenance research is a specialized activity requiring knowledge of many different areas. For example, there are training courses such as the Provenance Research Training Program (PRTP), a project of the European Shoah Legacy Institute; see at <http://www.culturalheritagelaw.org/events?eventId=502442&EventViewMode=EventDetails> accessed 12 May 2012.

21 Association of Art Museums Directors – The Monuments Men at <www.monumentsmenfoundation.org/user_docs/aamd_letter.pdf> accessed 6 June 2013.

22 Holocaust-Era Looted Art – Conference on Jewish Material Claims at <http://www.claimscon.org/forms/prague/looted-art.pdf> accessed 12 May 2012.

23 Stephen E. Weil, 'The American Legal Response to the Problem of Holocaust Art' (1999) 4 *Art Antiquity and Law* 285.

In most legal actions it is for the claimant or the prosecutor to prove the facts of his or her case. Some would wish this principle reversed where Holocaust material is the subject matter. For example, at the Terezin meeting, the Conference on Jewish Material Claims Against Germany together with the World Jewish Restitution Organization proposed the

- Sharing of evidence by both the current possessor and the claimant;
- Presumption of confiscation in favour of the claimant (the onus is on the later owner to rebut this presumption);
- Relaxed standards of evidence for the original owner;
- The burden of proof should not rest only on the claimant; the present possessor has also to prove the rightfulness of his possession.[24]

On the other hand, Kirk Varnedoe, Chief Curator of Painting and Sculpture at the Museum of Modern Art in New York, warns:

> It seems so clear-cut morally and ethically as to exceed mere legalisms. And that, I must say, is one of the things I have found most dangerous about the current debate. It is the sudden disaffection with the processes of law and the feeling that the moral claim of this issue itself is so imperative as to demand swifter justice and faster motion than can be provided for by the legal mechanisms at our disposal. These mechanisms are cumbersome, they are slow, they are tiresome, they're uncertain, and therefore they are inadequate for this task. But down that path lies significant danger, it seems to me.[25]

Recognition and/or Enforcement of Title

When an art object is stolen and identified in a foreign country, the court where proceedings for prosecution or recovery are brought will normally accept ownership as established by the rules of the home State. However, there is one situation where there has been debate and controversy. Some 41 States have legislation purportedly to the effect that they are the owners of undiscovered cultural objects buried in the subsoil within their jurisdiction. It is a matter for the State where legal proceedings are brought whether that claim is recognized or not. The issue is complicated by the fact that in many cases the law putting forth this claim is unclear.

---

24 Holocaust-Era Looted Art – Conference on Jewish Material Claims at <http://www.claimscon.org/forms/prague/looted-art.pdf> accessed 12 May 2012.

25 Kirk Varnedoe, 'Art, Law, and Ethics: Theory and Practice' (1999/2000) (Winter) *IFAR Journal* 14, 19.

A case in point is the English Court of Appeal decision in *Islamic Republic of Iran v Barakat Galleries*.[26] Iran alleged that it was the owner of 18 carved jars, bowls and cups said to date from 3000BC to 2000BC and originating from recent excavations in the Jiroft region of Iran. The excavations were unauthorized and unlawful under the law of Iran. Barakat had the antiquities in its possession claiming to have purchased them in France, Germany and Switzerland. The case involved two preliminary issues: whether Iran had title to the antiquities and if so by what means; secondly, if the court should recognize and/or enforce any such Iranian title. The trial judge found against Iran on both points. The Court of Appeal examined the Iranian law in detail and concluded that Iran was the owner of the antiquities even though it had never possessed them. But this required an extensive investigation of various pieces of Iranian legislation and an appeal to a higher court with its attendant costs.

But the case of *Iran v Barakat* is only one where the claim of state ownership was at issue.[27] Often legislation dealing with undiscovered antiquities is old and was never designed to deal with claims for return being made in foreign courts. Seeing the problems involved, many States will have received advice that it is not worthwhile taking legal proceedings.

Iran's claim in the Barakat case was based on the civil process of conversion,[28] not a criminal procedure. In the Common Law, the latter requires a higher standard of proof than the former. The case *United States v McClain* concerned antiquities smuggled from Mexico to the United States of America. The proceedings were under the National Stolen Property Act, but to be successful the prosecutors had to prove Mexico had unequivocally claimed ownership of the antiquities. It was found that Mexico had not done this till 1972 and it was not known when the antiquities had been exported. The Court considered that the Mexican law prior to 1972 was too vague in relation to the type of antiquities at issue to form the basis of criminal liability in the United States:

> It may well be, as testified so emphatically by most of the Mexican witnesses, that Mexico has considered itself the owner of all pre-Columbian artifacts for almost 100 years. If so, however, it has not expressed that view with sufficient clarity to survive translation into terms understandable by and binding upon American citizens.[29]

Against this background, UNESCO and UNIDROIT have promoted a set of Model Provisions on State Ownership of Undiscovered Cultural Objects. States are free to adopt these if they so desire and incorporate them in their law.

26 [2007] EWCA Civ 1374.

27 *United States v Schultz* (178 F. Supp.2d 445; 333 F.2d 393) is another important case.

28 In the Common Law, conversion is a tort committed when a person deals in chattels not belonging to him so as to deprive the owner of their use and possession.

29 *United States v McClain* 593 F2d 658 (1979) 670.

The Model Provisions cannot answer all questions raised by the legal status of undiscovered cultural objects. They are designed to be applied, adapted and supplemented where necessary by the issuance of regulations providing further details. They can either supplement or replace the relevant existing provisions to strengthen enforcement or to fill a gap.[30]

Provision 3 of the Model Provisions states:

> Undiscovered cultural objects are owned by the State, provided there is no prior existing ownership.

and number 4:

> Cultural objects excavated contrary to the law or licitly excavated but illicitly retained are deemed to be stolen objects.

These two provisions are simple and, if implemented exactly as set out in the Model Provisions, would provide a clear rule for establishing State ownership of undiscovered cultural objects in foreign jurisdictions.

Other Practical Problems

There are many other problems in investigating and prosecuting art crime when there is an international perspective. Some of these can also arise when the crime has purely national concerns. But an international element can heighten the difficulties and introduce new complexities.

Once objects are seized they must be stored. This can be difficult. For example, they may need to be kept at certain temperatures or levels of light. Customs and police have often relied on the good will of museums to provide appropriate storage conditions. This has been seen as part of the fight by museums against theft and illicit traffic. But the cost of storage for museums has risen greatly. Police and Customs could offer payment, but many museums have little space even for their own collections.

It is often difficult to predict how long storage facilities will be needed. The museum could be looking at years as the investigative phase is completed and then argument starts over responsibility for what has happened. If there are court proceedings there may be appeals. The *Yorke* case in Canada began in 1988 with seizure of the textiles but did not end till 2002 when some of the textiles were returned.

The *Yorke* case illustrates the type of problem that a museum or other holding institution could face. Some time after the textiles were seized, they were found

---

30 The Model Provisions and explanatory guidelines are reproduced in (2011) 16 *Uniform Law Review* 1024.

to be infested with moths. Various methods such as vacuuming and fumigation were tried to bring the infestation under control but they did not work. Eventually, a walk-in freezer unit had to be shipped to Halifax and the collection frozen. Technically, it would have been easier to move the textiles to a climate controlled facility in Ottawa, but the police thought the security precautions there would not meet their standards for control over evidence in a criminal proceeding.[31]

Language will create difficulties if there is more than one involved. For day-to-day operations in the police or Customs it may be possible for investigations to proceed even though the parties are not fluent in each other's language. However, when the matter advances to discussion of prosecution and legal claims both sides have to be absolutely certain of what they intend and understand. Interpreters will have to be hired to assist. Care must be taken to ensure that the interpreter is fluent in both languages. In the case *Bumper Development Corporation v Commissioner of Police* referred to above, the person who found the Shiva Nataraja, who spoke only the dialect of the village where he lived in Tamil Nadu, was brought to London to give evidence. He was subject to examination before the English High Court. However, the proceedings were two days underway when it was realized that the interpreter did not know the difference between 'ownership' and 'possession'. This was crucial to establishing the rights of the parties and so the taking of evidence had to begin again with a new interpreter leading to greatly increased costs.

Also significant will be the services of a translator. When allegations are made and claims introduced, documents will have to be translated from one language to the other. Translation is no easy task. When a translation is made, it should be read by a native speaker of that tongue before being put to official use to make sure that it is idiomatic.

Cultural differences will also play a role. Inhabitants of some countries have a much more casual approach to deadlines than those of others. While some work a full period of hours others frequently break for coffee or a cigarette. Attitudes to authority also differ. In some societies it would be rare for a subordinate to question a superior whereas in others it is regarded as the norm. Such differences can lead to confrontation unless both sides are aware of the issues and prepared to deal with them.

Once legal issues are raised there is the possibility of significant misunderstanding. There can be major differences in how different legal systems handle the same problem. An owner who makes a complaint in a foreign jurisdiction must expect procedures to be different from those in his or her own. The police will most likely handle the complaint in a different way. The public administration will be differently organized and the legal process will make different demands. For example, the claimant will have to be aware of the structure of government departments and where the real power lies to further his or her claim. If a lawyer is necessary, and most cases will require this even if legal proceedings are not taken,

31 Walden (n 3) 216.

care is needed to choose one with expertise in the subject. The law governing recovery actions is highly complex and a legal adviser must not only be aware of the national legal system in which he or she works but also that of the claimant and the international legal system in general. For example, if an object has been clandestinely excavated in State A and found in State B, it will be necessary to establish who the owner is under the law of State A. That State may have legislation claiming all undiscovered antiquities as state property. Will this claim of ownership be recognized in the courts of State B? Are there international instruments that can be used in the courts of State B to bolster A's claim? The person making the claim may not be experienced in such matters. For example, he or she may be a museum director with no previous involvement in international claims for objects stolen from their collections. They may well have had little contact with lawyers at all. Some of the demands of foreign lawyers may seem strange, such as for copies of old laws and detailed clarification of exactly who owns the museum and who has the power to sue. Here the director has to be able to trust the foreign lawyer and work to supply what is requested. It must be remembered that any change in instructions to the lawyer will almost certainly mean further costs.

It is essential that all concerned know the effect of any international legal instruments that are applicable. Those usually relevant are the two Protocols (1954 and 1999) to The Hague Convention on the Protection of Cultural Property in the Event of Armed Conflict 1954; the Convention on the Means of Prohibiting and Preventing the Illicit Import, Export and Transfer of Ownership of Cultural Property 1970 and the UNIDROIT Convention on Stolen or Illegally Exported Cultural Objects 1995. States party to these Conventions must apply them if the facts fall within their coverage but sometimes this is not done.

That occurred in The Netherlands in the case *Autocephalous Greek Orthodox Church in Cyprus v Lans*.[32] In 1998, the Church commenced legal proceedings in Rotterdam claiming return of four icons taken from the Antiphonitis church in occupied Northern Cyprus sometime after 1974. In the 1970s, Lans had bought the icons from a dealer in the Netherlands. The Church argued that the First Protocol to the Hague Convention 1954 applied and that under this Lans could not become the owner of the icons even if he had acted in good faith. Lans argued that, although the Netherlands had ratified the Protocol in 1958, this had never been implemented into local Dutch law. The Court held that the Protocol was not a provision with binding force upon any individual legal person in the Netherlands but was directed at States Parties. Therefore, Lans' rights under normal Dutch law were not affected. The Protocol has now been implemented into Dutch law by legislation.

---

32 Unreported decision of the District Court of Rotterdam, 4 February 1999. The case is discussed in more detail in Stephan Matyk, 'The Restitution of Cultural Objects and the Question of Giving Direct Effect to the Protocol to the Hague Convention for the Protection of Cultural Property in the Event of Armed Conflict 1954' (2009) 9 *International Journal of Cultural Property* 341.

It is appropriate here to make brief mention of when the instruments might be relevant.[33] The Protocols come into play when cultural objects as defined in the 1954 Convention are removed from occupied territory. The 1970 Convention applies specifically to objects stolen within the terms of Article 7; namely, 'from a museum or a religious or secular public monument or similar institution', provided they have been inventoried. States are required to prohibit their import and, at the request of the State Party of origin, 'take appropriate steps to return any such cultural property imported after the entry into force of this Convention in both States concerned'. There is also Article 3 which reads:

> The import, export or transfer of ownership of cultural property effected contrary to the provisions adopted under this Convention by the States Parties thereto, shall be illicit.

Article 3 should be taken as requiring States Parties to render 'illicit' in their national law imports, which are 'illicit' exports from another State. Exports are 'illicit' if the removal of the objects concerned from the territory of the State is prohibited. The UNIDROIT Convention on Stolen or Illegally Exported Cultural Objects 1995 states bluntly that '[t]he possessor of a cultural object which has been stolen shall return it'.[34] In respect of cultural objects unlawfully removed from the territory of a State Party (that is, smuggled), that State may request 'the court or other competent authority of another Contracting State' to order the return of that object.[35]

Cost will be a major factor in deciding whether to commence any process of recovery or prosecution in a foreign country. First, there will be the direct cost of hiring lawyers, translators, interpreters and other experts. For example, in the case *Bumper Development Corporation v Commissioner of Police*, experts were needed to provide evidence on the various scientific aspects proving the identity of the Shiva Nataraja. Experts usually charge high fees and will require travel and accommodation expenses. They may need compensation for income foregone on other activities.

The possibility of appeals also has to be considered as these will increase the legal costs enormously. Moreover, in certain countries such as England and Australia, if a person loses a court case, that person will usually be required to pay the costs of the other side as well. In *Bumper Development Corporation v Commissioner of Police*, the costs of the plaintiffs were calculated to amount to £303,489.67 and Bumper Development Corporation was ordered to pay this sum. It refused to do so. India and the other plaintiffs in the English action commenced

33 The text of these instruments and an analysis of each one can be found in Patrick J. O'Keefe and Lyndel V. Prott (eds), *Cultural Heritage Conventions and Other Instruments: A Compendium with Commentaries* (Institute of Art and Law 2011).

34 Article 3.

35 Article 5.

legal proceedings claiming these costs and interest in the courts of Alberta – where the company was incorporated. Bumper Development claimed that the English judgment was obtained through fraud. At the time of the proceedings in Alberta interest on the costs came to an additional £206,574.84. The Alberta court rejected Bumper Development's claim and ordered payment of the costs plus interest less a small amount the English courts had awarded Bumper.[36]

But direct costs are only part of what the investigation and prosecution of art crime will cost. Those thinking of pursuing such actions also have to take into account the time that officials will have to devote to running the necessary investigations and preparing for the proceedings. Many countries and collectors have small staffs devoted to management of collections and archaeological sites. They will have to prepare whatever documentation is required and give evidence in conjunction with, and under the guidance of, the legal authorities.

If the object is to be returned to the successful claimant, there will be further costs. It will have to be prepared for travel, often with special packaging. Insurance may well be advisable. Then there will be the cost of transport itself. The 1970 Convention requires a State Party that requests return of stolen cultural property under Article 7 to bear all expenses incident to the return and delivery.

Some assistance with costs may be obtained from the Fund of the Intergovernmental Committee for Promoting the Return of Cultural Property to its Countries of Origin or its Restitution in Case of Illicit Appropriation. This is administered by UNESCO. It was established in 1999 with the aim of supporting Member States in their efforts to pursue the return or restitution of cultural property and effectively fight illicit traffic in cultural property. Several aspects are specifically mentioned: the verification of cultural objects by experts, transportation, insurance costs, setting up of facilities to exhibit them in satisfactory conditions, and training of museum professionals in countries where cultural objects originate. The major problem of the Fund is that it has limited resources – in 2012 there was some €100,000 in the Fund donated by Greece.[37] Moreover, it only runs to the costs of Member States and non-State collections are not eligible to recover funds from it.

Conclusion

This chapter has emphasized the difficulties in investigating and prosecuting art crime from an international perspective. But the process should not be seen in a negative light. Anyone who wants to recover the proceeds of art crime can draw lessons on how to avoid the pitfalls. Certainly a successful prosecution or recovery

36 *Union of India v Bumper Development Corporation* 29 Alta LR (3d) 194.

37 Sixteenth Session of the Intergovernmental Committee for Promoting the Return of Cultural Property to its Countries of Origin or its Restitution in case of Illicit Appropriation at page 4; See at <http://portal.unesco.org/culture/en/ev.php-URL_ID=40585&URL_DO=DO_TOPIC&URL_SECTION=201.html> accessed 5 November 2013.

will often be difficult. One must know what to do and anticipate the problems that can arise. But a successful action must be seen not only for its own value but as acting as a deterrent to other thefts and illicit traffic in general. That is why a badly prepared case, or a case where there is little likelihood of success so that an adverse decision is highly possible, can hurt the prospects for other claims. Commentators are able to refer to such adverse decisions to discredit the prospects of legitimate claims.

Chapter 10
Immunity from Seizure for Works of Art on Loan: The Criminal Context

Craig Forrest*

Introduction

Increasingly lenders of works of art have become reluctant to loan them to institutions in other States fearing their seizure at the behest of third-party claimants taking advantage of the change in jurisdiction brought about by the movement of the art objects.[1] Claims by third parties may arise primarily in one of two ways. First, a claimant may seek to have the art seized to enforce a judgment made against the owner. Often the claim will not be related to the work of art in question and it is treated merely as an asset for the purposes of enforcing some other claim, most often a debt settlement.[2] Secondly, and perhaps most commonly, a claimant (whether a government, company or individual) may claim to be the owner, or entitled to possession, of the work of art, and bring legal proceedings to have that ownership or possession recognized and then to take possession of the work of art.[3] This civil

* Reader and Fellow, Centre for Public, International and Comparative law, TC Beirne School of Law, University of Queensland. The author thanks Rosanna Cuppaidge for her invaluable research assistance.

1 The meanings of the terms 'art', 'works of art', 'cultural property', 'cultural objects' and 'cultural heritage' are subject to much debate, and used differently in various national and international legal instruments. The term 'works of art' will be used in this chapter for the sake of consistency with other chapters, but should be interpreted broadly to cover what can be termed 'cultural property' or 'cultural heritage'. For discussion of the meaning of these terms, see Lyndel Prott and Patrick O'Keefe, 'Cultural Heritage or Cultural Property' (1992) 1 *International Journal of Cultural Property* 307; Craig Forrest, *International Law and the Protection of Cultural Heritage* (Routledge 2010) 1-30.

2 For example, Noga SA, a Swiss company, sought to seize a collection of 54 French masterpieces belonging to the Pushkin State Museum in Moscow when on loan to the Fondation Pierre Gianadda gallery in Switzerland. The seizure was to enforce a 1997 Arbitral ward by the Arbitration Institute of the Stockholm Chamber of Commerce for US $27 million arising out of a series of contracts for the shipment of foodstuffs and fertilizers to Russia in exchange for oil. See Nout van Woudenberg, *State Immunity and Works of Art on Loan* (Martinus Nijhoff 2012) 310-14.

3 Where a State is the defendant, sovereign immunity issues arise, and are addressed through international law and individual state legislation that gives effect to such immunity.

action may be complemented by a criminal action, requiring the seizure of the art as part of a criminal investigation.

The risk of loaned works of art being subject to such seizure, it is argued, undermines the significant cultural advantages of exchanges and loan arrangements.[4] Works of art have long been cultural ambassadors between nations, fostering understanding, co-operation and comity, which has been fostered and encouraged through international law instruments, such as the Declaration of Principles of International Cooperation, the Agreement on the Importation of Educational, Scientific and Cultural Material, Agreement For Facilitating the International Circulation of Visual and Auditory Materials of an Educational, Scientific and Cultural Character, and the Recommendation Concerning the International Exchange of Cultural Property.[5] To facilitate such exchange of works of art, a number of jurisdictions have enacted immunity from seizure legislation.

Immunity from seizure legislation essentially seeks to immunize a borrowed work of art from seizure by court order or from some other legally-imposed restraint on its physical movement.[6] The extent to which immunity should apply to seizures pursuant to a criminal investigation or breach of a criminal law requires a careful balancing of interests: the direct interest of facilitating the exchange of culture by providing immunity versus the need to fully investigate crimes and to give full effect to the criminal law. The role that a particular work of art plays in a criminal matter can vary considerably. The most obvious case is where the work of art lies at the heart of the crime, such as theft of a work of art. While unlikely, the work of art may have merely been used in the commission of a crime, perhaps used as a weapon in an assault, or it may be obscene, such as qualifying as child pornography. Moreover, works of art, often of staggering value and easily transportable, may be used for money laundering or may reflect the proceeds of crime.

This chapter will not address such immunity, but see, generally, Hazel Fox, *The Law of State Immunity* (2nd edn, Oxford University Press 2008). The question of immunity of State-owned property from seizure, whilst covered by immunity from seizure legislation may also be governed by international rules on immunity of States, including the 2004 United Nations Convention on Jurisdictional Immunities of States and Their Property (not yet in force).

4 See, for example, Commonwealth of Australia, *Parliamentary Debates*, House of Representatives, 28 November 2012, 13646.

5 United Nations Educational, Scientific and Cultural Organization (UNESCO) <http://portal.unesco.org/en/ev.php-URL_ID=12025&URL_DO=DO_TOPIC&URL_SECTION=-471.html> accessed 22 May 2013.

6 Norman Palmer, 'Value, Verity, and Validation: The Interplay of Legal and Economic Factors on the Security and Mobility of Art and Antiquities' in Susanna Pettersson, Monika Hagedorn-Saude, Teijamari Jyrkkiö and Astrid Weij, *Encouraging Collections Mobility: A Way Forward for Museums in Europe* (2010) <http://www.lending-for-europe.eu/fileadmin/CM/public/handbook/Encouraging_Collections_Mobility_A4.pdf> accessed 6 July 2012.

The provision of immunity from seizure in a criminal matter clearly has an impact on a State's ability to detect, investigate and prosecute art crime. This chapter examines the manner in which a number of States in Australasia, Europe and North America have addressed this issue in their national legislation.

Stolen Works of Art

The seizure of a work of art on loan usually arises when a person claims that the art had been stolen in a foreign State, but that, as the art (and possibly the thief, or person knowingly handling the stolen object) is within the jurisdiction of the loaning State, the appropriate criminal law enforcement authorities of that State should act in accordance with its criminal law. It might also be that the criminal investigation arises in another State, but the authorities in the State in which the art is found have powers to seize it as a product of some existing co-operative arrangement between the relevant States.

Attempts to seize works of art on loan have risen dramatically in recent years and a number of high-profile cases have raised acute concerns within the international museum and art gallery sector.[7] One case, above all, has been used by the museum and gallery community to illustrate the 'threat' of seizure for a borrowing institution and to urge States to adopt wide-ranging immunity statutes. That case involved the seizure in New York of Egon Schiele's *Portrait of Wally* and, given its notoriety, it is worth a detailed discussion.[8] At the heart of the case was the scope of the New York immunity from seizure legislation, and whether it extended beyond civil seizures to include criminal seizures as well.[9]

Bondi was a Jewish art dealer in Vienna who sold her art gallery in 1938 to Friedrich Welz, a Nazi party member, following the introduction of Aryanization laws in Austria and the designation of her gallery as non-Ayrian. During negotiations for the sale of the gallery, Bondi handed over a painting by Egon Schiele called *Portrait of Wally*, which she had as part of her private collection, to Welz. In these circumstances the voluntariness of the sale was questionable and the evidence supported the contention that the portrait was taken against Bondi's will.[10] Given the great number of works recovered at the end of the war, and the difficulties in assessing ownership, this painting, one amongst many seized by United States forces, was transferred to the Austrian government and then, incorrectly assumed to be part of another collection, was sold to the Austrian National Gallery. Bondi,

7 See generally van Woudenberg (n 2).

8 *People v Museum of Modern Art*, 93 NY. 2d 729; 719 N.E.2d 897 (N.Y. 1999).

9 See David Wissbroecker, 'Six Klimts, A Picasso and A Schiele: Recent Litigation Attempts to Recover Nazi Stolen Art' (2004) 14 *DePaul Journal of Arts and Entertainment* 39.

10 *United States v Portrait of Wally*, 663 F. Supp. 2d 232, 238, 252-9 (S.D.N.Y. 2009).

who had fled to London, attempted to recover the painting, and sought assistance from Dr Rudolph Leopold, an Austrian collector of Schiele paintings. However, without reference to Bondi's claim, Leopold acquired the painting on his own behalf by concluding an exchange with the National Gallery, exchanging one of his Schiele paintings for the *Portrait of Wally*. He subsequently refused to consider Bondi's claim.[11] In 1994 the Leopold Museum was established to house the collection and in 1997 it agreed to loan a number of paintings, including the *Portrait of Wally,* to the Museum of Modern Art in New York. When the portrait was exhibited in New York in 1998, Bondi's heirs sought to recover it.[12]

New York's Arts and Cultural Affairs Law[13] provided for automatic immunity from seizure for cultural objects loaned from foreign lenders to not-for-profit institutions in New York. Whilst the scope of this legislation was unclear at the time, it was very likely to apply to claims for possession from third parties. As such, Bondi's heirs could not have prosecuted their claim directly against the property in question as it clearly was immune from seizure. However, New York's Penal Code[14] makes it an offence to knowingly possess stolen property, and allows the court to order a third party to appear before the court and to produce specified physical evidence (*subpoena duces tecum*).[15] Such a subpoena was served on the Museum of Modern Art which directed it not to return the portrait to the Leopold Museum, as required by the loan contract. The Leopold Museum successfully challenged the seizure with the New York Court of Appeals holding that the immunity from seizure law should be read broadly to apply to both criminal and civil proceedings.[16] The subpoena, ultimately being considered a form of seizure, was prohibited by New York's immunity from seizure legislation.[17]

However, the United States Attorney's Office, on request from the United States Customs Service, immediately obtained a warrant of seizure for the painting, commencing a civil forfeiture action[18] on the basis that the portrait was stolen property and, knowing it to be so, was imported into the United States

11 *United States v Portrait of Wally*, 663 F. Supp. 2d 232, 252-9 (S.D.N.Y. 2009).

12 A second Schiele painting, *Dead City III*, was also seized at the behest of another claimant. Martha Lufkin, 'How do I sue thee? Let me count the ways' *The Art Newspaper*, November 1999.

13 *Arts and Cultural Affairs Law* s 12.03.

14 Penal Code (New York) article 165.54 (Criminal Possession of Stolen Property).

15 van Woudenberg (n 2) 185.

16 *People v Museum of Modern Art*, 93 NY. 2d 729; 719 N.E.2d 897 (N.Y. 1999).

17 The second Schiele painting, *Dead City III*, was also released, and no further action was taken in respect of that painting as the United States Attorney's office found no probable cause as to the illegality to support its seizure. For a criticism of this case, see Ronald B. Kowalczyk, 'Section 22.03 of the New York Arts and Cultural Affairs Law: Civil by Association' (2001) 10 *International Journal of Cultural Property* 95.

18 18 U.S.C. s 545 (Smuggling Goods into the United States); 19 U.S.C. s 1595(a) and (c) (Forfeitures and other Penalties) and 22 U.S.C. s 401(A) (Illegal Exportation of War Materials).

contrary to the federal National Stolen Property Act.[19] The Museum of Modern Art had not sought immunity pursuant to the federal Immunity from Seizure Act,[20] which, unlike the New York State legislation that applied automatically, required a specific application for immunity for the particular art on loan. The case turned on whether the portrait was stolen property and whether the Leopold Museum, knowing that it was stolen, nevertheless, together with the Museum of Modern Art, imported it into the United States.[21] The court was sufficiently satisfied that the property might be considered stolen, not only in relation to the confiscation of the property by the Nazi regime, but also by the wrongful conversion of the property by Leopold.[22] Moreover, there was evidence to suggest that Leopold knew that the painting was stolen and converted property when it was imported into the United States by him pursuant to the loan agreement.[23] This was sufficient as the basis for a trial on an issue of fact, and the portrait was therefore subject to seizure pending determination at trial.[24] Days before the commencement of the trial, the claimants, the United States government, and the Leopold Museum entered into an agreement resolving the case, which included the Leopold Museum paying the claimants US $19,000,000 (reflecting the true value of the painting) and the estate releasing its claim.[25]

This lengthy litigation caused significant disquiet in the museum and art gallery community, and resulted in a number of loan cancellations to New York institutions.[26] While dealing with the thorny issue of Holocaust looted art, and

19 18 U.S.C. s 2314 (Transportation of Stolen Goods, Securities, Moneys, Fraudulent State Tax Stamps, or Articles used in Counterfeiting).

20 22 U.S.C. s 2459 (Immunity from Seizure Under Judicial Process of Cultural Objects Imported for Temporary Exhibition or Display).

21 *United States v Portrait of Wally*, 663 F. Supp. 2d 232, 251 (S.D.N.Y. 2009). In its application to terminate the action without going to trial, the Leopold Museum had claimed that the portrait was not really stolen since Bondi had handed it over to representatives of the Nazi regime when demanded, as well as asserting that the claimants did not properly represent the Bondi Estate and that the statute of limitations had expired. *United States v Portrait of Wally*, 105 F.Supp 2.d 288 (S.D.N.Y 2000). See further Susan E. Brabenec, 'The Art of Determining "Stolen Property": *United States V. Portrait of Wally A Painting by Egon Schiele*, 105 F. Supp. 2d 288 (S.D.N.Y. 2000)' (2001) 69 *University of Cincinnati Law Review* 1369.

22 *United States v Portrait of Wally*, U.S. Dist. LEXIS 6445, 71-76. (S.D.N.Y. 2002).

23 *United States v Portrait of Wally*, U.S. Dist. LEXIS 6445, 80. (S.D.N.Y. 2002).

24 *United States v Portrait of Wally*, 663 F. Supp. 2d 232, 237 (S.D.N.Y. 2009).

25 Martha Lufkin, 'Portrait of Wally battle resolved: The case that changed everything' *The Art Newspaper*, September 2010, 4.

26 See James A.R. Nafziger, Robert Kirkwood Paterson and Alison Dundes Renteln, *Cultural Law: International, Comparative and Indigenous* (Cambridge University Press 2010) 513; Yin-Shuan Lue, Polly Clark and Marion R. Fremont-Smith, 'Countering a Legal Threat to Cultural Exchanges of Works of Art: The Malewicz Case and Proposed Remedies' *The Hauser Center for Nonprofit Organizations, Harvard University*, December 2007, Working Paper No. 42, 27.

having been resolved between the parties before judicial progress could be made on this issue, it did clarify the scope of the New York immunity from seizure law, extending it to seizure of property in relation to criminal matters.[27] The application of immunity to criminal seizures was, however, unexpected by the State of New York. This limitation on the State's application of its criminal law was of such a concern that the New York statute was amended in 2000 so that immunity would only apply in relation to civil seizures. However, for many borrowing and lending institutions, this shift in the balance was unacceptable,[28] and their intervention was sufficient to subject the amendment to a sunset clause, which allowed the broader immunity to re-apply from 2002.[29] This temporary 'loss' of immunity is symptomatic of the very real difficulty in balancing the interests of institutions with those of claimants, particularly when the claimants lost possession in the most egregious of circumstances such as the Holocaust. Moreover, it also illustrates the difficulties in investigating and prosecuting art crime, including Holocaust era art crime, when immunity from seizure legislation is brought into play.

Works of Art in Other Criminal Contexts

While the focus of this chapter is on the relationship between art crime, particularly stolen works of art, and immunity from seizure legislation, the impact of the latter may be broad enough to cover a range of criminal offences. A work of art may, for example, be seized where it is evidence in a criminal matter. This might arise where a work of art is used as a weapon (a statue for example) in an assault. Works of art may also be seized when their public display constitutes an offence. This arises primarily where the display is considered obscene. In 2008, for example, a number of photographic works by artist Bill Henson, on display in a New South

---

27 In 2012, *Christ Bearing the Cross Dragged by a Rogue* (1538) by Girolamo di Romano, borrowed by the Mary Brogan Museum of Art and Science in Florida from the Pinacoteca di Brera Museum of Milan, was seized by US Department of Homeland Security. The painting was claimed by descendants of Frenerico Gentili di Giuseppe, an Italian Jew, whose collection was seized and auctioned in France in 1941. As no immunity was sought pursuant to the *Immunity from Seizure Act*, the painting was seized and subsequently handed over to the heirs as the Italian Museum failed to make any claim to the painting. See Laura Gilbert, 'Government agency raids Florida museum: A work on loan from an Italian institution is seized with aim of returning it to heirs' *The Art Newspaper*, February 2012, 5; The Telegraph 'Italian masterpiece returned to Jewish man's heirs' <http://www.telegraph.co.uk/news/worldnews/europe/italy/9213138/Italian-masterpiece-returned-to-Jewish-mans-heirs.html> accessed 1 August 2012.

28 Two lenders, for example, cancelled an agreement to loan works to the Museum of Modern Art for a Pierre Bonnard retrospective a month after the initial seizure of the *Portrait of Wally*. See Nafziger, Kirkwood Paterson and Dundes Renteln (n 26) 513; and Lue et al. (n 26) 27.

29 van Woudenberg (n 2) 163.

Wales Gallery (Australia), were seized in accordance with the *Law Enforcement (Police Powers and Responsibilities) Act 2002* (NSW), following complaints from child advocacy groups.[30] The works included photographs of naked adolescents. Similar seizures have occurred in the United States, when photographic work by Jock Sturges depicting nudists and their children was seized in San Francisco[31] and in the United Kingdom when police threatened to seize work by Tierney Gearon on display at the Saatchi Gallery which featured nude photos of her young children playing.[32]

European Perspective

While the majority of States in Europe still do not have legislation that addresses immunity for works of art on loan, this is slowly changing.[33] One of the more recent States to adopt such legislation is the United Kingdom; rather surprising given its large art market.

The Tribunals Courts and Enforcement Act (2007) and Protection of Works of Art on Loan (Publication and Provision of Information Regulations) (2008) was introduced in response to concerns from museums that an increasing number of international lenders were refusing to lend items to United Kingdom museums without a guarantee of their safe return.[34] The Act provides protection for works of art loaned from abroad and temporarily exhibited in museums and public galleries in the United Kingdom. Conditions that must be satisfied for this 'protection' include; that the object is usually kept outside the United Kingdom; that it is not owned by a person resident in the United Kingdom; that its import does not contravene a prohibition or restriction on import; and that it is brought into the United Kingdom for temporary public display by an approved museum or gallery that has complied with the publication of information about the particular work of art being exhibited.

---

30 Josephine Tovey et al., 'Henson finds support over photos' *Sydney Morning Herald* <http://www.smh.com.au/news/arts/henson-finds-support-over-photos/2008/05/23/1211183097197.html> accessed 1 August 2012, and Dan Meagher, 'Investigating "indecent, obscene or pornographic" art: lessons from the Bill Henson controversy' (2009) 14 *Media and Arts Law Review* 292.

31 David Steinberg, 'Naked Truth' *Metroactive* <http://www.metroactive.com/papers/metro/03.19.98/cover/sturges 1-9811.html> accessed 27 August 2012.

32 Alan Travis, 'Police obscenity squad raid Saatchi Gallery' *The Guardian* <http://www.guardian.co.uk/uk/2001/mar/10/childprotection.society> accessed 27 August 2012.

33 van Woudenberg (n 2), 281.

34 Anna O'Connell, 'The United Kingdom's Immunity from Seizure Legislation' (2009) 72 *Modern Law Review* 783, 791. See also Janet Ulph and Ian Smith, *The Illicit Trade in Art and Antiquities: International Recovery and Criminal and Civil Liability* (Hart Publishing 2012) 176.

The Act creates a rather complex immunity. It provides that the work of art in question is 'protected'; by which it means that 'it may not be seized or forfeited under any enactment or rule of law, with the exception that such a seizure or forfeiture is under or by virtue of an order made by a court in the United Kingdom, and the court is required to make the order under, or under provision giving effect to, a Community obligation or any international treaty'.[35] The Act goes on to define 'seizure or forfeiture' in relation to a work of art to include: taking control of the object: execution or distress; diligence or sequestration; seizure, confiscation or forfeiture, or any other measure relating to the custody or control of the object, in the course of a criminal investigation or criminal proceedings (against the owner, the museum or gallery or any other person). While extending to seizure and forfeiture in criminal investigations (except those required by the United Kingdom's community or international treaty obligations), it does not affect liability for an offence of importing, exporting or otherwise dealing with the object. While this does not prevent prosecution for offences relating to the work of art, it does prevent the exertion of any power of arrest to prevent the object from leaving the United Kingdom, and therefore has a significant impact on the investigation and prosecution of a crime.

This inclusion of immunity to seizure in criminal matters and investigations is in contrast to that taken by the first European State to adopt an immunity statute – France in 1994.[36] The adoption of this legislation followed concerns raised when descendants of Russian collectors, whose collections had been nationalized, had claimed ownership of works of art loaned to the Pompidou Centre in Paris.[37] The legislation applies only to works of art on loan from an overseas public institution and to be shown publicly in France. Importantly, the immunity applies only in civil proceedings and does not prevent seizure pursuant to a criminal investigation.

The immunity legislation of many other European States is, however, much wider. The seizure in New York of the *Portrait of Wally* on loan from the Leopold Museum in Vienna gave rise, in 1993, to an Austrian immunity statute.[38] It applies to works loaned to an Austrian federal museum, and to a number of provincial museums, by both public and private lenders, and makes inadmissible any court action seeking possession or seizure, or measures of enforcement against it. Similarly, the German law[39] applies to any judicial procedure or interim measure, allowing for a legally enforceable return guarantee to be given ensuring that the

35 Tribunals Courts and Enforcement Act (2007), s 135.

36 Law 94-679 of 8 August 1994. See van Woudenberg (n 2) 282-9.

37 Ruth Redmond-Cooper, 'Disputed Title to Loaned Works of Art: The Shuchkin Litigation' (1996) 1 *Art Antiquity and Law* 73.

38 Bundesgesetz über die vorübergehende sachliche Immunität von Kulturgut-Leihgaben zum Zweck der öffentlichen Ausstellung. See van Woudenberg (n 2) 299-305.

39 Gesetz zum Schutz deutschen Kulturgutes gegen Abwanderung 1955 as amended by Gesetz zur Umsetzung von Richtlinien der Europäischen Gemeinschaften 1998. See van Woudenberg (n 2) 289-99.

cultural property on loan is returned to the lender on an agreed fixed date. It clearly covers seizure in criminal cases. The immunity legislation of Belgium[40] also extends to seizure pursuant to a criminal matter or investigation, as does the Swiss law[41] and that of Liechtenstein,[42] Finland[43] and the Czech Republic.[44]

North American Perspective

The United States, above all, has had to deal with third-party claims to works of art loaned from abroad. The federal Immunity from Seizure Act, the first of its kind, arose in the context of uncertainty as to ownership of works of art appropriated and nationalized in the Soviet Union. When the University of Richmond proposed to loan works of art from the Soviet Union, the latter insisted on a grant of immunity from seizure as a condition to the loan in order to prevent assertions of ownership by former Soviet citizens. The *Immunity from Seizure Act* was adopted to meet this end. It provides that whenever any work of art is imported into the United States in order to be part of a temporary exhibition operated by a United States non-profit organization, and where it has been determined that the object is of cultural significance and that the temporary exhibition is in the national interest, no court in the United States may 'enter any judicial process, or enter any judgment, decree, or order, for the purpose or having the effect of depriving such institution, or any carrier engaged in transporting such work or object within the United States, of custody or control of such object'. The possibly wide scope of this immunity is reflected in the United States Department of State's explanation as to the application of the Act, being to protect 'from seizure or *other judicial process* certain objects of cultural significance imported into the United States for temporary display or exhibition'. This wide scope to include immunity from seizure in criminal matters and investigations was affirmed in *Malewicz v City of Amsterdam*[45] when the court declared that the Act deprives all United States courts from 'taking any action to obtain physical custody of the Malewicz Collection or other cultural icons granted immunity while in this country'.

---

40 Law of 24 December 2002; Legal Code Modification Law 14 June 2004 (article 1412ter Judicial Code). See van Woudenberg (n 2) 306.

41 Bundesgesetz über den internationalen Kulturgütertransfer 2005. See van Woudenberg (n 2) 310.

42 Gesetz über die vorübergehende sachliche Immunität von Kulturgut, Liechtensteinisches Landesgesetzblatt, 15 January 2008, No. 9; See van Woudenberg (n 2) 320.

43 Laki eräiden Suomeen tuotavien näyttelyesineiden takavarikoinnin kielämisesetä No. 697/2011. See van Woudenberg (n 2) 321.

44 Zákon o státni památkové péči) 20/1987 Sb. See van Woudenberg (n 2) 323.

45 362 F. Supp. 2d 298 at 333.

As a federation, a number of individual States within the United States have adopted immunity from seizure legislation. As was evident in the litigation over the seizure of the *Portrait of Wally*, New York legislation (Arts and Cultural Affairs Law Act), for example, provides that 'no process of attachment, execution, sequestration, replevin, distress or any kind of seizure shall be served or levied upon any work of fine art' while the work is travelling to or from or while on exhibition, provided that it is on loan from a non-resident and part of a not-for-profit exhibition conducted within New York. Importantly, this immunity extended to cover criminal as well as civil seizures. Concerned that New York would become a safe-haven for art looted by the Nazi's, the legislation was amended in 2000 to narrow the scope of the immunity so as to exclude seizures in criminal cases. Inexplicably, to address concerns raised by museums, a sunset clause was introduced so that the amendment expired on 1 June 2002, and has not been re-enacted.[46] Tennessee's legislation[47] explicitly provides immunity for seizure for both civil and criminal matters, but does not grant immunity from suit against an owner of artwork in any court that has proper jurisdiction over such owner. Texas[48] on the other hand, excludes from its automatic immunity, instances where 'theft of the work of art from its owner is alleged and found proven by the court'.

Five Canadian provinces[49] have enacted immunity from seizure law. British Columbia's statute offers the broadest protection, providing automatic immunity from proceedings for possession of, or a property interest in, works of art brought into the province for a temporary public exhibit. The other four provinces all require application for immunity. Importantly, all provinces' immunity extends to immunity for criminal law seizures, including for cases of allegedly stolen works of art. Unlike in the United States, none of the Canadian provincial legislation has been raised in litigation.[50]

Australian Perspective

In 2013, Australia became the most recent State to adopt immunity legislation; in the form of the *Protection of Objects on Loan Act* 2013 (Cth). The adoption of this Act followed close consideration of the experiences of other jurisdictions.

---

46 O'Connell (n 34).

47 Tennessee Code ss 28-3-115.

48 Civil Practice and Remedies Code ss 3-61.

49 Manitoba (Foreign Cultural Objects Immunity From Seizure Act, C.C.S.M. 1987, c. F-140), Québec (Code of Civil Procedure R.S.Q. c. C-25), Ontario (Foreign Cultural Objects Immunity From Seizure Act, R.S.O. 1990, c. F.-23), British Columbia (Law and Equity Act, R.S.B.C. 1996, c. 253) and Alberta (Foreign Cultural Property Immunity Act, R.S.A. 2000, c. F-17).

50 See Daniel Getz, 'The History of Canadian Immunity from Seizure Legislation' (2011) 18 *International Journal of Cultural Property* 201.

The main object of this Act is 'to encourage lenders to lend objects for temporary public exhibition in Australia under arrangements involving certain institutions'.[51] In achieving this, the Act provides for a very broad immunity. Proceedings for an action *in rem* relating to works of art cannot be started;[52] nor can proceedings for an action *in personam* against a protected person relating to the work of art.[53] Moreover, works of art cannot be seized[54] or forfeited[55] under a law of the Commonwealth, a State or a Territory. These simply stated prohibitions cover a wide immunity from seizure and suit, including in the context of criminal seizures and forfeitures.[56] The broad immunity granted from seizure[57] or forfeiture[58] under a law of the Commonwealth, a State or a Territory is qualified in relation to a number of seizures pursuant to criminal laws, such as the *Crimes Act 1914*, which gives search, information gathering, arrest and related powers to police, is not prevented, and in particular, the *Proceeds of Crime Act 2002*.

The *Proceeds of Crime Act 2002* (Cth), addresses these issues by providing for a range of measures that allow for the seizure, forfeiture or restraining of use of property that represent the proceeds of crime. Its scope is considerably broad. It provides for the forfeiture of property to the Commonwealth on conviction of a serious offence where that property was acquired through proceeds of crime or was an instrument of the commission of a crime.[59] It also provides for forfeiture in some circumstances without a criminal conviction[60] if the court is satisfied that the property was an instrument of a serious offence or was the proceeds of one or more indictable offences, irrespective of whether that offence is a Commonwealth, State or foreign offence.[61] That this applies to foreign offences is of some import given the possibility that a work of art on loan from a foreign State may be the proceeds of crime in that State.[62] The Act also provides for restraining orders made against property which provides that the property must not be disposed of or otherwise

51 *Protection of Cultural Objects on Loan Act* 2013 (Cth) s 3(1).

52 *Protection of Cultural Objects on Loan Act* 2013 (Cth) s 9(2).

53 *Protection of Cultural Objects on Loan Act* 2013 (Cth) s 9(1).

54 *Protection of Cultural Objects on Loan Act* 2013 (Cth) s 11(1).

55 *Protection of Cultural Objects on Loan Act* 2013 (Cth) s 12(1).

56 *Protection of Cultural Objects on Loan Act* 2013 (Cth) s 5 provides that his section applies to the starting of proceedings in a federal court or a court of a State or Territory by claim, crossclaim or otherwise.

57 *Protection of Cultural Objects on Loan Act* 2013 (Cth) s 11(1).

58 *Protection of Cultural Objects on Loan Act* 2013 (Cth) s 12(1).

59 *Proceeds of Crime Act* 2002 (Cth) s 91.

60 *Proceeds of Crime Act* 2002 (Cth) ss 46, 66-8.

61 Proceeds of Crime Act 2002 (Cth) s 49. S 13 also provides that '[t]his Act extends, except so far as the contrary intention appears: (a) to acts, matters and things outside Australia, whether or not in or over a foreign country; and (b) to all persons, irrespective of their nationality or citizenship'.

62 See, for example, *Commonwealth v Garcia* [2004] QDC 523; *Ex Parte Commonwealth Director of Public Prosecutions* [2010] WASC 277.

dealt with by anyone or only by specified persons.[63] Importantly, 'dealt with' includes the removal of property from Australia.[64] Such a restraining order may prevent, for example, the return of works of art to lenders overseas.[65] Moreover, any law of the Commonwealth, a State or a Territory that gives a police officer (however described) a power of seizure and does not give that power to anyone other than a police officer, is not covered by the immunity.[66] The exceptions have been included to recognize that there may be circumstances where it is appropriate that police officers retain the ability to seize an object.

Immunity From Seizure and International Conventions on Stolen and Illicit Cultural Heritage

The 1970 Convention on the Means of Prohibiting and Preventing the Illicit Import, Export and Transfer of Ownership of Cultural Property addresses, in the main, the issue of export and import of cultural heritage, including work of art, but touches on the problem of stolen cultural objects in two articles.

Article 7 includes a provision that requires a State Party 'to prohibit the import of cultural property stolen from a museum or a religious or secular public monument or similar institution in another State Party to this Convention after the entry into force of this Convention for the States concerned, provided that such property is documented as appertaining to the inventory of that institution'. Article 13(c) of the Convention also requires States Parties to undertake to admit actions for recovery of stolen cultural objects brought by or on behalf of the rightful owners. Importantly, this obligation is made subject to the 'existing law of each State'. Some uncertainty exists as to the exact meaning of this phrase, though the United States has expressed the view that it requires each State to ensure the existence of 'a judicial remedy for the vindication of a property right if one exists'.[67] Uncertainty remains whether an immunity from seizure statute of a State Party that prevents the vindication of an existing property right is in contravention of this obligation since that immunity from seizure statute does not apply to all such claims and forms part of the laws of that State. Nevertheless, immunity statutes, particularly those that provide for immunity from suit, achieve the very opposite to what the spirit of this international obligation requires. This

63 *Proceeds of Crime Act* 2002 (Cth) s 17.

64 *Proceeds of Crime Act* 2002 (Cth) s 338.

65 Similar State and territory legislation exists, such as the *Criminal Proceeds Confiscation Act* 2002 (Qld), *Confiscation of Proceeds of Crime Act* 1989 (NSW), *Confiscation Act* 1997 (Vic), *Criminal Assets Confiscation Act* 2005 (SA) and *Criminal Property Confiscation Act* 2000 (WA).

66 *Protection of Cultural Objects on Loan Act* 2013 (Cth) s 11(2)(c).

67 For a detailed consideration, see Patrick J. O'Keefe *Commentary on the UNESCO 1970 Convention on Illicit Traffic* (2nd edn, Institute of Art and Law 2007).

difficulty also arises, perhaps more so, in relation to the International Institute for the Unification of Private Law (UNIDROIT) Convention on Stolen or Illegally Exported Cultural Objects, and for States within the European Union, with regard to Council Directive 93/7/EEC which addresses 'the return of cultural objects unlawfully removed from the territory of an EU country'.

The UNIDROIT Convention arose out of a concern that while the Convention on the Means of Prohibiting and Preventing the Illicit Import, Export and Transfer of Ownership of Cultural Property addressed the illegal export and import of cultural objects, it did not comprehensively address the problem of stolen cultural objects. This was due, partly, to the fact that UNESCO, strictly speaking, had no mandate to address private law issues. UNIDROIT's mandate, however allows for the adoption of conventions which seek to unify national laws, and in the case of stolen cultural objects, was able to deal with issues such as ownership, limitation periods, the position of the *bona fide* purchaser and the payment of compensation. The resulting convention applies to claims of an international character for the restitution of stolen cultural objects. Quite simply, it requires that the 'possessor of a cultural object which has been stolen shall return it', subject to certain limitation periods and the possible payment of compensation to *bona fide* purchasers. This international obligation is underpinned by the common law principle of *nemo dat quod non habet*; that is that a thief cannot give to another what the thief does not have – ownership of the work of art. The nature of cultural objects as unique and irreplaceable was such that this principle, though not fully developed in civil law systems, was appropriate and acceptable in all legal systems. Furthermore, the very uniqueness of the object drives the demand in the art market, and to side with the *bona fide* purchaser, even if compensation might have to be paid to the original owner, would effectively introduce a forced and artificial market, further encouraging theft.

Since the *nemo dat quod non habet* principle was adopted, the term 'possessor' was used to describe the person in whose hands the work of art is found. Article 3, however, does not actually indicate to whom the work of art is to be returned. This claimant may not necessarily be the owner, but may, for example, be a museum to which the work of art was loaned, and from which it was stolen. Since the Convention introduces a system for private and public entities to claim the restitution of cultural hertiage, it will be up to the national court to determine whether the claimant has a legitimate claim in accordance with the provision of the UNIDROIT Convention as implemented in that national law. Similarly, as to whether the work of art is stolen will depend on the national law of the State seized with the claim for restitution. Importantly, such a claim for the return of stolen works of art 'may be brought before the courts or other competent authorities of the Contracting State where the cultural object [work of art] is located, in addition to the courts or other competent authorities otherwise having jurisdiction under the rules in force in Contracting States'. It therefore envisages such a claim being brought in the State in which the work of art is located, which would include the State receiving a work of art on loan. The risk arises that return will be sought by a State other than that from which the work of art was loaned. The adoption of an immunity statute would directly affect this international obligation.

States with immunity legislation have reacted differently to this possible conflict. The United Kingdom and Australia, for example, while extending immunity to seizure and forfeiture in criminal investigations, excludes seizure or forfeiture necessary to give effect to their respective community or international treaty obligations, and does not affect liability for an offence of importing, exporting or otherwise dealing with the object. Belgian and Finnish legislation also provides that immunity cannot apply when it is necessary to give effect to an international obligation. The Swiss legislation, however, illustrates an alternative approach.[68] The legislation allows for a return guarantee to be issued following notification of the intended loan and an opportunity given for interested parties to oppose such a loan, including a State that might be considered a State of origin under the 1970 Convention (and, if Switzerland were to become a party to the UNIDROIT Convention, also from a State from which the work of art was stolen). A failure to make such an objection would result in the return guarantee overriding any international return obligation. A similar position exists in Germany and Austria. The United States approach is similar to the extent that once immunity arises under the federal Immunity from Seizure Act it overrides that which gives effect to the 1970 Convention. This might, in some circumstances, give rise to a conflict with the federal *National Stolen Property Act*. Uncertainty as to the interaction between an immunity statute and these international obligations appears to be one reason why Italy has failed to adopt a broad immunity statute for works of art on loan in Italy.[69]

Conclusion

A comparative consideration of the way in which a number of jurisdiction have addressed the criminal scope of immunity from seizure illustrates the very great difficulty in balancing the competing interest of fostering cultural exchange and giving effect to the criminal law and procedure of States.

The United Kingdom's immunity statute reflects this balancing of interests in that it does not prevent prosecution for offences relating to the work of art though it does prevent the exertion of any power of seizure to prevent the object from leaving the United Kingdom. While there is no question that immunity from seizure should not in any way prevent the prosecution for criminal offences, the exact scope of the immunity from seizure will directly affect criminal prosecutions

68 van Woudenberg (n 2) 317-20.
69 van Woudenberg (n 2) 324-31.

and the criminal investigation process. So, where States such as the United States, Canada, Belgium, Finland, Germany, Australia and Switzerland prevent seizure of works or art as part of a criminal matter or investigation, the detection, investigation and prosecution of art crime becomes substantially more difficult. Yet the interests that the immunity from seizure legislation seeks to protect, is part of the very interest that drives international art crime: the universal value and spirit inherent in works of art.

Part III

INTERNATIONAL AND REGIONAL OVERVIEWS

Chapter 11
Policing Art Crime in the European Union

Ludo Block

Introduction

In popular culture, such as the movie *Ocean's Twelve* about high-profile art heists, policing art crime tends to be portrayed as a thrilling area of police work performed by officers with seemingly unlimited resources. Reality, however, is, as usual, far less exciting. Even though worldwide treaties acknowledge the importance of cultural heritage protection[1] and recognize that the damage caused by such crimes as art theft and looting can be irreversible; in most countries, art crime policing is accorded little priority.

In the academic literature, in contrast, art crime has enjoyed rising popularity over the past decade, and a growing body of literature[2] now documents the different types of art crime – for example, looting and forgery – and the links between art crime and other crime areas such as the drug trade and organized crime. Regrettably, however, structured academic attention to art crime policing and transnational collaboration in this field is still lacking. There are, of course, some exceptions to this general picture, such as the 1974 book about the New York Police Department's first art crime detective[3]; the recent book by the former head of the FBI's art team[4]; and the contributions of practitioners to professional journals and conferences.[5] Nevertheless, the attention to art crime policing remains fragmented and piecemeal.

---

1 See, for example, the Convention for the Protection of Cultural Property in the Event of Armed Conflict [1954], the Convention on the Means of Prohibiting and Preventing the Illicit Import, Export, and Transfer of Ownership of Cultural Property [1970] and the Convention on Stolen or Illegally Exported Cultural Objects [1995].

2 See, for example, Noah Charney (ed), *Art and Crime: Exploring the Dark Side of the Art World* (Praeger Press 2009); Laurence Massy, *Le vol d'oeuvres d'art: Une criminalité méconnue* (Bruylant 2000); Edgar Tijhuis, *Transnational crime and the interface between legal and illegal actors: The case of the illicit art and antiques trade* (Wolf Legal Publishers 2006).

3 Laurie Adams, *Art Cop: Robert Volpe, Art Crime Detective* (Dodd, Mead and Company 1974).

4 Robert Wittman, *Priceless: How I Went Undercover to Rescue the World's Stolen Treasures* (Random House 2010).

5 See, for example, Roberto Conforti, 'The Carabinieri and the Protection of Italy's Heritage' (1994) 448 *International Criminal Police Review* 50; William Martin, 'Art Theft

This chapter thus attempts a broader analysis not only of art crime policing in the EU member states but also, because art crime cases often have a transnational component,[6] of the cooperation between EU police in the field of art crime and any overarching strategies they may employ. To do so, it draws not only on the (limited) existing literature but also on semi-structured interviews with police practitioners, as well as policy documents and primary (media) sources, in order to chart the practicalities of policing art crime in the EU.

The chapter begins with an overview of the current situation and activities related to art crime policing in 14 EU member states with a major emphasis on the significant interstate differences. The subsequent section then focuses on policy and policing efforts at the EU level in both the prevention and investigation of art crime, demonstrating especially that, despite a notable recent increase in attention, this issue has historically been assigned relatively low priority in the EU. This discussion is followed by a short review of the realities of transnational police cooperation on art crime in Europe, illustrating particularly the important role of Interpol and the obstacles met by police art crime specialists in their cross-border cooperation. Finally, the concluding section summarizes the key findings and highlights the importance of informal networks and the personal dedication of individual police officers, which together appear to be crucial factors in enabling and sustaining operational policing efforts in the prevention and investigation of art crime in the EU.

in the United States' (1994) 448 *International Criminal Police Review* 57; Jean-Michel Mimran, 'The French Central Office for Art Theft' (1994) 448 *International Criminal Police Review* 60; Annie Moulin, 'The Situation in Belgium' (1994) 448 *International Criminal Police Review* 55; Thomas Baker, 'Combating Art Theft: International Cooperation in Action' (1996) 63 *The Police Chief* 19; Brian Hanley, 'Law Enforcement Issues in Art Theft' (*Art Crime: Protecting Art, Protecting Artists and Protecting Consumers*, a conference convened by the Australian Institute of Criminology, Sydney, 2-3 December 1999); Richard Ellis, 'Investigating Stolen Art: The Reason Why' (AXA Art Conference, London, November 5, 2005); Gian-Luigi Nanni, 'Carabinieri for Protection of Cultural Heritage. Command: Structure and Tasks' (UNESCO regional meeting, *Prevention of Illicit Traffic and Other Illegal Actions Related to Cultural Properties*, Ohrid (Macedonia) 15-18 March 2006); Ramón Fernández Gallego, 'Falsificaciones y robo de obras de arte' (*La lucha contra el tráfico ilícito de bienes culturales*, Madrid, 18 October 2006); Tomás Rabadán, 'Las brigadas de patrimonio en el entorno jurídico de las Comunidades Autónomas' (*La lucha contra el tráfico ilícito de bienes culturales*, Madrid, 18 October 2006); Jean-Pierre Jouanny, 'The Role of Interpol in Countering the Traffic in Cultural Property' (2008) 45 *International Preservation News* 7; Anita Gach, 'Kunstdatenbank der Interpol' (2009) 11-12 Öffentliche Sicherheit 13; Andrea Ilari, 'Comando Carabinieri tutela patrimonio culturale' (*Governance of Cultural Property: Preservation and Recovery*, 30 September 2009, Basel Institute on Governance, Basel, Switzerland); Fred Kruijer, 'Kunstroof in Westeremden' (2011) 5 *Blauw* 26.

6 See, for example, Moulin (n 5); Baker (n 5); Gach (n 5); Blythe Bowman, 'Transnational Crimes against Culture. Looting at Archaeological Sites and the "Grey" Market in Antiquities' (2008) 24 *Journal of Contemporary Criminal Justice* 225.

Policing Art Crime in the Member States

As already mentioned, the extant literature offers few in-depth discussions of art crime policing, let alone any structured assessments. Hence, to open the door for such assessment, this section outlines the policing efforts by 14 EU member states to prevent and investigate art crime in the hope of identifying the common denominators in these efforts.

Austria

In Austria, since 2000, the police have maintained a website that displays stolen art for public viewing,[7] and the criminal investigation service at the national level has an art crime unit (*Re-ferat für Kulturgutdelikte*) staffed with two specialists supported by several case officers at the local level.[8] In addition, even though the Austrian police have no dedicated database on art crime, the national police information system, EKIS, allows the theft of cultural property (art and antiques) to be registered as a distinct category of stolen goods. The art crime unit also cooperates closely with the police in the adjacent countries of Germany and Switzerland, and since 2008, the forces from these three countries have collaborated on an eBay project to uncover the online sale of stolen cultural property.[9]

Belgium

In Belgium, a dedicated art crime unit, the Bureau of Art and Antiques, was established in 1988 within the Brussels judicial police.[10] After the Belgian police were reorganized in 2001, this bureau became part of Belgium's federal judicial police at the national level and was renamed Section ART. At that time, the section had a staff of seven; however, the section's current staff consists of only two specialists, one of whom is occupied full time with maintaining the ARTIST database. This database, a successor of the original art crime database established in 1993,[11] includes all art works reported stolen in Belgium, currently about 20,000 objects. To conduct actual investigations and provide support for international requests, however, the section must rely on its domestic network of correspondents in local federal police departments throughout Belgium, to whom it provides support in the form of knowledge and analyses.[12]

---

7 See Bundesministerium für Inneres – Bundeskriminalamt <http://www.bmi.gv.at/cms/bk/_fahndung/_fndg.aspx?b=KU_WE> accessed 12 March 2013.

8 Editorial, 'Schätze der Antike' (2006) 5-6 Öffentliche Sicherheit 40, see also Gach (n 5).

9 Gach (n 5).

10 Anne Beeckman, 'Het Bureau "Kunst & Antiek"' (2001) 3 *Magazine van de Federale Politie* 36.

11 Moulin (n 5).

12 Interview [1] with a Belgian police officer (7 May 2010).

Denmark

In Denmark where no more than 50 to 80 art crime offenses are registered annually,[13] the police have no dedicated unit on art crime nor do they maintain an art crime database. Some information on stolen art is published on the websites of local police districts, but there is no consistency in where and how the missing objects are listed.[14]

Finland

As in Denmark, in Finland, the level of reported art crime is very low and involves mostly the selling of forgeries.[15] Therefore, although the National Bureau of Investigation (NBI) employs a few specialists who deal with art crimes on a case-by-case basis, it has no full-time art crime unit, and the Finnish police maintain no dedicated database for stolen art. Art crime cases are registered at the national level in the NBI database – but not as a distinct category, which makes information on them difficult to retrieve.

France

In France, efforts against art crime are carried out by the Central Unit for the Fight against Trafficking in Cultural Goods (*l'Office central de lutte contre le traffic des biens culturels* or OCBC), originally established in 1975 as *l'Office central pour la répression des vols d'oeuvres et d'objets d'art* and renamed in 1997. Although located within the Central Directorate of the Judicial Police, the OCBC also acts on behalf of the gendarmerie and customs, as well as the ministries of culture, justice and foreign affairs. Staffed by approximately 30 officers, this office at the national level coordinates art crime investigations carried out by the regional criminal investigation departments and is directly involved in around 100 investigations a year into the most important cases.[16]

Since 1995, the OCBC has maintained the TREIMA database of stolen art, which includes photographs of cultural property stolen in France, as well as other art stolen abroad and reported missing through Interpol. To improve the recognition process, the OCBC modernized its database in 2005 (now called TREIMA II) to

---

13 Marzanna Cieślak and Katarzyna Zielinska, 'Threat of crime against cultural property. EU Member States and selected countries of the Eastern Partnership analysis 2007-2010' (EU Council Cultural Affairs Committee, Brussels, 31 October 2011).

14 Lars Korsell, Göran Hedlund, Sofia Elwér, Daniel Vesterhav and Anita Heber, *Cultural Heritage Crime: The Nordic Dimension* (Swedish National Council for Crime Prevention, Information and Publication 2006) 146.

15 Risto Rumpunen and Jyrki Seppälä, *Väärää Taidetta: Taiderikollisuus Suomessa* (Vammala Kirjapaino Oy 2004).

16 Mimran (n 5) 60.

allow image recognition searching and provide a web interface.[17] By the end of 2010, the database had referenced 86,000 stolen art objects in connection with 32,000 incidents.[18]

Germany

In Germany, section SO41-24 of the federal criminal investigation service (*Bundeskriminalamt* or BKA) employs a number of art crime specialists who coordinate and support art crime investigations[19] and maintain a database for works of art that have been stolen and/or offered in suspicious circumstances.[20] Actual investigations, however, are carried out by the individual state criminal investigation services (*Landeskriminalamt* or LKA). Three LKAs maintain dedicated art crime units: the LKA Baden-Württemberg and the LKA Bavaria, which both also maintain a database on stolen works of art,[21] and the LKA Berlin, which handled the famous Beltracchi case.[22] Together, the BKA and these three LKAs employ 15 officers who are especially involved in the prevention and investigation of art crime.[23]

Ireland

In Ireland, the former Arts and Antiques Unit[24] has been renamed the Garda Arts and Antiques Investigation Section and is attached to the National Bureau of Criminal Investigation (NBCI).[25] This section comprises one detective sergeant and one detective with extra assistance available from other members of the NBCI

17 Vincent Noce, 'Interpol élargit sa base' *Liberation* (22 August 2006).

18 Alain Bauer (ed), *La criminalité en France* (L'Observatoire national de la délinquance et des réponses pénales 2011), 233.

19 See, for example, Bundeskriminalamt, 'Erfolge bei der Bekämpfung der Kunstkriminalität: Bundeskriminalamt klärt Diebstähle von Heiligenfiguren auf' (Press release 7 August 2009); Bundeskriminalamt, 'Geraubtes Gemälde "Die Festnahme Christi" in Berlin sichergestellt' (Press release 20 June 2010).

20 CECOJI-CNRS, 'Study on preventing and fighting illicit trafficking in cultural goods in the European Union' (Centre d'études sur la coopération juridique internationale 2011) 86.

21 Ibid., 87; see also Landeskriminalamt Baden-Württemberg – Über uns <http://www.lka-bw.de/LKA/UeberUns/Seiten/ermittlungen.aspx> accessed 12 March 2013.

22 Deike Diening, 'Wie ein Berliner Kommissar den größten deutschen Kunstfälscherskandal enthüllte' *Der Tages-spiegel* (31 December 2012); see also Duncan Chappell and Saskia Hufnagel, 'The Beltracchi Affair: A Comment on the "Most Spectacular" German Art Forgery Case in Recent Times' (2012) Spring edn *Journal of Art Crime* 38.

23 Noah Charney, 'Q&A with Ernst Schöller' (2012) Spring edn *Journal of Art Crime* 96.

24 An Garda Síochána, *Annual Report 2000* (An Garda Síochána 2001) 47.

25 See An Garda Síochána – Criminal Investigation <http://www.garda.ie/controller.aspx?page=1645> accessed 12 March 2013.

as required.[26] The section's role is to investigate serious cultural property crime, and in this regard, advise and liaise with Garda colleagues, other police forces and outside agencies such as museums, galleries, experts and other persons or groups encountered during the course of its work. Apart from art and antique thefts and frauds, a major part of the section's enquiries involves criminal trans-border movement of cultural goods both in and out of Ireland.[27]

Italy

Undoubtedly the Italian Carabinieri, which has maintained a specialized commando force for the protection of cultural heritage (*Comando Carabinieri per la Tutela del Patrimonio Culturale*) since 1969,[28] is the most active police force in the EU, if not the entire world, in preventing and investigating art crime. Tasked with both preventing and fighting against the trafficking in cultural property, this unit has three divisions: Archaeology, Antiques and Contemporary Art Forgery. Functionally incorporated in 1975 within the Ministry for Cultural and Environmental Heritage, the unit has been gradually expanded to a total of 12 regional sections, each with its own regional expertise and investigative capacity but subordinated to the central unit. When it began 40 years ago, the commando had 16 staff members; now it and its subordinated sections have 300.[29] Its 'Leonardo' database of 'unlawfully removed cultural heritage goods', originally set up in 1980, is widely recognized as the largest dedicated database on art crime in the world and can be searched online.[30] Two other major tasks of the commando unit are the investigation of clandestine excavations and the return of looted artefacts.[31]

Lithuania

Although the Lithuanian Criminal Police maintains a Cultural and Art Values Theft Investigation Unit dedicated to cases of theft of cultural goods, this unit consists of only one person.[32] The unit does, however, maintain a database of registered stolen works of art that can be accessed online.[33]

---

26 Personal communication from the Garda press office (14 August 2012).

27 Ibid.

28 Conforti (n 5).

29 Comando Carabinieri, 'Il Comando Carabinieri per la Tutela Patrimonio Culturale' (Carabinieri 2010) <http://www.carabinieri.it/Internet/Cittadino/Informazioni/Tutela/Patrimonio+Culturale/> accessed 12 March 2013; Ilari (n 5).

30 See <http://tpcweb.carabinieri.it/tpc_sito_pub/simplecerca.jsp> accessed 12 March 2013.

31 Nanni (n 5).

32 CECOJI-CNRS, 'Annex to the Study on preventing and fighting illicit trafficking in cultural goods in the European Union' (Centre d'études sur la coopération juridique internationale 2011) 46.

33 See www.policija.lt/lt/kuriniai accessed 12 March 2013.

Norway[34]

In Norway, cultural heritage crime falls under the auspices of ØKOKRIM, the national authority for investigating and prosecuting economic and environmental crime. This responsibility, however, is not exclusive; for example, the investigation and recovery of Munch's *The Scream* after it was stolen for a second time in 2004 was in the hands of the Oslo Police District's organized crime division.[35] With respect to art crimes, ØKOKRIM's focus lies on cultural heritage crimes, which are defined as part of 'environmental crime' and account for only a few cases investigated each year.[36] Because of a lack of resources, ØKOKRIM has so far maintained no database on stolen art[37], although the agency does participate in the National Police Directorate's working group on a national database for recording stolen objects of art and cultural monuments.[38] Insufficient capacity, however, is seemingly not the only factor impeding the Norwegian police's prevention and investigation of art crime: according to one recent study, Norway's police officers perceive themselves as lacking sufficient knowledge to combat art crime.[39] Interestingly, however, in 1999, an ØKOKRIM officer acting undercover as a European buyer of Native American artefacts aided the FBI in a sting operation that put an end to a network dealing in stolen indigenous artwork.[40]

Spain

All three of Spain's different police agencies – the *Guardia Civil,* the *Cuerpo Nacional de Policía* and the *Mossos d'Esquadra* – maintain the capacity to prevent and investigate art crime. The art crime unit within *Guardia Civil* was established at the end of the 1970s, and in 1987, became a central operational unit named the *Grupo de Patrimonio Histórico*, which currently has about 20 staff members. The unit's key activities are the investigation of art crime and

34 Norway is not technically an EU member state; it is, however, part of the Schengen area under the Nordic Passport Union and participates in most EU police cooperative arrangements and agreements.

35 Nina Berglund, 'Munch Paintings Recovered' *Aftenposten* (1 September 2006).

36 ØKOKRIM, *Annual report 2008* (ØKOKRIM 2009), 10; ØKOKRIM, *Annual Report 2010* (ØKOKRIM 2011) 9.

37 Stortinget, *Skriftlig spørsmål fra Øyvind Håbrekke (KrF) til justisministeren* (Stortinget 2009-2010 15:228).

38 ØKOKRIM, *Annual Report 2010* (ØKOKRIM 2011) 26.

39 Hilde Madsø Jacobsen, Tanja Steen and Marie Ulsberg, Å jobbe med kulturminner (Albatrass 2008) 80.

40 Frans-Arne Stylegar, 'International Undercover Operation Recovers Native American Artefacts' (2007) *Arkeologi i nord* <http://arkeologi.blogspot.nl/2007/04/international-undercover-operation.html> accessed 12 March 2013; see also Wittman (n 4) 120.

the centralization of all art crime-related information submitted by the territorial units.[41] Overviews of stolen and recovered works are published on the *Guardia Civil* website.[42]

The *Cuerpo Nacional de Policía* established its art crime unit, the *Brigada de Investigación de Patrimonio Histórico*, in 1977. Located in the special and violent crime unit of the judicial police,[43] at its national level the brigade consists of two operational groups and an analytical group. In different regions of the country, the brigade's cumulative staff totals 124 representatives. The brigade is also responsible for maintaining the 'Dulcinea' database of stolen art works.[44]

Lastly, the *Mossos d'Esquadra*, the police force of the autonomous community of Catalonia, which was re-established in 1982 and obtained its current structure in 2002, includes an art crime unit, the *Grup de Patrimoni Històric,* within its Criminal Investigation Commissariat.[45] Although formal agreements do exist between these three law enforcement authorities, the cooperation and exchange of information between the specialized art crime units take place mostly based on unwritten informal arrangements.[46]

Sweden

In Sweden, art crime policing generally receives limited priority, although at the end of 2009, the National Criminal Police did appoint a dedicated coordinator for fighting art crime.[47] Nevertheless, the country maintains no art crime database and has no dedicated investigative capacity for art crime,[48] so cases that do involve police commitment to art crimes are the result of individual police officers acting out of personal drive.[49] Like the Norwegian respondents, Swedish police officers surveyed emphasized that their meagre resources and inadequate awareness of the cultural heritage crime area, as well as poor registration practices, obstruct the recovery of stolen art.[50]

---

41 See Ministerio del Interior, 'El Grupo de Patrimonio Histórico de la Guardia Civil recibe la Medalla de Oro de Bellas Artes' (press release 15 October 2008).

42 See <http://www.guardiacivil.es/es/prensa/especiales/objetos_artisticos_substraidos/index.html> accessed 12 March 2013.

43 See <http://www.policia.es/org_central/judicial/udev/udev.html> accessed 12 March 2013.

44 Fernández Gallego (n 5).

45 Rabadán (n 5).

46 Ibid.

47 Elin Törnqvist, *Samlat grepp mot kulturarvsbrotten* (2009) [November] *Svenks Polis*.

48 Tina Harr, 'De stjäl – och säljer tillbaka konsten' *Expressen* (23 June 2012).

49 Korsell et al. (n 14) 115.

50 Ibid., 34.

The Netherlands

With the 1974 establishment of a national administrative section to maintain a register on art and antique thefts, the Netherlands was among the first countries to pay structured attention to art crime. In 1979, this administrative section was transformed into an Arts and Antiques Unit within the National Criminal Intelligence Service.[51] However, in 2001, when the head of this unit went into early retirement, the unit was disbanded and the database no longer maintained. After pressure from the Netherlands parliament, the police did develop a new database; however, it only became fully operational in 2010, since when it has recorded 831 art thefts.[52]

This same parliamentary pressure also led in 2008 to the allocation of three (part-time) staff positions in the National Criminal Intelligence Section of the National Police to deal specifically with art crime. These officers, however, are primarily engaged in the collection and analysis of information on art crime: actual investigations of art crime cases remain the responsibility of regional police forces.[53] As yet, only the Amsterdam police force employs a dedicated art crime detective[54] and has on several occasions successfully prevented and investigated art crime.[55]

United Kingdom

In the United Kingdom, the London Metropolitan Police maintains the renowned Art and Antiques Unit within its Specialist Crime Directorate. This unit, which has national authority, currently includes three detective constables, two researchers, and ten part-time special constables known as ArtBeat officers.[56] Originally established in 1969 as a philatelic squad after a series of stamp dealer robberies,[57] the unit was disbanded for some time in the 1980s but was re-established in 1989 in its current form.[58]

---

51 Tweede Kamer der Staten-Generaal, *Het functioneren van de Centrale Recherche Informatiedienst* (TK 1984-1985, 19038) 1-2.

52 Cieślak and Zielinska (n 13).

53 Tweede Kamer der Staten-Generaal, *Kamervraag 1026* (TK 2009-2010, annex 2191-2192); see also Jos Klaren, 'Kunst en Antiek' (Fact sheet Dutch National Police, KLPD 2010).

54 Interview [3] with a senior Dutch police officer (13 April 2012).

55 See, for example, Amsterdam Police, 'Griekse iconen terug naar rechtmatige eigenaar' (Press release 5 December 2011); Amsterdam Police, 'Unieke, gestolen globes terug; één aanhouding' (Press release 27 June 2012); Henk Schutten, 'De jacht op de kunstcrimineel is geopend' *Het Parool* (13 July 2011) 14.

56 Metropolitan Police, 'Rogues' Gallery' (2010) [1017] *The Job* 14.

57 Metropolitan Police, 'Antiques Roadshow to Recovery' (2005) [951] *The Job.*

58 Matthew Hart, *The Irish Game* (Random House 2005) 91 and 134.

The Arts and Antiques Unit maintains the 'London Stolen Arts Database', which contains pictures and descriptions of over 54,000 items[59] and has on average 120 investigations running at any one time. The unit has been involved in a number of successful investigations, including the undercover operation to recover Edvard Munch's *The Scream* three months after it was stolen from Oslo's National Museum of Art in 1994.[60] Despite these successes, however, and notwithstanding the size of the illegal art market in Britain, the Metropolitan Police announced in 2007 that the unit was not a priority for the force and that a 50 per cent budget cut for the unit was imminent. A subsequent attempt to secure sponsorships from the private sector was unsuccessful[61]; however, although the unit did start supplementing its resources by recruiting part-time volunteer ArtBeat officers, the budget cuts were never carried out.

This outline of the activities related to art crime policing in the different EU member states clearly demonstrates that the priority assigned to these activities varies significantly: in some member states, art crime receives very little attention; in others, highly specialized units are fully dedicated to its prevention and investigation. Admittedly, because the above overview does not address all member states, the observations are insufficient for the drawing of any clear-cut conclusions; nevertheless, the discussion does point to three common elements in art crime policing efforts.

First, the policing of art crime appears to require some form of centralized expertise; that is, unlike other crimes like drug offenses, it is not the type of crime that any officer can work on with a little training. Secondly, effectively policing art crime calls for an adequate information management system, one that ideally facilitates the flow of information from local police to a centralized database that includes precise information on stolen works of art. Recent research by the EU Commission, for example, found that police in 18 of the 27 member states maintain one or multiple databases on stolen works of art, and in 16 member states, police have organized specific experts to investigate art crime.[62] The size of these units, however, differs significantly – from one officer in Lithuania to a few hundred in France and Italy. The third common element is the availability of actual (local) investigative capacity. This element appears paramount for the real-world investigation of art crime because maintaining expertise and a database alone do not catch art thieves and forgers – successful investigations require a great deal of legwork and persistence. A case in point is the recent attempt by the Amsterdam police to investigate art crime: despite the availability of expertise and a database at the national level, only after the Amsterdam criminal investigation department appointed an art crime specialist

59 See <http://www.met.police.uk/artandantiques/> accessed 8 August 2012.

60 Hart (n 58) 170-185.

61 Sandra Laville, 'Met's Art Theft Squad Has to Go Cap in Hand' *The Guardian* (London, 21 April 2007) 5.

62 CECOJI-CNRS (n 32) 3-79.

were investigations successful. In fact, the data collected for this analysis reveal that in only eight member states do police have investigative capacity explicitly allocated to art crime. It is therefore worth examining whether these commonalities at the member state level point to the existence (or absence) of overarching European strategies on art crime policing.

Policing Art Crime at the EU Level

Policy Level

Police cooperation as part of broader political cooperation on Justice and Home Affairs (JHA) in Europe was first discussed in the European political arena in 1975 when, prompted by several terrorist incidents, the intergovernmental TREVI forum was created. Although initially intended to coordinate effective anti-terrorism responses among European governments, TREVI extended its business to many other policing issues in and between the member states, especially after the TREVI Working Group III was established in 1985 to address serious crimes other than terrorism.[63] In 1990, the TREVI programme of action on the reinforcement of police cooperation explicitly designated 'valuable pictures, works of art [and] cultural property' as the subject of 'regular exchanges and permanent updating of rapidly acquired and detailed information' between member states.[64] Nevertheless, even though this designation represents the first time that art crime policing received political attention at the European level, the programme was in reality more a political statement and resulted in no tangible operational implementation.

With the coming into force of the Treaty on European Union[65] in 1993, 'strengthening police cooperation' became an explicitly expressed objective of EU policy-making, and the EU Council has since adopted numerous policy instruments in this field. Such instruments are aimed at such objectives as harmonizing existing – and introducing new – methods of investigation (joint investigation teams, witness protection); creating new methods and legal frameworks for information exchange; setting up centralized databases; and prioritizing cooperation in particular crime fields, such as counterfeiting and trafficking in drugs, human beings and arms. Nevertheless, although in the first decade after 1993 the topic of art crime was discussed on several occasions in both EU Council and Commission structures, these discussions did not lead to the inclusion of art crime in any formal

63 Ludo Block, *From Politics to Policing: The Rationality Gap in EU Policy-Making* (Eleven International Publishing 2011) 59.

64 TREVI, 'Program of Action relating to the reinforcement of police cooperation and of the endeavours to combat terrorism or other forms of organised crime' (Council of the European Communities 1990) para 4.

65 Treaty of Maastricht [1992] OJ C191.

instrument.[66] In 2002, however, art crime was included in the list of offenses for which the requirement for double criminality was removed under the European Arrest Warrant.[67]

Six years later, art crime appeared again on the political agenda when the French EU presidency proposed the creation and implementation of a European database of stolen cultural goods.[68] When the possibilities offered by Interpol and Europol's existing databases were first explored, Europol quickly announced that it could not design and manage such a system. Interpol, in contrast, did offer to examine the functionalities that EU member states wanted and the possibility of incorporating these functionalities into the Interpol stolen artwork database.[69] In November 2008, the Council adopted non-binding Conclusions on preventing and combating illicit trafficking in cultural goods. These conclusions emphasize the importance of close cooperation between those departments in member states that specialize in combating the illicit trafficking of cultural goods and suggest the designation of contact points. They also support Interpol's actions to improve its database based on the wishes of member states.[70]

In 2011, the Polish EU presidency re-opened the art crime debate in the Council and distributed a questionnaire on cultural property crimes among the member states. Based on an analysis of the responses,[71] the Council adopted new Conclusions on preventing and combating crime against cultural goods that called for an enhancement of the cooperation with Interpol on developing and implementing a system for urgent reporting of key events connected with

---

66 See Council, 'Meeting of the TREVI Working Group III on 18 and 19 October 1993 in Brussels' (EEC document 9768/93); Commission, 'Discussion paper on prevention of illicit trafficking of cultural goods' (First meeting of the EU forum on the prevention of organised crime, Brussels 17-18 May 2001); Council, 'Conclusions of the International Seminar on Falsification of and Trafficking in Works of Art and Cultural Property held in Santiago de Compostella (Spain) 11-13 June 2002' (Council document 10658/02); Commission, 'SIS II Project: Storage of alerts on stolen cultural goods in SIS II' (2004 document SIS2-SCG-005).

67 Council Framework Decision (EU) 2002/584/JHA on the European arrest warrant and the surrender procedures between Member States [2002] OJ L190/1.

68 Council, 'Draft conclusions on the creation and implementation of a European database of stolen cultural goods' (Council document 11246/08).

69 Council, 'Outcome of the proceedings of the Police Cooperation Working Party meeting of 15 and 16 September 2008' (Council document 13377/08). Interestingly Europol had developed a blueprint for an art crime database just a few years previously (Interview [1] (n 12)).

70 Council, 'Conclusions of the Council of the European Union on preventing and combating illicit trafficking in cultural goods' (Council document 14224/2/08).

71 Council, 'Analysis of the scale of the crime threat against cultural property in the Member States and the selected countries of the Eastern Partnership' (Council document 13867/2/11). The Council only makes this document partially available to the public; however, most of the censored contents are available in Cieślak and Zielinska (n 13).

crime against cultural goods. The Conclusions also endorsed the preparation, in cooperation with Interpol, of a handbook to increase the effectiveness of fighting crime against cultural goods.[72]

Operational Efforts on Policing Art Crime at the EU Level

In addition to the Council's policy efforts to enhance police cooperation in the Union, a number of agencies were established to facilitate and undertake police and judicial cooperation in the EU, two of which, Europol and CEPOL, have undertaken activities related to the investigation of art crime. The first, Europol, established in its current form in 1999,[73] is the EU law enforcement organization that handles information exchange and intelligence analysis and is fictionally represented in the movie *Ocean's Twelve* as having highly trained art crime experts among its staff. In reality, however, Europol has no investigative powers, and until 2002, it engaged in no activity whatsoever related to art crime.[74] In fact, the first reference to Europol activities on art crime appeared in Europol's 2004 annual report, which indicates that in that year, through its Working Group on Cultural Heritage Offenses,[75] Europol delivered training courses on cultural property crime, conducted a feasibility study on establishing an EU database on stolen cultural goods, and collected information for a *Europol Cultural Property Crime Handbook*.[76]

The Europol Work Programme for 2006 also lists two art crime-related objectives: the compilation of a handbook on investigating stolen cultural goods and the provision of training on cultural property crime.[77] After that, however, no further references to any art crime activities by Europol can be found. Seemingly, after the arrival of a new director in 2005, the Working Group on Cultural Heritage Offenses was disbanded, even though both a final draft of the projected handbook and a blueprint for a stolen art database were ready.[78] The handbook was never published and the database never built. Currently, there is neither a dedicated unit nor any specialist at Europol active in the field of art crime and no Analysis Work File[79] on art crime has been opened.[80]

---

72 Council, 'Conclusions of 13 December 2011 on preventing and combating crime against cultural goods' (Council document 15236/2/11).

73 Europol became an EU agency in 2010; for the history of Europol see <https://www.europol.europa.eu/content/page/history-149> accessed 31 July 2014.

74 Interview [2] with the head of the former Netherlands' art crime unit (Netherlands, 23 August 2010).

75 Interview [1] (n 12).

76 Europol, *Annual Report 2004* (Europol 2005) 14.

77 Council, 'Europol Work Programme 2006' (Council document 7611/05).

78 Interview [1] (n 12).

79 Analysis Work Files are the coordination and collaboration tools that Europol uses to collect and analyse information from the member states on specific types of crimes and criminal groups.

80 Personal communication from a senior Europol official (2 May 2010).

The second EU agency that has undertaken activities in the field of art crime is the European Police College, better known as CEPOL. This 'college' is in fact a network of national police training colleges from member states that was established in 2000 and became an EU agency in 2005. The courses it holds are dispersed over the EU at the various national training colleges, and the CEPOL website[81] lists the annual courses on art crime organized since 2007. In practice, however, these CEPOL 'courses' resemble more of an annual gathering of art crime experts from member states and to a large extent draw the same participants every year. Nevertheless, because these participants informally discuss actual cases between presentations, these meetings do constitute an important informal link in the international cooperation on art crime.[82] The next section therefore examines how that international cooperation works in practice.

Practices of Transnational Police Cooperation on Art Crime in Europe

Police cooperation in general can be characterized as a dynamic and complex endeavour.[83] In spite of member states' geographic proximity, the EU comprises 27 different jurisdictions with divergent legal systems, different cultures and languages, and significant disparity between the way policing is organized, all of which affect cooperation. Although the number of cooperative arrangements available to police in the EU has proliferated over the past three decades,[84] obstacles remain, and in spite of all the (multilateral) arrangements available for police cooperation, informal bilateral cooperation is still the preferred method in criminal investigations.[85] How, then, does police cooperation work in the field of art crime in which cases often have a transnational component? To address this question, this section highlights certain key issues in police cooperation practices in the art crime field, beginning with the significant role played by Interpol.

Interpol's Role in Policing Art Crime

The International Criminal Police Organization (ICPO), better known by its telex address Interpol, was established in 1923 and is the oldest existing multilateral arrangement for police cooperation. Comprised of 190 participating member countries, its core business is facilitating information exchange on a case-by-case

81 See <www.cepol.net>.

82 Interview [1] (n 12), Interview [3] (n 54).

83 Ludo Block, 'Combating Organized Crime in Europe: Practicalities of Police Cooperation' (2008) 2 *Policing* 74, 76.

84 Block (n 63) 51.

85 For example, Laure Guille, 'Police and Judicial Cooperation in Europe: Bilateral versus Multilateral Cooperation' in Frédéric Lemieux (ed), *International Police Cooperation: Emerging Issues, Theory and Practice* (Willan Publishing 2010) 27.

basis. Notwithstanding its other functions – which include a range of criminal databases, analytical services and proactive support for police operations throughout the world – communication remains the organization's primary function,[86] and in 2011 more than 16 million messages were transmitted through Interpol's I24/7 communication system.[87]

In fact, since 1925, Interpol has been at the forefront of the fight against art crime, and in 1963, the agency established a specialized unit to deal with stolen art works and cultural property and began issuing printed notices on stolen works of art.[88] In 1995, Interpol set up a computerized index of international art thefts, which grew into its stolen works of art database, which since 2005 has been available online for all law enforcement agencies through Interpol's I24/7 system.[89] Currently, Interpol is working together with Italy's Carabinieri on the so-called PSYCHE[90] project to modernize the database by enabling direct data insertion by member countries and adding image recognition software to simplify the checking process.[91]

Interpol also periodically organizes meetings related to fighting art crime, especially biannual meetings of the expert working group on art crime that, according to practitioners, have significantly facilitated cooperation.[92] These meetings, frequented by experts from around the world, provide a unique opportunity for the experts to forge the personal acquaintanceships that form the foundation of their informal network and close cooperation.[93]

Transnational Police Cooperation in Art Crime Cases[94]

Anecdotal evidence on art crime cases includes some accounts of elaborate cross-border undercover operations that successfully recovered high-profile stolen art – for example, Edvard Munch's *The Scream* and Vermeer's *Lady Writing a Letter with Her Maid*[95] – operations in which the involvement of two or more jurisdictions was frequently an essential ingredient.[96] It is such operations that

86 See <http://www.interpol.int/About-INTERPOL/Priorities> accessed 12 March 2013.

87 Interpol, *Annual Report 2011* (Interpol 2012) 19.

88 Fenton Bresler, *Interpol* (Sinclair-Stevenson 1992) 352-5.

89 Jouanny (n 5) 8; See Hufnagel, in this volume.

90 Protecting SYstem for Cultural HEritage.

91 Interpol, 'Safeguarding the World's Cultural Heritage Focus of Interpol Symposium' (Press release 21 October 2011).

92 Interview [1] (n 12).

93 Interview [2] (n 74); see also Interpol, 'Minutes of the 7th International Symposium on the Theft of and Illicit Traffic in Works of Art, Cultural Property and Antiques' (Interpol 2008).

94 This section is, unless otherwise indicated, based on interview [1] (n 12), interview [2] (n 74) and interview [3] (n 54).

95 Hart (n 58) 170-85.

96 See, for example, the case descriptions in Wittman (n 4).

appeal to the imagination and lead to popular portrayals of art crime policing. In reality, however, undercover operations require significant time and resources, and the cost of running them across borders is usually only justified in the case of high-profile works of art.[97] The majority of art crime cases involve lesser known art works and antiques, and the detective work done by most art crime investigators is unexciting, perhaps even dreary, even though close cooperation with colleagues across borders is daily practice.

The group of police art crime experts from EU member states that engages in cross-border cooperation in fact consists of approximately 30 persons, most of whom have known each other for over a decade. They meet annually at the CEPOL and Interpol meetings, which thus form the foundation for a close-knit network of specialists whose personal relations and mutual trust drive their cooperation. Members of this network exchange information informally and with a speed unmatched by formal channels. This rapid exchange is important because stolen art works are often moved across borders within days or even hours of the theft, and the chance of recovery is highest in the first month. Hence, swift cross-border information exchange is of utmost importance in the recovery of stolen items. Otherwise, it may be years before these works surface again at auctions or in the hands of art dealers.[98] Once a work of dubious provenance does resurface, quick checks across borders are often crucial.

In such international information exchange, the two most asked questions are whether a piece is stolen and whether it is fake or genuine. Answering either question, however, is seldom easy. Whether a certain work of art is (registered as) stolen is not always easy to determine because, as noted earlier, the majority of police databases at the local level do not allow the registration of stolen art works in sufficient detail. The information flow on art crimes from a local to a national centralized level is therefore incomplete, meaning that most existing databases at the national level are at best a repository of information on major cases rather than a representation of the actual level of art crime.[99] Such incomplete information presents a major stumbling block in the fight against art thefts in most EU member states.

The question of whether a work of art is genuine, which is also sometimes difficult to answer for the original artist,[100] is a tough question for the police art crime specialists. Even though they usually have a good knowledge of art, they are generally not art experts.[101] Rather, they maintain close contact with art dealers,

97 See also Ellis (n 5).

98 Ibid.; Interview [1] (n 12).

99 See also Edgar Tijhuis, 'Who Is Stealing All Those Paintings?' in Noah Charney (ed), *Art and Crime: Exploring the Dark Side of the Art World* (Praeger Press 2009).

100 See Henk Schutten, *Kunstmafia* (Meulenhoff 2000). Chapter eight details occasions where the famous painter Karel Appel provided contradictory judgement on the authenticity of (falsifications of) his own work.

101 But see Charney (n 23) interviewing a German art crime investigator who argues that any art crime team needs to have at least one staff member who can identify fakes.

experts, museums and national institutions and rely on these domestic informal networks for assistance. Building such networks, however, takes time and effort, especially given that the interests of, for example, art dealers are not always aligned exactly with those of the police.

Obstacles to Police Cooperation

The key obstacles to police cooperation across borders in the EU can be divided into three categories: linguistic and cultural, organizational and legal.[102] According to both the literature and practitioners' comments, the first are usually easily overcome in police cooperation on art crime because of the longstanding personal relations between the police practitioners involved and their shared passion for the profession. Organizational obstacles, however, can affect such cooperation because of the lack of priority accorded art crimes in many member states. This lack of priority is visible, for example, in suboptimal data management: the absence of appropriate data seriously hampers international cooperation but is also reflected by the limited resources made available for investigating art crimes and fulfilling enquiries from abroad. Although in general the limitations on police investigative resources can be a legitimate reason for police not following up on each and every international enquiry,[103] a request related to a low priority crime is particularly unlikely to be allocated resources. Often, the art crime specialists maintain contacts with a network of local police officers, an important link for securing sufficient support for any follow-up to an information exchange or for actual investigation. Here again, informal ties are paramount if anything is to be accomplished because there is no formal guarantee of swift allocation of needed resources in the case of art crime.

As regards legal obstacles, although the practitioners interviewed did not point to legal differences between member states as an insurmountable obstacle to their cooperation, they could all cite different instances of legal obstacles met in practice. One art crime specialist, for example, reported how art crime's low profile led a district magistrate to disallow the use of coercive measures against a suspected art fencer. In one such case, the magistrate did not see fencing stolen art as a serious matter and, despite ample evidence provided in an International Letter of Request (ILOR), allowed neither the arrest of the fencer nor a search of the fencer's premises, even though the exact same ILOR had convinced two other district magistrates to allow coercive measures against others involved in the same case.

Another art crime specialist recounted how the tardiness of the judicial system in another member state at some point hampered the investigation. The specialist's unit received a request to investigate and confiscate a number of stolen Greek

102 Block (n 63) 153-5. Generally also political obstacles to police cooperation exist but it is safe to say that within the EU these are minimal.

103 Block (n 83) 81.

icons that were put on auction in their jurisdiction. The ILOR needed as a basis to act upon took so long to clear the judicial channels in the requesting country, however, that a risk emerged that the icons would disappear again. Therefore, instead of acting upon an international request, it was decided to open a national investigation, which was possible because the icons, although not included in the Interpol database on stolen art works, had been displayed on a website as being stolen.

Nor are legal obstacles specific to cross-border cooperation; they are also encountered in national investigations. In the Netherlands, for example, privacy regulations could force the police to purge data after ten years even though it could easily take more than a decade for stolen works of art to resurface. As a result, when a work of art does suddenly reappear, all the data from the initial inquiry may have already been shredded, forcing the investigator who is trying to rebuild the case to rely on the memory of the officers that initially handled the investigation.[104]

Overall, as this brief analysis indicates, obstacles in cooperation encountered in the field of art crime tend to be tackled through direct informal contact between networked specialists. Such informal cooperation, although it may have certain disadvantages, is very similar to cooperation practices in other specialist areas of policing, for example, counter-terrorism.[105]

Summary and Conclusions

By outlining the efforts of European police forces in the prevention and investigation of art crime, including the overarching EU policy and operational efforts, this chapter aimed to provide useful insights into the practicalities of transnational cooperation in this field. Most particularly, examination of the preventive and investigative efforts of the police in the different EU member states reveals significant differences in the priority they assign to art crime. Although 18 of the 27 member states maintain centralized expertise, in only 8 member states is actual investigative capacity allocated to the investigation of art crime, again with sizeable differences between member states.

At the EU level, although the prevention and investigation of art crime has been discussed in the political arena on several occasions over the past three decades, only recently has such discussion led to tangible policy instruments. Moreover, Europol – in contrast to its popular image – in fact undertakes no activities in relation to art crime, while the courses organized by CEPOL, like the expert meetings held by Interpol, serve only as a get-together for art crime experts. Nevertheless, such meetings are a vital element in these experts' networked

104 Interview [1] (n 12); Interview [3] (n 54).

105 See Monica den Boer, Claudia Hillebrand and Andreas Nölke, 'Legitimacy under Pressure: The European Web of Counter-Terrorism Networks' (2008) 46 *Journal of Common Market Studies* 101; and Block (63) 58.

cooperation. Indeed, as in European police cooperation in general and other specialist policing fields in particular, informal cooperation between art crime specialists is paramount to success. Such informal networks are one of the key elements that enable cooperation even in the face of the low priority accorded art crime policing by many member states.

Another recurring and perhaps decisive element in art crime policing is the personal dedication of the art crime specialists. It is interesting, for example, that many have a background connection with art and/or antiques that goes far beyond a mere professional interest. One specialist interviewed, for instance, is an art collector[106] and, just as Robert Wittman's father was the owner of an antiques shop,[107] another is the child of an antiques dealer.[108] Similarly, Robert Volpe, the first art crime detective in New York, was himself not an unsuccessful painter,[109] and one of the German art crime experts is a renowned authority on forgeries and fakes.[110] The personal dedication of these art crime specialists can also be inferred from the fact that many have been working in this field for decades. Hence, although the current findings are an insufficient basis for any firm conclusions, the first glimpse they provide into this fascinating field of policing offers an interesting starting point for further investigation.

106 Interview [1] (n 12).
107 Wittman (n 4) 27.
108 Interview [3] (n 54).
109 Adams (n 3).
110 Charney (n 23).

Chapter 12
Art Crime in North America

Noah Charney

While the US Department of Justice and other reliable sources make clear the severity and extent of art crime worldwide (the estimated 3rd highest-grossing criminal trade worldwide, behind only drugs and arms and funding organized crime and terrorism), art crime remains little known and little regarded, even among police and governmental agencies. Efforts in recent years to promote the study of art crime have resulted in an increased understanding of the phenomenon, from better-informed media coverage to the addition of several new art squads in countries that never before had any dedicated art police. Two such relative new-comers to the field are the FBI Art Squad, founded in 2004, and the Quebec Art Squad, founded in 2008. This chapter will discuss the extent of art crime in North America, as well as the efforts to curb it. We will present three case studies, two from the US and one from Canada, and summarize the successes of the new art squads in both the United States and Canada.

Introduction

A gang of jewelry thieves wait for the lone night guard to step out for a cigarette. They slip into a museum wearing gas masks to disguise their faces, but also to ward off the cloud of high-powered bear spray with which they doused the entrance, just in case the guard should return early. They made off a haul of gold statues and jewelry, destined to be melted down and sold off for the value of the raw materials alone. A heroin addict regularly stole paintings from galleries, hospitals, libraries and offices, only to trade the artworks, some worth tens of thousands of dollars, for a day or two's worth of heroin. And a major museum launched a legal motion to firmly establish its ownership of a famous painting, pre-empting a possible lawsuit from a descendant of the original owner.

These three cases will be examined in this study of art crime in North America, which will also include summaries of the only two art-dedicated police units in North America, the FBI Art Squad and the Quebec Art Squad, both of which were founded only in the past eight years. Our goal will be to present a snapshot of the extent of art crime in North America, and what is being done to curb it, juxtaposing this to the successes of other countries with longer-established art units, as well as hundreds, if not thousands, more art crime cases reported each year.

Art Crime: A Brief Introduction

When one thinks of art crime, a Hollywood image is conjured, one of black-clad cat burglars, thieves in top hats and white gloves, and perhaps the occasional criminal collector twirling his waxed moustache as he cackles maniacally over a stolen horde in his Bavarian castle. But the truth behind art crime, a truth that is misunderstood by the general public and professionals alike, is far more sinister, and more intriguing. Art crime has its share of cinematic thefts and larger-than-life characters, but it is also the realm of transnational organized crime groups, the involvement of which results in art crime funding all manner of other serious crimes, including the drug trade and terrorism. Since the Second World War, art crime has shifted from a relatively innocuous, often ideological crime, into a major international plague, the third-highest grossing criminal trade worldwide.[1]

The United States Department of Justice ranks art crime behind only the drugs and arms trades, in terms of highest-grossing criminal trades. There are tens of thousands of artworks reported stolen each year, but despite this fact the general public is only attentive to the handful of big-name museum heists that make international headlines. In Italy alone there are 20,000-30,000 stolen artworks reported annually, and many more go unreported.[2] In fact, even though reported art crimes rank third in the list of criminal trades, it is estimated that significantly more art crime worldwide goes unreported than comes to the attention of authorities, making its true scale much broader, and more difficult to estimate.

Looted antiquities provide a funding source for Fundamentalist terrorist groups.[3] Mohammed Atta of Al-Quaeda tried to sell looted antiquities in 1999, in

---

1 This information came from US Department of Justice, the US National Central Bureau of Interpol, and was listed on the following website until 2012, when the site was redone and the content of this specific page was not again uploaded: <http://www.justice.gov/usncb/programs/cultural_property_program.php>. These statistics come from the UK National Threat Assessment, conducted by SOCA. The statistics were provided by Scotland Yard, but are classified. The report was submitted in 2006 or 2007 and it remained in the Threat Assessment for several years. The terrorist links to the Middle East come from the Interpol Tracking Task Force in Iraq and were reported at the annual Interpol Stolen Works of Art meeting in Lyon in either 2008 or 2009, after prior meetings were held in Lyon, Amman and Washington. The Head of IP Baghdad claimed to have proof of the link between Islamic Fundamentalist terrorist groups and art crime (primarily antiquities looting), but this was not shown explicitly to my contacts. However all of the major players, from Interpol to the US Department of Justice, believed the reports and still broadcast the claims of it, so there is no reason to doubt it – but the details are likely still classified.

2 The Carabinieri self-publishes annual yearbooks, in Italian, for internal distribution and for the media, from which this information was culled, along with numerous interviews with Colonel Giovanni Pastore and Colonel Luigi Cortellessa, the former and current Vice-Commandant of the art squad.

3 Matthew Bogdanos, 'Illegal Antiquities Trade Funds Terrorism' in *CNN World* (7 July 2011) <http://articles.cnn.com/2011-07-07/world/iraq.looting.bogdanos_1_

order to fund the 9/11 attacks.[4] In regions such as Afghanistan, local farmers dig up treasure troves that lie in wait beneath the soil, and sell them on to local criminal or governmental organizations for a tiny fraction of their actual value. The antiquities are then smuggled abroad, given a false provenance, and sold, often on an open market to unsuspecting museums and collectors, who would never imagine that their purchase might be indirectly funding the Taliban.[5]

Before the Second World War, much art theft adhered to this cliché of dramatic museum heists carried out by skilful cat burglars, a cliché that has been perpetuated by fiction and the media. But the reality is far more sinister, as the recent rash of 'blitz' thefts indicates. From the Stockholm Museum (2000) to the Munch Museum (2004) to the Bührle Collection (2008), the latest trend in art theft is for armed, masked thieves to burst into museums, threaten those in their path physically, grab objects near to the exit, and run off. They set off alarms, but the thieves depart before police have time to respond. Since 1960, when the television media began its love affair with reporting and glorifying both art crime and the exorbitant prices for which art sold at auction, organized crime groups have to a great extent taken over art crime, turning what was once essentially an individual, often ideological crime category into a major international plague that funds organized crime's other enterprises.[6]

Despite reliable agencies making clear the extent and severity of art crime, which is severe whether or not one is an art lover because of the numerous and explicit links between art crime and organized crime, from large international mafias to local gangs, annual statistics show that the general public still associates art crime with a handful of high-profile, cinematic museum heists. In truth, such poor data and statistics are available worldwide that authorities have only a vague idea of the total extent of the phenomenon worldwide in concrete terms. Aside from countries like Italy and France, which keep excellent and extensive data (but which is not available for analysis outside of their national police organizations), most countries have no dedicated art police at all. Information is often lost at a local level, as most national police do not ask their staff members to file a crime involving art in any distinct manner, lumping it in with general stolen property. Therefore information is lost early on, and cases may never make it to the attention of national police, or to Interpol. For every art theft that is reported, scores more will go unreported for a variety of reasons, from museums not wishing to advertise their vulnerability to the more practical fact that the vast majority of art crime involves illicit trade in antiquities that are looted directly from the

---

antiquities-trade-iraq-s-national-museum-looting?_s=PM:WORLD> accessed 16 June 2013.

4 'Kunst als Terrorfinanzierung' (*Der Spiegel*, issue 29, 2005): <http://www.spiegel.de/spiegel/print/d-41106138.html> accessed 16 June 2013.

5 *Blood Antiques* (Journeyman Pictures 2009).

6 Noah Charney, 'Art Crime in Context' in Noah Charney (ed), *Art & Crime: Exploring the Dark Side of the Art World* (Praeger 2009).

earth in clandestine excavations, and therefore will never appear on a stolen art registry because they have never been seen by modern humans before looters dug them up. Authorities might come across an empty Etruscan tomb in Umbria or a ransacked grave-site in the mountains of Peru, and one might guess at the category of objects that these sites once contained, but the specific objects are lost to us. These antiquities can therefore be sold on an open market, accompanied by forged provenance suggesting their legal excavation and exportation.

Though some have stated that art crime is worth $6 billion per year, it has never been made clear where this number comes from, and it is implausible to consider it an accurate estimate. The value of art at a legitimate, open-market level is so nebulous and protean, bending to the will of the stock market, changing tastes, and numerous other factors, that it is unrealistic to think that we can estimate the total value of art were it sold at a legitimate level, much less illicit art that is used least often for resale (antiquities looted from the earth aside), and more often for ransom, or barter and collateral between criminals. This number, $6 billion per year, might reflect the estimated black market value of art registered as stolen (meaning 7-10 per cent of its estimated auction value, which is itself an unscientific measurement). If that number is correct, then art crime cannot be the third highest-grossing criminal trade. The number is far too low, and human trafficking, even illegal traffic of plants and animals, might be considered higher. We simply don't know, which can be frustrating – it is also one of the reasons why art crime has gone relatively understudied until recent years. Criminologists tend to shy away from a field such as this, which lacks extensive and accurate empirical data, and relies on macro-analysis from anecdotal material and the experience of those in the field, often related orally or even through the unreliable filter of the media.

What is clear to all knowledgeable authorities is that art crime is indeed very serious: that much of it is perpetrated by, on behalf of, or involving organized crime groups of all sizes, from local gangs to international syndicates, and therefore it is not just the art that is at stake. This is what is important, and nit-picking over percentages and such is an exercise in frustration.

There are tens of thousands of art crimes reported per year, but despite this fact the general public only hears about the handful of big-name museum heists that make international headlines. In Italy alone there are around 20,000 art objects reported stolen annually, and many more go unreported. By far the biggest problem in terms of quantity, difficulty in preventing, and difficulty in policing, is the illicit excavation of antiquities directly from the earth, or in some cases the sea.

Much of the mechanics of art crime – precisely how and for what exact purpose it is committed – remains mysterious to the general public and police alike. The reasons for this are complex and fascinating. They require an understanding not only of organized crime, but also of the exclusive and often underhanded machinations of the international art community. The art trade has always been shady and unscrupulous, full of closed doors and lips, gentlemanly vows of silence and blind eyes. What other multi-million dollar market so rarely leaves a paper trail of transactions, regularly hides commodities to avoid luxury tax, and relies so heavily on the unscientific assurance of connoisseurs to determine authenticity and value, with fortunes in the balance? Few police understand the art world, and few members of the art community work as police officers.

Most countries have no dedicated art police, an important point to note, as it is evidence that the governmental administration of these countries do not consider art crime of sufficient severity to warrant a department of their own, despite numerous publications to the contrary. The reason for this is the relative paucity of sufficiently extensive empirical data and statistics on art crime – the result of a cyclical self-destructive pattern. The empirical data is sparse because governments do not dedicate resources to gathering and analysing data on art crime. They do not dedicate resources because the existing data has not proven its extent and severity to them.[7]

For this reason, it is useful to consider some of the more successful art squads as a point of reference for other countries and for future action. Some law enforcement bodies have recently established art squads, such as Canada and The Netherlands, the former of which is considered here.[8] The FBI only formed their art squad in 2004. These two North American art squads will be examined below.

It should be noted that the recovery rate for stolen art is particularly low, in some cases as low as 2-6 per cent: a study in 2010 estimated that only 1.5 per cent of stolen art is recovered.[9] It is even rarer to both recover stolen art and successfully prosecute. Because the greatest amount of data and subsequent analysis comes from solved cases, ideally involving both recovery of stolen goods and successful prosecution of the criminals, it is understandable that limited data is available on art crime.[10]

Definitions

In order to proceed from a point of mutual departure, it is useful to define terms for this essay. When art police say that most art crime, since the 1960s, has involved organized crime at some point in the life of the crime (theft, smuggling, laundering, fencing, etc), the general instinct is to assume that they mean large criminal syndicates, or 'mafias'. Of course such syndicates have been involved in numerous high-profile art crimes, several of which we will discuss below, from the Corsican Mafia's rash of thefts along the French Riviera in the 1960s and 1970s to

7 For more on this, see Noah Charney (ed), *Art & Crime: Exploring the Dark Side of the Art World* (Praeger 2009).

8 The Dutch Art Squad is still a small operation, run by one man, Martin Finkelnberg, and several part-time colleagues. Nevertheless, the very fact of its existence is notable, since most countries have no dedicated art squads at all.

9 Mark Durney, 'Art Theft Statistics: A Need for Reliability' (Fall/Winter, 2010) 1(2) *American Society of International Law, Cultural Heritage, and Arts Review*.

10 'Spirited Away: Art Thieves Target Europe's Churches' (*Time*, 10 January 2008) <http://www.time.com/time/nation/article/0,8599,1702155,00.html> accessed 12 November 2013.

the Russian mafia's involvement in several thefts of Edvard Munch paintings, to Balkan mafia's role in art thefts in Zurich to Cosa Nostra's famous 1969 theft of Caravaggio's *Nativity* from the church of San Lorenzo in Palermo. But those are the cases that make international headlines, and they represent only a fraction of what is actually reported each year. That is not to say that these high-profile cases are the only ones in which major criminal syndicates are involved – far from it. But the definition of organized crime used in discussions with police about art crime is significantly more expansive. Organized crime may be defined as any group of three or more individuals who work together in criminal enterprises aimed at collective, long-term goals.[11] This definition, which paraphrases the generally-accepted criminological definition, includes everything from a small local gang of jewelry and art thieves to the Japanese Yakuza. It is easier, in fact, to list what it does not include than what it does. This definition excludes street criminals, crimes of opportunity, independent thieves stealing for ideological reasons, most forgery and deception crimes (which tend to be perpetrated by individuals or pairs, without connection to larger criminal groups or other criminal activities), or those whose goal is maximizing immediate cash profit. The definition is otherwise inclusive, and it is therefore easy to understand how world art police agree on the role of organized crime in art crime.

Three Case Studies

In this chapter, we will examine several case studies in some depth that will serve as exemplary of the situation in North America. There are many case studies to choose from, but I have selected three main cases, one in Canada, two in New Haven, Connecticut in the United States.[12] We will discuss the 2008 theft of Bill Reid gold sculptures from Vancouver, in Canada. The two New Haven cases see the union of art theft, drug use and local organized crime leaders in the Dennis Maluk case from 2009, and a pre-emptive legal action brought by Yale University to firmly establish their ownership of Van Gogh's *Night Café*.

Bill Reid Gold Thefts (2008)

On 23 May 2008 thieves wearing gas masks stole 12 gold objects created by the Haida goldsmith Bill Reid as well as several antique Mexican gold objects from

11 United Nations Office on Drugs and Crime – *Introduction* <http://www.unodc.org/documents/data-and-analysis/tocta/Introduction.pdf> accessed 12 November 2013.

12 The reason for choosing two in New Haven out of all possible US cases (and there are over 1000 in the FBI's art crime database), is that they happened to coincide with my teaching a seminar in art crime at Yale University, in the spring of 2009. Life provided ideal case studies for my students, right in their hometown, and these cases are as exemplary as any.

the Museum of Anthropology at University of British Columbia, in Vancouver. Thieves had watched the museum for some time, noting when the security guards changed shifts. In the process they took note of the smoking habits of the only guard on duty at night – he regularly slipped outside for a cigarette, leaving the museum unguarded for the duration of his smoke.

The thieves waited until the guard stepped outside for his cigarette, and rushed into the museum. But they were prepared for the guard's return, should he finish his cigarette break early. They sprayed bear spray across the entrance to the museum, a high-powered form of mace used in emergencies to repel a bear attack, thereby blocking the entrance – had the guard returned he would have been, effectively, maced by the cloud of smoke that remained. Wearing gas masks to protect themselves and hide their identities, the thieves made off with a haul of gold artworks. The thieves also had significant knowledge of electronic security systems: they disabled the recording mechanisms of the surveillance cameras while the cameras were still on.[13]

The museum was particularly fearful that the gold objects would be melted down for their raw materials. Most stolen art has a high value through non-intrinsic reasons: that is to say that the value is not the sum of its constituent parts (which in paintings, for example, are often just wood and pigment), but rather how those humble parts are unified by the artist. For works of jewelry or in gold, there is a danger that the thieves will try to cash in only on the value of the raw materials, which are of reasonably high value in this case. While the art itself was valued at $2 million, we have discussed the difficulty and danger for the criminals to attempt to sell stolen, uniquely identifiable art. It is far safer to melt such gold artworks into unidentifiable lumps of raw material and sell those, thereby pocketing $15,000 (the value of the raw gold) without risk of being caught.

In hope of preventing this, the museum offered a reward for information leading to the recovery of the stolen art of $50,000 Canadian, a sum far higher than the value of the raw materials alone. The danger of offering a reward is that it teaches not only these criminals but others that crime does pay – that they can be rewarded by their victim in the form of cash for the return of the stolen art. For this reason in some countries, it is illegal to pay a ransom, whether to recover a kidnap victim or a work of art.

In 1975, thieves stole twenty-eight paintings from the Museum of Modern Art in Milan.[14] A reward was offered, and the paintings were returned by a colleague of the criminals, who thereby pocketed the reward. Shortly thereafter the same gang of criminals stole thirty-five paintings, including many of the same works, from the

---

13 'B.C. museum fears stolen Bill Reid gold pieces may be melted down' (CBCNews British Columbia, 25 May 2008) <http://www.cbc.ca/news/canada/british-columbia/story/2008/05/25/bc-ubc-museum-heist.html> accessed 12 November 2013.

14 Mark Durney, 'Ransoms and Stolen Art' (*Art Theft Central* blog, 2009) <http://arttheftcentral.blogspot.com/2009/02/ransoms-and-stolen-art.html> accessed 10 June 2010.

same museum. This time they kept the art, and it has never been recovered. That is the danger of paying a ransom.

In this case, however, the strategy paid off. The offer of a reward tempted the thieves, who were members of a small local criminal gang involved primarily in jewelry theft. Their intention had been to melt the stolen objects, but the reward had stayed their hand long enough for the police to arrest them in a suburb of Vancouver after an anonymous tip.[15]

All but two of the works were recovered, along with other stolen jewelry pieces.[16]

Dennis Maluk and Heroin for Paintings (2009)

The spring of 2009 saw a rash of art thefts in New Haven, Connecticut. A total of 39 recorded artworks (paintings, drawings, and photographs) were stolen from the greater New Haven area within a period of months.

This included three paintings taken from the Slifka Center at Yale, a Jewish community center, three photographs taken from the New Haven Public Library, three photographs taken from the New Haven Legal Assistance Association, and six works taken from the Yale New Haven Hospital. None of the works were of significant value, but those from the Slifka Center were worth in the high thousands of dollars each.

Examination of CCTV footage from the Slifka Center led local police to the thief: Dennis Maluk, a heroin addict. Maluk was arrested and told police that he had been stealing art in order to trade it for heroin. His dealer, Bruno Nestir, was a local member of a larger regional gang involved in small-scale sales of drugs and illicit firearms. When police raided Nestir's apartment, they found all 39 paintings, two shotguns, two rifles, two revolvers (all unlicensed), $947 in cash, and both heroin and marijuana packaged for sale on the street.

Only one of the stolen artworks was hanging on Nestir's wall. The others were stacked neatly on the floor of his apartment. He had taken to selling the frames for cash, and it is not clear what his intention was with the artworks themselves. Maluk said that Nestir would trade him $30-40 worth of heroin for each artwork. Maluk was essentially stealing art to exchange for a day or two's worth of his heroin fix.

Dennis Maluk is a typical example of a street criminal (sometimes called 'common thief') who happens to steal art, but who might have been just as content stealing DVD players, laptops, or cars – anything that will get him quick cash

---

15 'Career criminal paid $20,000 for helping recover stolen artwork' (CBCNews British Columbia, 30 January 2009) <http://www.cbc.ca/news/canada/british-columbia/story/2009/01/30/bc-reid-heist-reward.html> accessed 12 November 2013.

16 'Most of Bill Reid's stolen artifacts recovered' (*Vancouver Sun*, 10 June 2008) <http://www.canada.com/topics/news/national/story.html?id=88f0469a-a72b-47d4-83d8-fa1b127cea04> accessed 10 July 2008.

or, in this case, his next heroin fix. He stole paintings for no more thought-out reason than that they were relatively under-protected, relatively portable, and that he could get heroin for them. But the case is not quite so clear-cut, as Maluk was swapping the 39 paintings he happened to steal for heroin provided by a member of a local organized crime group, Bruno Nestir. Thus, the street criminal was being used by an organized crime group.

While this case is, in itself, not particularly remarkable and does not involve art of particular importance, it does provide an ideal microcosmic view into what happens with stolen art. In cases such as this, and on a larger scale like the Russborough House theft in 1986 by Martin Cahill (the most prominent example of the interchange between drugs, arms, and stolen art), we glimpse art crime followed by an exchange of illicit goods on a closed black market between criminals or criminal groups.[17] Stolen art may be used for barter or act as collateral in deals for other illicit goods for which there is criminal risk involved in cashing in on the good in question, whether it is drugs, arms or art. This case also illustrates a common theme: most thieves who steal art have no prior experience in art crime, and no knowledge of, or appreciation for, art. Art represents an easily-portable, often under-protected, high-value commodity, and nothing more.

Yale Art Gallery and Van Gogh's Night Café *(2009)*

The Internet era has seen a sudden increase in repatriation and reparations legal cases regarding stolen art. This is due to the simple fact of the world of information having become more accessible. Thanks to digitization we now know the location of artworks, particularly in public collections, from Seattle to Sri Lanka. In the past one would have had to travel to a collection to know what was inside it, or to rely on catalogues and books, which might not always show complete collections. A precedent has been set that art stolen during the Second World War in particular should be returned to the ancestors of those from whom it was stolen, as in the Maria Altmann case, in which five Gustav Klimt paintings that had been taken from her family during the Nazi era were restored to Altmann after a legal battle.[18]

A small but growing legal specialization has arisen, a subsection of art law, which focuses on art reparations. A settlement was recently struck on behalf of the descendants of Kazimir Malevich, in which five Malevich paintings, appropriated

17 This case involved the theft of 18 artworks from the Beit Collection at Russborough House, outside of Dublin. A Vermeer stolen by Cahill and his gang was used as collateral in a loan for drug money, while a Metsu painting was swapped for a shipment of drugs in a barter arrangement between organized crime groups. This case is well-documented in numerous sources, including Edward Dolnick's *The Rescue Artist* (Harper Perennial 2006) and Matthew Hart's *The Irish Game* (Walker Publishing 2004), as well as in Charney (n 7).

18 Hubertus Czernin, *Die Fälschung: Der Fall Bloch-Bauer und das Werk Gustav Klimts* (Czernin Verlag 2006).

by the Soviet Union when Malevich travelled abroad in 1927, were returned to the Malevich family, while a further 75 under consideration, would remain in the collection of the Stedelijkmuseum in the Netherlands, which had acquired these 80 works in 1958.[19]

This trend has also seen pre-emptive, defensive lawsuits. In 2009 the Yale Art Gallery brought a pre-emptive suit, seeking for a judge to reiterate that the jewel of their collection, *Night Café* by Vincent van Gogh, was the property of the museum.[20]

A rumour had preceded this action that a descendant of the original owner was making noises about reclaiming the painting for his family, which prompted Yale to this defensive action.

This action came shortly after the nation of Peru began to threaten legal action to recover the artifacts excavated from Machu Picchu by Yale archaeologist Hiram Bingham, circa 1911. This case is distinctive because there is no allegation of looting – Bingham led a well-documented, respectful archaeological expedition. At the time, Peru did not have the infrastructure to present the artifacts in a safe museum environment of their own, and it has been argued that Yale preserved treasures that would otherwise have fallen to looters or deteriorated. I have seen these artifacts, which are kept at the Yale Peabody Museum of Natural History. They are primarily pottery shards and textile fragments – there is hardly a first-rate, museum-worthy piece among them, and their interest is largely scientific, rather than as a museum draw. Had Peru's approach been less threatening and more cooperative, Yale might not have felt obliged to draw themselves up into a defensive formation, making it appear that they would lose face and admit a degree of guilt were they to acquiesce to Peru's demands and return the artifacts. There is a huge difference, psychologically, between a nation demanding that objects be returned (as Peru has done with Machu Picchu and Greece with the Parthenon Marbles), and requesting the return or sharing of objects, as Italy has done in many cases, far more successfully. When looting cannot be proven, the question becomes a moral rather than a legal one. For moral questions, better results would come about through polite cooperation, rather than public demand.

We will likely see more such lawsuits in the future, as more of the world's collections are digitized. Not only does this allow people to learn what art is where, but it also facilitates family history research, allowing victims of past art theft to discover the historical circumstance and therefore build a reasonable legal case for reparations or the return of looted art.

In addition to legal cases, the Internet era has made it far more difficult for thieves to sell stolen art. Most valuable fine art is unique and instantly recognizable

---

19 Howard Spiegler, 'Surviving War and Peace: the Long Road to Recovering the Malevich Paintings' (Spring 2009) 1 *The Journal of Art Crime*.

20 David Itzkoff, 'Yale Sues, Asserting Ownership of Van Gogh's "Night Café"' (*New York Times*, 25 May 2009) <http://artsbeat.blogs.nytimes.com/2009/03/25/yale-sues-asserting-ownership-of-van-goghs-night-cafe/> accessed 12 November 2013.

if it comes from an extant collection (antiquities looted directly from the earth or the sea are, of course, a different story, as we have discussed). Within hours of the discovery of a theft, photographs and descriptions of the stolen goods can be circulated around the world.[21]

This makes it very difficult for a potential buyer of stolen art to claim that he did not know that the work in question was stolen, and it makes it far more difficult for thieves to shop stolen art. This has driven criminals to use stolen art as barter or collateral, as we have discussed, in order to avoid the danger of looking for a buyer – for a large percentage of the stolen artworks that are recovered are found thanks to an undercover operation in which a policeman pretends to be a buyer of stolen art, luring the thieves into offering him the works.[22]

Art Squads in North America

To conclude, we will discuss the extent of art crime in the US and in Canada, and take a quick look at the art squads in each country.

FBI Art Squad

Founded in 2004, the FBI runs a team of 13 dedicated agents, supported by special trial attorneys for prosecutions. It also maintains the National Stolen Art File (NSAF), a computerized index of reported stolen art for the use of law enforcement agencies around the world.[23]

The FBI Art Squad has recovered over 2600 items valued approximately $142 million.[24]

Such statistics must be understood in context, however. The values for art cited are based on the estimated open market value, should a work of art with legitimate pedigree be offered at auction. Estimates of the black-market value of stolen art, based on the amount which undercover agents were asked to pay during sting operations, is 7-10 per cent of its perceived open market value, which we have already mentioned is an unreliable sum total – it really only serves to indicate that

21 One of the best sources for press releases about stolen art is the Museum Security Network.

22 The careers of Charlie Hill and Robert K. Wittman, two policemen who went undercover to recover stolen artworks, provide numerous examples of this. See Edward Dolnick, *The Rescue Artist* (Harper Perennial 2006) and Robert K. Wittman, *Priceless* (Broadway 2011).

23 FBI National Stolen Art File <http://www.fbi.gov/about-us/investigate/vc_majorthefts/arttheft/national-stolen-art-file> accessed 12 November 2013.

24 FBI Art Crime Team website <http://www.fbi.gov/about-us/investigate/vc_majorthefts/arttheft/art-crime-team> accessed 12 November 2013.

art crime is indeed a serious problem, far more serious than either the general public or government administrators realize.[25]

The FBI has been remarkably successful, despite the fact that a relatively small number of thefts occur in the United States. The US is rather a preferred venue to sell stolen art, and for this reason the FBI has helped other countries recover their stolen art, and has participated in numerous undercover operations in collaboration with foreign police forces.

There are some independent art police outside of the FBI, but they have largely turned to investigating art through the accumulation of experience in the field, rather than having been given special training or assignments. Don Hrycyk in Los Angeles is the leading investigator outside of the FBI, and Robert Volpe was the only such investigator in New York until his death.[26] Others include Thomas McShane and insurance agents, like Dorit Straus of Chubb. But we can count on one hand the number of art-specific investigators in the US, which is telling. The FBI stolen art database contains only a few thousand stolen objects, while the world's largest database, run by the Carabinieri and nicknamed Leonardo, contains over four million.

Quebec Art Squad

In 2008 the Sureté du Quebec, in collaboration with the Royal Canadian Mounted Police, established the first national art crime investigation team in Canada's history. The four-man team is now led by Jean-Francois Talbot, who has worked since 2003 with Alain Lacoursiere, an art historian and retired member of the Montreal police. Lacoursiere helped in the development of an art crime team in Canada and a system called Art Alert, which is an email bulletin sent out to 25,000 subscribers in 75 countries, largely members of the art community and police departments. Between 2004 and 2008, a combined force of agents from the Sureté du Quebec and the Montreal police department, investigated around 450 art crimes, made 20 arrests, and seized over 150 stolen or forged artworks, with a total estimated value of around $2 million. The newly-established art crime team handles an average of 90 art crime cases per year.[27]

Conclusion

It is safe to say that art crime in North America is a far more significant problem than most realize, including police, government officials, and the general public.

25 Mark Durney 'Ransoms Revisited Mocking Madonna' (*Art Theft Central* blog, 2010) <http://arttheftcentral.blogspot.com/2010/03/ransoms-revisited-mocking-madonna.html> accessed 6 June 2010.

26 For more on Don Hrycyk, see Joshua Knelman, *Hot Art* (Tin House 2012).

27 This information comes from an interview between Catherine Scofield Sezgin and members of the art crime team, published in the ARCA Blog (29 April 2011).

However while North America is a leading market territory for stolen and looted art and antiquities, with a significant portion of such goods smuggled to the United States or Canada for sale, neither country is a major source for stolen or looted objects. This is in part due to the shorter history of cultures that produce lasting plastic art of a high market value. Woodwork and textiles, made by Natives of North America, does not last centuries buried underground, and indeed burial rituals are very different among these cultures than, for example, Etruscans, who buried their dead in elaborate tombs, surrounded by valuable artifacts, intended to be preserved. As a source country for looted antiquities, taken in illicit archaeological excavations, North America might be considered along the lines of African nations, whose valuable plastic objects, certain bronzes and ceramics aside, tend to be made of wood and therefore neither sustain burial nor survive in non-ideal conditions for centuries. Likewise, there is not the same tradition of art decorating religious institutions in North America as there is in Europe, meaning that churches and temples, while occasionally targeted by art thieves, do not pose the same sort of potential for victimization. With around 90 cases investigated each year in Canada, and a few hundred per year in the United States, North America is more often the ultimate destination for illicit art that is intended for resale, rather than the origin of the theft or looted site. This is in stark contrast to the several thousand cases per year investigated in Germany, or the number in Italy, which investigates around 20,000 stolen artworks per year.

For this reason, a focus should be placed on ensuring that the art market is monitored, and Customs put an added emphasis on keeping questionable works out of the United States and Canada. The art market is so heavily weighted toward New York (with forays into Los Angeles, Montreal and Vancouver), that efforts could be concentrated there. At-risk sites are more practically limited to museums, galleries and private collections, with the largest problem worldwide, illicit looting of archaeological sites, hardly an issue in North America. Likewise, the frequent victimization of churches – as it happens in Europe – is hardly a problem. This information can allow US and Canadian efforts to focus for maximum effect.

But the issue remains, as the prominent criminologist Professor Petrus van Duyne has said on occasion, 'There is not enough fear about art crime.'[28] Because the general public still thinks of art crime in terms of Thomas Crown and *Ocean's Twelve*, rather than the truth relating to organized crime and terrorism, and because the majority of the public does not feel a personal connection to art (and therefore does not fear its disappearance), there is no pressure on governments and police departments to focus efforts and funding on art protection and recovery. For this reason it is useful, when discussing art crime in general or its presence in North America in particular, to emphasize the more sinister side of art crime, in order to impel those with the power to reinforce the efforts of the few passionate investigators and scholars to do so.

---

28 Interview conducted by the author, during van Duyne's teaching tenure on the ARCA Postgraduate Certificate Program in Art Crime and Cultural Heritage Protection (Summer 2010).

Chapter 13

Perspectives on the Investigation, Prosecution and Prevention of Art Crime in Asia

Stefan Gruber*

Art crime in Asia is an ever expanding phenomenon that has become increasingly difficult to police and prosecute. Asia is home to a vast number of culturally diverse and distinct communities, and boasts a rich history of significant ancient – and in some cases, continuous – civilizations that have left their traces in many regions, both urban and remote. Cultural heritage sites and artefacts represent the precious tactile legacies of these unique and distinct groups. Consequently, it is not surprising that the high quality of craftsmanship, value and sophistication of such treasures have long attracted looters, thieves and illicit art traders.

Art crime in Asia developed and adapted alongside political and social turmoil in the region. Throughout the centuries, countless wars and invasions in Asia frequently resulted in the deliberate destruction and pillaging of cultural property. Once Western forces began to colonize Asia, a new era of art trafficking took shape. The emergence of rival colonial powers on the Asian stage and the enforcement of their sovereign claims were accompanied by widespread destruction and looting of historic and cultural assets. During this period, the amassing of trophies and 'souvenirs' by soldiers, officials and wealthy travellers was widespread, and cultural goods were shipped overseas in large quantities. One of the most notorious examples is the ransacking and destruction of the Old Summer Palace in Beijing by Anglo-French troops during the Second Opium War in 1860. The Old Summer Palace was said to have hosted the most

---

* Associate Professor, Kyoto University. The author would like to thank Alice Gardoll, intern at the Sydney Centre for International Law, and Soung Takayama for their invaluable research assistance and support with the preparation of the final draft of this chapter. This chapter was drafted to a large extent while the author was a Visiting Fellow at the Centre for Comparative and Public Law (CCPL) at the University of Hong Kong. The author would therefore like to express his gratitude to CCPL and particularly its director Professor Simon N.M. Young, and the Faculty of Law of the University of Hong Kong for their generous support and hospitality.

magnificent collection of treasures ever collected at one place.[1] Items stolen during that incident still surface on a frequent basis at art auctions worldwide.

Other factors which caused the large-scale loss of cultural relics and promoted the uncontrolled export of cultural goods include civil wars and the collapse of Asian political systems in the twentieth century. A prominent example is the reign of the Khmer Rouge in Cambodia in the 1970s, during which time numerous ancient temples were damaged or demolished, and countless frescos, statues, and other cultural objects were looted, crudely removed from their original locations, and shipped overseas. A recent high-profile case of an artefact smuggled from Cambodia during that period involves the confiscation by American customs agents of a statue looted from the Prasat Chen Temple in Koh Ker from the possession of Sotheby's.[2] The counterpart of the statue is currently owned by the Norton Simon Museum in California, while the severed feet remain on the pedestal at the temple from which the figures were sawn off by looters.[3] Cambodia has sought the return of both artefacts from the United States under the 1970 UNESCO Convention.[4] In response, federal prosecutors and legal representatives of Sotheby's have raised many issues before the United States District Court for the Southern District of New York, including whether or not any laws which prohibit the removal of such items were in force in Cambodia during the relevant time.[5] Similar uncertainties substantially complicate the investigations and reparations of earlier incidences of looting in many Asian countries.

This chapter explores existing forms of art crime in parts of Asia, where looting and trafficking of regional artefacts have developed extensively in contemporary times. The sophisticated methods of looters and middlemen, the highly efficient smuggling networks which support them, and the involvement and resources of international art dealers collectively make the detection, investigation and prosecution of art crime very difficult. Factors contributing to such circumstances, which include the rising margins on the international art market, the opening of borders, and increased trade throughout the region, are also considered. Globalization, the simplified circulation of goods, and the diversity of political and legal systems in Asia are other aspects which add to the challenges facing cross-

1 Jack Beeching, *The Chinese Opium Wars* (Hutchinson 1975) 315.

2 'US Seeks Halt to Auction of Rare Cambodian Statue' *Australia Network News* (27 Feb 2013) <http://www.abc.net.au/news/2013-02-27/an-us-lawyer-seeks-return-of-rare-cambodian-statue/4543572> accessed 12 November 2013.

3 Ralph Blumenthal, 'Cambodia Is Seeking 2nd Statue' *The New York Times* (28 September 2012) <http://www.nytimes.com/2012/09/29/arts/design/cambodia-now-seeking-return-of-norton-simon-statue.html> accessed 12 November 2013.

4 Convention on the Means of Prohibiting and Preventing the Illicit Import, Export and Transfer of Ownership of Cultural Property (adopted 14 November 1970, entered into force 24 April 1972) 823 UNTS 231.

5 Tom Mashberg, 'Legal Tussle Over Statue Turns Nasty' *The New York Times* (14 September 2013) C1 <http://www.nytimes.com/2013/09/14/arts/design/legal-tussle-over-statue-turns-nasty.html?smid=fb-share&_r=0> accessed 12 November 2013.

border regulation of the art trade and the tracking of cultural artefacts. Following this discussion, the final part of the chapter examines several mechanisms and issues which are relevant to the prevention of art crime in Asia.

Pillaging of Archaeological Sites

Most forms of art crime are driven by the demands of the art market and collectors for 'fresh' items. With each legitimately obtained acquisition by museums and private collectors, the number of such items on the market decreases while their appeal remains on the rise.[6] The strong demand is often met by way of illegal excavations or art theft in contravention of export bans. This section focuses on the pillaging of heritage sites, rather than the theft of art from collections or museums, as it is the looting of cultural sites which primarily reflects the complexities involved in the prosecution and detection of art crime. This is particularly so in Asia, where several heritage sites are currently unprotected or not yet officially recorded.

Looting, one of the most destructive types of art crime, damages cultural heritage, destroys archaeological evidence, and culturally impoverishes the nations in which it occurs. In many regions archaeological items and sites are the only available sources of knowledge of ancient civilizations, particularly where no written records are available or ever existed.[7] It is estimated that 90 per cent of all archaeological material is destroyed during illegal excavations. This is due in part to the fact that most looters lack archaeological expertise and excavate sites within short periods of time in order to avoid detection. To an extent, the damage inflicted by such looting irreparably impedes the full recovery of those items and goes beyond their material loss. The knowledge of their exact locations and initial conditions, which would have added crucial information to the archaeological context, is permanently lost, even if the items are later retrieved.

Particularly in Asia, looting is a phenomenon of enormous scale. It is estimated that approximately 80 per cent of antiquities from Southeast Asia on the art market in the United States were illegally smuggled into the country, while allegedly ten million cultural artefacts have been transported out of China over the years.[8] Reports indicate that even concrete replicas meant to replace the looted authentic heads of statues at Angkor Thom in Cambodia have been stolen.[9] Such

6 James A.R. Nafziger, Robert Kirkwood Paterson and Alison Dundes Renteln, *Cultural Law: International, Comparative, and Indigenous* (Cambridge University Press 2010) 241.

7 Tom Bazley, *Crimes of the Art World* (Praeger 2010) 105.

8 See ibid., 103-9.

9 Seth Mydans, 'Raiders of Lost Art Loot Temples in Cambodia' *The New York Times* (1 April 1999) <http://www.nytimes.com/1999/04/01/world/raiders-of-lost-art-loot-temples-in-cambodia.html> accessed 12 November 2013.

occurrences not only illustrate the general lack of sophistication of local looters, but also highlight the alarming scale of the dilemma even at such prominent sites.

Art Forgery

A form of art crime that has become particularly widespread in Asia alongside theft, pillaging and illegal exporting of items is art forgery, a practice fuelled by the substantial monetary value of and consistent demand by the international art market for 'new' authentic items. Art forgery has consequently become a significant industry. For example, southern China has numerous factories that specialize in the reproduction of pieces of art and antiquities, although not necessarily always with the intention to mislead customers. Nonetheless, many of these factories have the expertise and resources to produce items that resemble antiquities from centuries ago. There are replicas which even pass scientific tests for authenticity because of their carefully arranged composition, which may include, for instance, fragments of genuine pieces.[10] Such items, consisting of various degrees of quality, are produced to deliberately scam purchasers and often evade detection by specialists. A variety of methods involve fabricating other 'proof' and producing ceramics with clay collected from the same pits as those used for the originals made centuries ago. Sophisticated forgers also often 'create' provenance for their items to make them appear authentic, again conning even experts in the field.[11] Because of the increasingly sophisticated methods of forgery, art markets in many regions of Asia are nowadays swamped with counterfeits. For example, in 2013 Chinese authorities closed the Jibaozhai Museum in Jizhou after discovering that almost all of its approximately 40,000 items on display were actually fakes.[12] Of course, vast numbers of fakes are not exclusively sold to 'honest' buyers on the 'genuine' local art markets. In fact, a substantial part of all smuggled and illegally traded antiquities appear to be counterfeit.[13] For instance, fakes produced in southern China for international export are often loaded in the Pearl River Delta, falsely declared, and shipped overseas via Hong Kong.

---

10 Toby Bull, 'Lack of Due Diligence and Unregulated Markets: Trade in Illicit Antiquities and Fakes in Hong Kong' in Noah Charney (ed), *Art and Crime: Exploring the Dark Side of the Art World* (Praeger 2009) 28-9.

11 Kenneth Polk and Duncan Chappell, 'Fakes and Deception: Examining Fraud in the Art Market' in Noah Charney (ed), *Art and Crime: Exploring the Dark Side of the Art World* (Praeger 2009) 74.

12 Jonathan Jones, 'Scandal in China over the Museum with 40,000 Fake Artefacts' *The Guardian* (18 July 2013) <http://www.theguardian.com/culture/2013/jul/17/jibaozhai-museum-closed-fakes-china> accessed 12 November 2013.

13 Bazley (n 7) 70-2.

Criminal Law and Prosecution of Art Crime

There is a wide range of repressive options available to prevent and prosecute offences related to art crime. Since most legislative systems regard undiscovered and buried items as the property of the state, excavating or removing such an item without permission would constitute theft and be punishable under the relevant criminal law.[14] However, looters and illicit antique traders must first be apprehended and linked to the evidence before prosecution may occur. Unfortunately, prosecuting and bringing offenders to justice have proved challenging because of the considerable difficulty involved in detecting thefts, especially in areas which are inadequately monitored and guarded.[15] Adding to these challenges is the fact that more thefts of cultural property, as with theft of any kind of property to a certain extent, occur than are reported to the police. Resultantly, offences arising from such instances are neither investigated nor prosecuted.[16] Furthermore, it is often difficult to link recovered items to specific sites once they are removed. These obstacles are amplified by the reality that many looters are organized professionals and act in coordinated operations. The hardest to link to looting operations are the illicit antique dealers who hire looters, request specific items, and pick sites to be pillaged. The string-pullers usually escape any prosecution as they are much better connected than the looters and take care not to leave any evidence which would allow for items to be traced back to their centres of operation or to the sites where the lootings were committed. The risk of being caught is considerably lessened once the item, or key evidence, is smuggled out of the country and is no longer within its jurisdiction.[17] These factors make successful investigations and convictions unlikely.

Penalties for offences related to art crime in Asia often reflect how serious the respective governments consider the problem to be. In the case of China, for example, serious punishments may be imposed when offenders are apprehended by authorities despite the presence of complications regarding the identification and prosecution of looters and other wrongdoers involved in illicit art trafficking. The Law of the People's Republic of China on Protection of Cultural Relics of 2007 lists several activities that are punishable under Chinese law. They include the illicit excavation of ancient sites, the damage

---

14 See, for example, Law on Cultural Heritage (Socialist Republic of Vietnam), arts 70-2.

15 Stefan Gruber, 'The Fight Against the Illicit Trade in Asian Cultural Artefacts: Connecting International Agreements, Regional Cooperation and Domestic Strategies' (2013) 3 *Asian Journal of International Law* 341, 346.

16 Guido Carducci, '"Repatriation", "Restitution" and "Return" of "Cultural Property": International Law and Practice' in Mille Gabriel and Jens Dahl (eds), *UTIMUT: Past Heritage – Future Partnerships, Discussions on Repatriation in the 21st Century* (International Work Group for Indigenous Affairs 2008) 122.

17 Ibid., 123.

to or destruction of any valuable cultural relics under state protection, the robbing or plundering of state-owned cultural relics, and the illegal sale, export or smuggling of protected cultural relics.[18] Furthermore, the Criminal Law of the People's Republic of China of 1997 imposes severe punishments for related crimes.[19] Depending on the nature and seriousness of the crime, criminals may have fines imposed for minor offences or receive a sentence of up to life imprisonment and confiscation of their property for the most serious offences.

In 1998, China implemented the death penalty in an attempt to crack down on the organized smuggling of cultural relics; this provision was ultimately repealed for all crimes related to cultural relics when the relevant provisions were revised in 2011.[20] While the provision was in effect, the application of the death penalty for such offences was not a hollow threat.[21] For example, in 1998 several men were executed and others imprisoned in Shanxi Province for stealing 15 frescos from the Zhaoling Museum in Xianyang City which were part of the Shaolin Tombs of the second emperor of the Tang Dynasty.[22] Another example concerns a case in 2010 involving the former chief of the cultural relics protection authorities of the Imperial Garden in Chengde in Hebei Province, who was executed after being convicted of stealing 259 cultural relics between 1993 and 2002 from the depository of the World Heritage-listed Mountain Resort and its Outlying Temples, replacing them with copies and inferior or incomplete objects, and ordering his subordinates to alter the records.[23] The thefts were discovered only after two cultural relics from the collection of the Palace Museum in Beijing were identified at an auction in Hong Kong in 2002, nearly a decade after the known criminal activities first began.[24]

Other countries take very different approaches to art crime. For example, in India, where the looting and illegal export of antiquities is severe, Section 25 of the Antiquities and Art Treasures Act (1972) provides for punishment with imprisonment or fines for certain offences related to the illegal export of antiquities. In contrast, section 30 of the Ancient Monuments and

---

18 2007 Law of the People's Republic of China on Protection of Cultural Relics (China Cultural Relics Law), art 64.

19 1997 Criminal Law of the People's Republic of China, arts 151, 264, 324-9.

20 Amendment VIII to the Criminal Law of the People's Republic of China, adopted at the 19th session of the Standing Committee of the Eleventh National People's Congress of the People's Republic of China on 25 February 2011.

21 See, for example, 'China Executes Three Men for Plundering Ancient Tombs' *Associated Press* (18 April 2003).

22 Jeanette Greenfield, *The Return of Cultural Treasures* (3rd edn, Cambridge University Press 2007) 275.

23 'China Executes Official for Plundering Cultural Relics' *Sify News* (19 November 2010) <http://www.sify.com/news/china-executes-official-for-plundering-cultural-relics-news-international-kltqkochjjb.html> accessed 12 November 2013.

24 Ibid.

Archaeological Sites and Remains Act (1958) provides for punishment with imprisonment for up to two years or a fine of up to 100,000 rupees (less than USD 2,000) or both for removing 'from a protected monument any sculpture, carving, image, bas-relief, inscription, or other like object'. As lawyers often take advantage of inconsistencies between the acts to defend their clients and attain lower sentences, looters and art dealers are hardly deterred by the soft penalties when lured by the comparatively sizeable profits that they would make through illegal dealings.[25]

Procedural and jurisdictional complications add to the difficulties surrounding the prosecution of criminals. Prosecutions are costly, time-consuming, and often exceed the resources available to heritage protection authorities, police investigators and public prosecutors. In addition, many cases are based in different jurisdictions, a fact which significantly impedes the successful prosecution of art crimes. Indeed, law enforcement agencies from jurisdictions where art crimes are committed have no authority to apprehend offenders who operate in foreign jurisdictions. Similar jurisdictional challenges arise in the context of illicit antique dealers who trade in countries where their actions would not constitute any violation of law. For example, the provisions of the 1961 Act on Ancient Monuments, Antiques, Objects of Art and Natural Museums of Thailand, which prohibit the export of any antique or object of art without a license[26] and provide for punishment of anyone who exports non-registered[27] or registered[28] antiques or 'objects of art', only apply to objects of Thai origin. Therefore, the trafficking of Cambodian artefacts in Thailand, for instance, would not be governed by the act.

Some countries in Asia function as areas of transit for looted antiquities.[29] Thailand, which has suffered significantly from the large-scale looting of its archaeological and cultural sites, remains an important hub for the trafficking of illegally exported cultural relics from other countries, predominantly Cambodia.[30] Looters in Cambodia, who are usually locals with knowledge about accessing valuable sites and pillaging them without being caught, often smuggle the looted items to Thailand via the many roads leading to its northern region; many such instances also involve middlemen from Thailand.[31] Once

25 Neeta Lal, 'India Blinks as Art Treasures Disappear' *Asia Times* (15 October 2011) <http://atimes.com/atimes/South_Asia/MJ15Df03.html> accessed 12 November 2013.

26 1961 Act on Ancient Monuments, Antiques, Objects of Art and Natural Museums (Thailand), s 22.

27 Ibid., s 38.

28 Ibid., s 39.

29 See also Simon Mackenzie, 'Trafficking Antiquities' in Mangai Natarajan (ed), *International Crime and Justice* (Cambridge University Press 2011) 143.

30 Sylvain Gharbi, 'Khmer Heritage Plundered' *7Days* (Phnom Penh, 18 January) <http://www.phnompenhpost.com/7days/2936-khmer-heritage-plundered> accessed 12 November 2013 19.

31 Ibid.

the items reach major cities, such as Bangkok, they enter the international art market and are sold, where they can hardly be tracked and virtually disappear.[32] The same occurs in other major transportation hubs with large ports and airports, such as Hong Kong and Singapore. The sheer amount of containers and other freight processed daily allows only for a small number of them to be checked for illegally exported or looted goods.[33] When such items are detected, customs officers are frequently unable to determine their true value and origin, whether they are exported legitimately, and whether they are genuine. Most looted items therefore remain undetected.

Certain countries have realized the necessity of tackling the cross-border smuggling of illegally exported antiquities by cooperating with other nations. For instance, Cambodia and Thailand signed an agreement in 2000 which focuses on increased bilateral cooperation in the fight against illicit art trafficking, the sharing of relevant information, sanctions against smugglers, the fostering of public awareness, and the establishment of a joint system of export certificates and provisions for the return of illegally exported cultural property.[34] Art crime involving cross-boundary operations can only be effectively prevented by cooperation between source countries and transit countries, and source countries and market states.[35] Relevant agreements which involve the sharing of intelligence and regulations regarding law enforcement and the penalization of related offences are particularly important in the context of this chapter.

Long-term Strategies for the Prevention of Art Crime in Asia

There are several aspects and strategies that should be considered when contemplating long-term approaches to address art crime in Asia. Although the investigation and prosecution of art crime is crucial in terms of deterrence and reparation, factors which contribute to the sources of the problem must also be examined. While collaboration between illicit art dealers and corrupt officials is one of the more obvious issues concerning crimes related to art, problems arising from the involvement of those who lack adequate understanding of their wrongdoing or act out of monetary necessity must also be addressed in order to alleviate the situation permanently.

---

32 Ibid.

33 Gruber (n 15) 355.

34 Agreement Between the Government of Cambodia and the Government of the Kingdom of Thailand to Combat Against Illicit Trafficking and Cross-border Smuggling of Movable Cultural Property and to Restitute it to the Country of Origin (signed and entered into force 14 June 2000).

35 Generally on this topic, see Gruber (n 15).

Capacity Building and Strengthening of Heritage Protection Agencies

The prevention of art crime in Asia requires effective capacity building and sufficient funds to support cultural heritage protection agencies that are responsible for the protection of sites and buried artefacts as well as the initial investigations into instances of looting and other offences related to art. In most Asian countries, these agencies are understaffed and underfunded. As a result, many sites in remote locations are not effectively patrolled and protected against looters.[36] Moreover, existing departments and staff often lack the training and authority to investigate and prevent such offences, and often cannot compete with the resources of professional looters and illegal art dealers. Additionally, even when general police forces are able to detect looting, they are often unable to investigate the damages caused by the looting or to gather evidence as effectively as specially trained staff would be able to do. The same dilemma applies to the trading of counterfeit items, for the detection of well-manufactured and forged pieces of art usually requires expert analyses and scientific tests, as detailed above. It is clear from these issues that prosecutions cannot be secured without appropriate staff and funding to detect offences and carry out investigations.

Establishing efficient systems of documentation and registration of heritage items and sites is another viable scheme which has the potential to substantially impair the illicit trafficking of antiquities. Ideally, further implementation of such arrangements in official repositories, museums and archaeological sites for the purpose of identifying and establishing the provenance of stolen items which surface on the international art market would be highly valuable to law enforcement agencies and the original owners requesting their return. Unfortunately, local and regional museums in many parts of Asia often do not have adequate registers of their items. Furthermore, where they do, the registrations do not conform to international standards for forms and descriptions, and are thereby rather ineffective for investigations concerning the repatriation of claims. For example, in January 2013 when thieves stole several priceless pre-Angkorian artefacts made of gold and bronze from the Rajabo Pagoda in Siem Reap province, some of which date back to the BCE era, only the pagoda committee knew about the exact number and kind of artefacts that were part of the collection.[37] In such cases, the exclusivity or lack of information and lack of any records significantly complicates the process of identifying the perpetrators and recovering the items once they are transported outside the region for sale on the international art market. Many existing systems of registration are undoubtedly in need of further development.

---

36 Stefan Gruber, 'Protecting China's Cultural Heritage Sites in Times of Rapid Change: Current Developments, Practice and Law' (2008) 10 *Asia Pacific Journal of Environmental Law* 253, 284.

37 Heritage Watch, 'Artifacts Stolen from Reach Bo Pagoda' (2013) <http://www.heritagewatchinternational.org/wat-bo-theft.html> accessed 12 November 2013.

Corruption, Greed and Lack of Responsibility

Another major, if not the primary, problem regarding art crime in Asia is the corruption or ignorance of local authorities. The officials are often unaware of the impact and relevance of art crime and relating legal regulations, or they deliberately ignore such cases.[38] In some areas, government officials even appear to be involved in the smuggling process. Certainly one of the most notorious looting operations involving the Cambodian army was the pillaging of the twelfth-century temple of Banteay Chhmar, which is located 15 kilometres from the Thai border. Under the commission of a Bangkok-based art dealer, a Cambodian army unit cut off over 500 square feet of reliefs, dismantled 12-metre-long walls and removed a large number of statues with heavy equipment over a period of four weeks.[39] Numerous pieces were put on sale in antique shops in Bangkok before the Thai police intercepted several trucks transporting further fragments of the reliefs into Thailand.

The structure of the international art market and the general attitudes of those involved towards unprovenanced items add to the difficulties of policing art crime.[40] To a certain extent, the collection of antiquities, the trade in cultural artefacts, and the supply of new items to the antique market have always involved the services of dubious characters and organized crime. As Bogdanos stated: 'Indeed, the patina of gentility we usually associate with the world of antiquities has always rested atop a solid core of criminal activity.'[41] This is particularly so for Asia, which has a vast number of heritage sites that are often unprotected or not yet officially recorded and constitute profitable targets for looters.

A large share of antiquities on the international art market is advertised with insufficient details as to their provenance, thereby precluding any proper assessment of their legitimacy.[42] This is common practice and seems to be the accepted norm rather than the exception within the art market. In many cases, art dealers tend to protect the seller and keep him or her anonymous.[43] This makes any investigation regarding the origins of allegedly stolen items and the potentially criminal circumstances surrounding the acquisitions very difficult to ascertain. That many items are in fact loot is often denied by art dealers. Some merchants avoid exploring this issue at

---

38 Gruber (n 15) 362.

39 Mydans (n 9).

40 Generally on the lack of due diligence amongst art dealers, see Bull (n 10).

41 Matthew Bogdanos, 'The Terrorist in the Art Gallery' *The New York Times* (10 December 2005) <http://www.nytimes.com/2005/12/10/opinion/10bogdanos.html?pagewanted=all> accessed 12 November 2013.

42 See the extensive research and interviews conducted by Mackenzie in Simon Mackenzie, *Going, Going, Gone: Regulating the Market in Illicit Antiquities* (Institute of Art and Law 2005) 32-62.

43 Carolyn Olsburgh, *Authenticity in the Art Market: A Comparative Study of Swiss, French and English Contract Law* (Institute of Art and Law 2005) 48-50.

all, while others overtly support looting as a means to supply the art market with stolen items. Many traders who are aware of the illegality of such activities either downplay the destructive impact of looting or justify it by maintaining that some stolen items would otherwise not have been discovered at all.[44]

One of the greatest challenges is to involve the art market in developing effective strategies and to convince art dealers and auctioneers to be part of the solution rather than the problem. As mentioned above, the margins in the international art market are significant and, due to the generally low cost of acquisition, apply particularly to stolen and looted items.

Education and Raising Awareness

Despite the problems of corruption discussed above, not everyone involved in the illicit art market is actually aware of the severity of his or her wrongdoings. In such cases, education can play an important role in addition to repressive measures.[45] Unlike punitive actions, education is non-threatening and achieves better long-term results. In many cases, unprofessional looters, such as local farmers, are not even aware of the value and significance of the items they loot. They also often lack knowledge of the relevant laws related to looting and heritage protection. Resultantly, they may not even be aware of the penalties that they would face if caught. A useful means of informing such persons of the criminality of pillaging and contributing to activities related to art trafficking is to circulate reports of recent prosecutions and relevant legal provisions in the affected regions. Cultivating an appreciation of the importance of preserving the local heritage and fostering pride in the local culture is also of great importance.[46] Long-term benefits are more likely to result where members of a population cooperate to protect their heritage.[47] Establishing a common respect for the local cultural heritage and support for the necessity of conservation will make the pillaging of heritage sites much more difficult for looters. For instance, members of the local community may stop looters from their illicit activities, inform the authorities, or assist with investigations. Tolerance of looting activities should decrease drastically when local populations understand that looters effectively rob them of tangible treasures of their cultural history.

Private recreational collectors must also be deterred from promoting the destruction of cultural heritage by purchasing from illicit art dealers. As with

---

44 Mackenzie (n 42) 60-1.

45 Thomas King, 'Some Dimensions of the Pothunting Problem' in George Smith and John Ehrenhard (eds), *Protecting the Past* (CRC Press 1991) 88.

46 Gruber (n 36) 295.

47 See in this context, for example, Shuzhong He, 'Illicit Excavation in Contemporary China' in Neil Brodie, Jennifer Doole and Colin Renfrew (eds), *Trade in Illicit Antiquities: The Destruction of the World's Archaeological Heritage* (McDonald Institute for Archaeological Research 2001) 24.

many local communities, several of these collectors are uninformed of the relevant provisions and are ignorant of the connections between illegally imported artefacts and organized crime. They are often unaware of the wrongdoing of their own dealings with illicit antique dealers and do not make sufficient inquiries as to the background of their purchases. By addressing these issues in the media, emphasizing the destruction caused by looting,[48] and approaching collectors in a non-repressive way, it may be possible to use their expertise and interest in the preservation of cultural heritage to assist authorities involved with heritage protection. Nevertheless, many private collectors are clearly very well aware of the impact of their wrongdoing and are actively involved in those destructive activities, which make them impervious to non-threatening and non-repressive strategies.

Improved education and training must also be provided to the police, customs officers and officials, including judges and prosecutors, who deal with heritage protection. Access to relevant information is a key issue in the effective implementation of policies and applies to government officials and private actors equally.[49] As mentioned above, effective prevention and investigation of art crime is very difficult where there is an insufficient number of trained specialist staff and a lack of awareness among relevant authorities who are involved in law enforcement, investigation units and customs.

Social Programs and Poverty Alleviation

Education cannot be sufficiently effective unless combined with programs to improve the social problems in heritage-rich regions where looting occurs. It is important to explore the circumstances and causes which promote the looting of artefacts. These considerations must be taken into account when structuring a sustainable and long-term solution for the looting and trafficking of cultural artefacts. This is especially pertinent to projects with objectives which aim to alleviate poverty and reduce the disparity between urban and rural areas as poverty is often the driving force behind looting and the wilful destruction of sites in order to obtain tradeable items.[50] Two of the primary obstacles impeding

48 Magnus Fiskesjo, 'Tomb Raiders and Destruction of History' *China Daily* (23 June 2010) 9 <http://www.chinadaily.com.cn/cndy/2010-06/23/content_10005909.htm> accessed 12 November 2013.

49 E. Somanathan and Thomas Sterner, 'Environmental Policy Instruments and Institutions in Developing Countries' in Ramón López and Michael A. Toman (eds), *Economic Development and Environmental Sustainability: New Policy Options* (Oxford University Press 2006) 229.

50 Generally regarding the connection between poverty and the loss of cultural heritage, see Stefan Gruber, 'Poverty and the Loss of Cultural Heritage Sites' in Yves Le Bouthillier and others (eds), *Poverty Alleviation and Environmental Law* (Edward Elgar 2012).

the effective prevention of looting in countries such as Cambodia are the poor economic conditions of many regions on the one hand and significant prices and high demand for cultural relics at the international level on the other.[51] In many cases, selling cultural relics is simply a practical source of income and means to feed families. Some looters either personally dig up the artefacts to sell them, act as participants in larger pillaging operations that are orchestrated by professional looters, or rent their properties to looters who then excavate anything that is discovered.[52] Other instances of looting relate to well-equipped professional grave robbers, who sometimes receive detailed orders and photos of sites from antique dealers[53] indicating which sites to loot and what items to steal. Such dealers are known to direct pillaging and smuggling operations from their offices, while much of the physical work is carried out by farmers and others who are paid by art dealers for their loot. Many looters may not even be aware of the value of the items.[54] This allows illicit art dealers to make lucrative profits while shifting the risk of apprehension by law enforcement authorities onto others.

It is important to note that any measure aimed at reducing poverty in heritage-rich regions will also help protect heritage and make it harder for illicit antique dealers to recruit looters. With decreased poverty, locals will be less likely to risk prosecution and penalties in order to sell their region's cultural treasures for profit. Likewise, guards would have less of an incentive to take bribes from looters if paid adequate wages.

In addition to penalties, several heritage protection laws also provide rewards for turning in discovered relics and notifying authorities of undiscovered sites and looting operations.[55] Such rewards are intended to prevent people from participating in illicit art trafficking.[56] Unfortunately, the weakness of these provisions lies in the fact that the monetary value of the proposed rewards fall far below the value of the profits which could be made by the sale of the cultural relics concerned. It is quite naive to expect someone to turn in a heritage item for a small reward if he or she could be paid many times that amount on the

---

51 Jane Perlez, 'A Cruel Race to Loot the Splendor That Was Angkor' *The New York Times* (21 March) <http://www.nytimes.com/2005/03/21/international/asia/21cambodia.html?_r=1&> accessed 12 November 2013.

52 Rachanie Thosarat, 'The Destruction of the Cultural Heritage of Thailand and Cambodia' in Neil Brodie, Jennifer Doole and Colin Renfrew (eds), *Trade in Illicit Antiquities: The Destruction of the World's Archaeological Heritage* (McDonald Institute for Archaeological Research 2001) 13.

53 Fiskesjo (n 48).

54 Michael L. Dutra, 'Sir, How Much Is That Ming Vase in the Window?: Protecting Cultural Relics in the People's Republic of China' (2004) 5 *Asian-Pacific Law & Policy Journal* 62, 71.

55 See, for example, China Cultural Relics Law, art 12.

56 Phillip Newell, 'The PRC's Law for the Protection of Cultural Relics' (2008) 13 *Art, Antiquity and Law* 1, 16.

illicit art market. Professional looters generally would also not be attracted by such small rewards as they are well aware of the fact that they are committing crimes when pillaging sites.[57] It is therefore preferable to provide adequate monetary rewards to people for assisting authorities in protecting national heritages and to threaten looters with grim penalties. String-pullers and corrupt officials must be punished with more severe penalties than hired local looters who act out of economic despair rather than criminal intent.

Conclusion

This chapter provided an overview of the primary problems relating to the investigation, prosecution and prevention of art crime in Asia. In particular, it focused on issues regarding the smuggling and selling of looted artefacts and to a lesser extent on art forgery. Many illegal art dealers operate across borders and are therefore difficult to link back to offences and be prosecuted. This is particularly due to the large scale of art crime in Asia and the enormous profits that are involved. Cooperation between neighbouring countries and assistance by market countries are of particular importance in this context. Additionally, it is crucial that particular source and transit countries collaborate closely in the gathering of intelligence, the regulation of exports, the punishment of relevant offences, and the repatriation of seized items. Particular care must be taken with international efforts, such as those concerning the administration of relevant laws which vary between countries in terms of penalties and enforcement.

The chapter also examined certain long-term measures for the prevention of art crime, which are of equal importance. Indeed, enhanced training of relevant government officials, the judiciary and other persons involved in the enforcement of related laws are as important as raising awareness among local populations. The benefits of introducing educational measures and programs to reduce poverty with regard to preventing illicit art trading was also considered. The tasks of preserving cultural heritage and fighting art crime will become much easier as poverty is diminished. When people are not prompted to act out of economic despair, they are much more likely to be receptive to the concept of heritage protection. The same results are anticipated in the contexts of harsh penalties imposed against corrupt officials and string-pullers who orchestrate the looting operations, and enhanced moral and economic rewards offered to those who assist in the protection of cultural relics. The effect of these dual measures is to disable the structures of organized art trafficking. The gravity of involvement in such activities must be reflected in legislative penalties, lest the high profits from looting, art theft, and illicit art trafficking otherwise prove to be too strong of incentives to ignore.

57 See further, Gruber (n 36) 296.

Issues relating to art crime in Asia are extremely complex and cannot be effectively addressed with isolated, singular strategies. Investigation and prosecution of art crime is hindered by numerous factors ranging from specific local and regional features in Asia to the structure of the international art market. Similarly, the prevention of art crime cannot be remedied by insulated stratagems; collaborative efforts are required. A range of approaches must be combined in a holistic manner in order to achieve long-term results. Regardless of the complexities and difficulties of corresponding issues, decisive action is crucial in this context, for art crime is wreaking havoc on Asia's cultural heritage. As the cultural heritage and archaeological contexts of different regions are non-renewable resources and generally cannot be fully recovered even if looted items are returned and perpetrators prosecuted, it is imperative that swift action and cooperation be effected in order to prevent further permanent harm and cultural impoverishment in Asia.[58]

58 Compare in this context similar ideas in Stefan Gruber, 'The Impact of Climate Change on Cultural Heritage Sites: Environmental Law and Adaptation' (2011) *Carbon and Climate Law Review* 209, 219.

Chapter 14
Protecting Cultural Heritage: A Review of Some Contemporary Developments in Australia and Near Environs[1]

Duncan Chappell[2] and Damien Huffer[3]

Introduction

Context and Trafficking Patterns

While the precise size and scope of the international trade in illicitly obtained cultural property within the Asian region remains a matter of some

1 This chapter is based upon an earlier paper presented by the authors at a conference on the Protection of Cultural Property in Asia, sponsored by the Norwegian Ministry of Foreign Affairs and Interpol, and held in Thimphu, Bhutan, on 18-19 February 2013.

2 Duncan Chappell, a lawyer and criminologist, is currently an Adjunct Professor in the Faculty of Law at the University of Sydney, and a Conjoint Professor in the School of Psychiatry at the University of NSW. He is also the Chair of the International Advisory Board of the Australian Research Council's Center of Excellence in Policing and Security. A past President of the NSW Mental Health Review Tribunal; a former Deputy President of the Federal Administrative Appeals Tribunal; and a former Director of the Australian Institute of Criminology he has also held senior academic posts in Australia, Canada and the US, and has been a consultant to government and international bodies including the UN, ILO and Commonwealth. Duncan Chappell has researched and published widely on a range of crime and criminal justice topics, including art crime and trafficking in cultural property. Among his most recent publications on this subject is a book, *Crime in the Art and Antiquities World: Illegal Trafficking in Cultural Property* (2011) published by Springer, New York, and co-edited with Stefano Manacorda of the University of Paris. Together with Damien Huffer, Duncan Chappell is at present involved in a research project examining patterns of illicit trafficking in cultural property in the South East Asian region with a particular emphasis on Vietnam.

3 Damien Huffer is a postdoctoral fellow at the Museum Conservation Institute and Department of Anthropology, National Museum of Natural History, Smithsonian Institution, Washington, DC, USA. He has recently completed his PhD in Archaeology/Bioarchaeology at the Australian National University. His thesis title was 'The Ties that Bind: Population Dynamics, Mobility and Kinship during the mid-Holocene in Northern Vietnam.' He has ongoing research interests in Southeast Asian archaeology, bioarchaeology, human osteology, and the design and use of 'learning games'/new-media methods as educational tools about complex issues; for example, the complex global antiquities trade.

conjecture,[4] there is compelling evidence that Australia, an affluent and developed Asia-Pacific nation, is an important destination for a significant volume of looted objects. In this chapter we examine two recent cases that illustrate this point and also demonstrate the difficult investigative and legal issues that arise in Australia in identifying and prosecuting those responsible for this illicit trade as well as seizing looted objects and repatriating them to their Asian countries of origin. It must be noted at the outset that the two authors were themselves involved in these cases in varying ways to be described, and that some of the information provided in this chapter results from that involvement.

Both cases arose as a result of seizures made in 2010 by Australian federal law enforcement officials from BC Galleries (BCG), a well-established art and antiquities dealership in Melbourne, Victoria, of various artefacts which were believed to have been illegally exported from Cambodia, China and the Philippines. These artefacts were being offered for sale in Australia, both through eBay and the BCG website. As will be seen in more detail below, under the provisions of the Commonwealth of Australia *Protection of Moveable Cultural Heritage Act 1986*[5] items believed to be illegally exported protected objects of a foreign country imported into Australia may be seized by authorities and returned to their rightful owners. However, before an object can be forfeited in this manner the importer may seek to challenge the seizure and recover it from Australian authorities. In the first case to be discussed, *BC Galleries (Vic) Pty Ltd v Commonwealth of Australia*,[6] such a challenge took place in the Federal Magistrates Court in Melbourne with a verdict in favour of the applicant importer. The challenge, which was the first case of its kind to come before an Australian court, raises significant issues which are explored in this chapter regarding the future ability of Australia to protect cultural property that is believed to have been plundered abroad from being imported into the country, as well as fulfilling its international obligations to return such property to the country from which it originated.

In the second case the outcome was different. The items involved were bronze bangles, bracelets, arm braces and earrings believed to have been taken illicitly from cemetery sites in Cambodia. The majority of the items still contained the partial or complete bones of the individuals on whose arms and

4 Neil Brodie, 'Illicit Antiquities: The Situation in South East Asia' (1999) <http://www.aic.gov.au/media_library/conferences/artcrime/brodie.pdf> accessed 9 March 2013; Christine Alder, Duncan Chappell and Ken Polk, 'Perspectives on the Organisation and Control of the Illicit Traffic of Antiquities in South East Asia' in Stefano Manacorda and Duncan Chappell (eds), *Organised Crime in Art and Antiquities* (ISPAC, Milan 2009) 119, 132; Tess Davis, 'Supply and Demand: Exposing the Illicit Trade in Cambodian Antiquities Through a Study of Sotheby's Auction House' (2011) 56 *Crime, Law, and Social Change* 155, 174.

5 PMCHA 1986.

6 [2012] FMCA 742.

legs they were placed in preparation for burial sometime between 2500 and 1500 years ago. The items had originally been advertised for sale on eBay and attracted the notice of the *Australian Archaeological Association* (AAA) which, in conjunction with the *World Archaeological Congress* (WAC), demanded their removal in accordance with eBay's own policy[7] of prohibiting the sale of human remains on its site.[8] The subsequent seizure of the objects was not challenged by the importer, BCG, and they were eventually repatriated to Cambodia. No criminal charges were laid in the matter, and it therefore remains a subject of conjecture whether or not any offences were committed either under the provisions of the *PMCHA 1986*, or the *Victorian Human Tissues Act 1982*[9] which among other things prohibits the unauthorized advertising for sale or purchase of human remains.

Before discussing these two cases in more depth we first provide some contextual information about the contemporary market in Australia for antiquities of the type seized as well as describing in more detail the role played by BCG in this market. The chapter concludes with some observations on the effectiveness or otherwise of the current legislative and allied measures in place in Australia designed to prevent the illicit trafficking of cultural heritage objects at large, and in particular those from the Asian region.

The Australian Antiquities Market

While no systematic or single source of information exists at present regarding the dimensions of the Australian market for antiquities and ethnographica, especially relating to artefacts sourced from Southeast Asia and Oceania, there has been a quite lengthy history of collecting such artefacts, from at least the late 19th century onwards.[10] Many of the collections gathered have found their way into public museums and galleries across the country[11] (see, for instance, *Museums and Collections of Antiquities in Australia and New Zealand*), although there

---

7 'Human Remains and Body Parts Policy'<http://pages.ebay.com/help/policies/remains.html> accessed 28 October 2012.

8 'World Archaeological Congress calls on eBay to halt sale of human remains' (Media release 2010) <http://www.australianarchaeology.com/mediarelease/> accessed 12 March 2013.

9 VHTA 1982.

10 William Anderson, 'Commodifying Culture: Ownership of Cambodia's Archaeological Heritage' (2007) 13 *Limina: A Journal of Historical and Cultural Studies* 103-12; Michael E. O'Hanlon and Robert Louis Welsch (eds), *Hunting the Gatherers: Ethnographic Collectors, Agents and Agency in Melanesia, 1870s-1930s* (Methodology and History in Anthropology, 6th edn, Berghahn Books 2000).

11 Australian Society of Classical Studies, 'Museums and Collections of Antiquities in Australia and New Zealand' <http://www.ascs.org.au/links/museums.html> accessed 5 March 2013.

remain significant but largely undocumented collections in the hands of private individuals and bodies.

At the public level several of the major Australian museums and galleries have accumulated specialized and significant collections of Asian artefacts including the country's National Art Gallery (NAG) located in Canberra,[12] the nation's capital, as well as the state-based Art Gallery of New South Wales (AGNSW) in Sydney and the National Gallery of Victoria (NGV) in Melbourne. The NGV Asian Art collection commenced as early as 1862[13] while the AGNSW collection was launched in 1879 by a gift of ceramics and bronzes by the Government of Japan.[14] Each of these institutions continues to acquire cultural objects of interest from the region, largely it would seem from overseas-based sources including auction houses and dealers.

Recent disclosures surrounding the arrest of the New York City-based dealer Subhash Kapoor suggest that some of these acquisitions may have dubious provenances.[15] Thus both the NGA and the AGNSW were reported to be among a number of prominent museums and galleries around the globe who had obtained objects from Kapoor that were possibly looted from various locations. The NGA acknowledged purchasing 21 objects from Kapoor and following the revelations about his alleged involvement in looting the NGA released a statement indicating that the Gallery had commenced a comprehensive re-examination by a panel of experts of the provenance of the works it had acquired from him. Former Getty Museum Director Michael Brand who took the helm of the AGNSW in June 2012 said that while the gallery had purchased six objects from Kapoor no one had made any suggestions that they were stolen or that there were any issues about their provenance.

To date the precise scope and intensity of the international fallout from the Kapoor affair on the collections of the museums and galleries who were his customers remains uncertain. Nonetheless, the affair is a timely reminder that even at the most elevated levels of collecting in Australia and elsewhere those involved must exercise the most rigorous due diligence in their purchase of cultural objects in order to avoid the opprobrium associated with the acquisition of looted antiquities. While drawing attention to this aspect of the Kapoor affair

---

12 'Asian Art' <http://nga.gov.au/asianart/index.cfm> accessed 5 March 2013.

13 'Asian Art' <http://www.ngv.vic.gov.au/whats-on/exhibitions/exhibitions/asian-art> accessed 5 March 2013.

14 'Asian Art' *Exhibitions* <http://www.artgallery.nsw.gov.au/collection/asian-art> accessed 5 March 2013.

15 Clare Morgan, 'Drama over National Gallery's Shiva Statue' *Sydney Morning Herald* (3 August 2012) <http://www.smh.com.au/entertainment/art-and-design/drama-over-national-gallerys-shiva-statue-20120803-23kfj.html> accessed 12 March 2013; Robin Pogrebin and Kevin Flynn, 'Museums studying dealers artefacts' *New York Times* (27 July 2012) <http://www.nytimes.com/2012/07/28/arts/design/us-asks-museums-to-examine-collections.html?_r=0> accessed 12 March 2013.

and its impact in Australia we are concerned in this chapter less with the collecting behaviours of the country's museums and galleries than we are with the acquisition practices and procedures of Australian-based dealers in cultural heritage objects. Not surprisingly, given Australia's comparatively small population of 22 million persons, the number of specialist dealers involved in the antiquities trade is nowhere as large as it is in the major markets for such goods in Europe and North America.

Within this operational framework there are several Australian antique and antiquities dealers in operation, almost entirely located in Sydney and Melbourne, who maintain an active presence in the national and international market. Preliminary research has identified eleven such businesses (including BC Galleries). This total includes a few dealers with online presences who indicate that they have a particular interest or specialty in Asian and/or Oceanic antiquities or antiques. Furthermore, those dealers who operate as generalist dealers of antiquities, antiques and ethnographica all include in their respective catalogues at least the occasional South and Southeast Asian material. A self-purported Gandharan specialist appears to conduct all business transactions online,[16] with no indicated storefront at all, while another dealer is located in Sydney but arranges all sales by appointment only and appears to only offer an infrequently updated blog by way of a catalogue.[17] This is contrasted with Guy Earl-Smith East Australia Trading Consolidated, Sydney's largest specialist dealer in regards to Asian antiquities.[18] Perhaps the most prominent independent dealers known on the Australian market, however, is BCG, which according to its website has been in operation in Melbourne since 1976.[19] Research by the authors that more completely addresses the scope of the Australian antiquities market in terms of the number of active dealers is ongoing.

In addition to these dealers the regional offices of Sotheby's and Christie's Auction Houses are located in Melbourne and Sydney, however their antiquities related activities are much less extensive than elsewhere in Asia, such as Singapore, Hong Kong and mainland China. They serve the Australian market together with a number of smaller auction houses with both local and international clientele. These various bodies conduct quite frequent auctions which from time to time include estate collections containing South Asian, Southeast Asian and Oceanic antiquities and ethnographica. For example, the Melbourne auction house Mossgreen Auctions sold several purportedly authentic South and Southeast Asian

16 'Gandhara' <http://www.gandhara.com.au/index1.html> accessed 10 March 2013.

17 Raymond Tregaskis and Victoria Tregaskis, 'Tregaskis Oriental Antiques – Buying and Selling Quality Objects' <http://tregaskis.blogspot.com.au/> accessed 19 March 2013.

18 'Guy Earl-Smith East Australian Trading Consolidated: International Tribal and Aboriginal Art, Artefacts and Antiquities' <http://www.guyearlsmith.com.au> accessed 11 March 2013.

19 'BC Galleries: Ancient Art and Antiquities, Tribal Art and Ethnographica' <http://bcgalleries.com.au/> accessed 10 March 2013.

derived antiques and antiquities within the larger category of 'Chinese & Asian Arts and European Antiques' as recently as 22 November, 2012.[20] Occasionally, confiscation and repatriation of sensitive material such as human remains has occurred before an auction took place.[21]

BCG and the Seizure of Cultural Heritage Objects

The range of objects offered for sale by BCG through its web site is immense and covers ancient art and antiquities, tribal art and ethnographica from most regions of the globe. Indeed, on its current website BCG claims that its site and catalogue of objects for sale is one of the largest of its kind on the Internet and contains art and artefacts 'of all cultures and regions'. An itemization and quantitative analysis by the authors of all antiquities and objects d'art listed in the BCG online catalogue is ongoing. Specifically, the regions of South and South East Asia (including Tibet, Nepal, Bhutan and artefacts from archaeological cultures that straddled today's Pakistan/Afghanistan border) are the foci of this analysis, and nothing listed as younger than the 19th century has been included, as such antiques (not antiquities) are much more likely to have well-documented and complete ownership histories and not to have appeared on the market due to archaeological site looting.

Preliminary analysis has revealed a total of 567 objects from the South Asian region (under the catalogue headings of 'Tibetan & Nepalese Art & Antiquities', 'South Asian Art & Antiquities', and 'Gandharan Art & Antiquities'. The combined price of all listed artefacts is $AUD 1,156,859.63, ranging in price from $AUD 46.00 (for a Kushan coin) to $AUD 87,465.00 (for a *c.* 7th century Gupta period sandstone sculpture of a deity and attendants). Regarding Southeast Asian antiquities (under the catalogue heading of 'Southeast Asian Art & Antiquities'), the total number is 298, with a combined price of $AUD 483,852.68, ranging in price from $AUD 51.00 to $AUD 49,392.00 (for a *c.* 12th century Khmer sandstone carving of a male divinity).

The total quantity of artefacts was calculated as of 30 March 2013, with new additions recorded in the database as they appeared, and the reservation or sale of specific items being noted as they occurred. The majority of objects from both regions were advertised for amounts below $AUD 10,000. In the case of the South Asian material, only 27 of 567 listed artefacts (4.7 per cent) have listed prices above that benchmark, while for the Southeast Asian material, only 9 of 298 (3 per cent) have markedly expensive prices.

---

20 Mossgreen Auctions, 'MA155 Spring Auction Series – Chinese & Asian Arts and European Antiques' <http://www.mossgreen.com.au/auctions/past.asp?idExhibition=1209162> accessed 19 March 2013.

21 'Recent Repatriation News' <http://sydney.edu.au/museums/research/repatriation.shtml> accessed 15 March 2013.

While a listed private company registered in Victoria the principal proprietor and founder of BCG would appear to be Frank Bottaro, now 65 years of age and a resident of Melbourne, although he is believed also to maintain an art and antiquities business presence in Bangkok, Thailand. In earlier press interviews Mr Bottaro is reported to have stated that from an early age he had a passion for archaeology and that following a successful career as a taxidermist he commenced his current art and antiquities business and went to Egypt in search of ancient artefacts. By 2002 he had more than 70 people who sourced antiques and art for him around the Middle East, China and New Zealand. 'Most dealers specialize in selected civilizations,' he said but 'we are interested in any cultures across the ages.' Mr Bottaro also said that 70 per cent of his acquired objects were sold to overseas customers. He had 'gone from struggling to make ends meet to being a rich man which is more fun'.[22]

Mr Bottaro's past activities in the art and antiquities trade have resulted in a number of brushes with authorities in several jurisdictions. In August 2004 Pakistani authorities in Lahore were reported to have seized more than 150 objects consigned as 'kitchen and table ware for BC Galleries in Melbourne, Australia'.[23] The objects recovered were in fact mostly 6000 year old prehistoric figurines, animal carvings, terracotta and a few statues of Buddha. The latter statues were judged to be fakes but the remainder of the objects seized was believed to have been illegally excavated from a major archaeological site at Mehrgarh in Baluchistan. No arrests or criminal proceedings occurred as a result of this seizure.

In 2005 Mr Bottaro was required to hand over to Australian Federal Police seven Egyptian tomb artefacts that had been listed for sale on the BCG website. The police noticed the items after they had been placed on the Interpol stolen art register. Mr Bottaro claimed to be an innocent scapegoat in the matter and while suspected of no wrongdoing elected not to challenge the seizure because of the legal expenses involved.[24] In December 2008 Mr Bottaro was again in the news when it was reported that he had been arrested at Cairo airport in Egypt for allegedly trying to smuggle two 2300-year-old animal mummies and 19 religious figurines out of the country. Mr Bottaro was subsequently released from custody without any charges being brought against him.

The two cases which are reviewed in this chapter involving BCG resulted from seizures of cultural objects believed to have been illegally exported from countries in the Asian region and imported to Australia. As noted earlier the

22 Selma Milovanovic, 'Egypt could jail Australian dealer for 15 years' *Sydney Morning Herald* (26 December 2008) <http://www.smh.com.au/news/world/egypt-could-jail-australian-dealer-for-15-years/2008/12/25/1229998662160.html> accessed 10 March 2013.

23 Zulqernain Tahir, 'Lahore: seized antiques are 6000 years old' *Dawn* (Lahore, Pakistan 27 August 2004) <http://archives.dawn.com/2004/08/27/local16.htm> accessed 2 March 2013.

24 Ibid.

seizures were made in 2010 from the premises of BCG in Melbourne. It would seem that the seizures were precipitated by local archaeologists after viewing certain pre historic human remains and associated jewelry advertised for sale on eBay. Eliciting the aid of both the Australian Archaeological Association and the World Archaeological Congress they were able to issue a call to eBay to remove from sale two 'Dong Son' votive bronze armlets from Northern Vietnam. 'The armlets contain human arm bones and there is concern about the cultural origin of the remains being offered for sale, as well as the affront to human dignity resulting from the sale of human body parts.'[25] The request also pointed to the policy which eBay already espoused of prohibiting the trading of human remains on its website. The call for action was in fact heeded by eBay and as we describe in more depth below the objects in question were eventually repatriated not to Vietnam but to Cambodia from where they most likely had been illicitly excavated and exported.

This action by the archaeological community to stop the sale of human body parts led to further investigation into the matter by the former Cultural Property Section of the Australian Federal Department of the Environment, Water, Heritage and the Arts (DEWHA), and in particular into the activities of BCG which was the listed supplier of the human remains. This investigation led to the seizures just referred to and the subsequent legal action by BCG to recover those items which were not associated with any human remains.

Case 1: *BC Galleries v The Commonwealth of Australia* 2012

As mentioned earlier BCG's recovery action was brought under the provisions of the Commonwealth of Australia *Protection of Moveable Cultural Heritage Act 1986.* This Act is designed to protect Australia's heritage of movable cultural objects as well as 'support the protection by foreign countries of their heritage of movable cultural objects'. More specifically, Section 14 of the *PMCHA 1986* states that 'where a protected object of a foreign country has been exported from that country' and that export was 'prohibited by a law of that country relating to cultural property, and the object is imported, the object is liable to forfeiture'. Section 34 of the *PMCHA 1986* gives an inspector specific power to seize protected objects believed to be subject to forfeiture.

The Commonwealth of Australia, through its officials in DEWHA, acted in the belief that seven objects seized by them at BCG's place of business in Melbourne were protected objects that had been illegally exported from their countries of origin, China (six objects) and the Philippines (one object). BCG disputed this claim and sought their return in accord with the provisions of Section 37 of the

25 'World Archaeological Congress calls on eBay to halt sale of human remains' (Media release 2010) <http://www.australianarchaeology.com/mediarelease/> accessed 12 March 2013.

PMCHA 1986 which states in part that 'the owner … of the object immediately before it was seized may bring an action against the Commonwealth in a court of competent jurisdiction for the recovery of the object on the grounds that the object is not forfeited or liable to be forfeited'. In this case the court of competent jurisdiction was the Federal Magistrates Court in Melbourne.

Remarkably, given the period during which the *PMCHA 1986* had been in existence, this would seem to be the first occasion in Australian legal history that such a recovery proceeding had been initiated by an owner of a seized object. Reliable statistics do not exist concerning the number of seizures by the Commonwealth of this type made over the period from 1986 to 2012. However, the Minister responsible for DEWHA indicated that, over the period from 2000, 19 seizures involving 43 objects had been affected, none of which had been challenged in court, and 34 of these objects had been successfully returned to their countries of origin.[26] It was into this unchartered legal territory that the BCG case sailed in June 2012 when the matter came before the Federal Magistrate's Court for a hearing. What follows in this section of the chapter is based upon a review of the subsequent published judicial decision in the case,[27] and the first author's participation in the hearing as one of several expert witnesses called to testify by the Commonwealth.

At that hearing BCG contended at the outset that the onus of proof, on the balance of probabilities, was upon the Commonwealth to show that (i) each of the objects seized was a protected object of a foreign country; (ii) that the object had been exported from the relevant foreign country; (iii) that the law of the relevant foreign country relating to cultural property prohibited the export; and (iv) that the object had been imported into Australia. Legal argument followed with the judicial officer involved in the matter, Judge Reithmuller, eventually ruling in favour of the applicant. The judge distinguished the forfeiture provisions of the *PMCHA 1986* from those contained in other associated Australian customs legislation where once goods were seized they were forfeited to the Commonwealth and the onus would be upon the applicant to justify their return. Here the onus was on the Commonwealth which would thus have to lead its evidence first and establish each of the points made above. Acting in accord with this initial ruling the Commonwealth then sought to establish each of the four points listed above with varying degrees of success as the court's ultimate judgment indicates.

(i) Protected object: Under the provisions of Section 3 of the *PMCHA 1986* the term 'protected object of a foreign country' means 'an object forming part of the moveable cultural heritage of a foreign country'. In determining whether or not the seven seized items fitted this description the court considered the types of object within Australia which were protected by the *PMCHA 1986* as well as the

26 Alexander 2012.

27 *BC Galleries (Vic) Pty Ltd v Commonwealth of Australia* [2012] FMCA 742.

definition given of such objects in Article 1 of the 1970 *UNESCO Convention on the means of prohibiting the illicit import, export and transfer of ownership of cultural property*.[28]

Based on expert evidence presented at the hearing the court concluded that five of the six objects said to originate from China and described originally on the BCG website as a 'Han buried stele'; 'a superb Northern Qi bull'; 'an important ceramic statue of a horse Northern Dynasties period'; an 'Eastern Han dynasty bronze and pottery money tree'; and a 'Han dynasty ceramic wall panel', did satisfy the definition of being part of that nation's moveable cultural heritage.[29] The sixth item, 'a rare Tang dynasty stone pillar with Buddhist scenes' was judged to be a replica or fake.

The single item said to originate from the Philippines was described by BCG as an 'Ifuagao head hunter trophy skull, flanked by pig skulls'. This object was also thought by an expert to be a fake, the human skull probably being that of a Japanese soldier from World War II rather than a Philippino male.[30]

(ii) Export: The court concluded that there was no question that each of the objects from China had been purchased by BCG in Hong Kong and then shipped to Australia. It was also clear that at some point they had each been exported from where they were originally located and that this was some place other than Hong Kong, and on the balance of probabilities most probably within the geographic limits of the former Han or Qi dynasties. However, the court noted that no evidence was led as to the geographic limits of each of these dynasties, nor of the relationship between these limits and those of the present day People's Republic of China (PRC) – accordingly the Commonwealth had failed to prove on the balance of probabilities that these objects 'actually originated from within the geographic area of the PRC'.[31]

The court also found that there was no evidence to show on the balance of probabilities that the objects, even if they had originated from within the PRC boundaries, had crossed the border within the time frame of the operation of the PRC laws relevant to the case, namely, since 19 November 1982.[32]

(iii) Prohibited export: In regard to the question whether or not under contemporary Chinese law these objects were prohibited from export the Commonwealth had sought at the hearing to rely upon the expert testimony of the first author. However, the court ruled that the first author was not an expert on Chinese law since he did

28 Convention on the Means of Prohibiting and Preventing the Illicit Import, Export and Transfer of Ownership of Cultural Property (adopted 14 November 1970, entered into force 24 April 1972) 823 UNTS 231.

29 [2012] FMCA 742, 13-14.

30 [2012] FMCA 742, 16.

31 [2012] FMCA 742, 18.

32 [2012] FMCA 742, 25.

not speak Mandarin or Cantonese, nor had he practiced law in China or made a special study of Chinese law. Thus the court, in the absence of expert testimony as to the operation of Chinese law was left with the statutory provisions to interpret on their face as best it could.

In fulfilling its interpretive task the court took the view that under Chinese law moveable cultural relics were classified into 'valuable' and 'ordinary' categories, and that the former category was further subdivided into three different grades.[33] The court seems to have also taken the view, incorrectly it is submitted, that the value of the items was a relevant factor in deciding whether or not they could be lawfully exported from China. The court observed that the genuine seized objects had each been purchased for very small amounts in Hong Kong and that 'the values of the items are not such that one could conclude on the balance of probabilities that they would be considered "valuable" for the purposes of the Chinese laws with respect to export restrictions, particularly if the restorations or repairs were done after they left China'.[34]

In reality contemporary Chinese laws regarding the protection of the nation's cultural heritage impose a virtual blanket ban on the export of any cultural relic made before or in 1911[35] The genuine objects seized were said to be from the Eastern Han (25-220 AD), Northern Han (400-500 AD) and Northern Qi (549-577 AD) dynasties which are clearly all well within the prohibited range of cultural relic exports regardless of their perceived value and grade.

(iv) Import into Australia: On the final point to be established the court had no difficulty concluding that the seized objects from China had been imported into Australia by BCG.

Based on these various findings the court ruled that the Commonwealth had failed to establish on the balance of probabilities that any of the seized objects were liable to forfeiture under the provisions of the *PMCHA 1986* and an order was made for the return of the objects to the applicant BCG. The Commonwealth elected not to appeal this decision so it now stands as an important precedent regarding the interpretation and operation of the *PMCHA 1986*, and will continue do so unless successfully challenged in a subsequent case or until legislative changes are made to the *PMCHA 1986* which will render it a more effective tool to deal with a situation like that presented in the BCG Case. More will be said shortly about what form these legislative changes might take but first consideration is given to the second case involving BCG where a more favourable outcome was reached from the perspective of those seeking to curb trafficking in cultural objects.

33 [2012] FMCA 742, 22-3.

34 [2012] FMCA 742, 23.

35 Paul Newell, 'The PRC's Law for the Protection of Cultural Relics' (2008) 13 *Art Antiquity and Law* 1, 48; Timothy Lau, 'The Grading of Cultural Relics in Chinese Law' (2011) 18 *International Journal of Cultural Property* 1, 35.

Case 2: Repatriation of Cambodian Artefacts and Human Remains

In the raid made by DEWHA officials in 2010 on the Melbourne premises of BCG, approximately 30 Cambodian Iron Age (*c.* 2500-1500 BP) mortuary objects, most still containing in-situ soil and human remains, were seized. Their subsequent documentation, analysis and eventual repatriation via an official hand-back ceremony held at the Cambodian Embassy, Canberra, Australia, on 10 March 2011 was deemed by all involved to represent a major victory for the international collaborative effort to curtail the illicit antiquities trade into Australia.

The items under contention in this case included several sets of thin bronze bangles (concreted together and still in-situ around the soil which came to cover the skeleton following soft-tissue decomposition), as well as finger rings, earrings, forearm and wrist guards fashioned from single sheets of decorated bronze. Most astonishingly, the assemblage even included paired lower legs fully encased in corroded bronze bangles and the intermediary soil matrix. In the course of the investigation following the seizures discussed above, the second author was asked to examine individually each of the Cambodian artefacts recovered, doing so under supervision within AQIS quarantine facilities.

All of the grave goods originally placed on the forearm contained, at the very least, the nearly complete diaphyses (midsection shaft of a long bone) of the ulna and radius. In a few instances, carpals (wrist bones) were visible. Many of the finger rings retained the phalanges (finger bones) that they were placed around. Finally, the paired lower legs contained nearly complete right and left tibiae and fibulae, representing at most two individuals, but most likely deriving from the same burial. Knowing this for certain is impossible due to loss of archaeological context as a consequence of looting. It was able to be determined that most of the human remains in question belonged to adults, with a few specimens belonging to younger sub adults (children). Only rough separation into adult and subadult age categories was possible based upon the dimensions and robusticity of the visible long bone shafts, as epiphyses (the rounded ends of long bones that develop separately and fuse with the shaft at varying, age-specific, rates) were seldom preserved.

The artefacts themselves were all constructed from bronze alloy, and included several types of relatively common Cambodian and Southeast Asian Iron Age grave goods.[36] Primarily, these consisted of thin and round, or thin and flat, circular bangles that would primarily have been mould-cast and characteristic of the majority of non-precious metal artefact production during Cambodian prehistory.[37]

---

36 Charles Higham, *Early Cultures of Mainland Southeast Asia* (River Books 2002); Andreas Reinecke, Vin Laychour and Seng Sonatra, *The First Golden Age of Cambodia: Excavations at Prohear* (Deutsche Archaeologische Institute, Bonn 2009).

37 Reinecke (n 36); Yoko Nojima, 'Non-Ceramic Grave Goods of Phum Snay in the Context of Socio-Political Development in Northwest Cambodia' in Yoshi Yasuda (ed), *Water Civilization: From Yangtze to Khmer Civilizations, Advances in Asian Human-Environmental Research* (Springer, Tokyo 2013) 116, 180; Dougald J.W. O'Reilly, Thuy

The forearm and wrist guards made from wrapped sheet metal were primarily undecorated (or exhibited heavily corroded surfaces), or were faintly embossed with cross-hatched or geometric patterns and folded sheet metal reinforcement along the edges to enhance the item aesthetically. The earrings seized were minimalistic in design and undecorated, hinge operated, and most likely to have been worn by pinching onto the earlobe. The finger rings consisted of spiral coils of thicker bronze with a circular cross-section. No artefacts made of precious or semi-precious stones or metal were seized together with those objects described above, nor were objects composed of iron, or any ceramics. This suggests that if these common Iron Age grave goods were encountered during the looting process, they were either retained in-country or sent to different destinations.

Cemetery sites dating to the still poorly-understood Iron Age remain the most important avenue available to understand the origins, and cost to human health, of the social hierarchies and militarization which facilitated the rise of early states and the subsequent Khmer Empire.[38] Iron Age cemeteries have been excavated or salvaged throughout Cambodia, but seem to be especially concentrated in the northwest and southeast, with an emerging picture of regional difference in mortuary and body modification practices and the raw material sources of grave goods.[39] Preliminary research has revealed that at least Northwestern communities appear to have engaged in frequent inter-personal violence; unsurprising given the numerous examples of weaponry in high status burials at this time.[40] More broadly speaking, other research has relied on quantitative analyses of inter-population variation in hereditary aspects of cranial and dental morphology to surmize that the genetic ancestry of Iron Age Cambodian populations (again, at least in the Northwest) was indigenous to Mainland Southeast Asia, irrespective of the increased contact with South Asia and Iron Age cultures of northern Vietnam

---

Chanthourn and Kate Domett, 'A Preliminary Report on the Excavation of an Iron Age Cemetery at Phum Snay, Banteay Meanchey, Cambodia, 2003' (2004) 5 *UDAYA: Journal of Khmer Studies* 219, 225.

38 Kate Domett and Dougald J.W. O'Reilly, 'Health in Pre-Angkorian Cambodia: A Bioarchaeological Analysis of the Skeletal Remains from Phum Snay' (2009) 48 *Asian Perspectives* 56, 78; Kate Domett and Hallie Buckley, 'Large Lytic Cranial Lesions: A Differential Diagnosis from Pre-Angkorian Cambodia' (2012) 22 *International Journal of Osteoarchaeology* 731, 739; Jennifer Newton, Kate Domett, Dougald J.W. O'Reilly and Louise Shewan, 'Dental Health in Iron Age Cambodia: Temporal Variation with Rice Agriculture' (2013) 3 *International Journal of Palaeopathology* 1, 10.

39 Reinecke (n 36); Kate Domett, Jennifer Newton, Dougald J.W. O'Reilly, Nancy Tayles, Louise Shewan and Nancy Beavan, 'Cultural Modification of the Dentition in Prehistoric Cambodia' (2013) 23 *International Journal of Osteoarchaeology* 274, 286; Simone Krais, Michael Franken and Andreas Reinecke, 'The Bioanthropology of the Early Iron Age Site of Prohear (Cambodia)' (2012) 4 *Zeitschrift für Archäologie Außereuropäischer Kulturen* 103, 125.

40 Kate Domett, Dougald J.W. O'Reilly and Hallie Buckley, 'Bioarchaeological Evidence of Conflict in Pre-Angkorian, Northwest Cambodia' (2013) 85 *Antiquity* 441-59.

and southern China suggested by the presence of exotic trade goods present in domestic and mortuary contexts.[41]

Each looted site represents not only knowledge lost about the lives and deaths of particular individuals from whose graves the antiquities or human remains derive, but also crucial information regarding how populations, communities and even families differed from each other in regards to status, connection to trade networks, mortality and fertility, health, diet, residential mobility, activity patterns, and even snapshots of unique customs. Archaeological and bioarchaeological investigation of these topics can only be carried out to its fullest when intact graves are able to be excavated. Retrospectively analysing partially looted assemblages or recovered artefacts already removed from archaeological context can provide only minimal, generalized information. Seizures and legal actions such as those discussed here are symptomatic of both the continued threat that looting poses,[42] and the need for concerted on-the-ground action[43] to curb the activities of those engaged in this illicit behaviour.

In 1996, and again in 2002, Cambodia passed laudable laws to afford meaningful legal protection to all monuments and archaeological sites within its borders, whether recorded and excavated or not, as well as to stipulate how the illicit excavation, destruction, exportation and occasionally importation of cultural property would be prosecuted when detected.[44] At the international level Cambodia is a signatory to all major United Nations sponsored conventions concerning cultural property, including the *1970 UNESCO Convention*, the *1995 UNIDROIT Convention*,[45] and the *2001 Convention on the protection of the underwater cultural heritage*.[46]

Bilateral Memoranda of Understanding (MOU) agreements or renewals have been signed or are pending with Thailand and the United States,[47] Australia,

41 Hirofumi Matsumura, Kate Domett and Dougald J.W. O'Reilly, 'On the Origin of Pre-Angkorian Peoples: Perspectives from Cranial and Dental Affinity of the Human Remains from Iron Age Phum Snay, Cambodia' (2011) 119 *Anthropological Science* 67, 79.

42 Dougald J.W. O'Reilly, 'Shifting Trends of Heritage Destruction in Cambodia: From Temples to Tombs' (2007) 20 *Historic Environment* 12, 16.

43 Dougald J.W. O'Reilly, 'The Tide is Turning: Battling Heritage Destruction in Cambodia through Social Marketing and Education' (2009) 9 *The SAA Archaeological Record* 11, 13.

44 'UNESCO Database of National Cultural Heritage Laws' <http://portal.unesco.org/culture/en/ev.php/URL_ID=33928&URL_DO=DO_TOPIC&URL_SECTION=201.html> accessed 28 August 2013.

45 UNIDROIT Convention on Stolen or Illegally Exported Cultural Objects (adopted 24 June 1995, entered into force 1 July 1998).

46 Convention on the Protection of the Underwater Cultural Heritage (adopted 3 November 2001, entered into force 2 January 2009).

47 'UNESCO Database of National Cultural Heritage Laws' <http://portal.unesco.org/culture/en/ev.php/URL_ID=33928&URL_DO=DO_TOPIC&URL_SECTION=201.html> accessed 28 August 2013

and even Ecuador.[48] Having such a MOU with Australia since 2011 means that a permit requirement imposed by the Cambodian Ministry of Culture and Fine Arts for the lawful export from the country of all 'cultural heritage dated from 3000 B.C. to 1900 A.D.'[49] will now be recognized and upheld by Australian authorities. With this MOU in effect the Cambodian government has in essence given permission to the Australian Government to seize all imports of cultural heritage from Cambodia which lack a valid export certificate.

The seizure of the mortuary objects from BCG in 2010 clearly preceded this MOU but the export certificate requirement for the lawful removal from Cambodia of any cultural heritage object falling within the time frame mentioned was very much in place and had been so since 1996. There is no evidence of such a certificate being obtained or requested and, given the already described condition of the various items seized, it would seem reasonable to assume that if they had been proffered for inspection and export certification purposes the local Cambodian authorities would have had reasonable suspicions that they had been illegally excavated and barred their exit from the country.

There is also no evidence as to how, when or where BCG originally acquired these mortuary objects and what due diligence they exercised in determining whether or not they were lawfully exported from their place of origin. It should be noted that under the provisions of the *PMCHA 1986* (Section 14 (2)), a person who knowingly imports an object that is a protected object of a foreign country, and whose export is prohibited by law, is guilty of an offence punishable by a fine of up to $100,000 or imprisonment not exceeding five years, or both, if a natural person and to a fine of up to $200,000 if a body corporate. However, as vividly illustrated by the circumstances and outcome of the BCG case, establishing the necessary elements of an offence under this provision, and in particular proving the requisite intent, would be a herculean task.

A somewhat easier prosecution route might have been taken using the provisions of Section 40 of the *Victorian Human Tissues Act 1982* which prohibit the publication or public display of an advertisement relating to the sale or purchase of human tissue, or the donation of tissue or the right to take tissue from the bodies of persons without ministerial approval. The penalty for such an offence is a maximum of 50 penalty units or imprisonment for three months, or both. As noted at the beginning of this chapter, BCG, perhaps mindful of this provision, elected not to seek the return of the mortuary items

48 University of Sydney Angkor Research Program, 'Submission to the Cultural Property Advisory Committee on Behalf of the Angkor Research Program of the University of Sydney' <http://www.savingantiquities.org/>. wpcontent/uploads/2013/03/University-of-Sydney-Angkor-Research-Program.pdf> accessed 28 August 2013.

49 Office of the Arts, 'Import of Cultural Heritage Objects into Australia' <http://arts.gov.au/movable/import> accessed 28 August 2013.

following their seizure. However, their zeal to advertise and display human tissue for sale seems largely undiminished, as evidenced by recent online catalogue advertisements for four Tibetan 'kangling' trumpets, three made of partial human femora (thigh bones), one of a human tibia, and described as 'tantric Buddhist instruments'.[50] They are being sold for between $AUD 463.00 and 772.00, and no information whatsoever regarding ownership history is provided to potential customers on the website. While these ritual instruments are traditionally made of human bone, Buddhist law proscribes specific rules as to the nature of the individual from whose bone a kangling can be made[51] with resultant legal and ethical difficulties inherent in sourcing, exporting, and importing authentic human bone from Nepal, Tibet, India or Bhutan. Kanglings made of wood can serve as suitable substitutes.[52]

Spasmodic Enforcement

From what has been described so far it should be apparent that the contemporary level of enforcement of the provisions of the *PMCHA 1986* which seek to give effect to Australia's international obligations to protect cultural heritage from the ravages of looting wherever it occurs are at the very best only being spasmodically utilized. To the best of our knowledge there have been no prosecutions brought under the terms of Section 14 of the *PMCHA 1986* referred to above while the number of seizures of protected objects illegally exported from their countries of origin and imported into Australia since 2000 have averaged about only two per year. At the same time private dealers in antiquities like BCG and other Australian-based operators we have identified have been conducting what would appear to be quite thriving businesses offering for sale a wide array of cultural objects from the Asian region and elsewhere.

It is in no way being suggested that all of these cultural objects are the products of looting but there would seem sufficient evidence from the BCG case alone to prompt a more rigorous examination of the source of these objects and their provenance when they are first brought into the country. However, in practice it is likely to be difficult to achieve the implementation of more stringent inspection procedures for cultural heritage goods at the border. It is the function of the Australian Customs and Border Protection Service (ACBPS) to oversee the state-level authorities who scrutinize all imports and to ensure they

---

50 'BC Galleries Ancient Art and Antiquities Catalogue: Tibetan & Nepalese Art & Antiquities-Item ID: 09694' <https://www.bcgalleries.com.au/antiquities/viewItem/09694> accessed 23 September 2013.

51 Om Chanda Handa, *Buddhist Monasteries in Himachal Pradesh* (Indus Publishing Company, New Delhi 2005).

52 'Shing Kangling' <http://www.damaruworks.com/kangling/wood-kanglings/> accessed 19 March 2013.

comply with both national and international laws.[53] The sheer volume of goods being imported at any time into Australia dictates that border control procedures rely to a substantial degree upon documentary import declarations rather than physical inspections of goods.[54] Thus in reality only if suspicions are raised, or there is some more tangible information about possible illicit trafficking, is it likely that ACBPS officials will look in person at a shipment of goods described as having some cultural heritage connection. Unlike narcotics and other illicit drugs, or a range of prohibited products posing a health or related risk, such goods are not in general on any frontline watch list for ACBPS officials.

Some confirmation of both the low priority given by ACBPS to issues associated with the import of cultural heritage objects from foreign countries, and the lack of any real expertise on the subject, can be gleaned from statements made by one of their officials at a landmark conference in 1999 on art crime in Australia.[55] At that time the official from the Australian Customs Service, as it was then known, acknowledged that 'a pertinent aspect of Customs role is our border responsibilities regarding protected objects' under the provisions of the *PMCHA 1986*.[56] However, his comments then referred to the control over cultural heritage objects of Australian origin and the enforcement of the export certificate regime for such objects rather than dealing with the import from foreign countries of illegally exported objects. He admitted that Customs had little experience with art crime in general and that during the preceding five years when he was responsible for all Customs investigations involving non-narcotic goods which were intended for prosecution 'not one case could be said to fall under the title of "art crime"'.[57]

We have no reason to believe that the circumstances described in 1999 by this official have changed in any significant way in regard to the approach now taken by ACBPS to this aspect of their responsibilities. The illicit trade in cultural objects remains a low priority item on the enforcement agenda of not only ACBPS but also other Australian law enforcement agencies. Efforts to change this situation are taking place but progress is slow and incremental.[58]

---

53 Craig Forrest, 'Australia's Protection of Foreign States' Cultural Heritage' (2004) 27 *University of New South Wales Law Journal* 605, 645.

54 ACBPS, 'Prohibited and Restricted Imports' <http://www.customs.gov.au/site/page4369.asp> accessed 23 September 2013.

55 Phil Burns, 'The Role of the Australian Customs Service' (Paper Presented at the Art Crime: Protecting Art, Protecting Artists and Protecting Consumers Conference, Australian Institute of Criminology, Sydney, 2-3 December 1999) <http://aic.gov.au/media_library/conferences/artcrime/burns.pdf> accessed 26 September 2013.

56 Ibid., 5.

57 Ibid., 2.

58 Duncan Chappell, 'Does the Mafia Collect Art? Exploring Some Questions About Organised Art Crime' (2011) 3 *CEPS Research Quarterly* 1, 2.

Conclusion

Before any meaningful protection and priority can be given in the future by Australian law enforcement agencies to protected cultural heritage objects illegally exported from other countries the *PMCHA 1986* will have to be amended to overcome the serious deficiencies it contains, as revealed by the decision in BCG 2012. This means placing the onus of proof firmly upon those who seek to import cultural heritage goods from elsewhere to show that they are lawfully obtained from their place of origin, and that all due diligence has been exercised to ensure that they are not the product of illicit excavation or theft. Insistence of the need for full documentation of the origin of goods and terms and place of purchase should also be part of the import procedures administered by ACBPS. Substantial penalties can follow if false declarations are made.

There is also a need to enhance the level of public awareness and concern about the nature and scope of the illicit market in trafficked cultural heritage objects. In the longer term it is likely to be a better informed and motivated public, rather than punitive measures, that reduces demand for looted objects. A promising start to educating the Australian public about their responsibilities when considering the purchase and importation of cultural heritage objects from abroad can be found in the *Make Sure It's Above Board* campaign launched in 2011 by DEWHA's Cultural Property Section in the Office for the Arts.[59] DEWHA produced a series of colourful and informative brochures and posters directed at Australians travelling overseas to advise them about the importance of ensuring they only purchased legitimate cultural heritage objects which could be lawfully exported from their country of origin. The campaign included references to the provisions of the *PMCHA 1986* and the possibility of seizure of any objects believed to have an illicit origin. Importantly, the ongoing investigation of the BCG cases at the time, and especially Case 2 discussed above, directly contributed to the shaping of this campaign, and a photograph of two of the seized bangles was added to the list of 'success stories'.

Australia still has a long road to traverse before it can claim to have in place a truly effective system which identifies and seizes looted objects of cultural significance that reach its shores. It is to be hoped that from the lessons learned from the two cases discussed in this chapter some progress will now be made down this road, and the repatriation of objects like those involved in the BCG 2012 will no longer be frustrated by inadequate laws and their spasmodic enforcement.

59 Office of the Arts, 'Make Sure It's Above Board' <http://arts.gov.au/movable/above-board> accessed 23 September 2013.

Chapter 15
Interpol and Advancements in International Police Cooperation on Art Crime

Saskia Hufnagel

Introduction

Interpol is probably the first manifestation of a coordinated international policing effort in the fight against cross-border crime and its roots can be traced to the late 19th century.[1] It was created as the first permanent international body of security cooperation in 1923, and established in Vienna as the International Criminal Police Commission (ICPC).[2] The aim of the organization was the creation of stability in Western Europe in the aftermath of the effects of WWI and the Russian Revolution.[3] In 1946, following the Nazification of the ICPC, the organization was re-established in Paris and emerged, in its current form, after 1989 in Lyon.[4] Interpol, unlike Europol,[5] is considered a truly international cooperation mechanism since it is open to all nations of the world to join. It comprised 190 member countries at the time of writing.[6] It is not a 'formal' police cooperation initiative as its constitution is not binding and its members are not states but police forces.

Since 1925 Interpol has been involved in the field of art crime. The Interpol art crime unit, until recently headed by Karl-Heinz Kind, seconded from the German police, was established in 1963. In its beginnings it focused mainly on stolen works of art and cultural property. Pictures and/or descriptions of works of art

---

1 Cyrille Fijnaut, 'International Policing in Europe: Its Present Situation and Future' in Jean-Paul Brodeur (ed), *Comparisons in Policing: An International Perspective* (Aldershot 1995) 115, 116.

2 John Occhipinti, *The Politics of EU Police Cooperation: Toward a European FBI?* (Lynne Rienner Publishers 2003) 29.

3 Fijnaut (n 1) 116.

4 Matthieu Deflem, *Policing World Society* (Oxford University Press 2002) 179.

5 See Ludo Block, this volume, who discusses the role of Europol in the area of art crime.

6 Interpol, *Structure and Governance* <http://www.interpol.int/About-INTERPOL/Structure-and-governance/National-Central-Bureaus> accessed 13 March 2013.

stolen from, for example, museums or collections were circulated in the form of Interpol print notices alerting to the loss of valuable pieces of art. The print notices evolved to become a computerized index of international art thefts in 1995. This index became the stolen works of art database in 2005 and has since then been available online for all law enforcement agencies through Interpol's I24/7 system. In 2009 the database went 'public' and access is today granted for every person with a legitimate interest.[7]

Before going into further detail with regard to Interpol's relevance and developments in the area of art crime, a hypothetical will be presented that shows a snapshot of the practice of Interpol in the field of art related crime.

Hypothetical

The hypothetical involves a museum in country A, a work of art (national treasure) lent to the museum from country B, which was stolen and transferred from the museum in country A to country C and – to make things more interesting – allegedly stolen by suspect nationals of country D. None of the countries involved belong to a region with specialized national legislation (for example, EU). Seeing that this is a hypothetical and only partly based on actual cases in this area, the suspects and the country the loot is transferred to are actually known to police. Unfortunately, many works of art in similar scenarios are never recovered.[8] The fact that the countries involved are remote and hence not subject to regional legislation in the field of art crime is, however, based on experiences in many similar cases.[9]

A first step of the investigation into the theft would be carried out by state A as the country in which the crime has occurred. However, interest in the investigation is also manifest in state B, as the country owning the work of art and hence the actual victim of the crime. Involvement of state B into the investigation of state A could occur through a liaison officer, provided state B had such an officer stationed in state A. Otherwise, state B could be involved through the Interpol National Central Bureau in state A, provided both states are member countries of Interpol. The National Central Bureau (NCB) links national police with the Interpol global

7 Vincent Noce, 'Interpol élargit sa base' *Liberation* (22 August 2006) <http://www.liberation.fr/culture/2009/08/22/interpol-elargit-sa-base_577169> accessed 19 November 2013.

8 See, for example, Vicki Oliveri, 'A Tale of Two Cities, A Tale of Two Art Thefts' in this volume and the recent art theft scandal in Rotterdam in David Ng 'Three Romanians plead guilty in 2012 Rotterdam art theft' *LA Times* (22 October 2013) <http://www.latimes.com/entertainment/arts/culture/la-et-cm-romanians-rotterdam-art-theft-20131022,0,5986313.story#axzz2l6lLtMgd> accessed 19 November 2013.

9 Janet Ulph and Ian Smith, *The Illicit Trade in Arts and Antiquities. International Recovery and Criminal and Civil Liability* (Hart Publishing 2012).

network. NCBs are typically a division of a national police agency or investigation service and serve as the contact point for all Interpol activities in the field.

NCBs also contribute to Interpol criminal databases and cooperate together on cross-border investigations, operations and arrests.[10]

In addition to investigations in state A with involvement of state B through their NCBs or liaison officers, police in state A, or the museum in state A and/or police in state B would also use another Interpol avenue to recover the stolen art work. Interpol hosts a Stolen Works of Art Database. The database was established in 1995 and since 1999 all member states have access to it. Furthermore, access to the database is today granted to institutions other than police to maximize the spread of information.[11] State A, state B and/or the museum itself could provide information on the stolen painting to the database. This information would have to be specific and is monitored through special forms asking for particulars on the work of art.[12] The reason for this procedure is to make it possible to match a possible find. If, for example, a dealer is asked to sell the work of art, he/she can go onto the database to make sure the piece is not stolen and if it is, can alert authorities to the find.

If publication through the Stolen Works of Art Database does not lead to recovery and the lost piece is of particular value or importance (in the present hypothetical we are dealing with a national treasure), the work of art would be included in the next issue of the Interpol poster series of the 'most wanted works of art' which is published every six months.[13] Provided the artwork is subsequently detected in country C, police in country C would be alerted and could seize the piece as an act of mutual assistance for country B, in the absence of any specific mutual legal assistance treaty or agreement, by using assistance of the Interpol NCBs.

With regard to the suspects, if their name and nationality, but not their location, is known, Interpol can issue an international wanted persons alert. This alert is, like the lost works of art database, distributed to national police and accessible generally over the internet.[14] If the suspects are arrested in their home country D, where they are nationals, this might prevent extradition as many countries do not extradite nationals. If they are arrested in country E, state A may request

10 Interpol (n 6).

11 Karl-Heinz Kind, 'The Role of Interpol in the Fight Against the Illicit Trafficking in Cultural Property' in Stefano Manacorda, *Organised Crime in Art and Antiquities* (International Scientific and Professional Advisory Council of the United Nations Crime Prevention and Criminal Justice Programme 2009) 205-6; Information is further based on an Interview and observations conducted at the Interpol Works of Art Unit in January 2012.

12 Interview and observations conducted at the Interpol Works of Art Unit, January 2012.

13 Kind (n 10) 205.

14 Interpol (n 6).

extradition. This procedure is now outside the realm of Interpol's competences as it concerns judicial cooperation.

Situations that require the involvement of Interpol are often governed by international rules established, for example, at the level of the United Nations (UN). These include, for example:

- 1929 International Convention for the Suppression of the Counterfeiting of Currency
- United Nations Convention against Corruption (UNCAC)
- United Nations Convention against Transnational Organized Crime (UNTOC)
- 1988 Drug Trafficking Convention

Relevant in relation to the Interpol example would here be the United Nations Convention against Transnational Organized Crime of 15 November 2000. Provided the above hypothetical would be construed as an instance of organized crime, Art 18 prescribes that 'the Parties are required to afford another the widest measure of mutual legal assistance in investigations, prosecutions and judicial proceedings in relation to offences covered by the Convention'. Mutual legal assistance can then be requested for the taking of evidence or statements, service of official documents, searches, seizures, freezing of assets, examining objects and sites, providing information and evidence (Article 18 (a)-(e)). However, limitations exist with regard to domestic law of the requested state party (Article 18 (g)). This means that any law enforcement action that is not provided for in the police procedure of the requested party, or prohibited under privacy laws of the requested party, cannot be requested.

If the case cannot be construed in terms of organized crime, another possibility is to apply the UNESCO Convention on the Means of Prohibiting and Preventing the Illicit Import, Export and Transfer of Ownership of Cultural Property 1970 or the UNIDROIT Convention on Stolen or Illegally Exported Cultural Objects 1995. Both legal frameworks deal with theft but with the focus on the return of cultural property to its owner rather than with the criminal issues.[15] Article 10(a) of the 1970 Convention requires States Parties to oblige dealers in antiquities subject to penal or administrative sanctions to maintain a registered recording of details on the item and supplier, as well as to inform the purchaser of the cultural property of an (if existing under national law) export prohibition. The effect of this section is to try to break the process of laundering stolen cultural goods. Because a number of the States Parties have not legislated on, or have not implemented, this provision it has not had the essential effect on the widespread practice of laundering stolen property. There is therefore now a move to draft a protocol to the United Nations

15 Patrick J. O'Keefe and Lyndel V. Prott (eds), *Cultural Heritage Conventions and Other Instruments: A Compendium with Commentaries* (Builth Wells: Institute of Art and Law 2011).

Convention against Transnational Organized Crime 2000 (UNTOC) to establish an international crime of conspiracy in relation to illicit traffic in cultural objects.[16]

It can be concluded in relation to the Interpol hypothetical that there is an assumption of shared responsibility in the area of art crime in the international community, justifying legally – if it can be construed as organized crime – an obligation on law enforcement cooperation, at least for parties to UNTOC. The Convention has so far 147 signatories and 179 parties to it. However, Barbados, Congo, Iran, Japan, Republic of Korea and Sierra Leone have not yet ratified it.

This hypothetical shows the complexities of the involvement of Interpol in art crime cases and it highlights that there is considerable room for improvement. A very recent, but rather Eurocentric attempt to improve Interpol activities in the area of art crime is the Protection System for Cultural Heritage (PSYCHE) Project, which will be outlined below.

International Partners

Interpol works together with a number of agencies and institutions to enhance its impact in the fight against art crime. One such agency is, for example, the Art Loss Register, which is a privately run database on mainly stolen, but also forged works of art. The Art Loss Register and Interpol are very similar in what they can provide, but according to Interpol complement each other in some aspects. Cooperation between the two has been perceived as positive by both actors.[17]

Interpol also collaborates with UNESCO. As UNESCO cannot deal with crimes for its lack of law enforcement powers, it includes Interpol in cases where it suspects criminal activity. It also uses the Interpol database and its 'Most Wanted Works of Art' list to alert to lost works of art.[18]

Interpol is further involved, together with UNESCO and the International Council of Museums (ICOM), in providing training initiatives in different regions of the world to improve awareness and knowledge of police practitioners with regard to art crime.

Referring back to the hypothetical, it is not only crucial that Interpol works together with international public and private organizations to recover art, create knowledge and exchange information and intelligence, but as the hypothetical has shown, some of the most crucial information for Interpol comes from the national level, which therefore also needs to be considered. If international art crimes are not detected at the national level there will be no involvement of Interpol. It is hence crucial that national police and customs detect stolen or unlawfully exported works of art from other countries.

16 See Lyndel V. Prott, this volume.

17 Interview and observations conducted at the Interpol Works of Art Unit, January 2012.

18 See Lyndel V. Prott, this volume.

It would be even more desirable (and important for international/Interpol involvement) if they could determine the origin of a piece. However, any law enforcement effort, whether national or international, relies on the country of origin wanting to take action.

International law enforcement action, such as an entry in the Interpol database, can be requested by a state if a theft from, for example, a museum or archaeological site is reported to the national police and it is suspected that the item has been brought out of the country. Before a state turns to involve the international level it can, if it has a suspicion as to where the item has been trafficked to, through diplomatic channels request authorities in the State where it suspects the object present to seize and return it. This might, however, not be the easiest option as most states, with the exception of southern Europe, do not have the law enforcement capacity and expertise to help with such requests.[19] Putting the object onto the Interpol database is hence a safe option, as it can prevent the legal sale of such objects and will certainly lower the price on the illegal market.

Reactions to international art thefts differ from state to state. While recent events in the Netherlands, Germany and Belgium were highly publicized and attracted both media and law enforcement attention internationally, in other countries such events might not trigger any publicity.[20] Beyond the actual detection and investigation of such crimes, the criminal prosecution is even more difficult and, as the recent Rotterdam thefts have shown, does also not necessarily lead to the recovery of the stolen art work.[21] While the thieves in the Rotterdam Kunsthal theft were caught and convicted, this is little consolation for the owner (Triton Foundation). Some of the paintings had allegedly been destroyed in an attempt by a thief's mother in Romania to cover up the offence and the others have so far not been found.

As was pointed out by Patrick O'Keefe in this volume, the element of embarrassment of private and state victims of art crime and considerations for political relations can also lead to international art crime not being reported, neither at the national, nor at the international level. Legal insecurities, like those discussed in the chapter by Duncan Chappell and Ken Polk in this volume, can further contribute to a reluctance to report theft and other art crimes. Generally, the market does not seem to trust police at the national level. However, the

19 See Ludo Block, this volume.

20 See, for example, Ng (n 8); Pierre-Yves Meughens and Florence Hainaut 'Des œuvres d'Ensor et de Van Dongen dérobées au Musée van Buuren' *rtbf.be info* (17 July 2013) <http://www.rtbf.be/info/regions/detail_des-uvres-d-ensor-et-de-van-dongen-derobees-au-musee-van-buuren?id=8049976> accessed 19 November 2013; DPA 'Bayern dringt auf Verständigung mit Gurlitt' *Handelsblatt* (15 November 2013) <http://www.handelsblatt.com/panorama/aus-aller-welt/kunstfund-bayern-dringt-auf-verstaendigung-mit-gurlitt/9082042.html> accessed 19 November 2013.

21 Ng (n 8).

possibility to put stolen works of art on the Interpol database is taken up frequently and is, according to the Interpol website, a very successful tool of art recovery.

If an owner wants to recover a stolen work of art and suspects it to have been brought out of the country, they can contact the Art Loss Register and/or Interpol. Both databases can assist in recovering the objects and making their legal sale difficult. The International Council of Museums (ICOM) can also issue a 'Red List' if the works of art concerned are archaeological objects from the most vulnerable areas of the world.[22]

Progress Made by Interpol

During its involvement in art crime one of the most significant improvements Interpol made in the field was reported to be the opening of the stolen works of art database to every person with a legitimate interest.[23] The Interpol database was thereby made accessible to museums, galleries and private collectors and the monopoly of the police in this area vanished. Fears of police practitioners that this could lead to misuse of the database were uttered, but so far no negative experiences have been reported.[24]

A European focus of Interpol started with the French EU presidency under which the creation and implementation of a European database of stolen cultural goods was put forward.[25] Europol declined the setting up of the system under its remit which opened up European opportunities for Interpol. This was the start of the PSYCHE idea, the **P**rotection **SY**stem for **C**ultural **HE**ritage, which should be implemented by Interpol in cooperation with other actors and institutions, such as the Italian Carabinieri. This project was further fostered when in November 2008 the Council adopted non-binding Conclusions on preventing and combating illicit trafficking in cultural goods which expressed approval of the improvements to the Interpol database if they were in accordance with the needs of EU member states.[26]

After some time of inactivity the Polish EU presidency put the debate about an art crime database back on the European agenda. It stressed in particular the importance of improving the existing system. The Council subsequently adopted

---

22 ICOM – Red List at <http://icom.museum/resources/red-lists-database/> accessed 19 November 2013.

23 Interview and observations conducted at the Interpol Works of Art Unit, January 2012.

24 Ibid.; see also Noce (n 7).

25 Council, 'Draft conclusions on the creation and implementation of a European database of stolen cultural goods' (Council document 11246/08).

26 Council, 'Conclusions of the Council of the European Union on preventing and combating illicit trafficking in cultural goods' (Council document 14224/2/08).

new Conclusions on preventing and combating crime against cultural goods. The Conclusions (again) aimed at improving cooperation with Interpol and the development and implementation of a system that enabled urgent reporting of key events connected to crimes against cultural goods.

As a result of these efforts Interpol is now finally working together with the Italian Carabinieri on the PSYCHE project to modernize the database. One improvement to the Interpol system is that PSYCHE enables direct data insertion by member countries and adds image recognition software to simplify the checking process. One of the main aims of the project is to help and encourage countries to participate in the Interpol system that so far have only supplied small amounts of data (few entries into the system), and that have no national database to support them in art crime investigations. To achieve easier access and participation in the database for them, PSYCHE developed a formatted message system for submission of information on stolen works of art directly from a country's National Central Bureau to the General Secretariat. While in the past the various Interpol National Central Bureaus had to send information relating to stolen works of art in free text messages, and the General Secretariat had to enter the information into the database manually, the new system significantly professionalizes this procedure. This is also the first step towards the fully automatic insertion of data into the Stolen Works of Art database.[27]

Another main aim of PSYCHE is the overcoming of problems relating to harmonization of different databases. At the moment, Interpol and national databases on stolen works of art are structured according to different criteria, making it impossible to exchange information automatically. Therefore, PSYCHE will develop an interface between them. This interface will be tested on the Italian 'Leonardo' database, owned and managed by the Italian Carabinieri Command for the Protection of Cultural Heritage. The interface will allow the creation of a platform for automatic data transfer from national databases to Interpol. All Interpol member countries can then access the information that will be transferred directly from the 'Leonardo' database to Interpol's new Stolen Works of Art database.

As mentioned above, an image-comparison component will be added to the existing text search engine for queries about stolen works of art. The aim of adding this component is to increase the possibility of positive hits and matches between works of art stored in the Interpol database and those on the market, thereby also enhancing the chances of recovering stolen works of art.[28]

Since the PSYCHE project started its operations in Rome under project leadership of Italy in March 2013 member countries benefiting from it have been listed as Austria, Belgium, Bulgaria, Cyprus, Estonia, France, Germany, Greece,

---

27 Interpol – General Assembly – 81st Session, *Report No 4: Improving International Cooperation and Enhancing Information Exchange on the Illicit Traffic in Cultural Property* (5-8 December 2012, Rome, Italy).

28 Ibid.

Hungary, Malta, Slovenia, Slovakia, Spain and Sweden.[29] Many of these countries, such as Austria, Belgium, Bulgaria, Cyprus, France, Hungary, Slovakia, Slovenia and Sweden, had also from the very beginning given their political support to the project and were integrated as partners. After submission of the proposal to the EU Commission in October 2012 more EU member states have become partners to the project, such as the Czech Republic, Estonia, Germany, Greece, Malta and Spain.

It is apparent from the list of countries partners to the project as well as from the funding body – the European Union – that PSYCHE is a rather Eurocentric initiative. Financial support for the project is provided by the European Commission which notified Italy on 3 May 2012 that it would fund the Project PSYCHE. The project proposal hence only allowed EU member countries to be integrated as official partners. In the Report on the 81st Interpol General Assembly on Improving International Cooperation and Enhancing Information Exchange on the Illicit Traffic in Cultural Property, held in Rome in December 2012, the results of the project (formatted message, access to the database, search tools and training modules) were said to 'benefit all Interpol member countries'.[30] The report pointed out in particular 'that several non-EU countries, including Australia, Canada and the United States, have expressed strong support for this project and have even started promoting it nationally to their specialized law enforcement agencies'.[31] According to an interview conducted at the Interpol Works of Art Unit in January 2012 the impact on Australia as a non-EU member state was rated very low. Australia's input in the Interpol database is, even considering its population size, negligible. Similarly low are its requests to the Stolen Works of Art Database.[32] As a non-EU member state it would not benefit from the facilitation of entry and search requirements which might encourage more engagement with the database and while there is strong enthusiasm by a handful of Australian police practitioners in the fight against art crime, one cannot claim that the project has been promoted nationally in this country. It therefore remains to be seen whether the new database will live up to the high hopes of Interpol and EU member states for improving cultural heritage protection in the EU and beyond.

One way of making the initiative a success is obviously to market it world-wide and teach practitioners in the EU how to use it. The last crucial component of the Project PSYCHE is therefore the training service (e-learning modules) which was developed as part of the project and provides information on how to use the new database.[33] The training will be provided through a number of

29 Formez – International Activities, *Kick off Meeting of the Project PSYCHE* <http://www.formez.eu/node/1499> accessed 20 November 2013.

30 Interpol – General Assembly – 81st Session (n 27).

31 Ibid.

32 Interview and observations conducted at the Interpol Works of Art Unit, January 2012.

33 Interpol – General Assembly – 81st Session (n 27).

different initiatives, such as an interactive e-learning platform which will provide users with multimedia training tools, accessible to all member countries inside and outside the EU, information seminars in EU member countries participating in the initiative and a handbook covering the database and the protection of international cultural heritage in general, such as national and international law, information exchange, international cooperation, case studies, and many other related issues.[34] In addition to these training initiatives, Interpol also organizes meetings related to the fight against art crime, such as the bi-annual meetings of the expert working group on art crime, on a regular basis. These meetings, by creating personal contacts between various countries and between a number of different agencies are hoped to enhance police cooperation in the field.

With a view to the future of PSYCHE it is hoped that this new initiative will improve the services provided to member states by the General Secretariat and make it possible for more tailored services based on the information received to be developed, such as analytical reports, delivering specific training and coordinating targeted operations.[35]

Conclusion

While the potential of the PSYCHE project to improve the fight against art crime seems great, reality will probably reveal many of its limitations. The hope that PSYCHE will have an effect on the recovery of stolen works of art globally will most likely not be justified. Even according to Interpol and police practitioners involved in art crime investigations, the effect of the new initiative is rather focused on Europe and the EU in particular. However, including one of the largest European databases – Leonardo, the Italian database on stolen works of art – into the Interpol system will very likely enhance the chances of discovering art thefts and might even lead to the inclusion of further European databases. Should the PSYCHE 'test' run prove to be an improvement to the existing system, other countries might want to contribute their knowledge. So, more than being successful as PSYCHE in the present form, the improvements could lead to a process of international cooperation and exchange that goes beyond the currently envisaged advantages.

Apart from PSYCHE, Interpol has shown significant developments in the area of art crime since the 1960s, not only with a view to improving databases, but also in relation to its networking and support capacity with national agencies, international institutions and even private initiatives in the field. According to the Interpol website, there have been a number of successful recoveries in recent years and the acceptance of the system is steadily increasing.

The most successful change to the Interpol stolen works of art database so far has been the opening up of the system to everyone with a legitimate interest.

34 Ibid.

35 Ibid.

According to practitioners, this has significantly broadened the information input and led to acceptance by more and more players in the field. It remains to be seen whether PSYCHE will have a similarly positive effect and live up to – at least European – expectations.

It needs to be concluded that the fight against art crime, despite the positive outlook in this chapter so far – is still not a fight of institutions, police forces or governments. It is mainly the fight of individuals. One of the problems individual practitioners face in this fight against art crime is that they are confronted with a system – the art market – that is nearly as 'closed shop', clandestine and exclusive as the police itself. Furthermore, art crime is not high on the list of priorities of most police forces (Italy being one of the outstanding exceptions). Practitioners with an interest in art crime often have to fight for their budget and personnel. Art crime units are often run by one to five members of staff per country and/or institution. However, considering this low number of staff, national and Interpol successes in the area of art crime should be even more valued. In most cases it is purely the dedication of highly skilled and motivated staff that creates positive outcomes.

Luckily, both Interpol and national art crime units receive significant support from the usual enemy of police, the media. Media coverage of art crime cases is extensive as the topic is extremely popular and makes very good news for police. Interpol receives a lot of positive publicity from its support in art crime investigations, however, its art crime unit is not being expanded. There seems to be a discrepancy between the successes of art crime investigations, the number of staff involved and police resources dedicated to art crime. This is not an Interpol specific issue, but a general observation. It would be desirable that national police further art crime investigations and allocate more resources and staff, for example, to Interpol as an institution staffed by police officers from its member states.

Index